BOOKS

IDENTIFICATION
AND PRICE GUIDE

FIRST EDITION

NANCY WRIGHT

D0047870

The CONFIDENT COLLECTOR™

AVON BOOKS ◆ NEW YORK

Important Notice: All of the information, including valuations, in this book has been compiled from the most reliable sources, and every effort has been made to eliminate errors and questionable data. Nevertheless, the possibility of error always exists in a work of such scope. The publisher and the author will not be held responsible for losses which may occur in the purchase, sale, or other transaction of property because of information contained herein. Readers who feel they have discovered errors are invited to *write* the author in care of Avon Books so that the errors may be corrected in subsequent editions.

THE CONFIDENT COLLECTOR: BOOKS (1st edition) is an original publication of Avon Books. This edition has never before appeared in book form.

AVON BOOKS
A division of
The Hearst Corporation
1350 Avenue of the Americas
New York, New York 10019

Copyright © 1993 by Nancy Wright
Cover art by Walter Wick
The Confident Collector and its logo are trademarked properties of Avon Books.
Interior design by Martha Schwartz
Published by arrangement with the author
Library of Congress Catalog Card Number: 92-21477
ISBN: 0-380-76941-7

Library of Congress Cataloging in Publication Data:

Wright, Nancy, 1927-
    The confident collector books identification and price guide /
Nancy Wright.
        p. cm—(The Confident Collector)
    Includes bibliographical references.
    1. Out-of-print books—Prices—United States. I. Title. II. Series.
Z1000.5.W75   1993   92-21477
017'.8—dc20   CIP

First Avon Books Trade Printing: September 1993

AVON TRADEMARK REG. U.S. PAT. OFF. AND IN OTHER COUNTRIES, MARCA REGISTRADA, HECHO EN U.S.A.

Printed in the U.S.A.

OPM 10 9 8 7 6 5 4 3

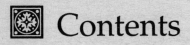 # Contents

Introduction   1

Market Report   3
Auction Results   4

Book Collecting   5
What Makes a Book Collectible?   6
Is It a First Edition?   9
Condition and Grading   13

About This Guide   19
How to Use This Guide   21
Price Structure   22
But What If My Book Isn't Here?   24

PRICE LISTINGS   27

Appendix A: Key to Categories   253
Appendix B: Key to Illustrators   280
Appendix C: Glossary   290
Appendix D: Abbreviations   295
Appendix E: References   297

Introduction

Most booksellers began as avid readers and book lovers—people to whom books were exciting and important. So it was with me. At the age of ten I realized that by patronizing all the branch libraries within walking distance of my home in Providence, I could borrow forty books to take away with me over my summer vacation. That discovery made my summers.

Later, I attended Penn State and the New School for Social Research. I married, had two sons, and went back to the New School for a degree and considerable graduate study. Over the years I majored at different times in writing, English literature, philosophy, and psychology. Many majors, many books.

After a colorful series of jobs (like those of a new author on the back of a 1940s dust jacket), I found myself crossing the line from book collector to bookseller. Until then, I had barely known such an occupation existed. (Adults ask, "What are you going to be when you grow up? A teacher? A doctor? A lawyer?" No one ever says, "Bookseller?")

At that time I was on the road as the co-owner and operator of a carnival ride, colorful job number seven. I seem not to have been previously aware of the existence of thrift shops and flea markets. I discovered them then, full of books, in and around some of the dozens of towns we traveled through.

Book collecting is a treasure hunt. First, I found, for twenty-five cents each (this was twenty years ago), books that I'd always wanted to read or to own. Then I discovered, for the same price, books I would never have gone looking for—some children's books with color plates, which I couldn't resist buying. Finally I found, at the same low prices, irresistible books that I didn't really want for myself (there's a limit), but had to buy anyway, that must, I thought, be worth five or ten dollars apiece, or more. Thus was begun my own personal treasure hunt for books, and almost simultaneously, my birth as a potential bookseller. I've been treasure hunting ever since. It's a treasure hunt that probably won't end until I do, and that for all book collectors is an endless and fascinating pursuit.

I've been selling books ever since also, the line between book collector and bookseller being a thin one; and I honestly can't say at what point I crossed it. But once it was crossed, I was in the process of discovering a way to support my habit. There was a bookseller in a bookshop in one of the towns who had shown me the first price guide to books I had ever seen, along with a copy of the out-of-print bookseller's companion— "AB Bookman's Weekly." But how could I ever have predicted that twenty years later I'd be writing a price guide myself!

Discovering the book business was something like a gourmet/gourmand suddenly realizing he can make a living as a cheese taster. I became a dealer in rare, used, and out-of-print books with my friend and partner, Marla Bottesch. Our business, Snowbound Books, operates out of the Northeast and runs an extensive out-of-print book search service, filling requests through the mail. We also exhibit at most of the bigger book shows in the Northeast.

In the summers, we operate a bookmobile that is set up at various fairs and festivals. If you should find yourself in Maine one summer attending one of these events, you may run into us. Please stop and say hello. When book enthusiasts meet, they rarely lack matter for conversation; the problem is usually not how to start but how to stop.

◼ Market Report

"Baby Boomers are redefining the market for rare books," says a February 1993 article in the Wall Street Journal publication "Smart Money." As the Baby Boomer generation has entered the market in recent years, it has brought a new mindset to the world of book collecting. It has turned the "popular" book into the collectible book. What's in and interesting has become what you collect; and "hot" new writers have become collectible overnight.

This new era of book collecting began with mysteries, detective stories, and science fiction, and now includes horror fiction and thrillers as well. Handsomely illustrated children's books, pop-ups, movie- and TV-related material, Disneyana, juvenile series books (meaning Nancy Drew, Tom Swift, and company), and early ("vintage") paperbacks, have now joined nineteenth-century literary first editions, fine bindings, color plate books, and others, at the active center of the book-collecting world.

The latest burst was led, some years ago, by Stephen King. The first editions of his earlier books (*Carrie, 'Salem's Lot, The Shining, Night Shift, The Stand*) go at the moment for $150 to $1,000. His limited editions can run up to $2,500.

First editions of Tom Clancy's *The Hunt for Red October* sell for $400 to $750, and Anne Rice's *Interview with the Vampire* for $250 to over $550. The first of Sue Grafton's "alphabet series" of mysteries, *"A" Is for Alibi*, can go for as much as $850, while *"B" Is for Burglar* is worth $200 to $400.

With children's books, the first editions of the beloved classics—*Winnie the Pooh, Charlotte's Web, The Secret Garden, Raggedy Ann, Anne of Green Gables*, and many more—continue to be bought and sold at high figures. Among nonfiction works, the first public edition of the government printing of "The Smyth Report" on atomic energy is now offered for around $750. Contemporary histories of the fighting units in World War II are valued at $75 to $200 or more, depending on the unit.

Auction Results

The "Smart Money" article stated that since 1987, Sotheby's, Christie's, and New York-based Swann Galleries have produced over $182 million in their US book auctions alone. In the past year at Sotheby's, a first edition of L. Frank Baum's *The Wonderful Wizard of Oz* sold for $39,600, and a first edition of Dashiell Hammett's *The Maltese Falcon*, estimated to go for about $5,000, brought $29,000 at the end of a bidding war; a presentation copy of Bram Stoker's *Dracula* sold for $44,000; F. Scott Fitzgerald's *The Great Gatsby* brought $14,300, and J.R.R. Tolkien's *The Hobbit*, $19,800.

The Swann Gallery's March 1992 sale of the Jack Gorlin collection drew tremendous attention. Mr. Gorlin was an amateur fencer and dueler, and during his travels amassed a rare and valuable collection of books in his area of interest.

At Swann's fiftieth anniversary auction in April 1992, the celebrated Raymond Epstein collection was on the block. The books collected by Mr. Epstein over a forty-year period brought a total of over $327,000. Highlights included original editions of *The Wealth of Nations* at $26,400; *Leaves of Grass*, $30,000; *The Tale of Peter Rabbit*, $55,000; *Gone With the Wind*, $4,180; and *Frankenstein*, $30,800.

◩ Book Collecting

For the treasure hunter, the world of book collecting is a wide, wide world: the world of books is enormous. There are 800,000 books in print right now in the United States alone, and most books stay in print for just a few years. For every book in print, how many books are there out of print? I don't think the number is calculable.

And the world of books is various. Whatever your own bent, you can follow it. You may have loved Dr. Seuss as a child. You may really be into the Beats. Or World War II. Or have a fascination with the history of radio. Maybe you love poetry. You may be an amateur—or a professional—magician. You may be hooked on the Far North. Or be enthralled with the history of sailing. Or the history of Judaism. Or the history of Ireland. You may collect Native American writers. Or maybe you were really turned on by "Star Trek" when you were ten years old. Whatever it is, there are books for it: books about it, books that do it, books that are there.

You may be a real mystery afficionado. Or maybe there's just one mystery writer that excites you. Raymond Chandler? Dashiell Hammett? Sue Grafton? Even in a field as comparatively narrow as the work of one writer, the possibilities can be endless. You can collect that writer's first editions, reprints, paperback editions, signed or presentation copies, limited editions, illustrated editions, magazine appearances, letters, photos, movie editions or movie versions, memoirs, biographies, critical works on the author, and more. (Each collecting path may not be absolutely endless, but by the time you get to the end you'll have a couple of other paths started anyway.)

Whatever it is that you personally care about, there's a path you can follow. And no matter what field you focus on, there will be rare books in that field, possible treasures at every turn—which is what treasure hunting is all about.

Books other than those that come new from the publisher fall into three common categories—used, out of print, and rare. Each category has its own distinct market. The person looking for a used book is looking for an inexpensive copy of a book that would cost him more if he bought it brand-new—like a dictionary, a novel, a bible, a classic, a cookbook. The person looking for an out-of-print book is trying to get hold of some particular title that he can't find otherwise. An out-of-print book can be expensive, but isn't necessarily so. The person interested in a rare book is often looking for a book to add to a collection, a book very limited in supply, and that can be quite expensive.

It is important to notice that the categories overlap. The student looking for an out-of-print book by a specific scholar of forty years ago may find it has become a rare and expensive book. The parent looking for an out-of-print childhood favorite to read to his child may find it's become very collectible and rare—or that it's been frequently reprinted and can be had as a used book for a dollar or two. Or you may have good luck and run across a rare book in a used book store.

What Makes a Book Collectible?

Everyone knows that a nineteenth-century edition of Dickens's *Oliver Twist* is valuable, right? Well, it might be valuable—in fact, it could be worth $1,500. Or it could be properly priced at one dollar at your local out-of-print bookstore. If the *Oliver Twist* is a cheap reprint edition, on poor paper, with poor illustrations or none, a dollar or two is all that it is worth. If it's a first edition, on the other hand, in the original binding, in good condition, it's worth $1,500 or so.

What is being discussed here are the grounds of value in books: what makes a book worth money, as well as which books are virtually worthless (monetarily speaking), and why. We will distinguish the question of specific price, which we can look up in a guide, from the more general question of what makes a book valuable.

The "Classics" got to be classics because they were well thought of, widely published, widely bought, and—before television—widely read. They came out sooner or later in very inexpensive editions and in great quantity. For every original edition, there are thousands and thousands of inexpensive reprints. Because of their quantity and quality, they are worth very little.

But a first edition of a classic, in nice condition, tends to be worth a great deal. Later printings of the original edition also have value, though the value is not really comparable, since the first printing of a first edition is highly sought after (see section titled "Is It a First Edition?").

Still other editions of a classic, if they are handsome volumes of good physical quality, in nice condition, and particularly if they are attractively designed and illustrated, can also be worth something. In this case, the publication date of the edition—whether it's from the 1880s or the 1930s or is a fine press edition from the 1970s—tends not to be of crucial importance in relation to price. Should the book be illustrated by a favored illustrator, then it is the valuation of that illustrator that will set the price range.

But a nineteenth-century reprint edition of *Oliver Twist* is not necessarily worth a thing. It is clear also from our example of *Oliver Twist* that age alone does not make a book valuable any more than its being a classic does. There are thousands and thousands of hundred-year-old books and fifty-year-old books that are virtually worthless. Attics are full of them. A bookseller, if he has any, might offer them for twenty-five cents to five dollars, and never find a buyer. They include out-of-date textbooks, book club editions, Reader's Digest Condensed Novels, out-of-date nonfiction, fiction by authors you've never heard of, old sets of encyclopedias and other outdated reference books, and books that are falling apart or are very shabby. Why these books are virtually worthless is because nobody wants them.

The value of a book is determined by (a) the social valuation of its contents and the reputation of its author; (b) its edition; (c) its condition; and (d) its physical and aesthetic qualities. The combination of these factors gives the book its collectibility, or (e) value— the measure of the demand for the book. Its price on the market, as distinct from its *value*, is determined by those same factors *plus* the economic factor of supply. If the book is scarce and its collectibility high, its price will be high. If the book is scarce, but its collectibility low, its price will be comparably low. The physical and aesthetic qualities, as distinct from condition, may be of great or little importance, depending on the type of book. In the modern first edition, these qualities are assumed and taken for granted, but in a limited edition, a fine press production, an art book, or in a handsome late nineteenth-century book, these may be the making of a valuable book.

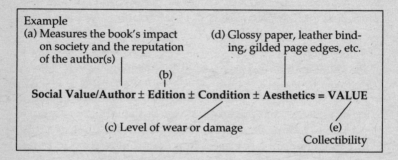

Example

(a) Measures the book's impact on society and the reputation of the author(s)

(d) Glossy paper, leather binding, gilded page edges, etc.

(b)

Social Value/Author ± Edition ± Condition ± Aesthetics = VALUE

(c) Level of wear or damage

(e) Collectibility

The social valuation of a book is based on its cultural and historical significance—the book's impact on society. Books like *The Origin of Species by Means of Natural Selection*, *The Adventures of Huckleberry Finn*, *The Great Gatsby*, and *Steal This Book* changed and enriched our consciousness, helped to shape the future, and are valued for having done so. Books written by great authors—such as Mark Twain, James Joyce, Jane Austen, and Nathanael West—remain highly collectible, as are works by individuals accomplished in other fields, like Frederick Douglass and Rockwell Kent.

The best way to get a quick grasp of the valuation of books and authors in terms of price is to do a once-over-lightly survey of the book price list. Since edition and condition are held constant in the guide, the survey will give you a picture of the comparative evaluation by the book-buying public of the various authors and their books.

The physical and aesthetic qualities of a volume are distinctions that you get a feel for by looking at and handling a lot of books, noticing the quality of the materials that went into making them, the attention given to design and detail, the quality of the illustrations, the neatness with which the books themselves were put together. The comparative weight of a book indicates the quality of paper used. Other frequent indications of quality are gilded page edges, glossy paper, illustrations with tissue guards, a binding of a high grade of leather or of decorated leather, etc. Pay attention to detail, exercise discrimination, and trust your instincts—you'll learn as you go.

Is It a First Edition?

The primary way to determine the edition of a book is to study all of the information given by the publisher. A date on the title page of a book is the *publication date*. The *copyright date* appears on the reverse side of the title page. The copyright date is the date on which the copyright was issued for a book. It is a date that does not change once it is received. The publication date is the date on which the physical book itself is published, so every edition of every book has a different publication date, but the copyright date remains the same. Not all books show a publication date. Virtually all modern American books show a copyright date.

The book *Gone With the Wind* has a copyright date of 1936. A copy of the book with the publication date of 1936, with "Published May, 1936" on the copyright page and no note of other printings (in excellent condition, in dust jacket) is worth up to $3,000. A copy of that very same book, in dust jacket, with a publication date of 1940 is worth about fifty dollars. Since its initial publication, *Gone With the Wind* has sold over twenty-one million copies and gone through hundreds of editions in thirty-one countries worldwide. But only the very early editions—particularly the first—are worth very much money.

When a book collector talks about a "first edition," he is actually referring to the first part of the first edition—the first printing—so much so that "first edition" has come to *mean* "first printing" when the term is used by collectors of literary firsts. But "edition" also has an older and more basic meaning, and the distinction between these two meanings should be made clear.

In its original meaning, an edition may have multiple printings. A first edition consists of all the printings of a book that come out originally, before editorial or design changes occur. A second edition is printed when there are substantial changes made to the text—paragraphs rewritten, a new chapter included, material updated, etc. This occurs most commonly with a textbook, or a new edition of a children's book or classic that may be printed with new illustrations, format, or binding. Therefore, a first edition, in this original and basic sense of the word, consists of all the printings of a book that come out before a specific set of significant changes is made.

But when booksellers or collectors refer to first editions, they are talking about the first printing of the first edition. A printing is all those copies of a book that are run off during one brief time period, and a first printing is the set number of books printed "first" of the first edition. When we say "first edition" in this book we will be following ordinary current usage and will almost always be using the term to mean "first printing."

For some of the most collectible books, much study has been given to distinguishing earlier and later parts of a single print run. This often involves finding that later copies show broken or imperfect print at some specific location in the book, have a spelling error corrected, or have some other minor changes. The first printing is then understood as being composed of one or more issues. The reason for this interest is that many collectors are concerned to find the very first of anything, and prices for books follow that fact. The distinguishing characteristics for an individual issue of a specific book are called "points," which is short for "points of issue." The term "points" now also designates those characteristics used to distinguish between printings. A list of reference books that include information on points is listed in "References" at the end of this book.

Often a book will say on its copyright page that it is a first edition or first printing or first impression. In these cases we know we have a first edition, and our task is simple—we are lucky. Unfortunately, this is not always the case.

There are thousands of publishers, and no law or adequate tradition that gives unity to their methods of distinguishing first editions and later printings. To make matters more confusing, many publishers are not self-consistent. There are several books on the market which list the information on the ways the various publishers denote first editions, and these books are listed in the chapter on resources at the end of the book.

There are certain common ways of indicating edition, however. Sometimes there will be a string of numerals or letters, from "1" to "9" or from "A" to "E" on the copyright page. If the "1" or the "A" is missing, the string will begin with a "2" or a "3," or a "B" or a "C"—indicating a second or third printing, respectively. An exception is for books published by Random House or Harcourt, Brace. If a Random House book says "First Edition" and also has a string beginning with "2," or if a Harcourt, Brace book says "First Edition" and has a string beginning with "B," these , contrary to the case with any other publisher, are first editions. With these two publishers, when the "First Edition" is removed, and the string begins with "2" or "B," we have a second printing. There is another kind of string, with "1" at the beginning and "2" at the end, so that the string might read "135798642." In this case, if the "1" alone is missing, the book is a second printing. If the "1" and "2" are missing, the book is a third printing, and so on.

Many publishers have their own special way of marking a first edition. Appleton indicates the number of the printing with a numeral placed just below the text on the last page of the book. Rinehart puts its monogram on the copyright page of its first editions—an "R" inside a circle. Scribner's puts an "A" there with its crest on the same page, but the crest alone does not indicate a first edition. Doran; Farrar & Rinehart; and Farrar & Straus also mark their first editions with their logos. Bobbs-Merrill sometimes puts a bow-and-arrow symbol on the copyright page of their first editions, but is very inconsistent in this practice.

Viking says "First published in _____," with the day and the year on the copyright page of its first editions, as do numerous British publishers, usually noting only the year. A number of publishers mark second, third, and further printings as such on the copyright page, omitting any mention of printing on their first editions. Among these are Boni; Boni and

Liveright; Covici, Friede; Coward-McCann; Dial Press; Dodd, Mead; Harvard University Press; Lippincott; Liveright; Macauley; McClure, Phillips; McDowell, Obolensky; Oxford University Press; Reynal & Hitchcock; Putnam's; Stokes; and Vanguard. Among the British publishers whose books are similarly marked are Hogarth, Jonathan Cape and Harrison Smith, Chatto & Windus, Grant Richards, and T. Fisher Unwin.

There are certain publishers—"reprint houses"—that publish reprints almost exclusively. The two largest in terms of the number of books they have reprinted are Grosset & Dunlap and A.L. Burt. They are followed by Tower, Sun Dial, Garden City Publishing, Federal, Altemus, Triangle, Donohoe, Colliers, Caldwell, International Fiction Library, International Association of Newspapers and Authors, Worthington, New York Book, Saalfield, Lupton, Mershon, and others. Books by these houses are immediately identifiable as non-firsts, with a very few exceptions, some of which appear in this book. None of these houses places a date on the title page of a book.

A pitfall to watch out for is the erroneously labeled first edition. Sometimes a book club copy may say "First Edition" on its copyright page, but this doesn't make it a first edition—it makes it a mistake. If the dust jacket is present, a book may be identified on the rear flap, or on the lower corner of the front jacket flap, as being from the Book-of-the-Month Club. If that corner is clipped, it may have been in order to remove the book club identification. Quite often a jacket will hold no clue at all except for the absence of a price on the top of the front flap. Virtually all dust jackets lacking a printed price can be considered book club editions. The exceptions are books from some university presses, which are not often selected by a book club, and books published very recently, when some publishers began omitting a price on the jacket. If the top flap has been price-clipped, it may be that it was clipped to conceal the fact that the book is a book club edition. But it may also be that someone clipped the price on a book bought as a gift. On the rear cover of the book itself, in the lower right-hand corner, a book club edition often has a "blind stamp," most often in the shape of an indented square, sometimes a dot or leaf shape. Book club editions, because of cheaper paper, are often thinner and of lighter weight, and before 1980, when plasticized book jackets were developed, had jackets of thinner and lower gloss paper.

Whether it's a current title or an older book, in many cases publisher's markings are not sufficient to determine its edition. In that case other distinguishing characteristics must be used. **Virtually all of the information given in the price list beyond the "vital statistics" of author-title-place-publisher-date-illustrations-number of volumes given with a first edition is given to assist in making that determination. All descriptive material, and aside from general commentary, is consistent with the book being a first edition, and in most cases the information given in the listings is sufficient to identify the edition.**

With a "hot" author expected to have a best-seller, the odds are very good that the publisher will have an initial print run of fifty to one hundred thousand copies. Later printings could run the number of copies of the book into a million or more. Buying a couple of copies and carefully storing them away in their mint condition does not mean the book will be more valuable *ever*. In this hot one minute, cold the next market, the current best-seller will often hit the remainder table of a bookstore for a tremendous discount to make way for the next trendy title. Changing tastes and values could mean that it would take an inordinate amount of time before this ultra-modern first will even appreciate to its original list price. Remember that scarcity factors into the selling price of collectible books—and a million-copy best-seller will probably never be scarce.

Condition and Grading

In the market valuation of books, the importance of condition can hardly be stressed enough. Particularly if you are buying to invest, but even if you simply want to be sure that your collection retains its value, don't ever forget condition. From a bookseller's point of view, a book in beautiful condition, if it's eighty years old or more, and was made out of good quality materials to begin with, will sell sooner or later, somewhere, to someone, regardless of its contents. (I'm talking about beautiful condition—not nice or pretty nice, but beautiful.) Condition is so important that it alone can sell a book, if the book is old enough, even though age alone, at least from 1820 or later, will rarely sell one. The superb copy of a book for which there is some demand not only brings a truly premium price, but it also sells quickly and easily, while the indifferent copy may sit on the bookseller's shelf forever.

In buying or selling "modern firsts" in particular, condition is the first thing to remember. The expression "modern first" is synonymous for booksellers and first edition collectors with "modern first edition in a dust jacket." The books that sell for the highest prices are expected to have no price clipping, owner's name, or remainder marks (ink stamp on page edges). A "modern first" published during the last twenty-five years or so is almost by definition virtually as new in dust jacket: if a bookseller is talking about a literary first edition published during the last fifty years or more and refers to it as "a first edition," he *means* "first edition in dust jacket." Should you tell a bookseller that you have a 1980 first edition for sale, and then it turns out that the book has no jacket, you will either have a visible case of exasperation on your hands or you have met a polite and self-contained bookseller.

A modern literary first edition *without* a dust jacket tends to sell for something like one-quarter of the price of the same book in the same condition *with* a dust jacket; this is the estimate of the specialist in modern first editions, as expressed by Allen and Patricia Ahearn in their *Collected Books: The Guide to Values* (see "References"). They also estimate there that for most books of nonfiction of the modern period, the lack of a jacket reduces the price to about eighty percent of the price of a jacketed copy. (The $100 book sells for eighty dollars without a jacket.)

In the case of nonfiction, the more the author is collected as "a first edition," because of his name, the more important the dust jacket will be, and the greater the price differential. The more generally the book is desired for strictly scholarly or similar purposes—i.e., as an out-of-print book, for its content alone—the less important the dust jacket will be to the price of the book.

If a literary first—say a first edition of *Tom Sawyer*—is in poor condition, the knowledgeable collector will buy it only at a great discount, and with the intention of having it rebound. One should understand that a rebound literary first edition from the mid-to-late nineteenth century, no matter how beautifully bound, is worth much less than the same book in the original binding. In the case of a work of nonfiction from the same period or earlier, binding tends to be of far less importance. Condition still matters, but a book should be rebound if the other characteristics that make a book valuable, like the social valuation of its contents, provides justification. Once rebound, the book will sell at some fair approximation of its value in original binding, though it may take longer to sell.

So, what do we mean specifically when discussing condition in a book? The books priced in this guide are priced as in nice condition. Nice condition is the standard in the world of collectible and widely marketable books and a guide has to be based on standards that can be held constant while other factors vary. The condition of the books listed in this guide is described as follows: as in essentially "as new" condition, with no defects, as they came from the publisher if published 1970 to today; as in "very nice" condition for books published 1950 to 1970; and as in "quite nice" condition for books published prior to 1950. "Quite nice" means certainly with no major defects, such as missing pages or gross wear and other defects I will describe, but there may be minor or possibly even moderate wear **so long as they remain structurally sound and aesthetically pleasing**. The terms being used here to describe condition and appearance in books are to be understood in their ordinary meanings in everyday language. There is always room for subjective interpretation, but I feel that the use of ordinary language is the safest and most communicative way to go.

In the book world, there are sets of descriptive terms for condition, words along the lines of "as new," "fine," "very good," "good," "fair," "poor," each with their own specific technical definition. The set most widely used is the one formalized at "AB Bookman's Weekly," the oldest, largest, and best-known journal for booksellers. The problem with this type of system is simple but profound. Terms from our everyday language receive a second set of meanings. For instance, the "AB" definition of "good" is "the average used and worn book that has all pages or leaves present, any defects must be noted." In other words, "good" has come to mean "pretty bad." When "good" means "bad," the system has broken down and become not just useless but unacceptably misleading. ("AB" didn't invent this terminology: it is simply recording the usage that has come to be).

Every good new bookseller conscientiously struggles to use these terms. As a result, when I once in a while receive a pathetic specimen of a book that has been described as "good" or "very good," it's difficult to complain since the dealer was just innocently following the rules. But as a matter of fact, after all my years in the business, when a bookseller's catalog description says "very good," I still expect him to mean very good, and he usually does. This means that despite all the manuals and magazines that discuss grading, in the world of respectable or valuable hardcover books only inexperienced booksellers, on the whole, use the system. I can't even imagine seeing a responsible bookseller (and the large majority of booksellers, though not absolutely all, are very responsible people) look a customer in the eye and tell him that the condition of a certain copy of a book he has back in his shop is "good," when in fact it's not very good. My advice is to use caution when reading written descriptions and to pay attention to your communications with booksellers, making sure that you understand each other. Ordinary language can be used with care, imagination, and honesty, and can serve our purposes well if used with respect.

Words like "superb" or "beautiful" are used for the older book, the standard for which has been described as "very nice" or "quite nice" (depending on its age), when these books markedly surpass those standards. (You would never hear a bookseller use words like "superb" or "beautiful" to describe a book published in 1980.) I have seen and sold books from the mid-nineteenth century that glowed, that still had a shine. This is where "superb" applies, or to a 1920s edition in dust jacket that meets the standards given here for the 1980 book. Although rare, it happens, and this kind of copy demands and receives an exceptional price. Minor defects are to be expected in anything less than a new book.

Almost no matter what the book, there are some characteristics that are simply unacceptable as long as we are talking about either price or salability. Among these are (a) missing pages or parts of pages; (b) missing or detached covers; (c) appreciable water or damp damage; (d) severe soil; (e) extreme wear or warping; and (f) badly broken hinges.

When it comes to damaged books, the policy should be *caveat emptor*. A good discount can be a fine way to get a hard-to-find book for reading or study, but otherwise a damaged book is not a worthwhile investment.

The publications listed in "References" at the end of this book are among the most reliable for collectors as well as booksellers.

◼ About This Guide

When the idea of a book price guide was presented to me, it occurred to me that the reason there had not been a really good (in my opinion) trade paperback price guide was that perhaps it was not possible to produce a good one. Scope, (along with reliability and ease of use) is a major criterion. If I need a roomful of tomes to help me research and price my own material, how could there be a general guide with only ten or twenty thousand entries that would be of any use?

The writers of the "tomes" have filled them with thousands of relevant entries, yet when I use them I still find only half of what I am looking for and need to price. Beyond those books, bookseller catalogs are available, and they will offer information on perhaps no more than another fifteen percent. How could anything I could do within the space limits be more than just a token price guide?

After much thought, illumination suddenly arrived—and the answer is so obvious, it's embarrassing. There are a tremendous number of books, hundreds of thousands surely, that relatively few people have any interest in at all. *But*, there is a group of books, maybe ten thousand or so, that people *are* interested in—*Little Black Sambo*, the "Gutenberg Bible," *Leaves of Grass*, Joseph C. Lincoln titles, Poe's first editions, Andrew Wyeth books, *Tom Swift*, Audubon's *Birds of America*, Zane Grey books, *Raggedy Ann*, titles and authors setting auction records, books rumored to be valuable, and whatever titles have been in the news lately. These are the books that "everyone" knows and wants to know more about, not the others. And there you have your list.

And this is just the list of authors and titles that any bookseller with broad experience can reel off, because these are the books that people want or are curious about. A bookseller already knows most of the titles on this list, because he is most frequently asked these questions.

Being able to price them is something else again. So as a matter of fact, this is exactly the kind of guide that booksellers themselves don't have and could use. Knowing how to price some of these things presents one of the most persistent and time-consuming minor frustrations for collectors and booksellers. As a class, these books are grossly underrepresented in the basic price guides. The prices can change fast because of demand and the fluctuating economy. Some booksellers are secretive about the prices in order to hold down their buying prices; the titles tend not to appear in catalogs because they are sold right off the shelf or to an anxious waiting list. Some, like Joseph C. Lincoln novels, or Gladys Tabor, or *Tom Swift*, seem to be treated as beneath notice. For these and other reasons, the prices for many of these books are not that easy for collectors or dealers to ascertain. I believe this book will fill a need that is rarely met, and never quite defined.

Within the scope of this guide, when a collector or dealer goes to look up a title, there's a good chance that it will be there. The guide covers the field in terms of price range—from the moderately priced novel to the record-setting auction sale price—and includes the specific categories of books that people collect, with a good sample of core books in each area.

There are many specific categories within which people collect books. Perhaps your interests lie in women's studies or children's books, maybe books that contain maps, maybe in one of several dozens of other classifications. To insure further ease of use, there is a "Key to Categories" included in the guide. This key, alphabetized by collecting categories, is a key to the entries in each of many of the most popular fields of book collecting. Under each category listed, the names of all of the authors included in this book with one or more works in that category are alphabetized. At a glance, you will be able to find all of the authors in the price guide who have titles listed in a special field.

How to Use This Guide

It is important to understand how the guide is organized, and the first thing to understand is exactly what's being priced. All of the books listed are hardcover books unless otherwise indicated. All nineteenth-century books listed are priced as in original cloth or paper-covered boards unless described otherwise. First editions of books published in 1970 or later are priced as in essentially "as new" condition—that is, with no defects, or as they came from the publisher. First editions of books published from about 1950 to 1970 are priced as in "very nice" condition, with dust jackets to match. All other books, unless otherwise specifically noted in their descriptions, are priced as in "quite nice" condition. A dust jacket is assumed from 1920 onward.

The primary way to find a book in this guide is to look it up by the name of its author. The core of the guide is one long listing of books alphabetized by the author's last name. Within that same alphabetized listing, special categories can be found. If you are looking for a specific category, whether it's Big Little Books or bibles, you'll find a selection of these books and their prices in the alphabetized price listings. For other categories—such as nautical or modern first editions—the entry for the category in the main listing refers you to the "Key to Categories" (Appendix A). The "Key to Categories" is alphabetized as well, from African-American books to women's studies. Under each category heading, such as nautical, there is a list of every author who has nautical books in the price listing. In all cases, the category will be found first in the main listing, which will then refer you to the "Key to Categories" if necessary.

In addition, the names of the most recognized illustrators are also found within the main listing, which will then refer you to an author and a title. In cases where there are a number of books illustrated by the same artist, the entry will refer you to the "Key to Illustrators." This key, in Appendix B, is alphabetized by the illustrator's last name. With each illustrator's name, the key cites all of the authors in the alphabetized price listing whose books contain the artist's work.

Now, what happens if you know the name of a book you loved as a child, like *Gulliver's Travels*, but don't know who wrote the book? There are many book titles that are known better by their titles than by their authors: *Uncle Wiggily*, *Gulliver's Travels*, *Raggedy Ann*, etc. In addition to being listed under the author's name, many of these books are also listed alphabetically by title.

With each entry in the price listing, there is information included to assist you in understanding what you have or are considering buying. Each entry begins with the author's name followed by the title (in italics), the city of publication, the publisher, the date of publication (or copyright date), number of volumes if there is more than one, the illustrator or illustrations, the edition, and the size of the book if particularly large or small. **It bears repeating that when a date is given in parentheses it is a copyright date, and when a date is given without parentheses it is the publication date as it appears on the title page of the book.** For a complete explanation of the meaning of these dates, see the chapter titled "Book Collecting."

In a very few cases in the guide, **a date has been provided in quotation marks. This has occurred where the edition being described was not in hand and where the catalog or other materials being used for the description of the edition failed to distinguish whether the dates given were copyright or publication dates** (an unacceptable failure as far as this bookseller is concerned).

In cases where a book has a dust jacket, the listing will indicate this by "DJ." If the listing does not contain a DJ, then the book is priced in the listing as having no dust jacket, an absence that must be noted since this is a fact that can affect the price dramatically.

Price Structure

One of the most important factors to understand in a price guide is what the price is based upon. In each case, the price given is the average price. By this, I mean the average price range of books sold at retail prices by out-of-print booksellers across the country, in bookshops, book barns, bookseller catalogs and lists, book shows, and books sold at auction. The fact that some books are not sold at the prices at which they were originally offered has also been taken into account.

In the case of a few important and very valuable books, a single recent auction price, rather than an average, has been used. This is so because of the scarce appearance of the book at recent auctions. The use of a single auction price has in these cases been noted in the description. But it is important to note that in most cases a single auction price has little reliability, since a single price may reflect simply a battle between two chronic rivals or a snowstorm that kept buyers away.

A group of auction prices is the most reliable basis of all for an average price. When auction prices have been available, they have been taken into account. For a given title, a group of auction prices could be somewhat higher or lower than a comparison group of catalog offering prices. Auction prices are on the whole available only for the more valuable and expensive books.

There are price guides on the market which show average prices considerably higher than those found in this guide. The differences in the guides are in precisely what prices are being averaged. In this guide, I attempt to use as our basis the prices of the whole range of professional booksellers, whether they run a small-town book shop or are part of the smaller percentage of the country's dealers in, for instance, the major cities. Prices are higher in this last group because more of the best material is available there, as well as the market to go with it. These booksellers handle perhaps sixty-five percent of the best and scarcest material, but maybe only five or ten percent of the total material sold in the country. Their prices are the pacesetters for the rest of the country. Obviously, prices vary widely across the geographical and hierarchical map. The goal of this guide, written for all potential buyers and sellers of out-of-print and rare books, is to mirror the whole range of the most frequently found prices for those books.

However, if the guide has a bias, it is in general toward the higher price rather than the lower. The reason for this is that catalogs and other printed material are heavily relied on when putting a guide of this nature together. This material tends to be a product of the most active and sophisticated dealers with the bulk of the choicest material.

The price spreads in the guide reflect the price spreads in the book world. But occasionally a price spread will seem ridiculous—$15 to $200. What can anyone do with that? A spread like this is a result not of taking every price to be found, exceptional or not, but of the fact that sometimes booksellers are not in agreement at all on the proper ballpark prices for an author. This can occur when the evaluation of an author is on its way up or on its way down, with half of the dealers not yet acting on that fact through ignorance or other causes. It could be that the author is new, or is of particular interest only in one geographical area, or maybe some bookseller knows something, or thinks he knows something, that is not generally known. At any rate, the occasional wide price spread simply reflects the realities of the book world at the moment.

But What If My Book Isn't Here?

Your own estimate, even for books not listed in this price list, can be fairly accurate when based on simple rules. Price structure is the orderly and consistent relationship between prices. If I have a first edition of Zane Grey's *The Thundering Herd* in nice condition in a DJ, it is worth less than an identical copy signed by the author. By the same token, a signed copy is worth less than an identical copy signed to the author's mother. On the other hand, this signed copy is worth more than an identical copy without a DJ and more than a signed reprint edition of the same title.

This all remains true whatever author and title I substitute for Zane Grey's *The Thundering Herd*.

It is important to understand that, other things being equal, the price of a signed Zane Grey first edition is based on the price of an unsigned Zane Grey first edition, and so on. Study the price range of first editions in nice condition with DJ of a given author. Once you have that range, you use the price structure to arrive at a price for the particular edition and condition in your hand.

This guide uses first editions in DJ as a standard. By repeatedly using one edition, in one condition, we provide ourselves with a constant, to which we can then relate everything else: other editions, conditions, titles, authors, prices. We use the constant as a tool. If we are consistent in edition and condition, it's like using a pitch pipe—everything else can be calculated in relation to it. The price guide may be used to study comparative pricing because the price structure and the pattern of prices remain the same.

Dust jacket or no dust jacket, first printing or later printing, reprint edition, cheap reprint edition, fine condition or poor condition, signed, association, advance or proof copy, limited edition, copy from a famous collection, or any combination of the above all have their place in the price structure. An author's first book, and an author's "great book" or most famous book, are ordinarily priced higher than his other first trade editions.

There are cases where an author has written for both adults and children, but is more renowned for his children's books. E.B. White and Dr. Seuss are authors whose first children's books are the most valuable and the most sought after—not their respective first books. Another exception is that sometimes an author's "great" book is worth as much or more than his first, such as Hemingway's *The Sun Also Rises* and T.S. Eliot's *The Waste Land*.

A limited edition consistently sells for a higher price than the ordinary first edition (the "first trade edition"). Limited editions are, as the name suggests, issued in limited quantities, and are often numbered. They may be signed by the author and/or illustrator and could be specially bound, made with special materials, or be accompanied with an original print. They cost much more as new books than the trade edition does, and their prices on the rare and out-of-print book market are correspondingly higher.

Before it is permanently bound, a book goes through several stages. Copies from these stages may be somewhat difficult for a person outside of the publishing industry to obtain except from an out-of-print bookseller, but if they can be obtained they are worth more than copies of the first trade edition. Uncorrected proofs and advance review copies are issued prior to publication of the book and are considered "even firster than firsts." Proof copies may sell for two to three times the price of the first edition of the same title. Advance reading copies are worth less than proof copies. First trade editions with review slips laid in are worth more than first trade editions but less than advance reading copies. Galley proofs, the long sheets of unproofed material, are the most valuable.

There are some books from famous collections, which you will see listed in auction records as the "Garden copy" or the "Epstein copy" as being worth a great deal. These books, because of their provenance, tend to sell for far more than an ordinary copy in equal or better condition, and often for several times more. Their prices cannot be used to judge the value of books that lack this kind of known history.

Some books are presented as groups in the price guide. Books by individual presses (such as Doves Press) and sets like Big Little Books are presented together so the internal price structure within each group can be understood. These books are then cross-referenced by author so that they can be compared with other samples of the author's work. The reader can compare a set of Kipling of a certain quality with sets by other writers of varying quality, and then compare the price of a Kipling set against a Kipling first edition and a Kipling reprint, which in turn can be compared against other authors' first editions and reprints. The condition of the book, of course, must also be taken into account when pricing.

This book may be considered a brief how-to manual as well as a price guide. For as long as I have been in the book business, I have been asked questions by interested people who had a sense of mysteries unexplained. This book has provided an opportunity to answer a few of the questions.

PRICE
LISTINGS

———————————————

The collectibility of a book is determined by combining (a) the **social valuation of contents** and the **reputation of author(s)**; (b) **edition**; (c) **condition**; and (d) **aesthetic qualities**, to equal (e) the **value or collectibility**.

The **price on the market**, as distinct from its collectibility, is determined by the factors above *plus* **scarcity**.

 A ────────────────────────

ABBEY, Edward. *Black Sun*. New York: Simon & Schuster 1971, 1st edition, DJ. $75.

ABBEY, Edward. *Desert Solitaire*. New York: McGraw-Hill (1968), 1st edition, DJ. $150.

ABBEY, Edward. *Slickrock*. San Francisco and New York: Sierra Club (1971), 1st American edition, photographs by Philip Hyde, folio, scarce, DJ. $250–$300.

ABBEY, Edward. *Slickrock: The Canyon Country of Southeast Utah*. San Francisco: Sierra Club (1971), 1st edition, photographs by Philip Hyde, wraps. $20–$50.

ABBEY, Edward. *The Monkey Wrench Gang*. Philadelphia: Lippincott 1975, 1st edition, DJ. $35–$50.

ABBEY, Edward. *The Monkey Wrench Gang*. Salt Lake City: Dream Garden Press 1985, special anniversary edition illustrated by R. Crum, 1st printing of this edition, thus a "first edition," or a "first thus," DJ. $75.

ABBOTT, Berenice. *The World of Atget*. New York: Horizon 1964, 1st edition, folio, 180 plates, DJ. $125.

ABBOTT, Berenice, and McCausland, Elizabeth. *Changing New York*. New York: Dutton 1939, 1st edition, DJ. $300.

ABBOTT, E.C. *We Pointed Them North*. New York: Farrar & Rinehart (1939), 1st edition, DJ. $90.

ABBOTT, E.C. *We Pointed Them North*. Norman: University of Oklahoma (1955), later printing of new edition. $15.

ABBOTT, E.C. *We Pointed Them North*. Norman: University of Oklahoma (1955), 1st printing, new edition, DJ. $27–$50.

ABRAHAM, Karl. *Selected Papers*. London: Hogarth Press 1927, 1st edition in English, translated by Douglas Bryan and Alix Strahey, DJ. $75–$85.

ACHEBE, Chinua. *Things Fall Apart*. London: Heinemann 1958, 1st edition of author's first book, DJ. $75–$125.

ACKERLY, J.R. *The Prisoners of War*. London: 1925, 1st edition, DJ. $60.

ADAMIC, Louis. *My Native Land*. New York: Harper & Brothers 1943, 1st edition, DJ. $25.

ADAMS, Ansel. *Examples: The Making of Forty Photographs*. Boston: Little, Brown (1983), 1st edition, 40 photographs, DJ. $45.

ADAMS, Ansel. *See also* "Key to Illustrators."

ADAMS, Franklin P. *The Melancholy Lute*. New York: 1926, limited and signed edition, leather binding. $35.

ADAMS, Henry. *Mont Saint Michel and Chartres*. Boston and New York: Houghton Mifflin: The Riverside Press, Cambridge 1916, 1st trade edition, 12 black and white plates. $65.

ADAMS, Henry. *Mont Saint Michel and Chartres*. Boston and New York: Houghton Mifflin: The Riverside Press, Cambridge (1926), later printing, illustrated. $25.

(ADAMS, Henry.) *Mont Saint Michel and Chartres*. Washington: privately printed 1904, 1st edition, folio, leather spine label, slipcase, rare. $1,500–$2,500.

ADAMS, Henry. *The Education of Henry Adams*. Boston and New York: Houghton Mifflin 1918, 1st trade edition. $60.

ADAMS, Leonie. *High Falcon and Other Poems*. New York: John Day (1929), 1st edition, DJ. $100.

ADAMS, Ramon. *Cowboy Lingo*. Boston: Houghton Mifflin 1936, 1st edition. $65.

ADAMS, Ramon. *Six Guns & Saddle Leather*. Norman: University of Oklahoma 1969, 2nd edition, DJ. $115.

ADAMS, Richard. *The Ship's Cat*. New York: Knopf 1977, 1st American edition, vividly illustrated, DJ. $45.

ADAMS, Richard. *Watership Down*. London: 1972, 1st edition, DJ, author's first book, scarce. $400.

ADAMS, Richard. *Watership Down*. Macmillan 1974, 1st American edition, author's first book, DJ. $100.

ADAMS, Samuel Hopkins. *Revelry*. New York: Boni and Liveright 1926, 1st edition, DJ. $35.

ADE, George. *Fables in Slang*. Chicago: Stone 1900, 1st edition. $20–$40.

ADE, George. *Forty Modern Fables*. New York: Russell 1901, 1st edition. Printed by Updike at Merrymount. $20–$40.

ADE, George. *More Fables*. Chicago and New York: Stone 1900, 1st edition. $20–$40.

ADNEY, Edwin Tappen, and Chapelle, Howard I. *The Bark Canoes and Skin Boats of America*. Washington, D.C.: Smithsonian Institute 1964. $30–$50.

AE. *See* Russell, George W., under Cuala Press.

AESOP. *The Fables of Aesop*. New York: Hodder & Stoughton (1909), 1st American edition, 23 mounted color plates by Detmold. $150–$200.

AFRICAN–AMERICANA. *See* "Key to Categories."

AFRICAN–AMERICAN PHOTOGRAPHERS. *See* "Key to Illustrators."

AGEE, James. *A Death in the Family*. New York: McDowell Obolensky (1957), 1st edition, 1st issue (1st issue identified by "walking" on page 80, mistakenly substituted for "waking"). $75–$100.

AGEE, James. *Let Us Now Praise Famous Men*. Boston: Houghton Mifflin 1941, 1st edition, photographs by Walker Evans, DJ. $325.

AGEE, James. *Let Us Now Praise Famous Men*. Boston: Houghton Mifflin (1960), later edition, photographs by Walker Evans, DJ. $25–$60.

AGEE, James. *Letters of James Agree to Father Flye*. New York: Braziller 1962, 1st edition, DJ. $20–$30.

AGRICOLA, Georgius. *De Re Metallica*. London: The Mining Magazine 1912, translated from the 1st Latin edition of 1556 by

Herbert Hoover. Original vellum, folio, woodcuts from the original. $300–$950.

AIKEN, Conrad. *The Jig of Forslin*. Boston: Four Seas Co. 1916, 1st edition, DJ. $60.

AIKEN, Conrad. *The Kid*. New York: Duell, Sloan & Pearce 1947, 1st edition, DJ. $35.

AIKEN, Conrad. *Ushant*. New York: Duell, Sloan & Pearce (1952), 1st edition, DJ. $20.

AIRCRAFT YEARBOOK 1941. New York: Aeronautic Chamber of Commerce 1941. $45.

AKERS, Floyd. *The Boy Fortune Hunters in Egypt*. Chicago: Reilly & Britton (1908), illustrated, 1st edition, 1st state, with drawing of an open book on title page, a listing of first three titles of this series on copyright page, and one ad for *The Girl Graduate* at the book's end. $150–$200.

ALBEE, Edward. *The Zoo Story, The Death of Bessie Smith, The Sandbox: Three Plays*. New York: Coward–McCann (1960), 1st edition, DJ. $85.

ALBEE, Edward. *Who's Afraid of Virginia Woolf?* New York: Atheneum 1962, 1st edition, DJ. $125–$150.

ALCOTT, Louisa May. *An Old–Fashioned Girl*. Boston: Little, Brown 1915, color plates by Jessie Wilcox Smith. $65–$85.

ALCOTT, Louisa May. *Little Men: Life at Plumfield With Jo's Boys*. Boston: Roberts Brothers 1871, green cloth, 1st American edition, 1st issue, with 4 pages of ads in front listing *Pink and White Tyranny* as "nearly ready." $75–$125.

ALCOTT, Louisa May. *Little Women*. Boston: Little, Brown 1915, illustrated in color by Jessie Wilcox Smith, cover with pictorial paste–on label, 1st printing of the Jessie Wilcox Smith edition. $125.

ALCOTT, Louisa May. *Little Women*. Boston: Little, Brown 1915, illustrated in color by Jessie Wilcox Smith, cover with pictorial paste–on label, later printing of the Jessie Wilcox Smith edition. $40.

ALCOTT, Louisa May. *Little Women*. Boston: Roberts Bros. 1868–69, 2 vols, 4 ills, including frontis, 1st edition, lacking "Part I" on spine of 1st volume, and with 2nd volume lacking the notice *"Little Women*, Part First" on page iv and priced $1.25 in ads, page 11. $100–$3,000.

ALDINGTON, Richard. *All Men are Enemies*. London: Chatto & Windus 1933, 1st edition, DJ. $35.

ALDISS, Brian W. *Greybeard*. New York: Harcourt, Brace & World (1964), 1st edition, DJ. $125.

ALDISS, Brian W. *The Hand–Reared Boy*. London: Weidenfeld & Nicolson (1970), 1st edition, DJ. $40.

ALEICHEM, Sholem. *Tevye's Daughters*. New York: Crown (1949), 1st edition, DJ. $15–$35.

ALGREN, Nelson. *The Man with the Golden Arm*. New York: Doubleday 1949, 1st edition, DJ. $60.

ALGREN, Nelson. *The Neon Wilderness*. Garden City: Doubleday 1947, 1st edition, DJ. $75.

ALGREN, Nelson. *See also* Vintage Paperbacks.

ALICE IN WONDERLAND. See Carroll, L.: *Alice's Adventures*...

ALLEN, Hervey. *Action at Aquila*. New York: Farrar & Rinehart 1938, 1st edition, DJ. $25.

ALLEN, Hervey. *Anthony Adverse*. New York: Farrar & Rinehart 1933, 1st edition, DJ. $65.

ALLEN, Hervey. *Anthony Adverse*, New York: Farrar & Rinehart 1934, 2 vols, 2 color frontis plates and ep's by N.C. Wyeth, 1st printing of this edition, slipcase. $75.

ALLEN, Hervey. *The Forest and the Fort*. New York: Farrar & Rinehart (1943), 1st edition, color frontis by Andrew Wyeth, DJ. $35–$50.

ALLEN, James Lane. *A Kentucky Cardinal*. New York: Harper's 1895, 1st edition. $20–$35.

ALLEN, William. *History of the Campaign of Gen. T. J. (Stonewall) Jackson in the Shenandoah Valley of Virginia*. Philadelphia: "1880". $175–$250.

ALLEN, William. *History of the Campaign of Gen. T. J. (Stonewall) Jackson in the Shenandoah Valley of Virginia*. Boston: "1892". $100–$175.

ALLEN, Woody. *Play it Again, Sam*. New York: (1969), 1st edition, DJ. $125.

ALMANACS. Bickerstaff, Isaac. *NEW–ENGLAND ALMANACK . . . FOR THE YEAR OF OUR LORD CHRIST 1800*. Providence: John Carter, nd. $25.

AMADO, Jorge. *Doña Flor and Her Two Husbands*. New York: Knopf 1969, 1st edition, DJ. $25.

AMBLER, Eric. *A Coffin for Dimitrios*. New York: Knopf (1939), 1st American edition, DJ. $200.

AMBLER, Eric. *Journey into Fear*. London: Hodder & Stoughton (1940), 1st edition, DJ. $750.

AMBLER, Eric. *Journey into Fear*. New York: Knopf 1940, 1st American edition, DJ. $125.

AMBLER, Eric. *Judgement on Deltchev*. London: Hodder & Stoughton (1951), 1st edition, DJ. $50.

AMERICANA. *See* "Key to Categories."

AMIS, Kingsley. *Lucky Jim*. London: Victor Gollancz, Ltd. 1953, 1st edition, DJ. $500.

ANDERSEN, Hans Christian. *Danish Fairy Legends and Tales*. London: William Pickering 1846, 1st English edition. This was translated from the Danish by Caroline Peachey, and contains many of the author's most famous stories. $225–$350.

ANDERSEN, Hans Christian. *The Fir Tree*. New York: Harper & Row (1970), illustrated by Nancy Ekholm Burkert in color and black and white, DJ. $25–$45.

ANDERSON, Maxwell. *Joan of Lorraine: A Play in Two Acts*. Washington: 1946, 1st edition, DJ. $20.

ANDERSON, Poul. *Agent of the Terran Empire*. Philadelphia and New York: Chilton (1965) 1st edition, scarce, DJ. $75–$125.

ANDERSON, Poul. *The Star Fox*. Garden City: Doubleday 1965, 1st edition, DJ. $65–$85.

ANDERSON, Sherwood. *Dark Laughter*. New York: Boni & Liveright 1925, 1st edition, DJ. $125.

ANDERSON, Sherwood. *Tar, A Midwest Childhood*. New York: Boni & Liveright 1926, 1st edition, DJ. $75.

ANGELO, Valenti. *Look Out Yonder*. New York: Viking Press 1943, frontis, illustrated by author, 1st edition, DJ. $25.

ANGELO, Valenti. *See also* "Key to Illustrators."

ANGELOU, Maya. *I Know Why the Caged Bird Sings*. New York: Random House (1969), 1st edition, 1st issue, with page tops stained red, author's first book, DJ. $50.

ANNE OF GREEN GABLES. See Montgomery, L.M.

ANTHOLOGIES. *A Book of Irish Verse*. 1895, introduction and notes by William Butler Yeats. $40–$60.

ANTHOLOGIES. *A Book of Princeton Verse II*. Princeton: Princeton University Press 1919. Has poetry by F. Scott Fitzgerald, John Peale Bishop, and Edmund Wilson. 1st edition. $75–$175.

ANTHOLOGIES. *American and British Verse from the Yale Review*. New Haven: Yale University Press 1920. $35.

ANTHOLOGIES. *American College Verse*. New York: Henry Harrison (1932), 1st edition, DJ. Includes material by Marianne Moore and Walter Van Tilburg Clark. Illustrated by Charles Cullen. $65.

ANTHOLOGIES. *An Anthology of Magazine Verse for 1922*. Boston: Small, Maynard 1922, 1st edition, DJ. $25.

ANTHOLOGIES. *An Anthology of the Younger Poets*. Philadelphia: Centaur Press 1932, 1st edition, DJ. Has work by Hart Crane, Kay Boyle, and William Faulkner. $150.

ANTHOLOGIES. *Anchor in the Sea: An Anthology of Psychological Fiction*. New York: Swallow/Morrow 1947, 1st edition, DJ. Includes 1st book appearances of Jean Stafford, John Berryman, Kay Boyle, and work by Delmore Schwartz. $35.

ANTHOLOGIES. De la Mare, Walter, editor. *Behold This Dreamer*. London: 1939, 1st edition, colored frontis and vignette by Barnett Freedman, DJ. $50.

ANTHOLOGIES. *Esquire. The Sixth New Year. A Resolution*. Chicago and New York: Esquire 1939, 1st edition. Includes Hemingway's *The Snows of Kilimanjaro*. Leatherbound. $25–$50.

ANTHOLOGIES. *Imagist Anthology 1930*. New York: Covici, Friede (1930), 1st edition, one of one thousand, with work by James Joyce, D.H. Lawrence, William Carlos Williams, H.D., and others, DJ. $150–$250.

ANTHOLOGIES. *Imagist Anthology 1930.* New York: Covici, Friede (1930), 1st edition, one of one thousand, with work by James Joyce, D.H. Lawrence, William Carlos Williams, H.D., and others. $85.

ANTHOLOGIES. *My Story That I Like Best.* New York: 1924, 1st edition, contributions by Edna Ferber, James Oliver Curwood, Irvin Cobb, and others, DJ. $10–$25.

ANTHOLOGIES. *New Directions 14.* New York: New Directions 1953, 1st edition, DJ. $20–$30.

ANTHOLOGIES. *New Directions in Prose and Poetry 1937.* Norfolk: New Directions 1937, 1st edition, DJ. $65–$100.

ANTHOLOGIES. *O. Henry Memorial Award Stories of 1939.* New York: Doubleday, Doran 1939, 1st edition, contains stories by Eudora Welty, William Faulkner, and Erskine Caldwell, DJ. $35–$75.

ANTHOLOGIES. *Prize Stories of 1947, The O. Henry Awards.* New York: Doubleday 1947, DJ. $20–$30.

ANTHOLOGIES. *The Best from "Playboy."* New York: (1954), the first annual issue, DJ. $75.

ANTHOLOGIES. *The Best from "Yank," The Army Weekly.* New York: E.P. Dutton & Co. 1945, DJ. $40.

ANTHOLOGIES. *The Best Humor of 1927.* Boston: Stratford Co. 1928, 1st edition, DJ. $20.

ANTHOLOGIES. *The Best Plays of 1942–43.* New York: Dodd, Mead 1944, 1st edition, DJ. $25.

ANTHOLOGIES. *The Best Plays of 1944–45.* New York: Dodd, Mead 1946, 1st edition, includes work by Tennessee Williams, George S. Kaufman, and others, DJ. $40.

ANTHOLOGIES. *The Best Plays of 1946–47.* New York: Dodd, Mead 1947, 1st edition, includes *The Iceman Cometh*, Lillian Hellman, Moss Hart, and Maxwell Anderson, DJ. $40.

ANTHOLOGIES. *The Best Poems of 1923.* New York: Harcourt, Brace (nd), 1st edition, DJ. $35–$50.

ANTHOLOGIES. *The Best Poems of 1926.* New York: Harcourt, Brace (nd), 1st edition, work by Robert Graves and others, DJ. $35–$50.

ANTHOLOGIES. *The Best Short Stories of 1938*. Boston: 1938, 1st edition, includes work by John Steinbeck, John Cheever, Robert Penn Warren, Jesse Stuart, and a first book appearance of Eudora Welty, DJ. $40–$50.

ANTHOLOGIES. *The Book of American Negro Poetry*. New York: Harcourt, Brace & Co. 1931, 1st revised edition, DJ. $50–$100.

ANTHOLOGIES. *The Hard-Boiled Omnibus*. New York: Simon & Schuster (1946), anthology of stories from "Black Mask" magazine, including work by Dashiell Hammett, Raymond Chandler, and others, 1st edition, DJ. $75–$100.

ANTHOLOGIES. *The Oxford Book of Modern Verse 1892–1935*. New York: Oxford University Press 1936, 1st American edition. $30.

ANTHOLOGIES. *The Pushcart Prize III*. (Yonkers): Pushcart Press (1978), 1st edition, DJ. $25–$40.

ANTIN, Mary. *The Promised Land*. Boston: Houghton Mifflin 1912, 1st edition. $25–$150.

ANTONINUS, Brother. *A Canticle to the Waterbirds*. Berkeley: for Lawton and Alfred Kennedy, San Francisco, Elizo 1968, 1st edition, quarto, photographs by Allen Say, limited edition of 200 copies, signed by Say and the author. Published without DJ. $75–$100.

ANTONINUS, Brother. *A Canticle to the Waterbirds*. Berkeley: for Lawton and Alfred Kennedy, San Francisco, Elizo 1968, 1st trade edition, quarto, photographs by Allen Say, DJ. $25.

APPLETON, Victor. *See* Juvenile Series Books.

APPLETON'S DICTIONARY OF MACHINES, MECHANICS, ENGINE-WORK, AND ENGINEERING. New York: D. Appleton 1862, 2 vols in 6, original cloth. $125–$250.

ARABIAN NIGHTS. *See* Wiggin, Kate Douglas.

ARBUS, Diane. *Diane Arbus*. Millerton: Aperture (1972), quarto, 1st edition, DJ. $50–$65.

ARDIZZONE, Edward. *Lucy Brown and Mr. Grimes*. New York: Oxford University Press (1937), 1st American edition, illustrated by the author. A little girl is approached by an old man who buys her ice cream; a nice story, but one that caused a stir among American librarians. DJ. $150–$250.

ARDIZZONE, Edward. *Tim's Last Voyage.* London: Bodley Head 1972, 1st edition, last of the "Tim" series, illustrated by the author, DJ. $45.

ARMSTRONG, Margaret. *See* "Key to Illustrators."

ARNOLD, H.H. *Global Mission.* New York: Harper 1949, a classic in World War II memoirs. $25.

ARNOLD, Matthew. *See* Ashendene Press: *Three Elegies.*

ARTZYBASHEFF, Boris. *See* "Key to Illustrators."

ASCH, Sholem. *Mottke the Thief.* New York: (1935), 1st edition, DJ. $16–$40.

ASCH, Sholem. *The Apostle.* New York: Putnam's (1943), 1st edition, DJ. $30–$50.

ASHBERY, John. *Some Trees.* New Haven: University Press 1956, 1st edition. This is the author's second book. Scarce. DJ. $125.

ASHBERY, John. *Three Poems.* New York: Viking (1972), 1st edition, DJ. $30.

ASHENDENE PRESS (London). *A Book of Songs and Poems from the Old Testament and Apocrypha.* London: Ashendene Press 1904, one of 150. $700.

ASHENDENE PRESS (London). Cervantes Saavedra, Miguel De. *Don Quixote.* London: Ashendene Press 1927–28, 2 vols, one of 225. $2,000.

ASHENDENE PRESS (London). Dante, Alighieri. *La Vita Nuova.* London: Ashendene Press 1895, one of 50, small quarto, original printed wrappers, box. $1,750.

ASHENDENE PRESS (London). Spenser, Edmund. *Minor Poems.* London: Ashendene Press 1925, one of 200. $500.

ASHENDENE PRESS (London). *The Song of Songs Which is Solomon's.* London: Ashendene Press 1902, illuminated by Valenti Angelo. $60.

ASHENDENE PRESS (London). *Three Elegies. "Lycidas" by John Milton. "Adonais" by Percy B. Shelley. "Thyrsis" by Matthew Arnold.* London: Ashendene Press 1899, one of 50. $600.

ASHENDENE PRESS (London). Thucydides. *The History of the Peloponnesian War.* London: Ashendene Press 1930, one of 260. $1,300–$1,600.

ASHENDENE PRESS (London). Tolstoy, Leo. *Where God Is Love Is*. London: Ashendene Press 1924, one of 200, translated by Louise and Aylmer Maude. $400.

ASHLEY, Clifford. *The Ashley Book of Knots*. Garden City: Doubleday, Doran 1944, 1st edition, illustrated. $30.

ASHLEY, Clifford. *The Yankee Whaler*. Boston: Houghton Mifflin 1938, 2nd edition. $110.

ASIMOV, Isaac. *Foundation*. New York: Gnome Press (1951), State A of the 1st edition, with cloth binding (dark blue stamped with red), and 1st edition so stated on copyright page, DJ. $150–$350.

ATHERTON, Gertrude. *The Conqueror*. New York: Macmillan 1902, 1st edition. $20–$25.

ATWELL, Mabel Lucie. *See* "Key to Illustrators."

ATWOOD, Margaret. *Surfacing*. New York: Simon & Schuster (1972), 1st edition, DJ. $25–$75.

ATWOOD, Margaret. *The Handmaid's Tale*. Boston: Houghton Mifflin 1986. $12–$20.

AUCHINCLOSS, Louis. *The Injustice Collectors*. Boston: Houghton Mifflin 1950, 1st edition, author's first book written under his own name, DJ. $20.

AUDEN, W.H. *The Age of Anxiety*. New York: Random House (1947), 1st edition, DJ. $45–$125.

AUDEN, W.H. *The Collected Poetry of*. London: Faber & Faber (1945), 1st British edition, DJ. $75–$200.

AUDEN, W.H. *The Collected Poetry of*. New York: Random House (1945), 1st edition, DJ. $100–$250.

AUDEN, W.H. *The Shield of Achilles*. New York: Random House (1955), 1st edition, DJ. $75–$125.

AUDUBON, John James. *The Birds of America*. London: 1827–1838, a copy from the Library of H. Bradley Martin, thus weighty with provenance. Stated price is not an average, but the price at which this went at auction in 1989. $3,960,000.

AUEL, Jean. *The Clan of the Cave Bear*. New York: Crown 1980, 1st edition, DJ. $50.

AUSLANDER, Joseph. *Hell in Harness.* New York: Doubleday 1929, 1st edition, scarce, DJ. $20–$45.

AUSTEN, Jane. *Love and Freindship* [sic], *& Other Early Works.* New York: Stokes 1922, now first printed from the original manuscript, preface by G.K. Chesterton, 1st American edition. $35.

AUSTEN, Jane. *Northanger Abbey: and Persuasion.* London: John Murray 1818, 4 vols, contemporary half calfskin, 1st edition of both titles, published posthumously. $3,000–$6,000.

AUSTEN, Jane. *Pride and Prejudice.* London: 1813, 1st edition, 3 vols, contemporary half calfskin, minor defects, one of three half-titles present after binding. $9,500–$12,000.

AUSTEN, Jane. *Sense and Sensibility.* London: Richard Bentley 1870, new edition, blind-stamped green cloth with gilt titling and decorative backstrip; hinge repaired, and backstrip slightly darkened. $60.

AUSTEN, Jane. *Sense and Sensibility.* London: T. Egerton 1811, 3 vols, 1st edition of author's first book, contemporary half calfskin. $12,000.

AUSTEN, Jane. *Sense And Sensibility.* London: T. Egerton 1813, 3 vols, 2nd edition of author's first book, contemporary half calfskin. $8,500.

AUSTEN, John. *See* "Key to Illustrators."

AUSTIN, A.B. *We Landed at Dawn.* New York: 1943, maps, the story of the Dieppe raid. $10.

AUSTIN, Mary. *The Land of Little Rain.* Boston and New York: Houghton Mifflin 1903, illustrated by E. Boyd Smith, frontis, 3 plates, decorative marginal drawings, author's first book, quite scarce. $95–$300.

AUSTIN, Mary. *The Land of Little Rain.* Boston and New York: Houghton Mifflin 1950, 48 photographs by Ansel Adams, 1st edition thus, DJ. $75–$135.

AUTOBIOGRAPHY OF AN EX-COLORED MAN. (By James Weldon Johnson). Boston: Sherman French and Co. 1912, author's first book. $200–$300.

AVEDON, Richard. *See* Baldwin, James: *Nothing Personal.*

AVEDON, Richard. *See* Capote, Truman: *Observations.*

AYLING, K. *They Fly to Fight.* New York: Appleton-Century 1944, the story of airborne divisions in World War II. $22–$25.

▧ B ——————————————————

BABAR. See De Brunhoff, Jean.

BABCOCK, Havilah. *My Health is Better in November.* Columbia: University of South Carolina Press 1948, 2nd printing, drawings by A.R. Wittkowsky, 35 stories of hunting and fishing in the south, author's first story collection. $75–$100.

BACHELLER, Irving. *Eben Holden's Last Day a-Fishin'.* New York: Harper 1907, 1st edition, pictorial cloth. $12.

BACHELLER, Irving. *Eben Holden: A Tale of the North Country.* Boston: (1900), 1st edition. $20.

BACHMAN, Richard (Stephen King). *See* Vintage Paperbacks.

BACON, Peggy. *Starting from Scratch: An Album of Drawings.* New York: Messner (1945), 1st edition, DJ. Scarce in DJ. $50–$75.

BACON, Peggy. *See also* "Key to Illustrators."

BADER. Barbara. *American Picture Books from Noah's Ark to the Beast Within.* New York: Macmillan (1976), 1st printing, DJ. $50–$100.

BAE (Bureau of American Ethnology). *16th Annual Report [for] 1894,95.* Washington: GPO 1897, 81 plates. $55–$75.

BAE (Bureau of American Ethnology). *5th Annual Report [for] 1883,84.* Washington: GPO 1887, 2 maps, 23 plates. $40–$60.

BAEDEKER, Karl. *Central Italy.* London: T. Fisher Unwin 1900, maps, plans, later edition. $20–$45.

BAEDEKER, Karl. *Egypt and the Sudan.* Leipzig: Baedeker, 1929 maps, later edition. $150.

BAEDEKER, Karl. *Paris and Environs.* London: T. Fisher Unwin 1910, later edition, maps and plans. $20–$45.

BAEDEKER, Karl. *Switzerland and Adjacent Portions of Italy, Savory and Tyrol.* Leipzig: 1905, maps, later edition. $20–$45.

BAGNOLD, Enid. *National Velvet.* New York: William Morrow 1935, 1st edition, drawings by Laurian Jones, DJ. $35–$75.

BAILEY, Carolyn. *Miss Hickory.* New York: Viking Press 1946, 1st edition, (Newbery winner 1947), no award notice on jacket, illustrated by Ruth Gannett, DJ. $18–$35.

BAILEY, Carolyn. *The Little Rabbit who Wanted Wings.* New York: Platt & Munk (1931). $10–$12.

BAILEY, H.C. *Mr. Fortune Speaking.* New York: Dutton 1931, 1st American edition, DJ. $40.

BAILEY, L.H. *Hortus Second, A Concise Dictionary of Gardening.* New York: 1956, DJ. $25.

BAILEY, L.H. *Standard Cyclopedia of Horticulture.* New York: 1930, 3 vols, plates. $100.

BAILEY, L.H. *The Pruning Manual.* New York: Macmillan 1916, later edition, DJ. $20.

BAILEY, Pearl. *Duey's Tale.* New York: Harcourt Brace Javanovich (1975), 1st edition, DJ. $15–$30.

BALDWIN, James. *Giovanni's Room.* New York: Dial (1956), the author's second book, 1st edition, DJ. $100–$200.

BALDWIN, James. *Go Tell it on the Mountain.* New York: Knopf 1953, 1st trade edition of author's first book, DJ. $200–$400.

BALDWIN, James. *Little Man, Little Man.* New York: Dial 1976, 1st American edition, quarto, illustrated by Yoran Cazac, DJ. $20–$35.

BALDWIN, James, and Avedon, Richard. *Nothing Personal.* New York: Atheneum 1964, folio, photographs by Richard Avedon, slipcase (issued without DJ), 1st edition. $150–$225.

BALLARD, J.G. *Why I Want to Fuck Ronald Reagan.* Brighton: Unicorn Book Shop 1968, one of 50 numbered and signed copies. First printing so stated. $300.

BAMBARA, Toni Cade. *Salt Eaters.* New York: Random House (1980), 1st edition, DJ. $10–$15.

BAMBARA, Toni Cade. *Sea Birds are Still Alive.* New York: Random House (1977), 1st edition, DJ. $25.

BANGS, John Kendrick. *The Bicyclers*. New York: 1896, 1st edition. $20.

BANKS, Russell. *Continental Drift*. New York: Harper & Row (1985), 1st edition, DJ. $20.

BANKS, Russell. *Trailerpark*. Boston: Houghton Mifflin 1981, 1st edition, DJ. $30.

BANNERMAN, Helen. *Little Black Sambo*, edited by Watty Piper. New York: Platt & Munk (1972), square octavo, color pictures throughout by Eulalie, DJ. $20–$35.

BANNERMAN, Helen. *Little Black Sambo*, edited by Watty Piper. New York: Platt & Munk (1972), square octavo, color pictures throughout by Eulalie. $12–$20.

BANNERMAN, Helen. *The Story of Little Black Sambo*. London: Grant Richards 1903, octavo, 1st edition in this larger format, preceded by the 1899 16mo, illustrated by the author. $500–$850.

BANNERMAN, Helen. *The Story of Little Black Sambo*. London: Grant Richards 1899, 1st edition, 16mo, illustrated by the author, original cloth. $850–$3,000.

BANNERMAN, Helen. *The Story of Little Black Sambo*. New York: Frederick A. Stokes (1901), original pictorial boards, illustrated by the author. $375.

BARAKA, Imamu Amiri. *Jello*. Chicago: Third World Press (1970), 1st edition, a play, wraps. $20–$35.

BARAKA, Imamu Amiri. *Raise Race Rays Raze Essays Since 1965*. New York: Random House (1971), 1st edition, DJ. $20–$35.

BARAKA, Imamu Amiri. *Afrikan Revolution*. Newark: Jihad 1973, in paper covers as issued, 1st edition. $20–$45.

BARAKA, Imamu Amiri. *Autobiography of LeRoi Jones*. New York: 1984, 1st edition, DJ. $10–$20.

BARAKA, Imamu Amiri. *See also* Jones, LeRoi.

BARBIER, George. *See* "Key to Illustrators."

BARKER, George. *Poems*. London: Faber & Faber (1953), 1st edition, DJ. $30–$75.

BARNARD, J.G. *Report on the Defenses of Washington*. Washington: "1871". $125–$200.

BARNES, Djuna. *Nightwood.* London: (1936), 1st English edition, DJ. $200–$300.

BARNES, Djuna. *Nightwood.* New York: (1937), 1st American edition, with an introduction by T.S. Eliot, DJ. $75.

BARRETT, Elizabeth. *Poems.* London: Edward Moxon 1844, 1st edition, 1st issue, original cloth, 2 vols (by Elizabeth Barrett Browning). $800–$1,200.

BARRETT, Elizabeth. *Poems.* London: Edward Moxon 1850, "new edition," original cloth, 2 vols (by Elizabeth Barrett Browning); includes 1st appearance in a book, of *Sonnets from the Portuguese.* $700–$1,000.

BARRIE, James. *Peter Pan and Wendy.* New York: Scribner's 1923 (1921), 12 color plates by Mabel Lucie Atwell, later printing of this edition. $45–$75.

BARRIE, James. *The Little Minister.* London: Cassell 1891, 1st edition, 3 vols, showing wear as usual. $100–$225.

BARRIE, James. *See also* Sets.

BARRINGTON, E. *The Gallants.* Boston: Atlantic Monthly Press 1924, 1st edition, DJ. $30.

BARROWS, R.M., editor. *The Kit Book for Soldiers, Sailors and Marines.* Chicago: Consolidated Book Publishers 1943, 12mo, paper-covered boards, contains J.D. Salinger's first book appearance, short story "The Hang of It," without mailing box. Issued without DJ. $75.

BARTH, John. *The End of the Road.* Garden City: Doubleday 1958, 1st edition of author's second book, DJ. $175–$225.

BARTH, John. *The End of the Road.* London: Secker & Warburg 1962, 1st British edition, 4 years after the American edition, DJ. $75.

BARTH, John. *The Floating Opera.* New York: Appleton, Century, Crofts (1956), 1st edition of author's first book, very scarce, DJ. $250.

BARTH, John. *The Sot-Weed Factor.* Garden City: Doubleday 1960, 1st edition, DJ. $250.

BARTHELME, Donald. *Come Back, Doctor Caligari.* Boston and Toronto: Little, Brown & Co. (1964), 1st edition of author's first book, DJ. $75–$125.

BARTON, Ralph. *See* "Key to Illustrators."

BATES, H.E. *Fair Stood the Wind for France.* London: 1944, 1st edition, DJ. $50.

BAUDELAIRE, Charles. *See* Limited Editions Club.

BAUM, L. Frank. *The Emerald City of Oz.* Chicago: Reilly & Britton (1910), 1st edition, illustrated by John R. Neill, 1st state, with blue cover (later printings of 1st edition are green), and bright metallic green on plates (later duller), 16 color plates. $400–$600.

BAUM, L. Frank. *The Emerald City of Oz.* Chicago: Reilly & Britton (1910), 1st edition, illustrated by John R. Neill, 1st state; spine and pictorial cover label rubbed, extremities worn, front hinge repaired, but a presentable copy. $125–$200.

BAUM, L. Frank. *The Emerald City of Oz.* Chicago: Reilly & Lee (1938), illustrated by John R. Neill, ills are in black and white, in very slightly defective DJ. $50.

BAUM, L. Frank. *The Emerald City of Oz.* Chicago: Reilly & Lee (1938), illustrated by John R. Neill, ills are in black and white. $25–$30.

BAUM, L. Frank. *The Wonderful Wizard of Oz.* Chicago: George M. Hill 1900, with pictures by W.W. Denslow, 1st edition, 2nd state, having no box around ads on page 2 and with first line of page 14 reading "low wail of," 24 color plates plus many 2-color ills. $3,000.

BAUM, L. Frank. *See also* Van Dyne, Edith, and Akers, Floyd (pseudonyms).

BAUM, Vicki, *Grand Hotel.* New York: Doubleday 1931, 1st American edition, DJ. $50.

BEACH, Rex. *Flowing Gold.* New York: Harper's 1932, 1st edition, DJ. $30.

BEAGLE, Peter S. *A Fine and Private Place.* New York: Viking Press 1960, 1st edition of author's first book, DJ. $50.

BEAGLE, Peter S. *The Last Unicorn.* New York: Viking 1968, 1st edition, DJ. $50–$75.

BEAR, Greg. *Eternity.* New York: Warner Books (1988), 1st edition, sequel to *Eon*, DJ. $20–$35.

BEARDSLEY, Aubrey. *A Second Book of Fifty Drawings*. London: Leonard Smithers 1899, folio, 50 full-page ills, frontis of Beardsley, limited to 1,000 copies. $100–$200.

BEARDSLEY, Aubrey. *The Uncollected Works of*. London: Bodley Head (1925), 1st edition, large quarto, 162 plates, DJ. $100–$200.

BEARDSLEY, Aubrey. *Under the Hill and Other Essays in Prose and Verse*. London: John Lane 1904, 1st edition, 16 ills by the author. $150–$200.

BEARDSLEY, Aubrey, *See also* "Key to Illustrators."

BEATON, Cecil. *An Indian Album*. London: Batsford 1946, introduction by Beaton, the rest is photographs, DJ. $50.

BEATON, Cecil. *Ashcombe—The Story of a Fifteen Year Lease*. London: Batsford 1949, 1st edition, drawing by the author, as well as by Rex Whistler, Pavel Tchelitchew, and Salvador Dali. $50–$125.

BEATON, Cecil. *The Book of Beauty*. London: (1930), 1st edition, drawings, photographs, and text. $100–$200.

BEATON, Cecil. *See also* Capote, Truman: *Local Color*.

BEATTIE, Ann. *Chilly Scenes of Winter*. Garden City: Doubleday 1976, 1st edition of her first novel. DJ. $75–$85.

BEATTIE, Ann. *Distortions*. Garden City: Doubleday 1976, 1st edition of author's first book of short stories, published simultaneously with her first novel, *Chilly Scenes of Winter*, DJ. $75–$85.

BEATTIE, Ann. *Secrets and Surprises*. New York: Random House (1978), 1st edition, DJ. $15–$25.

BECKETT, Samuel. *En Attendant Godot*. Paris: 1952, the scarce French edition, wrappers. $175–$250.

BECKETT, Samuel. *Murphy*. New York: Grove 1957, 1st edition, DJ. $75–$100.

BECKETT, Samuel. *Waiting for Godot*. New York: Grove Press (1945), 1st edition, DJ. $225–$400.

BEEBE, Lucius. *Hear the Train Blow: A Pictorial Epic of America in the Railroad Age*. New York: Dutton 1952, 1st edition, drawings by E.S. Hammack, DJ. $35–$65.

BEEBE, Lucius. *The Stork Club Bar Book.* New York: 1946, 1st edition. $15–$30.

BEERBOHM, Max. *Observation.* London: William Heinemann, Ltd. 1925, 1st edition, quarto, 50 plus plates by Beerbohm in color and black and white, DJ. $175–$300.

BEERBOHM, Max. *Rosetti and His Circle.* London: William Heinemann 1922, 22 color plates, brown paper DJ. $85–$200.

BEERBOHM, Max. *Zuleika Dobson, or An Oxford Love Story.* London: William Heinemann 1911, 1st edition. $100–$150.

BELL, Clive. *Proust.* London: 1928, 1st edition. $35.

BELL, Gertrude. *See* Golden Cockerel Press.

BELLAMY, Edward. *See* Limited Editions Club.

BELLOC, Hilaire. *Cautionary Tales for Children.* London: 1908, 1st edition, drawings by Basil Blackwood. $75.

BELLOC, Hilaire. *The Bad Child's Book of Beasts.* London: 1896, 1st English edition, drawings by Basil Blackwood. $70.

BELLOW, Saul. *Dangling Man: A Novel.* New York: Vanguard Press (1944), 1st edition of author's first book, DJ. $500.

BELLOW, Saul. *Henderson the Rain King.* New York: Viking 1959, 1st state of 1st edition, with top of page edges stained (colored), DJ. $125.

BELLOW, Saul. *The Adventures of Augie March.* New York: Viking 1953, 1st edition, 1st issue, with top of page edges orange, DJ. $100–$150.

BEMELMANS, Ludwig. *Hotel Bemelmans.* New York: Viking 1946, 1st edition, DJ. $25.

BEMELMANS, Ludwig. *Madeline.* New York: 1939, quarto, 1st edition, 1st issue, with twelve little girls (not eleven as later) in the illustration above the line, "They went home and broke their bread." Illustrated by the author, DJ. $150–$225.

BEMELMANS, Ludwig. *Madeline.* New York: Viking (1939, 1965) 5th printing of New Viking edition, DJ. $25.

BEMELMANS, Ludwig. *Sunshine.* New York: Simon & Schuster 1950, 1st edition, folio, colored ills by the author, DJ. $35–$60.

BENCHLEY, Robert. *20,000 Leagues Under the Sea or David Copperfield.* New York: Henry Holt (1928), 1st edition, drawings by Gluyas Williams, DJ. $20–$35.

BENCHLEY, Robert. *Chips Off the Old Benchley*. New York: Harper & Bros. (1949), 1st edition, ills by Gluyas Williams, DJ. $20–$35.

BENDA, W.T. *See* "Key to Illustrators."

BENET, Stephen Vincent. *John Brown's Body*. Garden City: Doubleday, Doran 1928, 1st trade edition, DJ. $35–$75.

BENET, Stephen Vincent. *The Devil and Daniel Webster*. New York: Farrar & Rinehart (1937), 1st edition, DJ. $30–$60.

BENET, Stephen Vincent. *See also* Limited Editions Club; Vintage Paperbacks.

BENNETT, Arnold. *The Old Wives' Tale*. London: Chapman & Hall 1908, 1st edition. $200–$300.

BENNETT, Robert A. *The Gun-Fighter*. New York: Washburn "1938", 1st edition, DJ. $20–$50.

BENSON, E.F. *Lucia in London*. London: Hutchinson (1927), 1st edition, DJ. $60.

BENSON, Sally. *Meet Me in St. Louis*. New York: Random House 1942, 1st edition, DJ. $35.

BENTLEY, E.C. *Trent's Last Case*. London: Thomas Nelson (1913), 1st edition. $100–$125.

BEOWULF. *See* Kelmscott Press: *The Tale of Beowulf*.

BERGER, Thomas. *Crazy in Berlin*. New York: Scribner's 1958, 1st edition, author's first book, DJ. $100–$125.

BERGER, Thomas. *Little Big Man*. New York: Dial 1964, 1st edition, DJ. $50–$125.

BERGER, Thomas. *Reinhart in Love*. London: Eyre and Spottiswoode 1963, 1st English edition, DJ. $60.

BERRY, Wendell. *Nathan Coulter*. Boston: Houghton Mifflin 1960, 1st edition of author's first book, DJ. $100–$200.

BERRY, Wendell. *November Twenty Six Nineteen Hundred Sixty Three*. New York: George Braziller (1964), oblong octavo, 16 ills by Ben Shahn, lettering by Shahn, 1st trade edition, slipcase. $25–$35.

BERRY, Wendell. *November Twenty Six Nineteen Hundred Sixty Three*. New York: George Braziller (1964), oblong octavo, 16 ills by Ben Shahn, lettering by Shahn, limited edition signed by artist and illustrator, slipcase. $125–$175.

BERRYMAN, John. *Homage to Mistress Bradstreet*. New York: Farrar, Straus & Giroux 1956, 1st edition, jacket design by Ben Shahn, DJ. $75–$125.

BERRYMAN, John. *Poems*. Norfolk: New Directions (1942), 1st edition, one of 500 hardbound copies of an edition of 2,000, signed by publisher James Laughlin, DJ. $150–$350.

BERRYMAN, John. *Poems*. Norfolk: New Directions (1942), 1st edition, one of 1,500 copies in wrappers, issued at the same time as the hardbound copies. $150–$400.

BERRYMAN, John. *The Dream Songs*. New York: Farrar, Straus & Giroux (1969), 1st edition. $75.

BESTER, Alfred. *The Demolished Man*. Chicago: Shasta (1953), 2nd printing, DJ. $30.

BESTER, Alfred. *The Demolished Man*. Chicago: Shasta 1953, 1st edition, winner of the Hugo award, DJ. $150–$200.

BETJEMAN, John. *First and Last Loves*. London: John Murray (1952), 1st edition, DJ. $50–$75.

BETTS, Ethel Franklin. *See* "Key to Illustrators."

BIBLES. Great Bible. London: Edward Whitechurch 1541, 6th edition of this version, folio, modern sheepskin, front cover detached, several leaves possibly supplied from another copy, price at auction. $2,800.

BIBLES. Gutenberg Bible, a leaf from. Mainz: Gutenberg, about 1450–55, single leaf, comprising Acts 25:24–27:24, framed. From the Sulzbach-Wells copy. Price at auction. $9,500.

BIBLES. Gutenberg Bible, a leaf from. Mainz: Gutenberg, about 1450–55, single leaf, comprising end of II Paralipomenon, Oratio manasse, St. Jerome's prologue to Esdras, and beginning of I Esdras, price at auction. $9,500.

BIBLES. Gutenberg Bible. Mainz: Gutenberg, about 1450–55. This set a world record price for a printed book sold at auction; from The Estelle Doheny Library. The most valuable [collection] ever sold at auction, totalling $34,402,507. $4,900,000.

BIBLES. First edition of the Douai New Testament, Rheims: John Fogny 1582, quarto, early eighteenth-century calfskin, rebacked, lacking last two leaves, price at auction (approximate). $1,000.

BIBLES. Tyndale's version. London: Richard Jugge (1553?), old calfskin, worn, rebacked, original spine preserved, first 2 and last leaves in facsimile, price at auction (approximate). $5,250.

BIBLES. Chamishah Chumshei Torah. Antwerp: Christopher Plantin 1580–82, quarto, contemporary leather, defective and worn, damp-stained, final leaves frayed at edges, price at auction. $800.

BIBLES. Szyk, Arthur. *The Book of Job*. New York: Heritage Press (1946), from the translation prepared at Cambridge in 1911, 8 full-page color plates by Szyk. $45.

BIBLES. Szyk, Arthur. *The Book of Ruth*. New York: Heritage Press (1947), from the translation prepared at Cambridge in 1911, 8 full-page color plates by Szyk. $45.

BIBLES. *See also* Ashendene Press and Golden Cockerel Press for *The Song of Songs*; Golden Cockerel for *Samson and Delilah*.

BICKERSTAFF, Isaac. *See* Almanacs.

BIERCE, Ambrose. *Fantastic Fables*. New York: Putnam 1899, 1st edition. $150.

BIERCE, Ambrose. *The Cynic's Word Book*. New York: Doubleday, Page & Co. 1906, first edition. $100–$150.

BIERCE, Ambrose. *See also* Sets.

Condition of the following Big Little Books is medium grade, with moderate wear to edges and moderate rounding of corners, unless condition specifically described otherwise. Higher figure in each price spread is that which would be asked by a specialist dealer in Big Little Books.

BIG LITTLE BOOKS. *Billy the Kid, Western Outlaw*. Racine: Whitman Cocomalt premium giveaway (1935), Cocomalt ad on rear cover. $21–$42.

BIG LITTLE BOOKS. *Blondie and Dagwood—Some Fun!* #703–10. Racine: Whitman (1949). $11–$22.

BIG LITTLE BOOKS. *Bonanza, The Bubble Gum Kid* #2002. Racine: Whitman (1967). $2.25–$4.50.

BIG LITTLE BOOKS. *Buck Rogers and the Doom Comet* #1178. Racine: Whitman (1935), average used copy, general wear at edges and spine, corners rounded, small spine tear. $20–$40.

BIG LITTLE BOOKS. *Buck Rogers and the Doom Comet* #1178. Racine: Whitman (1935). $37.50–$70.

BIG LITTLE BOOKS. *Buck Rogers and the Planetoid Plot* #1197. Racine: Whitman (1936). $45–$90.

BIG LITTLE BOOKS. *Bugs Bunny Accidental Adventure* #2029. Racine: Whitman (1969). $1.75–$3.50.

BIG LITTLE BOOKS. *Bugs Bunny and the Secret of Storm Island* #13. New York: Dell Publishing Co. (1942), Dell Fast Action. $25–$50.

BIG LITTLE BOOKS. *Chitty Chitty Bang Bang* #2025. Racine: Whitman (1968). $1.75–$3.50.

BIG LITTLE BOOKS. *Dick Tracy and the Boris Arson Gang* #163A. Racine: Whitman (1935). $27.50–$55.

BIG LITTLE BOOKS. *Dick Tracy and the Wreath Kidnapping Case* #1482A. Racine: Whitman (1946). $21–$42.

BIG LITTLE BOOKS. *Dick Tracy Out West* #723A. Racine: Whitman (1933). $35–$70.

BIG LITTLE BOOKS. *Dick Tracy Out West* #723A. Racine: Whitman (1933). A terrible copy, spine detached, bound by masking tape, loose pages. $5–$10.

BIG LITTLE BOOKS. *Flash Gordon and the Perils of Mongo* #1423C. Racine: Whitman (1940). $22.50–$45.

BIG LITTLE BOOKS. *G-Man Versus the Red X* #1147. Racine: Whitman (1936). $17.50–$35.

BIG LITTLE BOOKS. *Gene Autry and Raiders of the Range* #1409. Racine: Whitman (1946). $13–$26.

BIG LITTLE BOOKS. *Invisible Scarlet O'Neil Versus the King of the Slums* #1406. Racine: Whitman (1946). $17.50–$35.

BID LITTLE BOOKS. *Jack Armstrong and the Ivory Treasure* #1435B. Racine: Whitman (1937). $26.50–$53.

BIG LITTLE BOOKS. *Jack London's Call of the Wild* #L11. New York: Lynn Publishing Co. (1935), Lynn Books, movie edition with Clark Gable. $22.50–$45.

BIG LITTLE BOOKS. *Little Orphan Annie and Chizzler* #748. Racine: Whitman (1933), by Harold Gray. $32.50–$65.

BIG LITTLE BOOKS. *Lone Ranger and the Menace of Murder Valley* #1465B. Racine: Whitman (1937). $21.50–$43.

BIG LITTLE BOOKS. *Mandrake the Magician and the Midnight Monster* #1431. Racine: Whitman (1939). $17.50–$35.

BIG LITTLE BOOKS. *Mickey Mouse and the Seven Ghosts* #1475. Racine: Whitman (1940). $39.50–$79.

BIG LITTLE BOOKS. *Mickey Mouse and the Seven Ghosts* #1475. Racine: Whitman (1940), a quite worn copy, a slightly loose binding but no missing pages. $18.50–$37.

BIG LITTLE BOOKS. *Mickey Mouse in the Race for Riches* #1476B. Racine: Whitman (1938), a heavily worn copy, extremely worn edges, rounded corners, spine tear, tape. $10–$20.

BIG LITTLE BOOKS. *Popeye and the Deep Sea Mystery* #1499. Racine: Whitman (1939). $37.50–$75.

BIG LITTLE BOOKS. *Popeye and the Jeep* #1405C. Racine: Whitman (1937). $31.25–$62.50.

BIG LITTLE BOOKS. *Popeye and the Jeep* #1405C. Racine: Whitman (1937), average used BLB condition, general wear at edges and spine, corners rounded. $25–$50.

BIG LITTLE BOOKS. *Popeye and the Jeep* #1405C. Racine: Whitman (1937), quite worn, with slightly loose binding, but no loose pages. $17–$34.

BIG LITTLE BOOKS. *Red Ryder and the Western Border Guns* #1450C. Racine: Whitman (1942). $21–$42.

BIG LITTLE BOOKS. *Smilin' Jack and the Stratosphere Ascent* #1152A. Racine: Whitman (1937). $22.50–$45.

BIG LITTLE BOOKS. *Tailspin Tommy and the Hooded Flyer* #1423D. Racine: Whitman (1937). $21.50–$43.

BIG LITTLE BOOKS. *Tarzan and the Ant Men* #1444. Racine: Whitman (1945), by Edgar Rice Burroughs. $30–$60.

BIG LITTLE BOOKS. *Tarzan and the Jewels of Opar* #1495A. Racine: Whitman (1940), by Edgar Rice Burroughs. $37.50–$75.

BIG LITTLE BOOKS. *Tarzan and the Mark of the Red Hyena* #2005. Racine: Whitman (1967), by George S. Elrick. $2.50–$5.00.

BIG LITTLE BOOKS. *Tarzan, Lord of the Jungle* #1407C. Racine: Whitman (1946), by Edgar Rice Burroughs. $30–$60.

BIG LITTLE BOOKS. *The Return of Tarzan* #1102A. Racine: Whitman (1936). $15–$30.

BIG LITTLE BOOKS. *The Story of Skippy.* Racine: Whitman (1934), Whitman Phillips Milk of Magnesia premium with their ad on rear cover. $22.50–$45.

BIG LITTLE BOOKS. *Tom Mix and His Circus on the Barbary Coast* #1482. Racine: Whitman (1940), by Pete Daryl. $21.50–$43.

BIG LITTLE BOOKS. *Woody Woodpecker and the Meteor Menace* #2010. Racine: Whitman (1967). $2–$4.

BIGGERS, Earl Derr. *Charlie Chan Carries On.* Indianapolis: Bobbs-Merrill (1932), 1st edition, DJ. $200.

BIGGERS, Earl Derr. *Charlie Chan Carries On.* New York: Grosset & Dunlap nd, movie edition, contains stills from the movie starring Warner Oland, DJ. $50–$65.

BIGGERS, Earl Derr. *Keeper of the Keys.* Indianapolis: Bobbs-Merrill (1932), 1st edition, a Charlie Chan mystery, DJ. $50.

BIGGERS, Earl Derr. *The House Without a Key.* Indianapolis: Bobbs-Merrill (1928), 1st edition, with the Bobbs-Merrill bow and arrow symbol on verso. This is the first book in which Charlie Chan appears. DJ. $300–$400.

BILBO, Jack. *Famous Nudes by Famous Artists.* London: Modern Art Gallery 1946, 1st edition, 130 reproductions, some in color. $35–$50.

BILLINGS, John D. *Hardtack and Coffee, the Unwritten Story of Army Life.* Boston: 1887, 1st edition, original cloth. $175–$250.

BILLINGS, John D. *Hardtack and Coffee, The Unwritten Story of Army Life.* Chicago: Lakeside Press 1960, "the best of several editions of this classic." $50–$65.

BILLY THE KID. See Big Little Books.

BINYON, Laurence. *Japanese Color Prints.* London: Frederick Publishing Co. 1954, 1st edition, 46 plates. $75–$100.

BINYON, Laurence. *The Drawings and Engravings of William*

Blake. London: The Studio 1922, 106 plates including some in color, limited edition of 200 copies. $150–$300.

BINYON, Laurence. *The Drawings and Engravings of William Blake.* London: The Studio 1922, 106 plates including some in color, 1st trade edition. $100.

BIRCH, Reginald. *See* "Key to Illustrators."

BIRNEY, Catherine. *Sarah and Angelina Grimke.* Boston: Lee & Shepard 1885, 1st edition. $35–$50.

BISCHOFF, Ilse. *See* "Key to Illustrators."

BISHOP, Elizabeth. *Poems.* Boston: Houghton Mifflin 1955, 1st edition of author's second book, DJ. $100.

BISHOP, John Peale. *Green Fruit*, Boston: Sherman, French & Co. 1917, 1st edition. $150.

BISHOP, John Peale. *The Collected Poems.* New York: Scribner's Sons 1948, DJ. $35–$65.

BLACK PHOTOGRAPHERS ANNUAL, THE. New York: Black Photographers Annual (1972), 1st edition, wraps (also comes out in hardcover), forward by Toni Morrison. $20.

BLACKMORE, R.D. *Lorna Doone, A Romance of Exmoor.* New York: Thomas Y. Crowell & Co. (1893), 2 vols in 1. $15–$35.

BLACKMORE, Richard D. *Fringilla, or Tales in Verse.* Cleveland: The Burrows Brothers 1895, with sundry decorations and pictures by Will H. Bradley, one of 600 copies on handmade paper, very scarce. $250–$575.

BLACKMORE, Richard D. *Lorna Doone: A Romance of Exmoor.* London: Sampson Low, 1869, 3 vols, original blue cloth, 1st edition. $1,000–$1,500.

BLACKMORE, Richard D. *Lorna Doone: A Romance of Exmoor.* New York: Dodd, Mead 1924, modern edition, 16 color plates by Rowland Wheelright and Helen Sewell. $10–$25.

BLACKWOOD, Basil. *See* "Key to Illustrators."

BLAINE, John. *Rick Brant and the Lost City.* New York: Grosset and Dunlap (1957), 1st edition, DJ. $5–$7.50

BLAINE, John. *Rick Brant and the Lost City.* New York: Grosset and Dunlap (1957), pictorial cover. $4–$6.

BLAINE, John. *Rick Brant and the Wailing Octopus.* New York: Grosset and Dunlap (1957), 1st edition, DJ. $35.

BLAINE, Mahlon. *See* "Key to Illustrators."

BLAKE, William. *Songs of Innocence*. London: 1839, 12mo, original cloth (this title first published in 1789). $300–$750.

BLAKE, William. Drawings of. *See* Binyon, Laurence.

BLANDING, Don. *Hula Moon*. New York: Dodd, Mead 1930, color frontis, otherwise illustrated with silhouettes, 1st edition, DJ. $15–$35.

BLANDING, Don. *The Virgin of Waikiki*. (np): privately printed 1926, in gold and black, limited edition. $40.

BLEVINS, Winfred. *Give Your Heart to the Hawks: A Tribute to the Mountain Men*. Los Angeles: Nash 1973, 1st printing, DJ. $45.

BLIGH, William, and Fryer, John. *See* Golden Cockerel Press.

BLISH, James. *Jack of Eagles*. New York: Greenberg (1952), 1st edition of author's first book. $100.

BLOCH, Robert. *Psycho*. New York: Simon & Schuster 1959, 1st edition, DJ. $100–$300.

BLONDIE AND DAGWOOD. See Big Little Books.

BLUNT, Edmund M. *The American Coast Pilot*. New York: Edmund and George W. Blunt 1863, nineteenth edition, charts, calfskin binding. $125.

BOAS, Franz, editor. *Handbook of American Indian Languages*. Washington: Government Printing Office 1911 and 1922, 2 vols, 1st editions, comprising Parts I and II of Bureau of American Ethnology Bulletin 40. $100.

BOGAN, Louise. *Poems and New Poems*. New York: Scribner's 1941, 1st edition, scarce, DJ. $65.

BOND, Michael. *A Bear Called Paddington*. Boston: Houghton, Mifflin 1960, 1st US edition, line drawings by Peggy Fortnum. $20.

BOND, Nelson. *Mr. Mergenthwirker's Lobblies and Other Fantastic Tales*. New York: Coward-McCann 1946, 1st edition, DJ. $25–$35.

BOND, Nelson. *The Thirty-First of February*. New York: Gnome Press 1949, 1st edition, DJ. $25–$35.

BONHAM, Frank. *Snaketrack*. New York: Simon & Schuster "1952", 1st edition, DJ. $20–$30.

BONTEMPS, Arna. *You Can't Pet a Possum*. New York: Morrow 1934, 1st edition, illustrated by Ilse Bischoff, DJ. $100–$200.

BOOKS ABOUT BOOKS. *See* "Key to Categories."

BOOKS WITH PLATES, MAPS, ENGRAVINGS. *See* "Key to Categories."

BOOTH, Evangeline, and Hill, Grace Livingston. *The War Romance of the Salvation Army*. Philadelphia: (1919), 1st edition, DJ. $25–$50.

BORGES, Jorge Luis. *Deathwatch on the Southside*. Cambridge, Massachusetts: (1968), 1st edition, limited to 150 copies signed by author and translator, wraps. $65–$100.

BOULLE, Pierre. *The Bridge over the River Quai*. New York: Vanguard (1954), 1st edition, DJ. $50.

BOURKE-WHITE, Margaret. *Shooting the Russian War*. New York: Simon & Schuster 1943, 1st edition, DJ. $65–$125.

BOURKE-WHITE, Margaret. *See also* Caldwell, Erskine.

BOURKE-WHITE, Margaret, and Caldwell, Erskine. *Say, Is this the U.S.A.* New York: Duell, Sloan and Pearce 1941, 1st edition, folio, pictorial cloth. $150–$200.

BOWDITCH, Nathaniel. *The New American Practical Navigator: Being an Epitome of Navigation*. New York: E. & G.W. Blunt 1848, 18th new stereotype edition, charts and plates, calfskin binding. $175.

BOWEN, Elizabeth. *The Death of the Heart*. London: 1938, 1st edition, DJ. $35.

BOWEN, Elizabeth. *The House in Paris*. New York: Knopf 1936, 1st American edition, DJ. $20–$30.

BOWEN, R. Sidney. *See* Juvenile Series Books.

BOWER, B.M. *Shadow Mountain*. Boston: Little, Brown "1936", 1st edition, DJ. $20–$75.

BOWLES, Jane. *Two Serious Ladies*. New York: 1943, 1st edition of author's first book, DJ. $300–$500.

BOWLES, Paul. *The Delicate Prey and Other Stories*. (np): Random House (1950), 1st edition, DJ. $75–$125.

BOWLES, Paul. *The Sheltering Sky*. New York: New Directions (1949), 1st edition, DJ. $100–$175.

BOYD, James. *Drums*. New York: Scribner's (1928), ills by N.C. Wyeth, 1st illustrated trade edition. $35–$70.

BOYD, James. *Drums*. New York: Scribner's (1928), ills by N.C. Wyeth, edition limited to 520 numbered copies signed by the author and the artist, slipcase. $200–$400.

BOYD, James. *Drums*. New York: Scribner's 1925, 1st edition of author's first book, DJ. $75–$175.

BOYD, James. *Drums*. New York: Scribner's 1925, 1st edition of author's first book. $25–$35.

BOYD, William. *An Ice Cream War*. London: Hamish Hamilton (1982), 1st edition, DJ. $40–$100.

BOYER, Jane Allen. *See* "Key to Illustrators."

BRADBURY, Ray. *Dark Carnival*. Sauk City: Arkham House 1947, 1st edition of author's first book, DJ. $375–$700.

BRADBURY, Ray. *The Golden Apples of the Sun*. New York: Doubleday 1953, drawings by Joe Mugnaini, 1st edition, DJ. $100–$150.

BRADBURY, Ray. *The Illustrated Man*. Garden City: Doubleday 1951, 1st edition, DJ. $100–$150.

BRADBURY, Ray. *See also* Limited Editions Club.

BRADFORD, Roark. *John Henry*. New York 1931, 1st edition, DJ. $35.

BRADLEY, Will. *Bradley, His Book: Volume One, Number One*, 1896. $75–$150.

BRADLEY, Will. *See also* "Key to Illustrators."

BRAINE, John. *Room at the Top*. London: Eyre/Spottiswoode 1957, 1st trade edition, DJ. $100.

BRAMAH, Ernest. *The Eyes of Max Carrados*. London: Grant Richards 1923, 1st edition, DJ. $550.

BRAMAH, Ernest. *The Wallet of Kai Lung*. London: Richards 1900, 1st edition, DJ. $700.

BRAND, Max. *7 Trails*. New York: Dodd, Mead (1949), 1st edition, DJ. $20–$35.

BRAND, Max. *Happy Jack*. New York: Triangle (1928), reprint edition, DJ. $10–$20.

BRAND, Max. *Happy Jack*. New York: Triangle (1928), reprint edition. $4.

BRAND, Max. *Mistral*. New York: Dodd, Mead (1929), 1st edition, DJ. $20–$75.

BRAND, Max. *The False Rider*. New York: Dodd, Mead (1947), 1st edition, a "Silvertip" story, DJ. $20–$40.

BRAND, Max. *The Gun Tamer*. New York: Dodd, Mead (1929), 1st edition, DJ. $35–$100.

BRAND, Max. *The Night Horseman*. New York: Putnam "1920", 1st edition. $35–$75.

BRANDT, Bill. *See* Capote, Truman: *Local Color*.

BRANHAM, Ben P. *Automobile Reference Book*. New York: Ben P. Branham Co. (1925), all entries illustrated. $35–$50.

BRASSEY, Anne. *Around the World in the Yacht 'Sunbeam,' Our Home on the Ocean for Eleven Months*. New York: 1872, 1st American edition. $25.

BRAUTIGAN, Richard. *A Confederate General from Big Sur*. New York: Grove Press 1964, 1st edition, DJ. $100–$150.

BRAUTIGAN, Richard. *The Octopus Frontier*. San Francisco: Carp (1960), 1st edition, pictorial wrappers. $100–$200.

BRAUTIGAN, Richard. *The Pill Versus the Springhill Mine Disaster*. San Francisco: 1968, DJ. $200–$250.

BRIDGES, Robert. *The Shorter Poems*. London: George Bell & Sons 1890, 1st edition. $50.

BRIDGES, Robert. *The Testament of Beauty—A Poem in Four Books*. Oxford: Oxford University Press October 24, 1929, 1st edition, one of 250 copies. $65–$125.

BRIDGES, Robert. *The Testament of Beauty—A Poem in Four Books*. Oxford: Oxford University Press 1929, 1st English trade edition, DJ. $40.

BRIDGMAN, L.J. *See* "Key to Illustrators."

BROCK, C.E. *See* "Key to Illustrators."

BROCK, Stuart. *See* Vintage Paperbacks.

BROMFIELD, Louis. *Malabar Farm*. New York: Harper (1948), 1st edition, DJ. $15–$20.

BROMFIELD, Louis. *The Green Bay Tree*. New York: Stokes 1924, 1st edition of author's first book, DJ. $100–$200.

BRONTE, Charlotte. *The Professor*. New York: Harper 1857, 1st American edition in hard cover (published first by Harper in wraps), original brown cloth. $100–$200.

BRONTE, Emily. *Wuthering Heights*. New York: Random House 1943, illustrated with 15 full-page wood engravings by Fritz Eichenberg, with others as headpiece and title page decoration. Quarto, paper-covered boards with another Eichenberg engraving. $12.

BROOKE, Rupert. *The Collected Poems of*. London: 1915, frontis portrait of the author, 1st edition. $50–$75.

BROOKE, Rupert. *See also* Vintage Paperbacks.

BROOKS, Cleanth, and Warren, Robert Penn. *Understanding Fiction*. New York: Appleton (1943), later printing, DJ. $15–$35.

BROOKS, Gwendolyn. *A Street In Bronzeville*. New York: Harper 1945, 1st edition of author's first book, DJ. $100–$200.

BROOKS, Gwendolyn. *Bronzeville Girls and Boys*. New York: Harper & Row (1956), 1st edition, DJ. $125.

BROOKS, Gwendolyn. *Maud Martha*. New York: Harper (1953), 1st edition, DJ. $75–$125.

BROOKS, Van Wyck. *New England Indian Summer*. New York: Dutton 1940, 1st edition, DJ. $15–$25.

BROOKS, Van Wyck. *The World of Washington Irving*. New York: 1944, 1st edition, DJ. $10–$20.

BROWN, Alice. *Old Crow*. New York: Macmillan 1922, 1st edition. $20.

BROWN, Frederic. *The Fabulous Clipjoint*. New York: Dutton 1947, 1st edition of author's first book, DJ. $225–$275.

BROWN, Frederic. *What Mad Universe*. New York: Dutton 1949, 1st edition, DJ. $75–$125.

BROWN, Margaret Wise. *The Golden Egg Book*. New York: Simon & Schuster (1944), illustrated by Leonard Weisgard, early reprinting, DJ. $20.

BROWN, Margaret Wise. *The Winter Noisy Book*. New York: William Scott 1947, illustrated by Charles Shaw, probable 1st edition, DJ. $60–$85.

BROWNING, Elizabeth Barrett. *Aurora Leigh*. London: Chapman & Hall 1857, 1st edition, original cloth. $150–$300.

BROWNING, Elizabeth Barrett. *See also* Barrett, Elizabeth.

BROWNING, Robert. *The Pied Piper of Hamelin.* London: 1934, illustrated by Arthur Rackham, vellum binding, slipcase, one of 410 signed copies. $400–$900.

BROWNING, Robert. *The Pied Piper of Hamelin.* London: (1888), 35 colored ills by Kate Greenaway, pictorial boards. $200–$400.

BROWNING, Robert. *The Ring and the Book.* London: Smith, Elder 1868–69, original green cloth, 4 vols, 1st edition. $200–$400.

BROWNING, Robert. *See also* Doves Press; Limited Editions Club.

BRUNDAGE, Frances. *See* "Key to Illustrators."

BUCHAN, John. *Mountain Meadow.* Boston: Houghton Mifflin 1941, 1st edition, DJ. $20.

BUCHAN, John. *The Gap in the Curtain.* London: 1932, 1st English edition, DJ. $75–$90.

BUCK ROGERS. See Big Little Books.

BUCK, Pearl. *Dragonseed.* New York: John Day Co. (1942), 1st edition, DJ. $35.

BUCK, Pearl. *The Good Earth.* New York: John Day (1931), 1st edition, 1st state, DJ. $150–$400.

BUCK, Pearl. *The Water Buffalo Children.* New York: John Day (1934), drawings by William Arthur Smith, 1st edition, DJ. $30.

BUGS BUNNY. See Big Little Books.

BUKOWSKI, Charles. *Bring Me Your Love.* Santa Barbara: Black Sparrow Press 1983, 1st edition, folio, illustrated by R. Crum, limited edition of 350 copies signed by Bukowski and Crum, DJ. $75.

BUKOWSKI, Charles. *Crucifix in a Deathhand.* New York: Lyle Stuart 1965, illustrated by Noel Rockmore, decorated stiff paper wrappers, with wraparound band, limited 1st edition. $75–$100.

BULL, Charles Livingston. *See* "Key to Illustrators."

BULLEN, Frank T. *The Cruise of the 'Cachalot' 'Round the World After Sperm Whales.* London: Smith, Elder & Co. 1898, 1st English edition of author's first book. $150.

BUNIN, Ivan. *The Gentleman from San Francisco.* New York: Thomas Seltzer 1923, 1st American edition, translated by D.H. Lawrence and S.S. Koteliansky. $75–$125.

BURGESS, Anthony. *Honey for the Bears.* London: Heinemann 1963, 1st edition, DJ. $75.

BURGESS, Anthony. *A Clockwork Orange.* London: 1962, 1st edition, DJ. $250–$400.

BURGESS, Gelett. *Goops and How to be Them. A Manual of Manners for Polite Infants Inculcating Many Juvenile Virtues.* New York: Frederick A. Stokes 1900, 1st edition, square quarto, illustrated with goops by the author. $150–$250.

BURGESS, Gelett. *The Burgess Nonsense Book.* New York: Stokes (October, 1901), black and white ills by the author, 1st edition. $100–$200.

BURGESS, Thornton. *Little Joe Otter.* Boston: Little, Brown 1925, ills by Harrison Cady, 1st edition, 8 color plates, 2nd volume in the Smiling Pool series, small octavo, cover has pictorial paste-on label. $30–$40.

BURGESS, Thornton. *Little Joe Otter.* Boston: Little, Brown 1925, ills by Harrison Cady, 1st edition, 8 color plates, 2nd volume in the Smiling Pool series, small octavo, cover has pictorial paste-on label, DJ. $55–$100.

BURGESS, Thornton. *The Adventures of Paddy the Beaver.* Boston: Little, Brown 1917, 1st edition of the 15th Bedtime Story series, ills by Harrison Cady, gray cloth stamped in red and black. $35–$70.

BURGESS, Thornton. *The Adventures of Paddy the Beaver.* Boston: Little, Brown 1917, 1st edition of the 15th Bedtime Story series, ills by Harrison Cady, gray cloth stamped in red and black, DJ. $70–$150.

BURGESS, Thornton. *The Adventures of Paddy the Beaver.* New York: Grosset & Dunlap (1917), reprint edition of the 10th title in the 1949–1957 printing of the Bedtime Story series, illustrated, brown paper-covered boards stamped in black, DJ. $12–$15.

BURGESS, Thornton. *The Adventures of Paddy the Beaver.* New York: Grosset & Dunlap (1917), reprint edition of the 10th title in the 1949–1957 printing of the Bedtime Story series, illustrated, brown paper-covered boards stamped in black. $7.50–$9.00.

BURGESS, Thornton. *The Burgess Bird Book for Children.* Boston: Little, Brown 1919, illustrated by Louis Agassiz Fuertes, color plates, 1st edition, DJ. $85–$150.

BURGESS, Thornton. *The Burgess Bird Book for Children.* Boston: Little, Brown 1919, illustrated by Louis Agassiz Fuertes, color plates, 1st edition. $50.

BURGESS, Thornton. *The Burgess Bird Book for Children.* Boston: Little, Brown 1948, illustrated by Louis Agassiz Fuertes, color plates, later printing. $35–$40.

BURGESS, Thornton. *The Burgess Bird Book for Children.* Boston: Little, Brown 1948, illustrated by Louis Agassiz Fuertes, color plates, later printing, DJ. $50–$65.

BURGESS, Thornton. *Whitefoot the Woodmouse.* Boston: Little, Brown 1922, ills by Harrison Cady, cover has pictorial paste-on label, 8 color plates, 3rd volume in the Green Forest series. $30–$40.

BURGESS, Thornton. *Wildflowers We Should Know.* Racine: Whitman 1929, large color ills, quarto, wraps. $35.

BURKE, James Lee. *A Stained White Radiance.* New York: Hyperion (1992), 1st edition, DJ. $20.

BURKE, James Lee. *The Neon Rain.* New York: Henry Holt (1987), the first mystery with Dave Robicheaux, 1st edition, DJ. $35.

BURKE, Thomas. *Limehouse Nights.* London: 1916, 1st edition, very scarce in dust wrapper, DJ. $200.

BURKE, Thomas. *Limehouse Nights.* New York: McBride 1916, illustrated by Mahlon Blaine, 1st thus, DJ. $75.

BURKERT, Nancy Ekholm. *See* "Key to Illustrators."

BURNETT, Frances Hodgson. *A Little Princess.* New York: Scribner's 1905, 1st edition, illustrated by Ethel Franklin Betts. $50–$150.

BURNETT, Frances Hodgson. *A Little Princess.* Philadelphia: Lippincott (1963), 1st of this edition, illustrated by Tasha Tudor with color plates and black and white, DJ. $20–$35.

BURNETT, Frances Hodgson. *A Little Princess.* Philadelphia: Lippincott (1963), 1st of this edition, illustrated by Tasha Tudor with color plates and black and white. $8–$15.

BURNETT, Frances Hodgson. *Little Lord Fauntleroy*. New York: 1886, 1st edition, 1st issue, with symbol of De Vinne Press after the last pages of text, illustrated by Reginald Birch. $100–$200.

BURNETT, Frances Hodgson. *The Secret Garden*. New York: Stokes (1911), color plates by Maria Kirk, green cloth cover with pictorial paste-on label. $60–$400.

BURNETT, W.R. *Asphalt Jungle*. New York: Alfred Knopf 1949, 1st edition, DJ. $50.

BURNETT, W.R. *High Sierra*. New York: (1940), 1st edition, DJ. $125.

BURNETT, W.R. *Little Caesar*. New York: 1929, 1st edition of author's first book, scarce, DJ. $200–$400.

BURROUGHS, Edgar Rice. *Escape on Venus*. Tarzana: Burroughs (1946), 1st edition, DJ. $50–$100.

BURROUGHS, Edgar Rice. *Tarzan and the Jewels of Opar*. Chicago: McClurg 1918, 1st edition, 1st issue, with "W.F. Hall" printed bottom of verso, DJ. $1,200–$2,500.

BURROUGHS, Edgar Rice. *Tarzan and the Jewels of Opar*. New York: A.L. Burt (1919), reprint edition, DJ. $35.

BURROUGHS, Edgar Rice. *Tarzan, Lord of the Jungle*. Chicago: McClurg 1928, 1st edition, DJ. $1,200–$1,500.

BURROUGHS, Edgar Rice. *Tarzan, Lord of the Jungle*. Chicago: McClurg 1928, 1st edition, 2nd printing, DJ. $800.

BURROUGHS, Edgar Rice. *Tarzan of the Apes*. Chicago: McClurg 1914, 1st edition, 1st issue, with Old English type on copyright page, and without acorn on spine. $1,000–$1,500.

BURROUGHS, Edgar Rice. *Tarzan of the Apes*. Chicago: McClurg 1914, 1st edition, 1st issue, with Old English type on copyright page, and without acorn on spine, DJ. $20,000–$30,000.

BURROUGHS, Edgar Rice. *Tarzan of the Apes*. Chicago: McClurg 1914, 1st edition, 2nd issue, without Old English type on copyright page, and with acorn on spine. $900–$1,200.

BURROUGHS, Edgar Rice. *Tarzan of the Apes*. New York: A.L. Burt (1914), early reprint edition, DJ. $75–$150.

BURROUGHS, Edgar Rice. *The Chessmen of Mars*. Chicago: McClurg 1922, illustrated by J. Allen St. John, 1st edition, DJ. $1,500–$1,700.

BURROUGHS, Edgar Rice. *The Girl from Hollywood*. New York: Macauley Co. 1923, 1st edition, 1st state of binding, coarse mesh weave red cloth lettered in yellow-green, DJ. $1,000–$1,500.

BURROUGHS, Edgar Rice. *The Girl from Hollywood*. New York: Macauley Co. 1923, 1st edition, 1st state of binding, coarse mesh weave red cloth lettered in yellow-green. $125.

BURROUGHS, Edgar Rice. *The War Chief*. Chicago: McClurg 1927, 1st edition. An acorn symbol on copyright page. $100–$250.

BURROUGHS, Edgar Rice. *See also* Big Little Books.

BURROUGHS, John. *Bird and Bough*. Boston: Houghton Mifflin 1906, 1st edition. $15–$25.

BURROUGHS, William S. *The Naked Lunch*. Paris: Olympia Press (1959), 1st edition, 1st issue, with a green border on title page, DJ. $200–$375.

BURROUGHS, William S. *The Soft Machine*. Paris: Olympia Press (1961), 1st edition, with "Printed in France. . . June 1961" on copyright page, paper covers, DJ. $150.

BURROUGHS, William S. *See* Vintage Paperbacks: Lee, William.

BURT, Katherine Newlin. *A Man's Own Country*. Boston: Houghton, Mifflin "1931", 1st edition, DJ. $20–$45.

BURT, Struthers. *The Diary of a Dude-Wrangler*. New York: Charles Scribner's Sons 1938, 1st illustrated edition, 1st thus, many plates, DJ. $30.

BURTON, Virginia Lee. *Mike Mulligan and his Steam Shovel*. Boston: Houghton, Mifflin 1939, illustrated by the author, 1st edition, DJ. $85–$175.

BURTON, Virginia Lee. *The Little House*. Boston: Houghton, Mifflin 1942, illustrated by the author, 1st edition, DJ. $65–$125.

BURTON, Virginia Lee. *See also* "Key to Illustrators."

BUSH, Christopher. *The Case of the Heavenly Twin*. London: (1963), 1st edition, DJ. $20.

BUSTER BROWN. See Outcault, F.

BUTLER, Ellis Parker. *Pigs is Pigs*, later printings. (See listing of *Pigs is Pigs* for the 1st edition of this title, printed without author's name on cover or title page.) $8–$25.

BUTTS, Mary. *Imaginary Letters.* Paris: E.W. Titus (nd), Black Manikin Press, copper engravings from drawings by Jean Cocteau, limited edition of 250 copies. $150.

BYNNER, Witter. *An Ode to Harvard and Other Poems.* Boston: Small, Maynard 1907, 1st edition of author's first book. $35–$75.

BYRNE, Donn. *Blind Rafferty and his Wife Hilaria.* New York: (1924), 1st edition, early state, with perfect type in last lines of pages 108 and 138, DJ. $35–$50.

BYRON, George Gordon, Lord. *The Prisoner of Chillon and Other Poems.* London: Murray 1816, 1st edition, original wrappers. $100–$250.

 C ———————————————————————

CABELL, James Branch. *Hamlet had an Uncle, a Comedy of Honor.* New York: Farrar & Rinehart (1940), 1st edition, DJ. $30–$40.

CABELL, James Branch. *Jurgen: Comedy of Justice.* London: Golden Cockerel Press 1949, one of 500 numbered copies, 16 wood engravings by John Buckland Wright, purple morocco and red buckram. $150.

CABELL, James Branch. *Jurgen: Comedy of Justice.* New York: McBride 1919, 1st edition, 1st issue, with "Published August, 1919" on copyright page, and unbroken rule on page 144, DJ. $150.

CABELL, James Branch. *Something about Eve.* New York: McBride 1927, 1st edition, DJ. $25.

CABELL, James Branch. *See also* Golden Cockerel Press.

CABLE, George W. *Old Creole Days.* New York: Scribner's 1879, 1st edition, author's first book. $65–$150.

CABLE, George W. *The Creoles of Louisiana.* New York: Scribner's 1884, 1st edition, scarce. $150.

CABLE, George W. *The Creoles of Louisiana.* New York: Scribner's (1884), later printing. $15–$35.

CABLE, George W. *The Grandissimes*. New York: Scribner's 1880, 1st edition. $50–$100.

CABLE, George W. *See also* Limited Editions Club.

CADY, Harrison. *See* "Key to Illustrators."

CAIN, James M. *Mildred Pierce*. New York: Knopf 1941, 1st edition, DJ. $100–$250.

CAIN, James M. *Serenade*. New York: Knopf 1937, 1st edition, DJ. $150–$200.

CAIN, James M. *The Postman Always Rings Twice*. New York: Knopf 1934, 1st edition, DJ. $300–$400.

CALDECOTT, Randolph. *See* "Key to Illustrators."

CALDWELL, Erskine. *God's Little Acre*. New York: The Modern Library Edition (1934), 1st Modern Library edition, DJ. $50.

CALDWELL, Erskine. *God's Little Acre*. New York: Viking Press 1933, 1st edition, DJ. $150–$300.

CALDWELL, Erskine. *Tobacco Road*. New York: Scribner's 1932, 1st edition, with "A" on copyright page, DJ. $300–$700.

CALDWELL, Erskine, and Bourke-White, Margaret. *You Have Seen Their Faces*. New York: Viking 1937, 1st edition, photographs by Margaret Bourke-White, DJ (scarce in dust wrapper). $150–$300.

CALDWELL, Taylor. *Dynasty of Death*. New York: Scribner's 1938, 1st edition of author's first book, DJ. $50.

CALISHER, Hortense. *In the Absence of Angels*. Boston: Little, Brown 1951, 1st edition of author's first book, DJ. $75–$100.

CALLAGHAN, Morley. *Strange Fugitive*. New York: Scribner's 1928, 1st edition of author's first book, DJ. $125–$225.

CAMBRIDGE BIBLIOGRAPHY OF ENGLISH LITERATURE. New York and Cambridge: 1941, 5 vols. $65.

CAMBRIDGE HISTORY OF ENGLISH LITERATURE. Cambridge: 1907 to 1916, 14 vols. $175–$250.

CAMPANELLA, Roy. *It's Good to be Alive*. Boston: Little, Brown 1959, 1st edition, DJ. $22.50.

CAMPBELL, Lang. *See* "Key to Illustrators."

CAMPBELL, Roy. *The Flaming Terrapin*. London: Jonathan Cape 1924, 1st edition of poet's second book, DJ. $75–$150.

CAMPBELL, V. Floyd. *See* "Key to Illustrators."

CAMUS, Albert. *La Peste*. Paris: Gallimard (1947), 1st edition, with printed wraps and in slipcase, one of 30 numbered copies. $1,500.

CAMUS, Albert. *The Outsider*. London: Hamish Hamilton 1946, author's first book, published as *The Stranger* in the US during the same year ; 1st English edition, DJ. $35–$75.

CAMUS, Albert. *The Plague*. New York: Knopf 1948, 1st American edition, DJ. $40–$50.

CAMUS, Albert. *The Stranger*. New York: Knopf 1946, 1st American edition, DJ. $25–$65.

CANETTI, Elias. *Auto-Da-Fe*. London: 1946, 1st English edition, DJ. $75.

CANFIELD, Dorothy. *The Deepening Stream*. New York: Harcourt, Brace 1930, 1st edition, DJ. $20.

CANFIELD, Dorothy. *Understood Betsy*. New York: Henry Holt 1917, 1st edition. $20.

CANIFF, Milton. *Terry and the Pirates*. New York: 1946, author-illustrated, illustrated cover, DJ. $40.

CAPA, Robert. *Images of War*. New York: Grossman Publishers 1964, 1st edition, folio, more than 100 photographs, DJ. $75–$125.

CAPA, Robert. *Slightly out of Focus*. New York: Henry Holt 1947, 1st edition, quarto, DJ. $50–$75.

CAPEK, Karel. *Letters from Spain*. New York: Putnam's 1932, 1st edition, DJ. $55.

CAPEK, Karel. *R.U.R.* Garden City: Doubleday 1923, 1st American edition of author's first book, DJ. $75.

CAPEK, Karel. *War with the Newts*. New York: Putnam (1937), 1st American edition, DJ. $40.

CAPOTE, Truman. *Breakfast at Tiffany's*. New York: Random House (1958), 1st edition, DJ. $75–$125.

CAPOTE, Truman. *Local Color*. New York: Random House (1950), 1st edition, illustrated with photographs by Henri Cartier-Bresson, Cecil Beaton, and Bill Brandt, DJ. $100.

CAPOTE, Truman. *Other Voices, Other Rooms.* New York: Random House (1948), 1st edition of author's first book, DJ. $85–$175.

CAPOTE, Truman. *The Grass Harp.* New York: Random House (1951), 1st edition, 1st issue, in the rough binding, DJ. $100–$200.

CAPOTE, Truman, and Avedon, Richard. *Observations.* New York: Simon & Schuster 1959, 1st edition, folio, photographs by Avedon, slipcase (issued without DJ). $150–$225.

CARAS, Roger. *Monarch of Deadman Bay.* Boston: Little, Brown 1959, 1st edition, DJ. $10.

CARAS, Roger. *The Custer Wolf.* New York: 1966, later printing, DJ. $8.

CARAS, Roger. *Wild Animals.* Philadelphia: (1964), 1st edition. $6–$8.

CARLETON, Will. *City Ballads.* New York: 1886, 1st edition. $12.50.

CARLETON, Will. *Farm Ballads.* New York: 1873, 1st edition. $12.50.

CARLYLE, Thomas. *See* Doves Press.

CARMAN, Bliss. *Ballads of Lost Haven.* Boston: Lamson, Wolffe and Co. 1897, 1st edition. $50.

CARMER, Carl. *Dark Trees to the Wind.* New York: William Sloane Associates (1949), 1st edition, DJ. $25.

CARPENTER, Edward. *Homogenic Love.* Manchester: Labour Press Society 1894, paper covers, 1st edition. $150.

CARPENTER, Edward. *The Intermediate Sex.* New York and London: Mitchell Kennerly 1912, 1st edition. $30.

CARR, John Dickson. *Captain Cut-Throat.* New York: Harper (1955), 1st edition, DJ. $25.

CARR, John Dickson. *He Who Whispers.* New York: Harper (1946), 1st edition, DJ. $45–$75.

CARRIGHAR, Sally. *Icebound Summer.* New York: Knopf 1956, later printing, DJ. $8.

CARRIGHAR, Sally. *Wild Heritage.* Boston: Houghton Mifflin 1965, 1st edition. $7.

CARRINGTON, Hereward. *Physical Phenomena of Spiritualism.* Boston: Herbert B. Turner 1907, 1st edition. $30.

CARRINGTON, Hereward. *The Problems of Psychical Research.* New York: 1914, 1st edition. $30.

CARROLL, Lewis. *Alice's Adventures in Wonderland.* Garden City: Doubleday, Doran (nd), facsimile edition, red cloth, John Tenniel ills. $15–$30.

CARROLL, Lewis. *Alice's Adventures in Wonderland.* New York: Appleton 1866, 1st American edition, from the sheets of the suppressed (by the author) London edition, 42 ills by John Tenniel, red cloth. $3,500–$6,500.

CARROLL, Lewis. *Alice's Adventures in Wonderland.* New York: Harper & Brothers, 1901, illustrated by Peter Newell with numerous full page ills, bound in white boards with gold lettering. $100.

CARSE, Robert. *The Twilight of Sailing Ships.* New York: Gallahad Books (1965), reprint. $17.50

CARSON, Rachel. *Silent Spring.* Boston: Little, Brown 1962, 1st edition, DJ. $25–$75.

CARSON, Rachel. *The Sea Around Us.* New York: (1951), later printing. $4–$7.

CARSON, Rachel. *Under the Sea-Wind.* New York: Simon & Schuster 1941, 1st edition of author's first book, DJ. $100–$150.

CARSON, Rachel. *See also* Limited Editions Club.

CARTER, Forrest. *The Education of Little Tree.* New York: Delacorte (1976), 1st edition, the best-selling "memoir" that turned out to be fiction, very scarce in the first edition, DJ. $50–$200.

CARTER, John. *ABC for Book Collectors.* London: Rupert Hart-Davis 1952, 1st edition, DJ. $45.

CARTER, John, and Muir, Percy, editors. *Printing and the Mind of Man.* London: Cassell; New York: Holt, Rinehart & Winston (1967), 1st edition, DJ. $125.

CARTIER-BRESSON, Henri. *From One China to the Other.* New York: Universe Books (1956), 144 photographs, buckram. $125.

CARTIER-BRESSON, Henri. *The Europeans.* New York: Simon & Schuster (1955), 1,114 photo plates, 1st American edition, DJ. $250–$350.

CARTIER-BRESSON, Henri. *The People of Moscow.* New York: Simon & Schuster (1955), 1st edition, DJ. $100.

CARTIER-BRESSON, Henri. *See also* "Key to Illustrators."

CARVER, Raymond. *At Night the Salmon Move.* Santa Barbara: Capra 1976, one of 100 numbered, signed, hardbound copies, issued without DW. $65–$175.

CARVER, Raymond. *What We Talk About When We Talk About Love.* New York: Knopf 1981, 2nd printing, which came out a month after the 1st. $20.

CARVER, Raymond. *Will You Please Be Quiet, Please.* New York: McGraw-Hill (1976), 1st edition of Carver's first regularly published book, DJ. $100–$300.

CARY, Joyce. *The African Witch.* London: Gollancz (1936), 1st edition, DJ. $100.

CARY, Joyce. *The Horse's Mouth.* New York: Harper 1950, 1st American edition, DJ. $20–$50.

CASANOVA, Jacques. *See* Sets.

CASSELL'S. New Dictionary of Cookery. London and New York: 1912, 12 color plates, pictorial cover. $150.

CASTANEDA, Carlos. *Journey to Ixtlan, The Lessons of Don Juan.* New York: (1972), 1st edition, DJ. $15.

CASTANEDA, Carlos. *Tales of Power.* New York: Simon & Schuster 1974, 1st edition. $7.

CASTANEDA, Carlos. *The Teachings of Don Juan: A Yaqui Way of Knowledge.* Berkeley: University of California 1968, 1st edition, DJ. $50–$75.

CASTLE, Agnes. *Our Sentimental Garden.* London: William Heinemann (1914), ills in color by Charles Robinson, 1st edition. $65.

CATHER, Willa. *A Lost Lady.* New York: Grosset & Dunlap (1925), movie edition, 1st thus, DJ. $40.

CATHER, Willa. *Death Comes for the Archbishop.* New York: Knopf 1927, 1st edition, DJ. $200–$350.

CATHER, Willa. *Lucy Gayheart.* New York: Knopf 1935, 1st edition, DJ. $50–$75.

CATHER, Willa. *Shadows on the Rock.* New York: Knopf 1931, 1st edition, DJ. $75–$125.

CATLIN, George. *North American Indians.* Edinburgh: Grant 1926, 2 vols, 320 color plates. $475.

CATLIN, George. *North American Indians*. Edinburgh: Johnston 1926, 2 vols, later edition, 400 illustrations in color by the author, boxed. $200.

CAZAC, Yoran. *See* "Key to Illustrators."

CELINE, Louis-Ferdinand. *Journey to the End of Night*. Boston: Little, Brown 1934, 1st American edition, DJ. $100.

CELINE, Louis-Ferdinand. *Voyage au bout de la Nuit*. Paris: Danoel et Steele 1932, 1st trade edition, printed wrappers, tissue DJ. $185.

CENDRARS, Blaise. *Sutter's Gold*. New York: Harper and Brothers 1926, translated from the French by Henry Longan Stuart, woodcuts by Harry Cimino, 1st American edition, DJ. $35–$50.

CERVANTES. *See* Ashendene Press.

CHAGALL, Marc. *The Jerusalem Windows*. New York (or Monte Carlo): 1962. $1,200.

CHAGALL, Marc. *Chagall's Posters*. New York: Crown Publishing (1975), folio, 60 color plates plus black and white, DJ, and slipcase. $65–$85.

CHAMBERLAIN, Joshua L. *The Passing of the Armies*. New York: 1915. $125–$200.

CHAMBERS, Robert W. *The Firing Line*. New York: D. Appleton & Co. 1908, 1st edition, $30.

CHAMBERS, Robert W. *The King in Yellow*. Chicago and New York: Neely 1895, 1st edition, preferred binding of green cloth with lizard on cover. $150.

CHANDLER, Raymond. *Farewell My Lovely*. New York and London: Knopf 1940, 1st edition, DJ. $1,200–$2,000

CHANDLER, Raymond. *Farewell My Lovely*. New York and London: Knopf 1940, 1st edition. $100–$150.

CHANDLER, Raymond. *Farewell My Lovely*. New York: World, 1st Tower edition (1940), DJ. $20.

CHANDLER, Raymond. *Killer in the Rain*. Boston: Houghton Mifflin 1964, 1st edition, DJ. $75–$175.

CHANDLER, Raymond. *Killer In the Rain*. Boston: Houghton Mifflin 1964, 1st edition of this collection. $25.

CHANDLER, Raymond. *Red Wind: A Collection of Short Stories.* Cleveland and New York: World (1946), 1st edition of this collection, DJ. $35–$50.

CHANDLER, Raymond. *Red Wind: A Collection of Short Stories.* Cleveland: World (1946); 1st edition thus. $5–$20.

CHANDLER, Raymond. *The Big Sleep.* Cleveland and New York: World (1946), 1st movie edition, 1st edition thus, jacket and ep's illustrated with scenes from the movie, DJ. $20–$60.

CHANDLER, Raymond. *The Big Sleep.* New York: Knopf 1939, 1st edition of author's first book, introducing Philip Marlowe, DJ. $1,500–$2,200.

CHANDLER, Raymond. *The Big Sleep.* New York: Knopf 1939, 1st edition of author's first book. $150–$300.

CHANDLER, Raymond. *The High Window.* New York: Alfred Knopf 1942, 1st edition, DJ. $650–$1,500.

CHANDLER, Raymond. *The High Window.* New York: Alfred Knopf 1942, 1st edition. $135.

CHANDLER, Raymond. *The Long Goodbye.* London: Hamish Hamilton (1953), 1st English edition, precedes 1st American edition, DJ. $150–$350.

CHANDLER, Raymond. *See also* Vintage Paperbacks.

CHAPELLE, Howard I. *Boatbuilding.* New York: W.W. Norton 1941, first edition, photographs, drawings. $25–$50.

CHAPELLE, Howard I. *History of American Sailing Ships.* New York: W.W. Norton 1935, 1st edition, plates and photographs, some soiling. $50.

CHAPELLE, Howard I. *The Baltimore Clipper, Its Origin and Development.* Salem: Marine Research Society 1930. 1st edition, 35 plates and 49 plans. $200.

CHAPMAN, Charles. *Piloting, Seamanship and Small Boat Handling.* New York: Motor Boating 1961. $12–$30.

CHASE, Mary Ellen. *Silas Crockett.* New York: Macmillan 1935, 1st edition, DJ. $12–$25.

CHASE-RIBOUD, Barbara. *Echo of Lions.* New York: Morrow (1989), 1st edition, DJ. $25.

CHATTERTON, E.K. *Whalers and Whalings.* London: T. Fisher Unwin, Ltd. 1925, 1st edition. $30.

CHAUCER, Geoffrey. *See* Golden Cockerel Press.

CHEEVER, John. *The Wapshot Chronicle*. New York: Harper (1957), 1st edition, DJ. $50–$100.

CHESTERTON, G.K. *Alarms and Discursions*. London: Methuen 1910, 1st edition. $35.

CHESTERTON, G.K. *The Innocence of Father Brown*. London: Cassell 1911, 1st edition. $125–$175.

CHESTERTON, G.K. *The Scandal of Father Brown*. London: Cassell (1935), 1st edition, chipped and slightly torn DJ. $350.

CHESTERTON, G.K. *The Secret of Father Brown*. London: Cassell (1927), 1st edition. $35–$125.

CHESTNUT, Mary Boykin. *A Diary from Dixie*, edited by Ben Ames Williams. Boston: "1949", a new edition, supplanting the first, which had been heavily censored; this is now essentially the whole diary, DJ. $25–$35.

CHESTNUT, Mary Boykin. *A Diary from Dixie*, edited by Isabelle D. Martin and Myrta Lockett Avary. New York: "1905". $30–$50.

CHESTNUTT, Charles W. *The Conjure Woman*. Boston: Houghton Mifflin 1899, 1st edition of author's first book, scarce. $125–$200.

CHESTNUTT, Charles W. *The Marrow of Tradition. Conjure Woman*. Boston: Houghton Mifflin 1901, 1st edition. $75–$150.

CHICHESTER, F. *Gypsy Moth Circles the World*. New York: Coward-McCann (1967). $12.

CHILDREN'S BOOKS. *See* "Key to Categories."

CHILD'S GARDEN OF VERSES, THE. *See* Stevenson, Robert Louis.

CHITTENDEN, Hiram. *History of the American Fur Trade*. Stanford: Stanford University Press (1954), 2 vols, map, DJ. $75–$100.

CHITTENDEN, Hiram. *The American Fur Trade of the Far West*. New York: Harper 1902, 1st edition, 3 vols, map, illustrated. $450–$700.

CHITTY CHITTY BANG BANG. *See* Fleming, Ian; *See also* Big Little Books.

CHRISTIE, Agatha. *13 for Luck.* New York: Dodd, Mead 1961, 1st American edition, DJ. $25.

CHRISTIE, Agatha. *Death Comes as the End.* London: Crime Club (1945), 1st edition, DJ. $85–$135.

CHRISTIE, Agatha. *Murder on the Orient Express.* London: Collins 1934, 1st edition, DJ. $1,200–$1,500.

CHRISTIE, Agatha. *The Adventure of the Christmas Pudding.* London: Crime Club (1960), 1st edition, DJ. $40–$75.

CHRISTIE, Agatha. *The Murder of Roger Ackroyd.* London: Collins 1926, 1st edition. $400.

CHRISTIE, Agatha. *See also* Vintage Paperbacks.

CHRISTY, Howard Chandler. *See* "Key to Illustrators."

CHURCHILL, Winston S. *The Second World War.* London: Cassell 1949–54, 1st English edition, 6 vols, DJs. $200.

CHURCHILL, Winston S. *The Second World War.* London: Cassell 1949–54, 1st English edition, 6 vols. $50–$75.

CHURCHILL, Winston Spencer. *A History of the English Speaking Peoples.* London: Cassell & Co. 1956–58, 4 vols, 1st English edition, DJs. $150–$250.

CHURCHILL, Winston Spencer. *A History of the English Speaking Peoples.* London: Cassell & Co. 1956–58, 4 vols, 1st English edition. $75–$150.

CHUTE, Carolyn. *Letourneau's Used Auto Parts.* New York: Ticknor & Fields 1988, 1st edition, DJ. $20.

CHUTE, Carolyn. *The Beans of Egypt, Maine.* Boston: Ticknor & Fields, 1985, 1st edition, the first printing was a small one, signed by the author, DJ. $75.

CIMINO, Harry. *See* "Key to Illustrators."

CLANCY, Tom. *The Hunt for Red October.* Annapolis: Naval Institute Press (1984), 1st edition of author's first book, DJ. $400–$750.

CLAPP, George Wood. *Prosthetic Articulation.* New York: (1914), illustrated. On how to make dentures. $35.

CLARK, Walter Van Tilburg. *The Ox-Bow Incident.* New York: (1940), 1st edition, DJ. $125.

CLARKE, Arthur C. *2001: A Space Odyssey.* (New York): The

New American Library (1968), 1st edition, 1st printing so stated, DJ. $100.

CLAVELL, James. *King Rat.* Boston: Little, Brown (1962), 1st edition of author's first book, DJ. $100–$150.

CLAVELL, James. *Noble House.* New York: Delacorte (1981), 1st trade edition, DJ. $20.

CLAVELL, James. *Tai-Pan: A Novel of Hong Kong.* New York: 1966, 1st edition of author's second book, DJ. $50–$75.

CLEAVER, Eldridge. *Soul on Ice.* New York: McGraw-Hill (1968), 1st edition, DJ. $20–$35.

CLEMENS, Samuel. *See* Twain, Mark.

CLOWES, G.S. Laird. *The Story of Sail.* New York: Henry Holt 1935. $20.

COATES, Robert M. *The Outlaw Years.* New York: Macauley (1930). $75–$125.

COBB, Irvin. *Speaking of Operations.* New York: Doran (1915), 1st edition, illustrated by Tony Sarg, DJ. $35.

COCTEAU, Jean. *Enfants Terribles.* New York: Brewer & Warren 1930, 1st American edition. The first book in the US to be set in Eric Gill's sans serif type. $25.

COCTEAU, Jean. *Les Enfants Terribles.* Paris: Grasset 1929, 1st edition, limited edition, beige wrappers. $70.

COCTEAU, Jean. *Orphee.* London: 1933, 1st edition in English, frontis by Picasso. Limited edition of 100 numbered copies signed by both Cocteau and Picasso. $300–$1,500.

COCTEAU, Jean. *See* "Key to Illustrators."

COFFIN, Robert Tristram. *John Dawn.* New York: Macmillan 1936, 1st edition, DJ. $12–$25.

COHEN, Leonard. *Beautiful Losers.* New York: Viking Press (1966), 1st edition, DJ. $30–$35.

COLERIDGE, Samuel Taylor. *Christabel: Kubla Kahn, A Vision.* London: printed for John Murray 1816, 1st edition, 1st issue with February ads. $650–$900.

COLERIDGE, Samuel Taylor. *See also* Eragny Press.

COLETTE, Sidonie-Gabrielle. *Claudine at School.* New York: Boni 1930, 1st American edition, illustrated by H. Marande, DJ. $50.

COLETTE, Sidonie-Gabrielle. *See also* Limited Editions Club.

COLLIER, John (born 1884, American). *Patterns and Ceremonials of the Indians of the Southwest.* New York: 1949, 1st edition, over 100 lithographs and drawings by Ira Moskowitz, limited edition, signed by author and artist. $75–$100.

COLLIER, John (born 1901, English). *His Monkey Wife, or Married to a Chimp.* New York: Appleton 1931, 1st American edition of author's first book, DJ. $100–$150.

COLLIER, John (born 1901, English). *No Traveller Returns.* London: The White Owl Press 1931, 1st edition, limited to 210 signed copies, decorated cloth binding. $125.

COLLODI, Carlo. *Pinocchio.* Garden City: Doubleday 1932, illustrated by Maud and Miska Petersham. $25.

COLUM, Padraic. *Creatures.* New York: Macmillan 1927, illustrated by Boris Artzybasheff, limited to 300 copies, signed by artist and author, DJ. $65–$85.

COLUM, Padraic. *The Forge in the Forest.* New York: Macmillan 1925, 1st edition, illustrated by Boris Artzybasheff. $30–$40.

COMPTON-BURNETT, Ivy. *Daughters and Sons.* New York: W.W. Norton 1938, 1st American edition, DJ. $75.

CONNELL, Evan S. *Mrs. Bridge.* New York: Viking 1959, 1st edition of author's second book and first novel, DJ. $75–$100.

CONNELLY, Marc. *The Green Pastures.* New York: Farrar & Rinehart (1929), 1st edition, DJ. $75.

CONNOLLY, Cyril. *The Condemned Playground: Essays 1927–1944.* London: Routledge 1945, 1st edition, DJ. $40–$75.

CONNOLLY, Cyril. *The Unquiet Grave.* New York: Harper & Brothers 1945, 1st American edition, DJ. $75–$100.

CONRAD, Joseph. *A Conrad Argosy.* Garden City: Doubleday 1942, quarto, illustrated, DJ. $25.

CONRAD, Joseph. *An Outcast of the Islands.* New York: Appleton 1896, 1st American edition of author's second book in the original terracotta wrappers. $250–$350.

CONRAD, Joseph. *Lord Jim. A Tale.* Edinburgh and London: Blackwood 1900, 1st edition, green cloth, stamped and lettered in black and gold. $125–$250.

CONRAD, Joseph. *Lord Jim. A Tale.* New York: Doubleday & McClure 1900, 1st American edition. $100–$150.

CONRAD, Joseph. *Suspense.* London: J.M. Dent 1925, 1st edition. $60.

CONRAD, Joseph. *Typhoon and Other Stores.* New York: The Book League of America (1921), reprint edition. $2.50–$4.

CONRAD, Joseph. *See also* Limited Editions Club.

COOKBOOKS. *See* "Key to Categories."

COOK, Canfield. *See* Juvenile Series Books.

COOK, Captain James. Author unknown. *Journal of a Voyage Around the World, in HMS "Endeavor," IN THE YEARS 1768, 69, 70, 71.* London: for T. Becket & P.A. de Hondt 1771, 1st edition, 1st issue. Published almost 2 years before official version by Hawkesworth. $4,000.

(COOK, Captain James.) *See also* Hawkesworth, John.

COOK, Frederick. *My Attainment of the Pole.* New York: Polar Publishing 1911, 1st edition, quarto. $80.

COOPER, James Fenimore. *The Deerslayer: or The First Warpath.* Philadelphia: Lea & Blanchard 1841, 2 vols, original cloth, 1st edition, rare. $450.

COOPER, James Fenimore. *See also Last of the Mohicans, The.*

COOTES, F. Graham. *See* "Key to Illustrators."

COPPARD, A.E. *Collected Poems.* London: Jonathan Cape 1928, 1st edition, DJ. $20–$30.

CORELLI, Marie. *Barabbas, A Dream of the World's Tragedy.* London: Methuen 1893, 3 vols, 1st edition, with publisher's ads dated October, 1893 at rear. $200.

CORELLI, Marie. *Innocent. Her Fancy and His Fact.* London: Hodder & Stoughton (1914), frontis, original cloth, 1st edition. $20.

CORNELL, Catherine. *I Wanted to be an Actress.* New York: 1939, 1st edition, photographs, limited and signed edition. $50.

CORSO, Gregory. *The Vestal Lady on Brattle and Other Poems.* Cambridge, MA: Brukenfeld 1955, 1st edition of author's first book, wrappers, signed. $125–$175.

CORVO, Baron. (Frederick William Rolfe). *Chronicles of the House of Borgia.* London: Grant Richards 1901. $100–$150.

CORVO, Baron. *In His Own Image.* London: 1924. New edition. $20–$30.

COSTLER, Dr. A. *The Practice of Sex. The Crisis of Civilization and the Sexual Mass Misery of our Time.* London: np (1936), by Arthur Koestler with the name spelled "Coester" on the title page, portfolio of erotica in rear flap, very scarce. $100–$250.

COVARRUBIAS, Miguel. *Indian Art of Mexico and Central America.* New York: Knopf 1957, illustrated by the author with color plates and within text, also photographs, quarto, DJ, publisher's box. $75–$150.

COVARRUBIAS, Miguel. *Negro Drawings.* New York: Knopf 1927, 1st edition. $75–$150.

COVARRUBIAS, Miguel. *See also* "Key to Illustrators."

COWARD, Noel. *Blithe Spirit.* New York: Doubleday, Doran 1941, 1st American edition, DJ. $40–$50.

COWLES, Fleur. *See* "Key to Illustrators."

COX, Palmer. *Queerie Queers with Hands, Wings and Claws.* New York: Larkin 1887, illustrated boards. $35–$60.

COX, Palmer. *The Brownies around the World.* London: T. Fisher Unwin 1894, 1st English edition, illustrated by the author. $85–$200.

CRANE, Hart. *The Bridge.* New York: Liveright 1930, 1st trade edition, photograph of Brooklyn Bridge by Walker Evans. This edition was published 3 months after the Paris limited editions and was revised, DJ. $225–$650.

CRANE, Hart. *The Bridge.* New York: Liveright 1930, 1st trade edition, photograph of Brooklyn Bridge by Walker Evans. This edition was published 3 months after the Paris limited editions and was revised. $125–$175.

CRANE, Hart. *The Bridge.* Paris: Black Sun Press 1930, quarto, wrappers, 3 photographs by Walker Evans, one of 200 numbered copies on Holland paper, in glassine DW and silver slipcase. $900–$1,700.

CRANE, Hart. *The Bridge.* Paris: Black Sun Press 1930, quarto, wrappers, 3 photographs by Walker Evans, one of 50 numbered copies on Japanese vellum, signed, in glassine DW and silver slipcase. $3,600–$6,000.

CRANE, Nathalia. *The Janitor's Boy and Other Poems*. New York: Seltzer 1924, 1st trade edition of author's first book in rose–colored boards. $35.

CRANE, Stephen. *Maggie: A Girl of the Streets*. (New York): no publisher (1893), 1st edition, very rare, mustard yellow wrappers, published under the name of Johnston Smith, with chips and tears. $4,200–$15,000.

CRANE, Stephen. *The Black Riders*. Boston: Copeland and Day 1895, 1st edition, gray pictorial boards or yellow cloth, one of 500. $350–$500.

CRANE, Stephen. *The Open Boat and Other Stories*. New York: Doubleday 1898, 1st edition with silver–stamped, green pictorial cloth. $125–$200.

CRANE, Stephen. *The Red Badge of Courage*. New York: Appleton 1895, 1st edition, 1st issue with inserted title page on laid paper, with text on woven paper. $575–$3,000.

CRANE, Stephen. *The Red Badge of Courage*. New York: Appleton 1896, 2nd edition. $75–$100.

CRANE, Stephen. *The Red Badge of Courage*. New York: Macmillan 1962, The Macmillan Classics, afterword by Clifton Fadiman, black and white illustrations by Herschel Levit; binding is the modern hard washable pictorial plasticized cloth of the yellow Nancy Drew and blue Hardy Boys. $1.50–$3.50

CRANE, Stephen. *See also* Grabhorn Printing; Limited Editions Club; Sets.

CREELEY, Robert. *Gold Diggers*. np: Divers Press 1954, 1st edition, wrappers, DJ. $100–$150.

CREVECOEUR, Michel-Guillaume St. Jean de. *Letters from an American Farmer, Describing Certain Provincial Situations, Manners and Customs*. Philadelphia: Mathew Carey 1793, 1st American edition. $300–$400.

CREWS, Harry. *A Feast of Snakes*. New York: Atheneum 1976, 1st edition of an early work, DJ. $75–$125.

CREWS, Harry. *The Gospel Singer*. New York: William Morrow 1968, 1st edition of author's first book, DJ. $150–$350.

CRONIN, A.J. *The Citadel*. Boston: Little, Brown 1937, 1st American edition, DJ. $75.

CROSBY, Caresse. *Graven Images*. Boston: Houghton Mifflin 1926, DJ. $175–$300.

CROSBY, Harry. *Sleeping Together: A Book of Dreams*. Paris: Black Sun Press 1931, in wrappers, limited edition. $350–$500.

CROSBY, Harry. *The Collected Poems*. Paris: 1931, 4 vols, wraps, 1st edition. $900.

CROWLEY, Aleister. *Diary of a Drug Fiend*. New York: E.P. Dutton 1923, 1st American edition. $75.

CROWLEY, Aleister. *Magick in Theory and Practice by the Master Therion*. London: 1929, privately printed. $225–$300.

CROWLEY, Aleister. *Moonchild: A Prologue*. London: The Mandrake Press 1929, 1st edition, DJ. $75–$200.

CROY, Homer. *They Had to See Paris*. New York: 1926, 1st edition. $25.

CRUIKSHANK, George. *The History of Jack and the Beanstalk*. London: David Bogue (1854), 1st edition, 1st issue, pictorial wrappers, 6 etchings by Cruikshank. $150–$250.

CRUIKSHANK, George. *See also* "Key to Illustrators."

CRUM, R. *See* "Key to Illustrators."

CUALA PRESS (Churchtown and Dublin, Ireland). Gogarty, Oliver St. John. *Elbow Room*. Dublin: Cuala Press 1939, one of 450. $80.

CUALA PRESS (Churchtown and Dublin, Ireland). Gregory, Lady. *The Kiltartan Poetry Book: Prose Translations from the Irish*. Dublin: Cuala Press 1918, one of 400. $120.

CUALA PRESS (Churchtown and Dublin, Ireland). Kavanagh, Patrick. *The Great Hunger*. Dublin: Cuala Press 1942, one of 250. $150.

CUALA PRESS (Churchtown and Dublin, Ireland). O'Connor, Frank. *The Wild Bird's Nest*. Poems from the Irish. Dublin: Cuala Press 1932, one of 250, inscribed. $300.

CUALA PRESS (Churchtown and Dublin, Ireland). Parnell, Thomas. *Poems*. Dublin: Cuala Press 1927, one of 200. $90.

CUALA PRESS (Churchtown and Dublin, Ireland). Russell, George W. ("AE"). *By Still Waters.* Dublin: Cuala Press 1906, one of 200. $200.

CUALA PRESS (Churchtown and Dublin, Ireland). Synge, John Millington. *Deirdre of the Sorrows.* Dublin: Cuala Press 1910, one of 250. $250.

CUALA PRESS (Churchtown and Dublin, Ireland). Tynan, Katherine. *Twenty One Poems.* Dublin: Cuala Press 1907, one of 200. $550.

CUALA PRESS (Churchtown and Dublin, Ireland). Yeats, John Butler. *Early Memories: Some Chapters of an Autobiography.* Dublin: Cuala Press 1923, one of 500. This is by the father of W.B. Yeats, not by his brother Jack, as some sources have it. $50–$125.

CUALA PRESS (Churchtown and Dublin, Ireland). Yeats, William Butler, and Johnson, Lionel. *Poetry and Ireland.* Dublin: Cuala Press 1908, one of 250. $350.

CUALA PRESS (Churchtown and Dublin, Ireland). Yeats, William Butler. *If I Were Four-and-Twenty.* Dublin: Cuala Press 1940, one of 450. $100–$300.

CUALA PRESS (Churchtown and Dublin, Ireland). Yeats, William Butler. *In the Seven Woods.* Dun Emer Press 1903, one of 325. This was one of the 11 books published by Dun Emer before it was moved to Churchtown and renamed "Cuala." $100–$300.

CUALA PRESS (Churchtown and Dublin, Ireland). Yeats, William Butler. *Michael Robartes and the Dancer.* Dublin: Cuala Press 1920, one of 400. $125–$150.

CUALA PRESS (Churchtown and Dublin, Ireland). Yeats, William Butler. *The Wild Swans at Coole.* Dublin: Cuala Press 1917, one of 400. $200.

CUALA PRESS (Churchtown and Dublin, Ireland). Yeats, William Butler. *Words for Music Perhaps.* Dublin: Cuala Press 1932, one of 450. $140.

CULLEN, Charles. *See* "Key to Illustrators."

CULLEN, Countee. *Color*. New York and London: Harper 1925, 1st edition of author's first book, DJ. $150–$300.

CULLEN, Countee. *Copper Sun*. New York: Harper and Brothers 1927, 1st trade edition. $35.

CULLEN, Countee. *The Ballad of the Brown Girl*. New York: Harper and Brothers 1927, illustrated by Charles Cullen, 1st edition, in slipcase. $75–$125.

CULLUM, Ridgewell. *The Saint of the Speedway*. New York: George Doran "1924", 1st edition, DJ. $20–$40.

CULPEPPER, Nicholas. *The Complete Herbal*. London: 1815, quarto, contemporary calfskin, with portrait and all 40 hand-colored plates. $200.

CULPEPPER, NICHOLAS. *The English Physician Enlarged*. London: (1798?), ("Culpepper's English Physician and Complete Herbal.") 2 vols, quarto, contemporary calfskin gilt, extremities worn, 12 tinted anatomical plates and 29 hand-colored plates of plants. $350.

CUMMINGS, e.e. *Collected Poems*. New York: Harcourt, Brace (1938), 1st edition, DJ. $35–$50.

CUMMINGS, e.e. *Eimi*. (New York: Covici Friede, 1935), one of 1,381 numbered copies signed by author, DJ. $100–$225.

CUMMINGS, e.e. *Puella Mea*. Mount Vernon: Golden Eagle Press (1949), 1st separate edition, DJ. $35–$50.

CUMMINGS, e.e. *The Enormous Room*. New York: Boni and Liveright 1922, 1st edition, 1st state, with the word "shit" censored on page 219, DJ. $300–$400.

CUMMINGS, e.e. *Tulips and Chimneys*. New York: Thomas Seltzer 1923, 1st edition. $75–$150.

CUNARD, Nancy. *Sublunary*. London: Hodder & Stoughton 1923, frontis sketch by Wyndham Lewis, 1st English edition. $60.

CUNNINGHAM, Eugene. *Quick Triggers*. Boston: Houghton, Mifflin 1935, 1st edition, DJ. $20–$65.

CUPPY, Will. *How to Attract the Wombat*. New York: Rinehart 1949, 1st edition, DJ. $35.

CURRY, John Stuart. *See* "Key to Illustrators."

CURWOOD, James Oliver. *The Alaskan*. New York: Cosmopolitan "1923", 1st edition, DJ. $25–$65.

CURWOOD, James Oliver. *The Black Hunter*. New York: Cosmopolitan 1926, 1st edition, DJ. $25–$65.

CURWOOD, James Oliver. *The River's End*. New York: Grosset & Dunlap (1919), reprint edition. $3.50–$8.

CURWOOD, James Oliver. *The River's End*. Philadelphia: The Blakiston Company (1946), reprint edition. $2.50–$4.

CURWOOD, James Oliver. *The River's End*. Philadelphia: The Blakiston Company (1946), reprint edition, DJ. $3–$5.

CUSTER, Elizabeth. *Boots and Saddles*. New York: 1885, 1st edition, 1st issue, without the portrait or map. $50–$100.

CUTLER, Carl C. *Greyhounds of the Sea: The Story of the American Clipper Ship*. New York: Halcyon House 1930, 1st edition, illustrated, some in color. $50.

 D ————————————————————————————

DA VINCI, Leonardo. *The Notebooks*. New York: Reynal & Hitchcock 1938, 1st English language edition, DJ. Halftone ills from Leonardo. $85.

DAHL, Roald. *Charlie and the Great Glass Elevator*. New York: Knopf (1972), 1st edition, illustrated by Joseph Schindelman, DJ. $20–$30.

DAHL, Roald. *Some Time Never*. New York: Charles Scribner's Sons 1948, 1st edition, DJ. $50.

DAHL, Roald. *The Gremlins*. London: Collins (1944), illustrated by the Walt Disney Studios in color and black and white, 1st English edition of author's first book, DJ. $350.

DAHLBERG, Edward. *Do These Bones Live?* New York: Harcourt, Brace (1941), 1st edition, DJ. $35.

DAHLBERG, Edward. *The Sorrows of Priapus*. (New York): Thistle Press (1957), 1st edition of 150 copies signed by author and artist, full-page and half-page drawings by Ben Shahn, with an extra signed lithograph laid in, glassine dust wrapper and slipcase. $175–$400.

DALI, Salvador. *See* "Key to Illustrators" under Whistler, Rex.

DANA, E[dmund]. *Geographical Sketches on the Western Country: Designed for Emigrants and Settlers: Being the Result of Extensive Researches and Remarks.* Cincinnati: Looker, Reynolds and Co. 1819, 1st edition, 12mo, moderately worn. $850.

DANA, Richard Henry. *Two Years Before the Mast.* New York: Grosset & Dunlap (1935), reprint edition, DJ. $6.

(DANA, Richard Henry.) *Two Years Before the Mast. A Personal Narrative of Life at Sea.* New York: (Harper's Family Library) 1840, 1st edition of author's first book. (Author's name does not appear.) 1st issue with the letter "i" in copyright notice properly dotted. $2,500–$3,500.

DANA, Richard Henry. *Two Years Before the Mast.* Chicago: Lakeside Press 1930, limited edition, color ills. $65.

DANA, Richard Henry. *Two Years Before the Mast.* Los Angeles: Ward Ritchie 1964, 2 vols, color plates, maps, boxed, fine special edition. $160.

DANA, Richard Henry. *See also* Heritage Press.

DANE, Clemence. *Broom Stages.* London: Heinemann 1931, title page and dust wrapper designed by Rex Whistler, 1st edition, DJ. $40–$75.

DANTE, Alighieri. *See* Ashendene Press.

DARLING, Esther Birdsall. *Baldy of Nome.* San Francisco: A.M. Robertson 1913, original pictorial boards with cloth spine, frontis, and plates, scarce. $50.

DARLING, Esther Birdsall. *Navarre of the North.* Garden City: Doubleday 1931. $50.

DARWIN, Charles. *Descent of Man and Selection in Relation to Sex.* London: John Murray 1871, 2 vols; 1st edition, 1st issue in green cloth with errata on verso in 2nd volume, illustrated. $450–$1,000.

DARWIN, Charles. *Descent of Man and Selection in Relation to Sex.* New York: Appleton 1871, 2 vols, 1st American edition. $85–$250.

DARWIN, Charles. *Expression of the Emotions in Man and Animals.* New York: Appleton 1873, 1st American edition. $150.

DARWIN, Charles. *On the Origin of Species by Means of Natural Selection.* London: John Murray, 1858, 1st edition, original green cloth. $8,000–$20,000.

DARWIN, Charles. *On the Origin of Species by Means of Natural Selection.* New York: Appleton 1860, 1st American edition, 1st issue with two quotations after the half-title page. $500–$1,000.

DARWIN, Charles. *Origin of Species and Descent of Man.* New York: Random House (1936), 1st Modern Library edition, DJ. $15–$35.

DARWIN, Charles. *See also* Heritage Press.

DAUGHERTY, James. *Andy and the Lion.* New York: Viking Press 1938, illustrated by the author, 1st edition, Caldecott medal, boxed, DJ. $75.

DAUGHERTY, James. *Daniel Boone.* New York: Viking Press 1939, illustrated by the author, 1st edition, Newbery winner. $27.50.

DAUGHERTY, James. *Daniel Boone.* New York: Viking Press 1939, illustrated by the author, 1st edition, Newbery winner, DJ. $50–$65.

DAVIES, Rhys. *The Song of Songs and Other Stories.* London: E. Archer (1927), 1st trade edition, wraps. $20–$35.

DAVIES, Rhys. *See also* Golden Cockerel Press.

DAVIES, W.H. *The Soul's Destroyer.* London: 1907, 1st published edition of author's first book (privately printed first in 1905), wrappers. $50–$75.

DAVIS, H.L. *Honey in the Horn.* New York: Harper 1935, 1st American edition, DJ. $50–$75.

DAVIS, Richard Harding. *Soldiers of Fortune.* New York: Scribner's 1897, 1st edition, pictorial cloth, illustrated by Charles Dana Gibson. $20–$50.

DAY, Clarence. *Life with Father.* Made into a Play by Howard Lindsay and Russel Crouse, New York: 1942, 1st edition. $20.

DAY, Clarence. *Life with Father.* New York: Knopf 1935, 1st edition, DJ. $40.

DAY-LEWIS, Cecil. *A Time to Dance and Other Poems.* London: The Hogarth Press 1935, 1st edition, DJ. $35–$100.

DE ANGELI, Marguerite. *Bright April*. New York: Doubleday (1946), 1st edition, illustrated throughout by the author in color and black and white, DJ. $30–$45.

DE ANGELI, Marguerite. *Bright April*. New York: Doubleday (1946), 1st edition, illustrated throughout by the author in color and black and white. $8–$15.

DE ANGELI, Marguerite. *Skippack School*. New York: Doubleday (1939), 1st edition, illustrated throughout by the author in color and black and white, DJ. $35–$50.

DE BEAUVOIR, Simone. *The Mandarins*. Cleveland: World (1956), one of 500 signed copies, of which 325 were for private distribution, slipcase. $75–$150.

DE BRUNHOFF, JEAN. *Babar and Father Christmas*. New York: Random House (1940), 1st American edition, illustrated throughout in color by the author, large quarto, illustrated boards with cloth spine. $150–$250.

DE LA MARE, Walter. *Down a Down Derry*. London: Constable (1922), quarto, 3 color plates by Dorothy Lathrop, also black and white, 1st edition. $80.

DE LA MARE, Walter. *Peacock Pie—A Book of Rhymes*. London: Constable & Co., Ltd. 1913, 1st edition. $75–$125.

DE LA MARE, Walter. *Peacock Pie—A Book of Rhymes*. New York: Henry Holt (1924), illustrated by C. Lovat Fraser with 16 color plates. $75–$125.

DE LA MARE, Walter. *Peacock Pie—A Book of Rhymes*. New York: Henry Holt (1925), illustrated by W. Heath Robinson, 1st American edition thus. $40.

DE LA MARE, Walter. *The Three Mulla-Mulgars*. London: Duckworth & Co. 1910, 1st edition, DJ. $250–$300.

DE LA MARE, Walter. *The Three Mulla-Mulgars*. London: Duckworth & Co. 1910, 1st edition. $50–$100.

DE LA MARE, Walter. *See also* Anthologies.

DE MONVEL, Boutet. *See* "Key to Illustrators."

DE SOTO, Hernando. *See* Grabhorn Printing.

DE VINNE, Theodore. *See* Grolier Club.

DECARAVA, Roy. *See* Hughes, Langston: *The Sweet Flypaper of Life*.

DEFOE, Daniel. *Robinson Crusoe.* New York: Cosmopolitan Book Corporation 1920, 16 color plates by N.C. Wyeth. $125.

DEIGHTON, Len. *The Ipcress File.* London: Hodder & Stoughton 1962, 1st edition of author's first book, DJ. $175.

DELAND, Margaret. *Dr. Lavender's People.* New York: Harper 1903, 1st edition, frontis, plates, illustrated by Lucius Hitchcock, green pictorial cloth. $20

DELILLO, Don. *Americana.* Boston: Houghton Mifflin 1971, 1st edition of author's first book, DJ. $75.

DELILLO, Don. *Great Jones Street.* Boston: Houghton Mifflin 1973, DJ. $35.

DELL, Floyd. *Love in Greenwich Village.* New York: George H. Doran Co. (1926), 1st edition, DJ. $50.

DEMING, Edward. *See* "Key to Illustrators" under Remington, Frederick.

DENISON, Muriel. *Susannah of the Mounties.* New York: Random House (1950s), movie edition, ills from the Shirley Temple movie, DJ. $35–$65.

DENISON, Muriel. *Susannah of the Mounties.* New York: Random House (1950s), movie edition, ills from the Shirley Temple movie. $15–$35.

DENNIS, Wesley. *See* "Key to Illustrators."

DENSLOW'S MOTHER GOOSE. Being the Old Familiar Rhymes and Jingles of Mother Goose. New York: McClure, Philips & Co. 1901, 1st edition, 1st state, with the text ("Humpty Dumpty") beginning on the verso of the dedication leaf, illustrated throughout in color by W.W. Denslow, who also selected and edited the rhymes. $250–$300.

DENSLOW, W.W. *See also* "Key to Illustrators."

DERLETH, August. *The Memoirs of Solar Pons.* Sauk City: Mycroft & Moran 1951, 1st edition, DJ. $85.

DERLETH, August. *The Reminiscences of Solar Pons.* Sauk City: Mycroft & Moran 1951, 1st edition, DJ. $75.

DERLETH, August. *The Night Side.* New York and Toronto: Rinehart (1947), 1st edition. $45.

DERLETH, August. *Village Daybook.* Chicago: Pelligrini & Cudahy (1947), ills by Frank Utpatel, DJ. $25.

DERRYDALE PRESS. Haig-Brown, Roderick L. *The Western Angler*. New York: Derrydale Press (1939), 1st edition, 2 vols, many plates, color and black and white, one of 950 sets, with folding map, in box. $500–$800.

DETMOLD, E.J. *Pictures from Birdland*. London and New York: Dent and Dutton 1899, 1st edition, illustrated by the author with his twin brother Maurice, their first book, 24 color plates, quarto. $300–$600.

DETMOLD, E.J. *The Book of Baby Pets*. London: Henry Frowde, Hodder & Stoughton ca 1913, thick quarto, 19 tipped-in color plates by Detmold, 1st edition. $150–$350.

DETMOLD, E.J. *See also* "Key to Illustrators."

DETMOLD, Maurice and Edward. *See* "Key to Illustrators."

DEUTSCH, Babette. *Honey Out of the Rock*. New York: Appleton 1925, 1st edition, DJ. $60.

DEVRIES, Peter. *Angels Can't Do Better*. New York: Coward-McCann, 1st edition, DJ. $150.

DI PRIMA, Diane. *Memoirs of a Beatnik*. New York: Traveller's Companion Series (1969), wraps. $35.

DI PRIMA, Diane. *The Calculus of Variation*. San Francisco: (privately published) 1972, wraps, 1st edition. $20.

DI PRIMA, Diane. *This Kind of Bird Flies Backward*. (New York: Totem Press 1958), 1st edition of author's first book, wraps. $50.

DICK TRACY. *See* Big Little Books.

DICK, Philip K. *Humpty Dumpty in Oakland*. London: Gollanzc 1986, 1st edition, DJ. $25–$35.

DICK, Philip K. *The Game-Players of Titan*. London: White Lion (1974), 1st British edition, 1st hardcover edition, DJ. $75–$100.

DICK, R.A. *The Ghost and Mrs. Muir*. Chicago and New York: (1945), 1st American edition of author's first book, DJ. $35.

DICKENS, Charles. *A Christmas Carol*. Philadelphia: Lippincott (1915), 1st printing of this Rackham edition, 12 color plates by Arthur Rackham, plus many black and white ills, lettered tissue guards. $150–$200.

DICKENS, Charles. *Oliver Twist*. Boston: Houghton, Osgood & Co., Riverside Press, Cambridge 1880, Globe edition, illustrated from designs by Darley and Gilbert, reprint edition, decorative nineteenth-century cloth binding, book printed on fairly inexpensive paper. $3.50–$8.

DICKENS, Charles. *Oliver Twist.* London: Richard Bentley 1838, 3 vols, 1st edition, ills by Cruikshank, half-morocco. $500–$800.

DICKENS, Charles. *Oliver Twist.* London: Richard Bentley 1838, 3 vols, 1st edition, ills by Cruikshank, modern calfskin gilt by Bayntum. $1,000.

DICKENS, Charles. *Oliver Twist.* London: Richard Bentley 1838, 3 vols, original cloth, 1st edition, ills by Cruikshank, 1 vol rebacked with original spine preserved, minor wear and staining, very scarce in original cloth. $1,000–$1,500.

DICKENS, Charles. *The Life and Adventures of Nicholas Nickleby.* London: Chapman and Hall 1839, 1st book edition, 1st issue, plates by Phiz (H.K. Browne), early decorative fine binding. $250–$350.

DICKENS, Charles. *The Life and Adventures of Nicholas Nickleby.* London: Chapman and Hall 1839, 1st book edition, 1st issue, plates by Phiz (H.K. Browne), original cloth. $450–$600.

DICKENS, Charles. *The Life and Adventures of Nicholas Nickleby,* London: Chapman and Hall 1838-39, 1st edition, 1st issue, 20 parts in 19, green wraps, illustrated by Phiz (H.K. Browne). $1,500–$2,000.

DICKENS, Charles. *The Life and Adventures of Nicholas Nickleby.* New York: Worthington Co. 1890, reprint edition, decorative nineteenth-century cloth binding, stamped black on green, inexpensive paper. $2–$4.

DICKEY, James. *Drowning with Others.* Middletown: Wesleyan University Press (1962), 1st edition, DJ. $90.

DIDION, Joan. *Run River.* New York: Ivan Obolensky, Inc. 1963, 1st edition of author's first book. $85.

DIDION, Joan. *Slouching Towards Bethlehem.* New York: Farrar, Straus & Giroux 1968, 1st edition, DJ. $40–$60.

DINESEN, Isak. *Out of Africa.* New York: Random House 1938, 1st edition, DJ. $75–$125.

DINESEN, Isak. *Seven Gothic Tales*. New York: Harrison, Smith and Robert Hass 1934, 1st trade edition. $8–$15.

DINESEN, Isak. *Seven Gothic Tales*. New York: Harrison, Smith and Robert Hass 1934, 1st trade edition of author's first book, DJ. $85–$150.

DISNEY. *Heath Reader: Donald Duck Sees South America*, by Marion Palmer, Heath Publishing Co. (1945). $18–$35.

DISNEY. *Walt Disney's Uncle Remus Stories. A Giant Golden Book*. New York: Simon & Schuster (1947), 1st edition, quarto. $30–$45.

DISNEY, Walt. *Mickey Mouse Book No. 4*. Philadelphia: David McKay (1934), large quarto, consists of comic strips. $150–$300.

DISNEY, Walt. *See* Big Little Books.

DISNEY, WALT, STUDIOS. *See* "Key to Illustrators."

DIXON, Maynard. *See* "Key to Illustrators."

DOCTOR DOLITTLE. See Lofting, Hugh.

DOCTOROW, E.L. *Loon Lake*. New York: Random House 1980, 1st trade edition, DJ. $25.

DOCTOROW, E.L. *Ragtime*. New York: Random House (1975), 1st edition, DJ. $40.

DODGE, M.E. *Hans Brinker; or The Silver Skates*. New York: James O'Keane 1866, by Mary Mapes Dodge, 1st edition, illustrated by Thomas Nast. $250–$350.

DODGE, Mary Mapes. *See* Dodge, M.E.

DONLEAVY, J.P. *The Ginger Man*. New York: McDowell, Obolensky (1958), 1st US edition of author's first book, DJ. $50–$65.

DONNE, John. *Poems... with Elegies on the Author's Death*. London: M.F. for John Marriot 1633, 1st edition. $4,000–$5,000.

DOS PASSOS, John. *The 42nd Parallel*. New York: Harper and Brothers 1930, 1st edition, DJ. $150.

DOS PASSOS, John. *USA*. New York: Harcourt 1938, 1st of this trilogy, 1st thus, DJ. $65–$125.

DOUGHTY, Charles Montague. *Travels in Arabia Deserta*. Cambridge: Cambridge University Press 1888, 2 vols, map, illustrated, 1st edition, original binding. $1,500.

DOUGLAS, Aaron. *See* "Key to Illustrators."

DOUGLAS, Lloyd C. *The Robe*. Boston: Houghton Mifflin 1942, 1st edition, DJ. $35.

DOUGLAS, Lord Alfred. *My Friendship With Oscar Wilde*. New York: 1932, 1st edition, DJ. $100.

DOUGLAS, Norman. *South Wind*. London: 1917, 1st edition, with the transposed lines on page 335. $85–$150.

DOUGLAS, Norman. *South Wind*. New York: Dodd Mead, 1928, 1st American edition, illustrated by Valenti Angelo, DJ and slipcase. $55–$75.

DOVES PRESS (London). Browning, Robert. *Dramatis Personae*. London: Doves Press 1910, one of 250. $125.

DOVES PRESS (London). Browning, Robert. *Men and Women*. London: Doves Press 1908, one of 250, 2 vols, hand-flourished by Robert Johnston and signed by him. $550.

DOVES PRESS (London). Carlyle, Thomas. *Sartor Resartus*. London: Doves Press 1907, one of 300. $375.

DOVES PRESS (London). Milton, John. *Areopagitica*. London: Doves Press 1907, one of 300. $550.

DOVES PRESS (London). Ruskin, John. *Unto this Last*. London: Doves Press 1907, one of 300. $200.

DOVES PRESS (London). Shakespeare, William. *Antony and Cleopatra*. London: Doves Press 1912, one of 15 on vellum. Morocco Doves binding 1914. $4,200.

DOVES PRESS (London). Shakespeare, William. *Coriolanus*. London: Doves Press 1914, one of 15 printed on vellum, bound in elaborate gilded morocco by the Doves bindery in 1919. $3,500.

DOVES PRESS (London). Shakespeare, William. *Lucrece*. London: Doves Press 1915, one of 175. $450.

DOVES PRESS (London). Shakespeare, William. *Venus and Adonis*. London: Doves Press 1912, one of 200. $325.

DOVES PRESS (London). Tennyson, Alfred. *Seven Poems and Two Translations*. London: Doves Press 1902, one of 25 on vellum. $2,750.

DOVES PRESS (London). Tennyson, Alfred. *Seven Poems and Two Translations*. London: Doves Press 1902, one of 325. $160.

DOWSON, Ernest. *The Poems of Ernest Dowson*. London: 1905, illustrated by Aubrey Beardsley. $275–$350.

DOYLE, A. Conan. *A Study in Scarlet.* New York and London: Street & Smith nd, Select Fiction Library, reprint edition. $7–$10.

DOYLE, A. Conan. *Conan Doyle's Best Books.* New York: P.F. Collier & Son, nd, 3 vols, reprint edition, black and white ills, tinted frontis. $20–$35.

DOYLE, Arthur Conan. *The Adventures of Sherlock Holmes.* London: George Newnes 1892, and *The Memoirs of Sherlock Holmes* 1894, 2 vols, 1st editions, original cloth, illustrated by Sidney Paget. $1,500–$2,000.

DOYLE, Arthur Conan. *The Adventures of Sherlock Holmes.* London: 1899, pictorial wrapper. $20.

DOYLE, Arthur Conan. *The Hound of the Baskervilles.* London: George Newnes 1902, original pictorial cloth, 16 ills by Sidney Paget, 1st edition. $600–$1,500.

DOYLE, Arthur Conan. *The Hound of the Baskervilles.* New York: McClure, Phillips & Co. 1902, original cloth, ills by Sidney Paget, 1st American edition, 1st issue, without ":published 1902" on the copyright page. $150–$500.

DOYLE, Arthur Conan. *The Hound of the Baskervilles.* New York: McClure, Phillips & Co. 1902, original cloth, ills by Sidney Paget, 1st American edition, 3rd issue, with "illustrated" on title page, which is tipped in. $85–$135.

DOYLE, Arthur Conan. *The Memoirs of Sherlock Holmes,* New York: Harper and Brothers 1894, 1st American edition, 1st issue. $500.

DOYLE, Arthur Conan. *The Memoirs of Sherlock Holmes.* New York: Harper and Brothers 1894, 1st American edition, 2nd (revised) issue. $25–$75.

DOYLE, Arthur Conan. *The New Revelation.* New York: George H. Doran (1918), 1st American edition. $35.

DOYLE, Arthur Conan. *See also* Limited Editions Club; Heritage Press.

DREISER, Theodore. *An American Tragedy.* New York: Boni and Liveright 1925, 2 vols, 1st edition, DJs. $100–$200.

DREISER, Theodore. *An American Tragedy.* New York: Boni and Liveright 1925, 2 vols, 1st edition. $40–$65.

DREISER, Theodore. *Sister Carrie*. New York: Doubleday, Page 1900, 1st edition of author's first book, only 1,008 of which were printed. $1,000–$2,000.

DREVENSTEDT, Amy. *See* "Key to Illustrators."

DRINKWATER, John. *New Poems*. Boston: Houghton Mifflin 1925, 1st American edition. $20.

DU BOIS, W.E.B. *Suppression of the American Slave Trade*. New York: Longmans Green 1896, 1st edition of author's first book. $500.

DU BOIS, W.E.B. *The Souls of Black Folk*. Chicago: McClurg 1903, 1st edition. $250–$325.

DU BOIS, W.E.B. *Worlds of Color*. New York: Mainstream 1961, 1st edition, 3rd book of the Mansart trilogy, DJ. $30.

DU MAURIER, Daphne. *Rebecca*. London: Gollancz 1938, 1st edition, DJ. $125–$175.

DUNBAR, Paul Laurence. *Candle Lightin' Time*. New York: Dodd Mead 1901, 1st edition, 1st issue, with photographic ills by the Hampton Institute Camera Club and decorations by Margaret Armstrong, original ornate, decorated pictorial cloth. $75–$150.

DUNBAR, Paul Laurence. *Folks from Dixie*. New York: Dodd Mead 1898, illustrated by E.W. Kemble, original pictorial brown cloth, 1st edition. $75–$150.

DUNBAR, Paul Laurence. *Li'l Gal*. New York: Dodd Mead 1904, 1st edition, original decorative cover by Margaret Armstrong, photographs by L.R. Miner. $75–$100.

DUNBAR, Paul Laurence. *The Complete Poems*. New York: Dodd Mead 1913, 1st edition. $50.

DUNCAN, Gregory. *See* Juvenile Series Books.

DUNNE, Peter Finley. *Mr. Dooley: In Peace and in War*. Boston: Small, Maynard 1898. $35.

DUNSANY, Lord. *Plays of Gods and Men*. Boston: Luce & Co. (1917), cloth and gilt boards, 1st American edition, DJ. $40–$65.

DUNSANY, Lord. *Tales of War*. Boston: Little, Brown 1918, 1st American edition. $20–$40.

DUNSANY, Lord. *Tales of War*. Dublin: (1918), 1st edition, DJ. $50–$100.

DURRELL, Lawrence. *The Alexandria Quartet: Justine and Balthazar and Mountolive and Clea.* London: Faber & Faber 1957–60, 4 vols, 1st edition, DJs. $350–$450.

DURRELL, Lawrence. *The Black Book.* New York: 1960, 1st American edition, DJ. $35–$50.

DURRELL, Lawrence. *The Black Book.* Paris: The Obelisk Press 1938, wraps, 1st edition. $500–$700.

 E ─────────────────────────────

EARHART, Amelia. *The Fun of It: Random Records of My Own Flying and of Women in Aviation.* New York: 1932, record in rear, DJ. $500.

EARLY, Eleanor. *New England Cookbook.* New York: (1954), 1st printing, DJ. $27.50

EASTLAKE, William. *Go in Beauty.* New York: Harper & Brothers (1956), 1st edition of author's first book, DJ. $100–$150.

EASTMAN, Max. *Enjoyment of Living.* New York: Harper 1948, 1st edition, DJ. $35.

EATON, Seymour. *The Roosevelt Bears: Their Travels and Adventures.* Philadelphia: Edward Stern & Co. 1906, illustrated by V. Floyd Campbell, 1st edition, profusely illustrated, with 16 color plates plus black and white throughout. $100–$275.

EBERHART, Mignon. *See* Vintage Paperbacks.

EBERHART, Richard. *Collected Poems 1930-1960.* New York: Oxford 1960, 1st American edition, DJ. $50–$75.

EDDINGTON, Sir Arthur S. *Mathematical Theory of Relativity.* Cambridge: Cambridge University Press 1930, 2nd edition. $50.

EDDINGTON, Sir Arthur S. *Report on the Relativity Theory of Gravitation.* London: 1918, paper covers, 1st edition. $500.

EDDISON, E.R. *The Worm Ouroboros.* New York: Boni 1926, 1st American edition of author's first book. $40.

EDMONDS, Walter D. *Chad Hanna.* Boston: 1940, 1st edition, DJ. $25.

EDMONDS, Walter D. *Drums Along the Mohawk.* Boston: Little, Brown 1936, 1st edition, DJ. $50–$125.

EICHENBERG, Fritz. *See* "Key to Illustrators."

EINSTEIN, Albert. *Relativity: The Special and General Theory.* New York: Henry Holt 1921, 1st American edition. $40.

EISELY, Loren. *Notes of an Alchemist.* New York: (1972), later printing, DJ. $12.

EISELY, Loren. *The Firmament of Time.* New York: Atheneum 1960, 1st edition, scarce, DJ. $30–$65.

EISELY, Loren. *The Mind as Nature.* New York: Holt & Rinehart (1962), 1st edition, DJ. $30–$50.

EISENSTAEDT, Alfred. *See* "Key to Illustrators."

ELIOT, T.S. *Ash Wednesday.* London: Faber & Faber 1950, 1st edition, jacket designed by Baldwin, DJ. $75–$125.

ELIOT, T.S. *Four Quartets.* London: Faber & Faber 1944, 1st English edition, DJ. $45.

ELIOT, T.S. *Four Quartets.* New York: Harper & Brothers 1943, 1st American edition, one of 788 copies preserved from the 1st printing, the remainder having been destroyed because of incorrect margin, DJ. $750.

ELIOT, T.S. *Four Quartets.* New York: Harper & Brothers 1943, 1st American edition, 2nd impression, DJ. $75.

ELIOT, T.S. *Murder in the Cathedral.* (Canterbury): 1935, 1st edition, wraps. $150–$300.

ELIOT, T.S. *Murder in the Cathedral.* London: Faber & Faber, 1st trade edition, DJ. $50–$125.

ELIOT, T.S. *Old Possum's Book of Practical Cats.* London: Faber & Faber (1939), quarto, pictorial cloth, 1st edition, DJ. $250.

ELIOT, T.S. *The Family Reunion.* New York: Harcourt, Brace (1939), later printing, DJ. $12–$20.

ELIOT, T.S. *The Wasteland.* New York: (1971) 1st trade edition, DJ. $40.

ELIOT, T.S. *The Wasteland.* New York: Boni & Liveright 1922, 1st edition, approximately 500 copies in 1st state, with "mountain" correctly spelled in line 339 and with 5-mm-high figures on colophon and flexible black cloth binding, DJ. $3,000–$3,500.

ELIOT, T.S. *The Wasteland: A Facsimile and Transcript of the Original Drafts Including the Annotations of Ezra Pound.* (London): Faber & Faber (1971), one of 500 numbered copies, slipcase. $100–$200.

ELLISON, Ralph. *Invisible Man.* New York: Random House (1952), 1st edition of author's first book, DJ. $250–$400.

ELLSON, Hal. *Duke.* New York: Scribner's 1949, 1st American edition, DJ. $35.

ELOISE. See Thompson, Kay.

ELSIE DINSMORE. See Finley, Martha.

EMERSON, Ralph Waldo. *English Traits.* Boston: Phillips, Sampson & Co. 1856, 1st edition, original cloth. $50–$150.

EMERSON, Ralph Waldo. *Representative Men: Seven Lectures.* Boston: Phillips, Sampson and Co. 1850, 1st edition, 1st issue, original brown cloth. $75–$200.

ENRIGHT, Elizabeth. *Thimble Summer.* New York: Farrar & Rinehart 1938, 1st edition, 2nd printing (no publisher's symbol on copyright page), DJ. $20–$35.

EPSTEIN, Brian. *A Cellarful of Noise.* Garden City: Doubleday 1964, 1st edition, DJ. $60.

EPSTEIN, Jacob. *See* "Key to Illustrators."

ERAGNY PRESS (London). Coleridge, Samuel Taylor. *Christabel, Kubla Khan, Fancy in Nubibus and Song from Zapolya.* London: Eragny Press 1904, one of 226. $150.

ERAGNY PRESS (London). Jonson, Ben. *Songs by Ben Jonson.* London: Eragny Press 1906, one of 175. $700.

ERAGNY PRESS (London). Rosetti, Christina. *Verses by Christina G. Rosetti.* London: Eragny Press 1906, one of 175. $1,200.

ERAGNY PRESS (London). Villon, Francois. *Les Ballades.* London: Eragny Press 1900, one of 222. $175.

ERDRICH, Louise. *Baptism of Desire.* New York: Harper 1989, 1st edition of the author's first book of poetry, DJ. $20–$35.

EULALIE. *See* "Key to Illustrators."

EVANS, Abbie Huston. *Collected Poems.* (Pittsburgh): University of Pittsburgh Press (1970), 1st edition, DJ. $20.

EVANS, Abbie Huston. *Fact of Crystal.* New York: Harcourt, Brace (1961), 1st edition, DJ. $35.

EVANS, Abbie Huston. *Outcrop.* New York and London: Harper and Brothers 1928, 1st edition of author's first book, DJ. $150.

EVANS, Abbie Huston. *The Bright North.* New York: Macmillan "1938", 1st edition, DJ. $50.

EVANS, Walker. *American Photographs.* New York: Museum of Modern Art (1938), 1st edition. $75–$150.

EVANS, Walker. *Message from the Interior.* New York: Eakins 1966, limited 1st edition, issued without DJ. $200.

EVANS, Walker. *See also* Agee, James: *Let Us Now Praise Famous Men.*

EVANS, Walker. *See also* "Key to Illustrators."

 F ———————————————————————

FABRE, Jean Henri. *Fabre's Book of Insects.* New York: Tudor (1937), reprint edition, color plates by E.J. Detmold. $35–$75.

FAIRBROTHER, Nan. *New Lives, New Landscapes.* London: Architectural Press 1970, 2nd impression. $40.

FAIRBROTHER, Nan. *New Lives, New Landscapes.* New York: Knopf (1970), later printing. $30.

FAIRBROTHER, Nan. *The House in the Country.* New York: Knopf 1965, 1st American edition, DJ. $17.50.

FAIRCHILD, David. *Garden Islands of the Great East.* New York: Scribner's 1943, photos, later printing. $15.

FAIRCHILD, David. *The World Grows Round My Door.* New York & London: Scribner's 1947, 1st edition, many photographs. $15.

FANNING, Edmund. *Voyages and Discoveries in the South Seas 1792-1832*. Salem: Marine Research Society Publication 6, 1924, one of 97 copies, 32 plates, original marbled boards with 1/4 cloth. $100–$275.

FANNING, Edmund. *Voyages Round the World*. New York: Collins & Hanney 1833, 1st edition, original half-leather, worn, joints cracking. $500–$900.

FANTASY ARTISTS, ELEVEN. *See* "Key to Illustrators."

FARADAY, Michael. *A Course of Six Lectures on the Chemical History of a Candle to which is Added a Lecture on Platinum*. London: Griffin, Bohn 1861, 1st edition. $100–$300.

FARADAY, Michael. *A Course of Six Lectures on the Chemical History of a Candle to which is Added a Lecture on Platinum*. New York: Harper & Brothers 1861, 1st American edition. $75.

FARMER, Fannie Merritt. *The Boston Cooking-School Cookbook*. Boston: Little, Brown 1924, new, revised edition, tan cloth, worn. $35.

FARMER, Philip José. *Dark is the Sun*. New York: Ballantine Books 1979, 1st edition, DJ. $20–$25.

FARMER, Philip José. T*he Fabulous Riverboat*. New York: Putnam (1971), 1st edition, DJ. $150–$200.

FARNAN, Dorothy J. *Auden in Love*. New York: Simon & Schuster 1984, 1st edition, DJ. $10–$20.

FARNOL, Jeffrey. *The Money Moon*. New York: Dodd, Mead & Co. 1911, 1st edition, illustrated by Arthur Keller, brown cloth cover with color pictorial insert and bold gilt decoration. $25.

FARRELL, James T. *A World I Never Made*. New York: Vanguard Press (1936), 1st edition, DJ. $45.

FARRELL, James T. *Studs Lonigan*. New York: Random House 1938, 1st Modern Library Giant edition, DJ. $25.

FARRELL, James T. *Young Lonigan: A Boyhood in Chicago Streets*. New York: 1932, 1st edition of author's first book, DJ. $300.

FARRINGTON, S. Kip, Jr. *Pacific Game Fishing*. New York: Coward-McCann 1942, 1st edition, illustrated in color and black and white, by Lynn Bogue Hunt, also photographs, DJ. $50–$80.

FAST, Howard. *The American.* New York: Duell, Sloan and Pearce (1946), 1st edition, DJ. $35.

FAST, Howard. *The Children.* New York: Duell, Sloan and Pearce (1947), 1st edition, DJ. $40.

FAULKNER, William. *Absalom, Absalom!* New York: Random House 1936, 1st trade edition, DJ. $300–$450.

FAULKNER, William. *As I Lay Dying.* New York: Jonathan Cape & Harrison Smith (1930), 1st edition, 1st issue, DJ. $400–$600.

FAULKNER, William. *Go Down, Moses and Other Stories.* New York: Random House (1942), 1st trade edition, DJ. $150–$350.

FAULKNER, William. *Intruder in the Dust.* New York: Random House (1948), 1st edition, DJ. $100–$200.

FAULKNER, William. *Light in August.* New York: Harrison Smith & Robert Haas (1932), 1st edition, 1st issue, with "Jefferson" for "Mottstown," DJ. $350–$550.

FAULKNER, William. *Requiem for a Nun.* New York: Random House (1951), 1st trade edition, DJ. $65–$125.

FAULKNER, William. *Sanctuary.* New York: Jonathan Cape & Harrison Smith (1931), 1st edition, DJ. $500–$1,500.

FAULKNER, William. *The Sound and the Fury.* New York: Jonathan Cape & Harrison Smith (1929), 1st edition, 1st issue, DJ. $3,000.

FEARING, Kenneth. *The Big Clock.* New York: Harcourt, Brace (1936), 1st edition, DJ. $20–$40.

FERBER, Edna. *Saratoga Trunk.* Garden City: Doubleday 1941, 1st edition, DJ. $20.

FERBER, Edna. *Show Boat.* New York: Doubleday, Page 1926, 1st edition, DJ. $35.

FERDINAND (THE BULL). See Leaf, Munro.

FERLINGHETTI, Lawrence. *Pictures of the Gone World.* San Francisco: City Lights Pocket Bookshop (1955), 1st edition, 1st printing, of author's first book and #1 in the City Lights Pocket Poets series, stiff wraps, one of 500 copies, without the wrap-around band. $100–$200.

FEUTCHWANGER, Leon. *Success: Three Years in the Life of a Province.* London: Secker 1930, 1st edition, DJ. $25–$35.

FIELD, Eugene. *Poems of Childhood*. New York: Scribner's 1904, 8 full-page plates by Maxfield Parrish, plus title page and pictorial paper label on cover. $50–$125.

FIELD, Eugene. *The Love Affairs of a Bibliomaniac*. New York: Scribner's 1896, decorated cloth, 1st edition. $25–$35.

FIELD, Eugene. *The Sugar Plum Tree and Other Verses*. Akron: Saalfield 1930, quarto, 1st edition, 8 full-page color plates by Fern Bisel Peat, plus many black and white ills, DJ. $65.

FIELD, Eugene. *Wynken, Blynken and Nod and Other Verses*. Akron: Saalfield 1930, folio, pictorial wrappers, illustrated by Fern Bisel Peat with 12 full pages in color, plus covers. $35–$45.

FIELD, Eugene. *See also* Sets.

FIELD, Peter. *Powder Valley Plunder*. New York: Jefferson House "1962", 1st edition, DJ. $10–$25.

FINLEY, Martha. *Elsie's Womanhood*. New York: Dodd, Mead (1875, 1903, 1917), a later printing of one of the first few Elsie Dinsmore titles. $10.

FIRBANK, Ronald. *Prancing Nigger*. New York: Brentano's (1924), 1st American edition, first of the author's works to be published in the US, black cloth, introduction by Carl Van Vetchen, DJ. $125–$150.

FIRBANK, Ronald. *The Artificial Princess*. London: Centaur Press 1934, 1st trade edition, DJ. $150.

FIRBANK, Ronald. *The Princess Zoubaroff. A Comedy*. London: Richards 1920, 1st edition, one of only 513 bound copies, frontis and decorations, DJ. $200–$300.

FISHER, M.F.K. *The Gastronomical Me*. New York: Duell, Sloan, & Pearce (1943), 1st printing, DJ. $40.

FISHER, Vardis. *Children of God*. New York and London: Harper and Brothers 1939, 1st trade edition, DJ. $35–$65.

FISHER, Vardis. *In Tragic Life*. Caldwell: Caxton 1932, 1st edition, DJ. $35.

FITZGERALD, F. Scott. *Tender is the Night*. New York: Scribner's 1934, 1st issue, DJ. $1,200.

FITZGERALD, F. Scott. *The Beautiful and the Damned*. New York: Scribner's 1922, 1st edition, 1st printing, DJ. $1,200–$1,500.

FITZGERALD, F. Scott. *The Beautiful and the Damned.* New York: Scribner's 1922, 1st edition, 1st printing. $100–$125.

FITZGERALD, F. Scott. *The Beautiful and the Damned.* New York: Scribner's 1922, 1st edition, 1st state of second printing. $60.

FITZGERALD, F. Scott. *The Great Gatsby.* New York: Scribner's 1925, 1st edition, 1st issue, with the reading "sick in tired" on page 205. $200–$350.

FITZGERALD, F. Scott. *See also* Limited Editions Club.

FIVE LITTLE PEPPERS, THE. See Sidney, Margaret.

FLACK, Marjorie. *Angus and the Ducks.* New York: Doubleday (1930), early printing, illustrated in color and lithographs by the author, scarce. $35–$50.

FLACK, Marjorie. *The Story About Ping.* New York: Viking 1943, 1st edition, illustrated by Kurt Wiese, scarce, DJ. $50–$150.

FLASH GORDON. See Big Little Books.

FLAUBERT, Gustave. *See* Golden Cockerel Press.

FLEMING, Ian. *Casino Royale.* London: Jonathan Cape (1953), 1st edition in 1st state DJ with no quote from the Sunday Times. $1,200–$1,500.

FLEMING, Ian. *Chitty Chitty Bang Bang.* New York: Random House 1964, 1st American edition, DJ. $75.

FLEMING, Ian. *Goldfinger.* London: Jonathan Cape 1959, 1st edition, DJ. $75.

FLEMING, Ian. *Live and Let Die.* London: Jonathan Cape 1954, 1st edition, DJ. $400–$500.

FLEMING, Ian. *Live and Let Die.* New York: Macmillan Co. 1955, 1st American edition, DJ. $125.

FLEMING, Ian. *See also* Big Little Books; *Chitty Chitty Bang Bang.*

FLOETHE, Richard. *See* "Key to Illustrators."

FORD, Ford Madox. *No More Parades.* New York: Boni (1925), 1st American edition, DJ. $60–$75.

FORD, Ford Madox. *The Good Soldier.* London: John Lane, Bodley Head 1915, 1st edition, scarce. $250–$450.

FORD, H.J. *See* "Key to Illustrators."

FORD, Paul Leicester. *Wanted—A Matchmaker.* New York: Dodd, Mead 1900, 1st edition, 5 full-page ills by Howard Chandler Christy, green cloth with decorated cover and spine by Margaret Armstrong. $75–$85.

FORESTER, C.S. *Lord Hornblower.* Boston: Little, Brown 1946, 1st American edition, DJ. $25.

FORESTER, C.S. *Lord Hornblower.* London: Joseph (1946), 1st edition, DJ. $35–$55.

FORESTER, C.S. *Poo-Poo and the Dragons.* Boston: Little, Brown 1942, 1st edition, illustrated by Robert Lawson, boxed, scarce, DJ. $150–$300.

FORESTER, C.S. *The African Queen.* Boston: 1935, 1st American edition, DJ. $500.

FORESTER, C.S. *The African Queen.* London: (1935), 1st edition, DJ. $1,000.

FORSTER, E.M. *A Passage to India.* London: Edward Arnold & Co. 1924, original cloth, 1st edition, DJ. $350–$650.

FORSTER, E.M. *A Room with a View.* London: 1908, 1st edition. $150–$400.

FORSTER, E.M. *Howards End.* New York: Putnam's 1910, 1st American edition of author's first book to be published in the US, maroon cloth. $125.

FORSTER, E.M. *Where Angels Fear to Tread.* Edinburgh and London: William Blackwood and Sons 1905, 1st edition of author's first book; 1st issue, with this title not referred to in ads in rear. $400–$500.

FORSTER, E.M. *Where Angels Fear to Tread.* Edinburgh and London: William Blackwood and Sons 1905, 1st edition of author's first book; 2nd issue, with this title listed in the ads. $200–$350.

FORSTER, E.M. *Where Angels Fear to Tread.* New York: 1920, 1st American edition, in black cloth, DJ. $200–$350.

FORTNUM, Peggy. *See* "Key to Illustrators."

FOURNIER, Alain. *The Wanderer.* London: Le Grand Meulnes 1929, 1st English edition, DJ. $350.

FOWLES, John. *The Collector.* Boston: Little, Brown (1963), 1st American edition, DJ. $85–$150.

FOWLES, John. *The Collector.* London: Jonathan Cape, 1963, 1st English edition, DJ. $450–$650.

FOWLES, John. *The Ebony Tower.* Boston: Little, Brown (1974), 1st American edition, DJ. $50.

FOWLES, John. *The Ebony Tower.* London: Jonathan Cape (1974), 1st edition, DJ. $100–$200.

FOWLES, John. *The French Lieutenant's Woman.* Boston: Little, Brown (1969), 1st American edition, DJ. $75.

FOX, John. *The Little Shepherd of Kingdom Come.* New York: Charles Scribner's Sons 1931, illustrated with 16 mounted color plates by N.C. Wyeth, one of 512 copies, signed by the artist, original vellum-backed cloth, bow, and DJ. $800.

FRANCE, Anatole. *Filles et Garcons.* Paris: Hachette (1900), quarto, pictorial boards, many color plates plus black and white, by Boutet de Monvel. $60.

FRANCE, Anatole. *See also* Limited Editions Club.

FRANCIS, Dick. *Dead Cert.* New York: Holt (1962), 1st American edition, DJ. $150–$300.

FRANCIS, Dick. *For Kicks.* New York: Harper 1965, 1st American edition, DJ. $100.

FRANCIS, Dick. *The Sport of Queens.* London: Joseph 1957, 1st edition of author's first book, DJ. $175.

FRANCIS, Dick. *The Sport of Queens.* New York: Harper 1969, 1st American edition, DJ. $75.

FRANKLIN, John. *Narrative of a Journey to the Shores of the Polar Sea, in the Years 1819-20-21-22.* London: John Murray 1823, quarto, 1st edition, maps and plates, some of them hand-colored, leather binding. $400–$650.

FRANKLIN, John. *Narrative of a Journey to the Shores of the Polar Sea, in the Years 1819-20-21-22.* London: John Murray 1824, 2 vols, 2nd edition, maps, leather binding. $275–$350.

FRANKLIN, John. *Narrative of a Second Expedition to the Shores of the Polar Sea.* New York: Greenwood Press "1969". London reprint of the 1828 edition, published with no DJ. $25.

FRASER, Claude Lovat. *See* "Key to Illustrators."

FRASER, George MacDonald. *Flashman at the Charge.* New York: Knopf 1973, 1st edition, DJ. $45.

FREEMAN, Donald Southall. *Lee's Lieutenants.* New York: Charles Scribner's Sons 1942-44, 3 vols, 1st edition, DJs. $150–$200.

FREEMAN, Donald Southall. *R.E. Lee: A Biography.* New York: Charles Scribner's Sons 1934-35, 4 vols, 1st edition, glassine DJs and publisher's box. $150–$250.

FREEMAN, Mary E. Wilkins. *The People of our Neighborhood.* Philadelphia: Curtis Publishing Co.; New York: Doubleday and McClure (1898), decorated green cloth, top edge gilt, gilt lettering, untrimmed. $40.

FREUCHEN, Peter. *Arctic Adventures. My Life in the Frozen North.* New York and Toronto: Farrar & Rinehart (1935), map ep's. $15.

FREUCHEN, Peter. *Book of the Eskimos.* Cleveland: NY World Publishing Co. (1961), book club edition, DJ. $8.

FREUD, Sigmund. *Collected Papers.* New York: Basic Books, Inc. (1959), 5 vols, 1st American edition. $50–$100.

FRIEDMAN, Bruce Jay. *Stern.* New York: Simon & Schuster 1962, 1st edition of author's first book, DJ. $75.

FRIEL, Arthur. *Forgotten Island.* New York: 1931, 1st edition, DJ. $25.

FROST, Robert. *A Boy's Will.* London: David Nutt 1913, author's first published book, 1st edition, 1st issue with collation as follows: (x), (50) pages + (1) page publisher's ad, 1st binding of bronzed-brown pebbled cloth, original green cloth slipcase. $2,000–$3,500.

FROST, Robert. *A Further Range.* New York: Henry Holt (1936), 1st trade edition, DJ. $50.

FROST, Robert. *A Further Range.* New York: Holt, Rinehart (1936), later printing. $15.

FROST, Robert. *In the Clearing.* New York: Holt, Rinehart (1962), 1st trade edition, DJ. $50.

FROST, Robert. *North of Boston.* London: David Nutt 1914, "first edition, 1914" so stated, 1st issue with olive green cloth stamped in gilt and blind-stamped. $1,500–$2,000.

FROST, Robert. *North of Boston*. New York: Holt 1914, 1st American edition, with "first edition 1914" on copyright page, sheets from the British edition with Henry Holt title page. $500–$1,000.

FROST, Robert. *West-Running Brook*. New York: Holt, Rinehart (1928), 1st edition, 2nd state, with "first edition" on copyright page (1st state lacks the "first edition" notice), DJ. $75.

FRYER, Jane Eayre. *The Mary Frances Sewing Book*. Philadelphia: Winston (1913), illustrated by Jane Allen Boyer, patterns uncut and complete. $85–$150.

FRYER, John (with William Bligh). *See* Golden Cockerel Press.

FUJIKAWA, Gyo. *See* "Key to Illustrators."

FULLER, R. Buckminster. *Nine Chains to the Moon*. Philadelphia: Lippincott (1938), 1st trade edition of author's first book, DJ. $85.

FULLER, R. Buckminster. *Nine Chains to the Moon*. Philadelphia: Lippincott (1938), 1st edition, limited to 5,000 copies of author's first book, DJ. $375.

FULLER, Roy. *Epitaphs and Occasions*. London: 1949, 1st edition, DJ. $35.

 G ──────────────────────────

G-MAN. *See* Big Little Books.

GADDIS, William. *The Recognitions*. New York: Harcourt, Brace (1955), 1st edition of author's first book, DJ. $200.

GAG, Wanda. *Millions of Cats*. New York: Coward-McCann 1928, 1st edition, illustrated by the author, DJ. $150–$250.

GALLICO, Paul. *Manxmouse*. New York: Coward-McCann 1968, 1st American edition, DJ. $25.

GALLICO, Paul. *Mrs. 'arris Goes to Parliament*. Garden City: Doubleday 1965, 1st American edition, DJ. $20.

GALLICO, Paul. *The Snow Goose—A Story of Dunkirk*. London: 1941, 1st edition, DJ. $75.

GALLICO, Paul. *The Snow Goose—A Story of Dunkirk*. London: 1946, quarto, 4 color plates and many ills in the text by Peter Scott, 1st edition thus, buckram and gilt, limited to 750 copies, signed by author and artist, DJ. $125–$175.

GANNETT, Ruth. *See* "Key to Illustrators."

GARCIA MARQUEZ, Gabriel. *Love in the Time of Cholera*. New York: Knopf 1988, 1st American trade edition, DJ. $35–$50.

GARCIA MARQUEZ, Gabriel. *One Hundred Years of Solitude*. New York: Harper & Row (1970), 1st American edition, 1st issue, translated by Gregory Rabassa, DJ. $250–$500.

GARDNER, John. *Grendel*. New York: Knopf 1971, 1st edition, DJ. $125–$175.

GARDNER, John. *The Dory Book*. Camden, Maine: International Marine 1978. $35.

GARDNER, John. *The Sunlight Dialogues*. New York: Knopf 1972, 1st edition, DJ. $50–$100.

GARDNER, John. *The Wreckage of Agathon*. New York: Harper and Row 1970, 1st edition, DJ. $50–$75.

GARIS, Howard. *Uncle Wiggily and the Cowbird*. Sandusky: American Crayon Co. (1943), quarto, ills by Mary and Wallace Stover, paper covers. $8–$18.

GARIS, Howard. *Uncle Wiggily and the Littletails*. New York: Platt & Munk (1942), about 4 ills by Elmer Rache, including color frontis, DJ. $8–$18.

GARIS, Howard. *Uncle Wiggily's Fortune*. New York: Platt & Munk (1942), about 4 ills by Elmer Rache, including color frontis. $6–$15.

GARIS, Howard. *Uncle Wiggily's Holidays*. Newark: Charles E. Graham 1922, ills by Lang Campbell; one of the series with 3 stories per book, with a colored picture on each page and color pictorial label on cover. $15–$40.

GARIS, Howard. *Uncle Wiggily's Picture Book*. New York: Platt & Munk (1940), ills by Lang Campbell, 12 color plus black and white ills. $15–$30.

GARIS, Howard. *Uncle Wiggily's Picture Book.* New York: A.L. Burt (1924), ills by Lang Campbell, 32 color plus black and white ills, quarto. $15–$40.

GARIS, Roger. *My Father was Uncle Wiggily.* New York: McGraw Hill 1966, photographs, 1st edition, DJ. $12–$25.

GARLAND, Hamlin. *Back Trailers from the Middle Border.* New York: 1928, 1st edition, DJ. $25–$45.

GARLAND, Hamlin. *Forty Years of Psychic Research.* New York: 1936, 1st edition. $30.

GARLAND, Hamlin. *Main Travelled Roads.* Boston: Arena Publishing Co. 1891, 1st edition of author's first book, 1st issue, with "first thousand" at foot of cover, wraps. $75–$175.

GARLAND, Hamlin. *The Book of the American Indian.* New York and London: Harper & Brothers 1923, 1st edition, 35 plates, boxed, very scarce. $250.

GARNETT, David. *The Grasshoppers Come.* (New York): Brewer, Warren & Putnam (1931), 1st American edition, DJ. $20.

GASCOYNE, David. *Poems 1937-1942.* London: 1943, 1st edition, large 8vo, decorated boards, dust wrapper designed by Graham Sutherland, DJ. $50–$65.

GASS, William. *Willie Master's Lonesome Wife.* New York: Knopf 1971. $25–$50.

GATES, Josephine Scribner. *Live Dolls' House Party.* Indianapolis: Bobbs-Merrill (1906), illustrated by Virginia Keeping. $40–$50.

GATES, Josephine Scribner. *More About Live Dolls.* Toledo: Franklin (1903), probable 1st edition, illustrated by Virginia Keeping, cover has pictorial paste-on. $50–$60.

GATES, Josephine Scribner. *The Live Dolls in Wonderland.* Indianapolis: Bobbs-Merrill (1946), later printing. $20.

GATTY, Harold. *The Raft Book.* New York: Grady Press (1943), charts, boxed. $30–$50.

GAUGUIN, Paul. *Intimate Journals.* New York 1921, 27 plates by Gauguin, 1st American edition, 1st edition in English, issued without DJ, edition limited to 530 copies. $200–$300.

GAUGUIN, Paul. *Noa Noa. My Voyage to Tahiti*. New York: Leap Publishers 1947, 14 color plates and 36 text ills, large 8vo, cloth DJ. $20.

GENE AUTRY. See Big Little Books.

GENET, Jean. *Our Lady of the Flowers*. Paris: Morihien 1943, one of 475 copies, top edge gilt, red leather. $100.

GENTHE, Arnold. *Isadora Duncan: Twenty-Four Studies*. New York and London: Mitchell Kennerly 1929, quarto, frontis and 24 full-page photographs, box lacking. $100–$200.

GENTHE, Arnold. *The Book of the Dance*. New York: Mitchell Kennerly (1916), 1st edition, buckram with gilt vignette, over 100 photographs by Genthe. $110.

GIBBINGS, Robert. *Lovely is the Lee*. New York: 1945, wood engravings by the author. $17–$20.

GIBBINGS, Robert. *See* Golden Cockerel Press.

GIBBINGS, Robert. *The Wood Engravings of... with some Recollections by the Artist*. London: J.M. Dent & Sons 1959, 1st English edition, over 1,000 engravings and 9 pages of halftones, publisher's prospectus laid in, full buckram cover, glassine DJ. $100–$200.

GIBBINGS, Robert. *See also* "Key to Illustrators."

GIBBON, Edward. *The History of the Decline and Fall of the Roman Empire*. New York: 1834, 5th American edition, 4 vols, octavo, original calfskin, edges worn and scuffed, a few corners scraped, 3 folding maps, one of which is torn. $110.

GIBRAN, Kahlil. *Prose Poems*. New York: Knopf 1934, 1st edition, original black cloth. $8–$20.

GIBSON, Charles Dana. *A Widow and Her Friends*. New York and London: 1901, large quarto, 78 pages of drawings by Gibson, 1st edition. $125–$150.

GIBSON, Charles Dana. *Our Neighbors*. New York and London: 1905, large quarto, 68 pages of drawings by Gibson, 1st edition. $135.

GIBSON, Charles Dana. *See also* "Key to Illustrators."

GIDE, André. *The Journals of André Gide*. New York: Knopf 1947, 1st American edition, DJ. $25.

GILBERT, Michael. *Smallbone Deceased.* New York: Harper 1950, 1st American edition, DJ. $25.

GILL, Brendan. *The Trouble of the House.* Garden City: Doubleday 1950, 1st edition, DJ. $35–$45.

GILL, Eric. *Art and Manufacture. Handworker's Pamphlet #4.* London: Fanfare Press 1929, white printed wrappers with 2 wood engravings by the artist. $65–$85.

GILL, Eric. *It All Goes Together.* New York: Devin Adair 1944, 28 pages of ills plus text, DJ. $20–$35.

GILL, Eric. *The Engravings of Eric Gill.* Wellingborough: Christopher Skelton 1983, 1,200 or more prints, some in color, large quarto, back of ivory cloth and sides of black cloth. Limited to 1,350 copies, in slipcase. $150–$200.

GILL, Eric. *See also* Golden Cockerel Press.

GILL, Tom. *Wildcat 13.* New York: Putnam "1941", 1st edition, DJ. $10–$35.

GILMAN, Caroline. *Oracles from the Poets: A Fanciful Diversion for the Drawing Room.* New York and London: Wiley & Putnam 1845, amounts to a parlor game, very decorative binding, rebacked. $35–$40.

GILOT, Francoise. *See* "Key to Illustrators."

GINSBERG, Allen. *Howl and Other Poems.* San Francisco: The City Lights Pocket Bookshop (1956), 1st edition. $250–$350.

GINSBERG, Allen. *Howl for Carl Solomon.* (San Francisco: Grabhorn-Hoyem 1971), quarto, pictorial cloth, printed on handmade paper and signed by the poet, beige cloth with colored ills by Robert Lavigne, 1st edition thus. $150–$225.

GINSBERG, Allen. *Kaddish and Other Poems.* San Francisco: City Lights Books 1961, 1st edition, wraps. $50–$75.

GIOVANNI, Nikki. *Black Feeling Black Talk Black Judgement.* New York: (1970), author's first book, 1st edition, DJ. $35–$65.

GIOVANNI, Nikki. *Re:Creation.* Detroit: (1970), in wraps as issued, 1st edition. $35–$65.

GIRADOUX, Jean. *Amphitryon 38.* New York: Random House (1938), 1st American edition, DJ. $25.

GISSING, George. *New Grub Street.* London: Smith, Elder 1891,

3 vols, 1st edition, original dark blue-green cloth, gilt-lettered spine. $1,000–$2,000.

GISSING, George. *The Private Papers of Henry Rycroft.* Westminster: Constable 1903, original cloth, 1st edition. $50–$125.

GLANZMAN, Louis. *See* "Key to Illustrators."

GLASGOW, Ellen. *In This Our Life.* New York: Harcourt and Brace (1941), 1st edition, DJ. $30.

GLASGOW, Ellen. *Vein of Iron.* New York: Harcourt, Brace (1935), 1st edition, DJ. $25.

GLASGOW, Ellen. *See also* Sets.

GODDEN, Rumer. *Take Three Tenses.* Boston: 1945, 1st American edition, DJ. $15–$35.

GODDEN, Rumer. *The Chinese Puzzle.* London: Peter Davies (1936), 1st edition of author's first book. $35–$65.

GOGARTY, Oliver St. John. *Going Native.* New York: Duell, Sloan & Pearce 1940, 1st American edition, DJ. $20–$35.

GOGARTY, Oliver St. John. *Mr. Petunia.* London: Constable (1946), 1st edition, DJ. $25–$40.

GOGARTY, Oliver St. John. *See also* Cuala Press.

GOLD, Michael. *120 Million.* New York: International Publishers (1929), 1st edition of author's first book. $40–$60.

GOLDBERG, Isaac. *Tin Pan Alley.* New York: John Day 1930, 1st edition. $25.

GOLDEN COCKEREL PRESS (Waltham St. Lawrence). Bell, Gertrude. *The Arab War.* Waltham: Golden Cockerel Press 1940, one of 30 copies specially bound in Morocco. $250.

GOLDEN COCKEREL PRESS (Waltham St. Lawrence). Bligh, William and Fryer, John. *The Voyage of the Bounty's Launch.* Waltham: Golden Cockerel Press 1934, one of 300 copies. $250.

GOLDEN COCKEREL PRESS (Waltham St. Lawrence). Cabell, James Branch. *Jurgen.* Waltham: Golden Cockerel Press 1949, one of 100 copies specially bound and with an extra engraving. $300–$900.

GOLDEN COCKEREL PRESS (Waltham St. Lawrence). Chaucer, Geoffrey. *The Canterbury Tales.* Waltham: Golden Cockerel Press 1929-31, one of 15 copies on vellum. $2,000.

GOLDEN COCKEREL PRESS (Waltham St. Lawrence). Davies, Rhys. *Daisy Matthews and Three Other Tales.* Waltham: Golden Cockerel Press 1932, one of 325 copies, original half-morocco. $150.

GOLDEN COCKEREL PRESS (Waltham St. Lawrence). Flaubert, Gustave. *Salambo.* Waltham: Golden Cockerel Press 1931, one of 500. $75.

GOLDEN COCKEREL PRESS (Waltham St. Lawrence). Gibbings, Robert. *The Seventh Man, a True Cannibal Tale of the South Seas.* Waltham: Golden Cockerel Press 1930, one of 500 copies. $150.

GOLDEN COCKEREL PRESS (Waltham St. Lawrence). Gill, Eric. *Clothing Without Cloth.* Waltham: Golden Cockerel Press 1931, one of 500 copies. $125–$275.

GOLDEN COCKEREL PRESS (Waltham St. Lawrence). Herrick, Robert. *One Hundred and Eleven Poems.* Waltham: Golden Cockerel Press 1955, one of 105 specially bound copies and with an additional set of ills not in the book. $400.

GOLDEN COCKEREL PRESS (Waltham St. Lawrence). Keats, John. *Endymion.* Waltham: Golden Cockerel Press 1947, one of 400. $300.

GOLDEN COCKEREL PRESS (Waltham St. Lawrence). La Rochefoucauld. *Moral Maxims.* Waltham: Golden Cockerel Press 1924, one of 325. $150.

GOLDEN COCKEREL PRESS (Waltham St. Lawrence). Lawrence, T.E. *Secret Despatches from Arabia.* Waltham: Golden Cockerel Press 1939, one of 1,000. $200–$650.

GOLDEN COCKEREL PRESS (Waltham St. Lawrence). *Mabinogion.* Waltham: Golden Cockerel Press 1948, one of 475 copies, translated by Gwyn Jones and Thomas Jones, "The Golden Cockerel Mabinogion." $250–$450.

GOLDEN COCKEREL PRESS (Waltham St. Lawrence). Milton, John. *Paradise Lost.* Waltham: Golden Cockerel Press 1937, one of 200. $500.

GOLDEN COCKEREL PRESS (Waltham St. Lawrence). More, Sir Thomas. *Utopia.* Waltham: Golden Cockerel Press 1929, one of 500. $200.

GOLDEN COCKEREL PRESS (Waltham St. Lawrence). Napolean I. *Napoleon's Memoirs*. Waltham: Golden Cockerel Press 1945, one of 450, edited by Somerset de Chair. $200.

GOLDEN COCKEREL PRESS (Waltham St. Lawrence). Omar Khayyam. *The Golden Cockerel Rubaiyat*. Waltham: Golden Cockerel Press 1958, one of 75 specially bound and with an extra set of plates, including 2 not used in the book. $375.

GOLDEN COCKEREL PRESS (Waltham St. Lawrence). Ovid (Publius Ovidius Naso). *The Amores*. Waltham: Golden Cockerel Press 1932, one of 350 copies. $75–$175.

GOLDEN COCKEREL PRESS (Waltham St. Lawrence). Plato. *The Phaedo*. Waltham: Golden Cockerel Press 1930, one of 500 copies. $100.

GOLDEN COCKEREL PRESS (Waltham St. Lawrence). Powys, Lleweyn. *The Book of Days*. Waltham: Golden Cockerel Press 1937, one of 300 copies. $250.

GOLDEN COCKEREL PRESS (Waltham St. Lawrence). Powys, Theodore Francis. *Goat Green*. Waltham: Golden Cockerel Press 1937, one of 150 copies. $75–$200.

GOLDEN COCKEREL PRESS (Waltham St. Lawrence). *Samson and Delilah*. Waltham: Golden Cockerel Press 1925, one of 325 copies. $125–$300.

GOLDEN COCKEREL PRESS (Waltham St. Lawrence). *Sir Gawain and the Green Knight*. Waltham: Golden Cockerel Press 1952, one of 360 copies. $250.

GOLDEN COCKEREL PRESS (Waltham St. Lawrence). Sterne, Lawrence. *A Sentimental Journey*. Waltham: Golden Cockerel Press 1928, one of 500 copies. $110.

GOLDEN COCKEREL PRESS (Waltham St. Lawrence). Swift, Jonathan. *Gulliver's Travels*. Waltham: Golden Cockerel Press 1925, 2 vols, one of 450 copies. $600–$700.

GOLDEN COCKEREL PRESS (Waltham St. Lawrence). Swinburne, Algernon Charles. *Lucretia Borgia*. Waltham: Golden Cockerel Press 1942, one of 250 copies. $85.

GOLDEN COCKEREL PRESS (Waltham St. Lawrence). *The Song of Songs*. Waltham: Golden Cockerel Press 1925, one of 30 hand-colored copies. $3,000.

GOLDEN COCKEREL PRESS (Waltham St. Lawrence). Thoreau, Henry David. *Where I Lived and What I Lived For.* Waltham: Golden Cockerel Press 1924, one of 350 copies. $120.

GOLDEN COCKEREL PRESS (Waltham St. Lawrence). Wells, H.G. *The Country of the Blind.* Waltham: Golden Cockerel Press 1939, one of 280 copies. $175–$225.

GOLDING, Louis. *The Miracle Boy.* New York: 1927, 1st American edition, DJ. $25.

GOLDING, William. *Lord of the Flies.* London: Faber & Faber (1954), author's first book, 1st edition, DJ. $500–$800.

GOLDING, William. *Lord of the Flies.* New York: Coward-McCann 1955, author's first book, 1st edition, DJ. $150–$200.

GOLDSCHMIDT, Lucien and Naef, Weston. *See* Grolier Club.

GOLLIWOGS. See Upton, Bertha and Florence.

GOODIS, David. *See* Vintage Paperbacks.

GOODMAN, Paul. *Communitas: Means of Livelihood and Ways of Life.* Chicago: University of Chicago Press (1947), quarto, 1st and only printing of 1st edition, illustrated by Percival Goodman, DJ. $100–$300.

GOODMAN, Paul. *Kafka's Prayer.* New York: Vanguard Press (1947), 1st edition, DJ. $35–$50.

GOODMAN, Percival. *See* "Key to Illustrators."

GOODWIN, Philip R. *See* "Key to Illustrators."

GORDIMER, Nadine. *Six Feet of the Country.* New York: 1954, 1st edition, linen-backed boards, scarce, DJ. $65.

GORDON, Elizabeth. *Bird Children.* Chicago: Volland (1912), 13th edition, illustrated by M.T. Ross, paper-covered boards. $40–$60.

GORDON, Elizabeth. *Flower Children.* New York: Wise-Parlow (1910) (revised 1939), ills by M.T. Ross. $25–$35.

GOREY, Edward. *Amphigorey.* New York: 1972, 1st trade edition, DJ. $50–$75.

GOREY, Edward. *The Unstrung Harp: or, Mr. Earbrass Writes a Novel.* New York/Boston: Duell, Sloan & Pearce/Little, Brown (1953), illustrated by the author, 1st edition of author's first book, DJ. $100–$150.

GOREY, Edward. *The Vinegar Works.* New York: Simon & Schuster 1963, 3 vols, oblong 12mo, 1st edition, in slipcase, fairly scarce. $75–$100.

GORKI, Maxim. *Autobiography of.* New York: Citadel Press (1949), translated by Isadore Schneider, 1st American edition, DJ. $30–$50.

GORKI, Maxim. *Reminiscences of Tolstoy, Chekhov, and Andreyev.* London: Hogarth Press 1934, 1st collected edition, translated by S.S. Kotelianski, Leonard Woolf, and Katherine Mansfield, photographs, DJ. $75–$100.

GOSSE, Edmund. *Father and Son. A Study of Two Temperaments.* London: Heinemann 1907, 1st trade edition, frontis portrait, scarce. $30–$125.

GOULD, John (1804-81). *Hummingbirds.* London: published by the author (1849-61) ("A Monograph of the Trochilidae or Family of Hummingbirds"), 5 vols plus 1887 supplement, folio, morocco gilt, with 418 hand-colored plates, many highlighted with gold. $80,000–$90,000.

GOULD, John (1804-81). *John Gould's Birds of Paradise: Birds of New Guinea, Volume I.* London: 1988, folio, 56 colored plates with descriptive text, cloth. $350.

GOULD, John (1804-81). *The Birds of Europe.* London: published by the author (1832-37), 5 vols, folio, modern half-morocco gilt, with 448 hand-colored plates, a few repaired edge tears and some cancellation stamps. $50,000–$70,000.

GOULD, John (1804-81). *The Birds of Great Britain.* London: published by the author (1862-73), 5 vols, folio, contemporary morocco gilt, with 367 hand-colored lithographs, some soiling, repair to one tear through text. $50,000–$70,000.

GOULD, John (1804-81). *Trogons.* London: published by the author (1835-38) ("A Monograph of the Trogonidae, or Family of Trogons"), folio, contemporary half-morocco gilt, joints and corners worn, with 36 hand-colored plates, 10 of them heightened with gold. $25,000

GOYEN, William. *The House of Breath.* New York: Random House (1950), 1st edition of author's first book, says "first printing" on the copyright page, DJ. $40–$50.

GRABHORN PRINTING (San Francisco). Crane, Stephen. *The Red Badge of Courage*. San Francisco: Grabhorn Printing 1931, one of 980 copies. $50–$125.

GRABHORN PRINTING (San Francisco). De Soto, Hernando. *The Discovery of Florida*. San Francisco: Grabhorn Printing 1946, one of 280 copies. $100–$225.

GRABHORN PRINTING (San Francisco). Harte, Bret. *The Luck of Roaring Camp*. San Francisco: Grabhorn Printing 1948, one of 300 copies. $50–$75.

GRABHORN PRINTING (San Francisco). Hawthorne, Nathaniel. *The Scarlet Letter*. San Francisco: Grabhorn Printing 1928, one of 980 copies. $50–$100.

GRABHORN PRINTING (San Francisco). Jeffers, Robinson. *Poems*. San Francisco: Book Club of California 1928, 1st edition, frontis portrait signed by Ansel Adams, initials by Valenti Angelo, one of 300 copies signed by Jeffers, slipcase. $600–$1,000.

GRABHORN PRINTING (San Francisco). Kaiser, Henry J. *Twenty-Six Addresses Delivered During the War Years*. San Francisco: Grabhorn Printing 1945, one of 30 copies. $100–$250.

GRABHORN PRINTING (San Francisco). Melville, Herman. *The Encantadas, or, The Enchanted Isles*. San Francisco: Grabhorn Printing 1941, one of 550. $70–$90.

GRABHORN PRINTING (San Francisco). Miller, Henry. *13 California Towns from the Original Drawings*. San Francisco: Grabhorn Printing 1947, one of 300. $110.

GRABHORN PRINTING (San Francisco). Poe, Edgar Allan. *The Journal of Julius Rodman*. San Francisco: Grabhorn Printing 1947, one of 500. $80.

GRABHORN PRINTING (San Francisco). Saroyan, William. *Hilltop Russians in San Francisco*. San Francisco: Grabhorn Printing 1941, one of 500, in DJ. $60–$80.

GRABHORN PRINTING (San Francisco). Shakespeare, William. *King Lear*. San Francisco: Grabhorn Printing 1959, one of 180. $120.

GRAFTON, Sue. *"A" is for Alibi*. New York: Holt, Rinehart and Winston (1982), 1st edition, DJ. $450–$750.

GRAFTON, Sue. *"B" is for Burglar.* New York: Holt (1985), 1st edition, DJ. $200–$400.

GRAFTON, Sue. *"C" is for Corpse.* New York: Holt (1986), 1st edition, DJ. $100–$200.

GRAFTON, Sue. *"D" is for Deadbeat.* New York: Holt (1987), 1st edition, DJ. $65–$85.

GRAFTON, Sue. *"F" is for Fugitive.* New York: Holt (1989), 1st edition, DJ. $40–$60.

GRAHAM, Tom (Sinclair Lewis). *Hike and the Aeroplane.* New York: (1912), 1st edition, worn, one plate missing. $150–$200.

GRAHAME, Kenneth. *The Wind in the Willows.* London: Methuen 1951, illustrated by Arthur Rackham, 12 color plates, white calfskin with gilt, limited edition of 500 copies, in slipcase. $500–$1,200.

GRAHAME, Kenneth. *See also* Limited Editions Club.

GRANT, Gordon. *See* "Key to Illustrators."

GRANT, Ulysses S. *Personal Memoirs of U. S. Grant.* New York: Charles L. Webster & Co. 1885-86, 2 vols, 1st trade edition, cloth. $45–$75.

GRASS, Gunther. *The Tin Drum.* New York: Pantheon Press (1962), 1st American edition of author's first book, DJ. $75–$125.

GRAVES, Robert. *Good-Bye to All That; An Autobiography.* London: Jonathan Cape 1929, 1st edition, 1st state, with poems by Sassoon on pages 341-343, DJ. $500–$800.

GRAVES, Robert. *Good-Bye to All That; An Autobiography.* New York: Jonathan Cape and Harrison Smith (1930), 1st American edition, DJ. $50–$100.

GRAVES, Robert. *I, Claudius.* London: Barker 1934, 1st edition, DJ. $150–$250.

GRAVES, Robert. *I, Claudius.* New York: Smith & Haas 1934, 1st American edition, DJ. $75–$150.

GRAVES, Robert. *Poems (1914-1926).* Garden City: Doubleday Doran 1929, 1st American edition. $50–$250.

GRAVES, Robert. *Poems (1914-1926).* London: Heinemann 1927, 1st edition, DJ. $100–$250.

GRAVES, Robert. *The White Goddess: A Historic Grammar of Poetic Myth.* London: Faber (1948), 1st edition, DJ. $35–$150.

GRAVES, Robert. *The White Goddess: A Historic Grammar of Poetic Myth.* (New York): Farrar, Straus and Cudahy, Inc. (1948), 1st American edition, DJ. $35–$75.

GRAYSON, David. *Hempstead. A Novel.* New York: 1915, 1st edition of author's first novel, DJ. $35.

GREEN, Anna Katherine. *The Circular Study.* New York: McClure, Phillips 1900, decorated cloth, 1st edition. $25–$40.

GREEN, Anna Katherine. *The Filigree Ball: Being a Full and True Account of the Mystery Concerning the Jeffrey-Moore Affair.* Indianapolis: Bobbs-Merrill Company (1930), 1st edition, frontis. $35–$40.

GREEN, Henry. *Loving.* New York: Viking Press 1949, 1st American edition, DJ. $25.

GREEN, Julian. *The Closed Garden.* New York: 1928, translated from the French by Henry Logan Stuart, 1st edition in English, 1st edition with introduction by André Maurois, wraps. $30.

GREENAWAY, Kate. *Under the Window.* London: George Routledge and Sons (1878), 1st edition, pictorial boards with cloth, Greenaway's ills in color throughout. $150–$200.

GREENAWAY, Kate. *See also* "Key to Illustrators."

GREENE, Graham. *Brighton Rock.* London: Heinemann (1938), 1st English edition, DJ, (preceded by US edition), "Published July 1938." $750–$2,000.

GREENE, Graham. *Brighton Rock.* New York: Viking 1938, 1st American edition, DJ, (precedes the British edition), "Published in June 1938." $225–$500.

GREENE, Graham. *Our Man in Havana.* London: Heinemann (1958), 1st edition, DJ. $75.

GREENE, Graham. *The Confidential Agent.* New York: The Viking Press 1939, 1st American edition, DJ. $225.

GREENE, Graham. *The Heart of the Matter.* New York: Viking 1948, 1st American edition, DJ. $35–$65.

GREENE, Graham. *The Power and the Glory.* London: Heinemann 1940, 1st edition. $225–$600.

GREENE, Graham. *The Power and the Glory.* London: Heinemann 1940, 1st edition, DJ. $2,500.

GREENE, Graham. *The Quiet American.* London: Heinemann (1955), 1st edition, with Book Society wraparound band, DJ. $75–$150.

GREENE, Graham. *The Quiet American.* New York: Viking Press 1956, 1st American edition, DJ. $35–$50.

GREGORY, Horace. *The Shield of Achilles.* New York: 1944, 1st edition, DJ. $35–$50.

GREGORY, Jackson. *Secret Valley.* New York: Dodd, Mead "1939", 1st edition, DJ. $20–$45.

GREGORY, Lady (Isabella Augusta). *Poets and Dreamers: Studies and Translations from the Irish.* Dublin: Hodges, Figgis 1903, 1st edition, scarce. $35–$50.

GREGORY, Lady. *See also* Cuala Press.

GRESHAM, William. *Nightmare Alley.* New York: Rinehart 1946, 1st edition, DJ. $45.

GREY, Zane. *Knights of the Range.* New York: Harper 1939, 1st edition with code letters M-N on copyright page and "first edition" so stated, DJ. $100–$125.

GREY, Zane. *Knights of the Range.* New York: Grosset & Dunlap (1939), reprint, DJ. $7–$12.

GREY, Zane. *Tales of Fresh Water Fishing.* New York: Harper & Brothers 1928, quarto, over 100 photographs by the author and others, drawings by Wilhelm Smith, 1st edition, DJ. $250.

GREY, Zane. *Tales of Southern Rivers.* New York: Grosset & Dunlap (1924), reprint edition. $25.

GREY, Zane. *Tales of Southern Rivers.* New York: Harper & Brothers (1924), 1st edition, photographs. $55–$75.

GREY, Zane. *Tales of Southern Rivers.* New York: Harper and Brothers (1924), 1st edition, photographs, DJ. $125–$175.

GREY, Zane. *The Code of the West.* New York: Harper and Brothers 1934, 1st edition, DJ. $125.

GREY, Zane. *The Hash Knife Outfit.* New York: Grosset & Dunlap (1933), reprint. $3.50–$7.

GREY, Zane. *The Light of the Western Stars.* New York: Grosset

& Dunlap (1914), reprint edition, black and white frontis. $3.50–$7.

GREY, Zane. *The Light of the Western Stars.* New York: Grosset & Dunlap (1914), reprint edition, black and white frontis, DJ. $7–$12.

GREY, Zane. *The Thundering Herd.* New York: Grosset & Dunlap (1925), reprint edition, DJ. $7–$12.

GREY, Zane. *The Thundering Herd.* New York: Grosset & Dunlap (1925), reprint. $3.50–$7.

GREY, Zane. *The Thundering Herd.* New York: Harper & Bros. 1925, 1st edition. $12.

GREY, Zane. *The Thundering Herd.* New York: Harper & Bros. 1925, 1st edition, DJ. $100.

GREY, Zane. *The Thundering Herd.* New York: Grosset & Dunlap (1925), reprint. $3.50–$7.

GREY, Zane. *Twin Sombreros.* New York: Harper & Bros. (1940), 1st edition. $15.

GREY, Zane. *Wild Horse Mesa.* New York: Grosset & Dunlap (1928), reprint edition, DJ. $7–$12.

GREY, Zane. *Wild Horse Mesa.* New York: Harper 1928, 1st edition, DJ. $100.

GRIEVE, Maud. *A Modern Herbal.* New York: 1931, 2 vols, 1st American edition. $350–$500.

GRIMM, Jakob Ludwig Carl, and Grimm, Wilhelm Carl. *German Popular Stories,* translated from the *Kunder und Haus Marchen,* collected by M.M. Grimm from oral tradition. London: Baldwyn/Robins 1823-26, 1st editions, 1st issues, with all points; contemporary binding, 20 full-page ills by George Cruikshank, 55 tales. $1,500–$3,000.

GRIMM, THE BROTHERS. *Grimm's Fairy Tales.* New York: Grosset & Dunlap (1945), reprint edition, color and black and white ills and endpapers by Fritz Kredel. $5–$8.

GRIMM, THE BROTHERS. *Grimm's Fairy Tales,* New York: Grosset & Dunlap (1945), reprint edition, color and black and white ills and ep's by Fritz Kredel, DJ. $8–$12.

GRIMM'S FAIRY TALES. See Grimm, Jakob: *German Popular Stories.*

GROLIER CLUB (New York). *Catalogue of Ornamental Leather Bookbindings Executed in America Prior to 1850.* New York: Grolier Club 1907. $130.

GROLIER CLUB (New York). De Vinne, Theodore. *Notable Printers of Italy.* New York: Grolier Club 1910, one of 400. $150.

GROLIER CLUB (New York). Goldschmidt, Lucien and Naef, Weston. *The Truthful Lens: A Survey of the Photographically Illustrated Book, 1844-1914.* New York: Grolier Club 1980, one of 1,000. $175-$325.

GROLIER CLUB (New York). Henderson, Robert W. *Early American Sport: A Chronological Check-List.* New York: Grolier Club 1937, one of 400. $100.

GROLIER CLUB (New York). Horblit, Harrison D. *One Hundred Books Famous in Science.* New York: Grolier Club 1964, one of 1,000. $350.

GROLIER CLUB (New York). Matthews, William F. *Modern Book Binding Practically Considered.* New York: Grolier Club 1889, one of 300. $90.

GROLIER CLUB (New York). Omar Khayyam. *Rubaiyat.* New York: Grolier Club 1885, one of 150. $120.

GROLIER CLUB (New York). *One Hundred Books Famous in English Literature.* New York: Grolier Club 1902, one of 305, introduction by George E. Woodberry. $130.

GROLIER CLUB (New York). *One Hundred Influential American Books Printed Before 1900.* New York: Grolier Club 1947, one of 600. $125-$325.

GROLIER CLUB (New York). Wroth, Lawrence C. *The Colonial Printer.* New York: Grolier Club 1931, one of 300. $120.

GRONVOLD, H. *See* "Key to Illustrators."

GROSS, Milt. *He Done Her Wrong.* Garden City: Doubleday, Doran & Co. 1930, 1st edition, DJ. $65.

GROSZ, George. *A Little Yes and a Big No.* New York: The Dial Press 1946, small quarto with 38 plates by the artist, some in color, and many text ills, DJ. $200.

GROSZ, George. *Ecce Home.* New York: Jack Brussel 1965, folio, with 16 watercolors and 84 black and white drawings, white boards with gold, slipcase. $75.

GROVER, Eulalie Osgood. *The Overall Boys*. Chicago: Rand, McNally & Co. (1905), illustrated by Grover, the creator also of the Sunbonnet Babies, 1st edition. $35–$75.

GROVER, Eulalie Osgood. *The Sunbonnet Babies*. Chicago: Rand, McNally & Co. (1902), illustrated by Grover, 1st edition. $40–$75.

GRUBER, Frank. *Fighting Man*. New York: Rinehart "1948", 1st edition, DJ. $15–$40.

GRUELLE, Johnny. *Raggedy Ann and Andy*. New York: Johnny Gruelle Co. (1920), illustrated by the author. $45–$55.

GRUELLE, Johnny. *Raggedy Ann and Andy*. New York: Volland (1920), illustrated by the author. $55–$65.

GRUELLE, Johnny. *Raggedy Ann and Andy*. New York: Donahue (1920), illustrated by the author. $25–$35.

GRUGER, F.R. *See* "Key to Illustrators."

GRUMBACH, Doris. *Chamber Music*. New York: Dutton (1979), 1st edition, DJ. $20–$35.

GRUMBACH, Doris. *The Company She Kept*. New York: Coward-McCann (1967), 1st edition, DJ. $35–$75.

GRUMBACH, Doris. *The Ladies, A Novel*. New York: Dutton 1984, 1st edition, DJ. $15–$30.

GRUMBACH, Doris. *The Missing Person*. New York: Putnam's (1981), 1st edition, DJ. $20–$35.

GRUMBACH, Doris. *The Short Throat, The Tender Mouth*. Garden City: Doubleday 1964, 1st edition, DJ. $50–$125.

GRUMBACH, Doris. *The Spoil of the Flowers*. Garden City: Doubleday 1962, 1st edition of author's first book, DJ. $100–$150.

GUDERIAN, Heinz. *Panzer Leader*. New York: Dutton "1952", translated from the German by Constantine Fitzgibbon. $30–$40.

GUEST, Edgar. *Friends*. Chicago: Reilly and Lee Co. (1925), 1st edition, bright, decorated boards, in publisher's box. $35.

GUINEY, Louise Imogen. *Happy Ending, The Collected Lyrics of*. Boston and New York: Houghton Mifflin 1909, 1st edition. $40–$100.

GULLIVER'S TRAVELS. See Golden Cockerel Press.

GUNN, Thom. *To the Air.* Boston: Godine 1974, 1st edition, issued without DW. $25.

GUNN, Thom. *Touch.* Chicago: University of Chicago Press 1967, 1st edition, issued without DJ. $35.

GURY, Jeremy. *The Wonderful World of Aunt Tuddy.* np (New York): Random House (1958), 1st printing, illustrated by Hilary Knight, DJ. $50.

GUTHRIE, A.B. *The Big Sky.* New York: Sloane 1947, 1st edition, DJ. $45–$100.

GURTHRIE, A.B. *The Way West.* New York: William Sloane Associates (1949), 1st edition, DJ. $45–$100.

 H ——————————————————————————

HAGGARD, H. Rider. *Ayesha: The Return of She.* London: Ward, Lock 1905, 1st edition, original cloth. $50–$75.

HAGGARD, H. Rider. *Heart of the World.* New York: Longmans & Green 1895, 1st American edition,which preceded the English edition by 10 months, includes 2 ills which did not appear in the later edition. $35–$70.

HAGGARD, H. Rider. *Jess.* New York and London: Street & Smith nd, Select Fiction library, reprint edition. $3.50–$8.

HAGGARD, H. Rider. *King Solomon's Mines.* London: Cassell and Co. 1885, 1st edition, original cloth, folding frontis, scarce. $125.

HAGGARD, H. Rider. *The People of the Mist.* New York: Longman's, Green and Co. 1894, 1st American edition, original cloth, decorated boards. $50.

HAIG-BROWN, Roderick L. *See* Derrydale Press.

HALEY, Alex. *Roots.* Garden City: Doubleday (1976), 1st trade edition, DJ. $35–$150.

HALL, Donald. *Exiles and Marriages.* New York: 1955, 1st edition, DJ. $50–$60.

HALL, James Norman. *Doctor Dogbody's Leg*. Boston: Little, Brown 1940, 1st edition, DJ. $35–$50.

HALL, James Norman. *Faery Lands of the South Seas*. New York: Harper & Brothers 1921, 1st edition of the author's second book, DJ. $35–$50.

HALL, James Norman. *See also* Nordhoff, Charles B.

HALL, Radclyffe. *Poems of the Past and Present*. London: Chapman & Hall 1910, 1st edition. $100–$200.

HALL, Radclyffe. *Songs of Three Countries and Other Poems*. London: Chapman & Hall 1913, 1st edition. $100–$150.

HALL, Radclyffe. *The Well of Loneliness*. London: Jonathan Cape (1928), 1st edition, 1st state, with, on page 50, "whip" instead of "whips," DJ. $100–$250.

HALL, Radclyffe. *The Well of Loneliness*. Paris: nd, 1st edition, uncensored. $40–$60.

HALL, Trevor. *A Bibliography of Books on Conjuring in English From 1580 to 1850*. Minneapolis: 1957, illustrated. $80–$200.

HALLET, Jean-Pierre. *Congo Kitabu*. New York: Random House (1968), later printing, photographs, map ep's, DJ. $20.

HAMMACK, E.S. *See* "Key to Illustrators."

HAMMETT, Dashiell. *Red Harvest*. New York: Knopf 1929, 1st edition of author's first book, DJ. $1,750–$2,250.

HAMMETT, Dashiell. *Red Harvest*. New York: Knopf 1929, 1st edition of author's first book. $125–$350.

HAMMETT, Dashiell. *The Big Knocker*. New York: Random House 1966, 1st edition, DJ. $100–$125.

HAMMETT, Dashiell. *The Maltese Falcon*. New York and London: Knopf 1930, 1st edition, DJ. $2,000–$3,000.

HAMMETT, Dashiell. *The Maltese Falcon*. New York and London: Knopf 1930, 1st edition. $350–$500.

HAMMETT, Dashiell. *The Maltese Falcon*. New York: Modern Library 1934, 1st Modern Library edition, DJ. $20–$50.

HAMMETT, Dashiell. *The Thin Man*. New York: Knopf 1934, 1st edition, DJ. This is the green dust wrapper with publisher's label on front, but no priority exists for DW. $400–$1,200.

HAMMETT, Dashiell. *The Thin Man*. New York: Knopf 1934, 1st edition. $100–$200.

HAMMETT, Dashiell. *See also* Vintage Paperbacks.

HANLEY, James. *The Furys*. London: 1935, 1st edition, DJ. $135.

HANNAH, Barry. *Airships*, New York: Knopf 1978, 1st edition, DJ. $50–$75.

HANNAH, Barry. *Geronimo Rex*. New York: Viking (1972), 1st edition of author's first book, DJ. $75–$125.

HANS BRINKER AND THE SILVER SKATES. See Dodge, M.E.

HANSEN, Joseph. *The Boy who was Buried this Morning*. New York: Viking 1990, 1st printing, DJ. $20.

HARDING, A.R. *Deadfalls and Snares*. Columbus: A.R. Harding (1907), later printing, paper covers. $20.

HARDING, A.R. *Ginseng and Other Medicinal Plants*. Columbus: A.R. Harding (1936), later printing. $22.50.

HARDING, A.R. *Steel Traps*. Columbis: A.R. Harding nd, paper covers. $15.

HARDWICK, Elizabeth. *The Ghostly Lover*. New York: Harcourt (1945), 1st edition of author's first book, DJ. $100–$150.

HARRIS, Frank. *My Life and Loves*. Paris: Obelisk Press (1945), 1st printing of this 1st trade edition (printed privately in Paris in 1922 in 3 vols), printed wraps, 4 vols. $150.

HARRIS, Frank. *Oscar Wilde: His Life and Confessions*. New York: Printed and published by the author, 1918, 1st edition, 2 vols, original cloth. $75.

HARRIS, Joel Chandler. *On the Plantation*. New York: Appleton 1892, 1st edition, illustrated by E.W. Kemble. $300–$500.

HARRIS, Joel Chandler. *Uncle Remus: His Songs and His Sayings*. New York: Appleton 1881, 1st edition, 1st issue of author's first book, with "presumptive," rather than "presumptuous" on page 9, bottom line. $300–$500.

HARRIS, Mark. *The Southpaw*. Indianapolis: Bobbs-Merrill (1953), 1st edition so stated, DJ. $75–$100.

HARRISON, Jim. *A Good Day to Die*. New York: Simon &

Schuster (1973), 1st edition of Harrison's scarce second novel (but not his second book), DJ. $150.

HARRISON, Jim. *Locations.* New York: Norton (1968), 1st edition of author's second book, DJ. $50–$125.

HART, Moss. *Winged Victory; The Air Force Play.* New York: Random House (1943), 1st edition, pictorial DW designed by Steiner-Prag. $25–$50.

HART, William S. *Pinto Ben.* New York: Britton (1919), first book by this early movie star, 1st edition., DJ. $20–$35.

HARTE, Bret. *See* Grabhorn Printing.

HARTLEY, Marsden. *Twenty-Five Poems.* (Paris: Contact Editions 1923), 1st edition, wraps. $300.

HAWKER, Sir Peter. *Instructions to Young Sportsmen in All that Relates to Guns and Shooting.* London: (1833), 7th edition, crimson crushed morocco, all edges gilt. $150.

HAWKES, John. *Second Skin.* (New York): New Directions (1964), 1st trade edition, DJ. $30–$60.

HAWKESWORTH, John. *An Account of the Voyages... for Making Discoveries in the Southern Hemisphere [First Voyage]* np: W. Strahan & T. Cadell 1773, 3 vols, 1st edition, imperfect—lacking several plates, joints cracking, cover detached. $1,275–$1,600.

HAWKESWORTH, John. *The Voyages of Captain James Cook Around the World.* Printed verbatim from the original editions. London: Phillips 1809, 7 vols, charts and engravings, calfskin binding. $250–$550.

HAWKINS, Anthony Hope (Anthony Hope). *The Dolly Dialogues.* New York: R.H. Russell 1901, 1st printing of this edition (an earlier one was illustrated by Rackham), 18 ills by Howard Chandler Christy, highly decorative binding with morocco, gilt panels, raised bands. $75–$125.

HAWTHORNE, Nathaniel. *The Blithedale Romance.* Boston: Ticknor, Reed and Fields 1852, original brown cloth, 1st edition. $75–$150.

HAWTHORNE, Nathaniel. *The Marble Faun: or, The Romance of Monte Beni.* Boston: Ticknor and Fields 1860, 2 vols, 1st edition, 12mo, original cloth. $75–$200.

HAWTHORNE, Nathaniel. *The Scarlet Letter, A Romance.* Boston: Ticknor, Reed and Fields 1850, 1st edition, modern fine binding. $500–$700.

HAWTHORNE, Nathaniel. *The Snow-Image, and Other Twice-Told Tales.* Boston: Ticknor, Reed and Fields 1852, 1st edition, original cloth. $50–$150.

HAWTHORNE, Nathaniel. *See also* Grabhorn Printing.

HAYCOX, Ernest. *Pioneer Loves.* Boston: Little, Brown "1952", 1st edition, DJ. $15–$50.

HEANY, Seamus. *Death of a Naturalist.* London: Faber & Faber (1966), 1st English edition of the author's first regularly published book, DJ. $225–$300.

HEANY, Seamus. *Death of a Naturalist.* New York: Oxford University Press 1966, 1st American edition, a very small printing, DJ. $150–$250.

HEANY, Seamus. *Door into the Dark.* London: Faber & Faber (1969), 1st English edition, DJ. $125–$200.

HEANY, Seamus. *Door into the Dark.* New York: Oxford University Press 1969, 1st American edition, DJ. $75–$150.

HEARD, H.F. *Doppelgangers.* New York: Vanguard 1947, 1st American edition, DJ. $35.

HEARN, Lafcadio. *Creole Sketches.* New York and Boston: Houghton Mifflin 1924, illustrated by the author, DJ. $35–$65.

HEARN, Lafcadio. *Japanese Fairy Tales.* New York: Boni 1918, 1st American edition, cloth-backed boards. $35–$50.

HEARN, Lafcadio. *Japanese Fairy Tales.* Tokyo: (1898-1903), 5 vols, pictorial wrappers, in rice paper sleeves and protective folder, 1st edition, crepe paper. $500–$700.

HEARN, Lafcadio. *Karma.* New York: Boni & Liveright 1918, printed boards with cloth, 1st edition. $35.

HEARN, Lafcadio. *Occidental Gleanings.* New York: Dodd, Mead 1925, 2 vols, original cloth with paper labels, 1st editions. $30–$50.

HECHT, Ben. *Count Bruga.* New York: Liveright 1926, 1st edition, DJ. $25–$125.

HECHT, Ben. *I Hate Actors.* New York: Crown Publishers 1944, 1st edition, DJ. $50–$125.

HECHT, Ben. *The Cat that Jumped Out of the Story.* Philadelphia: Winston (1947), 1st edition, illustrated by Peggy Bacon. $35–$50.

HEIDI. See Spyri, Johanna.

HEINLEIN, Robert. *The Green Hills of Earth.* Chicago: Shasta (1951), 1st edition, DJ. $100–$200.

HEINLEIN, Robert. *The Puppet Masters.* New York: Doubleday 1951, 1st edition, DJ. $50–$100.

HELBRANT, Maurice. *See* Vintage Paperbacks: Lee, William.

HELLER, Joseph. *Catch-22.* New York: Simon & Schuster 1961, 1st edition of the author's first book, rare, DJ. $350.

HELLER, Joseph. *Something Happened.* New York: Knopf 1974, 1st trade edition, DJ. $35–$50.

HELLMAN, Lillian. *Another Part of the Forest.* New York: Viking 1947, 1st edition, DJ. $35–$75.

HELLMAN, Lillian. *The Little Foxes.* New York: Random House 1939, 1st edition, DJ. $35–$50.

HELLMAN, Lillian. *Watch on the Rhine: A Play in Three Acts.* New York: Privately printed 1942 for the Joint Anti-Fascist Rescue Committee, one of 349 numbered copies, 1st illustrated edition, full-page ills by R. Kent, F. Eichenberg, DJ. $50–$200.

HEMINGWAY, Ernest. *A Farewell to Arms.* London: Jonathan Cape (1929), 1st English edition, DJ. $125–$200.

HEMINGWAY, Ernest. *A Farewell to Arms.* New York: Scribner's 1929, 1st edition, 1st issue, which is without the legal disclaimer that appears later, DJ. $500–$700.

HEMINGWAY, Ernest. *A Farewell to Arms.* New York: Scribner's 1929, 1st edition, 1st issue, without the legal disclaimer. $75.

HEMINGWAY, Ernest. *Death in the Afternoon.* New York: Charles Scribner's Sons 1932, 1st edition, DJ. $250–$650.

HEMINGWAY, Ernest. *For Whom the Bell Tolls.* New York: Scribner's 1940, 1st edition, 1st issue, with the "A" on copyright page, DJ. $175–$250.

HEMINGWAY, Ernest. *The Old Man and the Sea.* New York: Scribner's 1952, 1st edition, 1st issue, with proper 1st issue DJ with Hemingway portrait printed in blue, DJ. $75–$125.

HEMINGWAY, Ernest. *To Have and Have Not.* New York: Scribner's 1937, 1st edition, DJ. $250–$450.

HEMON, Louis. *Maria Chapdelaine. A Tale of the Lake St. John Country.* New York and Toronto: Macmillan 1924, drawings and decorations by Wilfred Jones. $25.

HENDERSON, Robert W. *See* Grolier Club.

HENDRYX, James B. *Murder at Halfaday Creek.* New York: Doubleday, Doran "1951", 1st edition, DJ. $25–$45.

HENDRYX, James B. *Outlaws of Halfaday Creek.* Garden City: Doubleday, Doran 1935, later printing. $5–$10.

HENDRYX, James B. *The Yukon Kid.* New York: Doubleday, Doran "1934", 1st edition, DJ. $25–$65.

HENRY, O. *The Complete Works of O. Henry.* Garden City: Doubleday & Company 1953, 2 vols, later printing. $9–$15.

HENRY, O. *The Complete Works of O. Henry.* Garden City: Doubleday & Company 1953, 2 vols, later printing, DJ. $15–$25.

HENRY, O. *The Four Million.* New York: McClure, Phillips 1906, 1st edition. $50–$100.

HENRY, Robert S. *On the Railroad.* Akron & New York: The Saalfield Pub Co. (1936), colored ills by Otto Kuhler, quarto, wrappers. $35–$40.

HERBERT, A.P. *The Water Gypsies.* London: (1930), 1st English edition, DJ. $25.

HERBERT, Frank. *Dune.* Philadelphia: Chilton (1965), 1st edition, DJ. $350–$600.

HERFORD, Oliver. *The Rubaiyat of a Persian Kitten.* np: Bickers and Son 1904, 1st edition, small quarto, 35 tinted plates, original cloth. $35.

HERGESHEIMER, Joseph. *The Bright Shawl.* New York: 1922, 1st edition, DJ. $10–$25.

HERITAGE PRESS. Dana, Richard Henry. *Two Years Before the Mast.* New York: Heritage Press 1947, boxed, special edition. $12.50.

HERITAGE PRESS. Darwin, Charles. *The Voyage of the Beagle.* New York: Heritage Press (1957), boxed. $12–$20.

HERITAGE PRESS. Doyle, Arthur Conan. *The Adventures of Sherlock Homes.* New York: Heritage Press (1950), illustrated with a selection of the original ills, 3 vols, publisher's slipcase. $35.

HERITAGE PRESS. Housman, A.E. *A Shropshire Lad.* New York: The Heritage Press 1935, decorations by E.A. Wilson, and 25 color ills, full brown pigskin, slipcase. $30–$50.

HERITAGE PRESS. Hudson, W.H. *Green Mansions.* New York: The Heritage Club (1937), illustrated by Miguel Covarrubias, designed by Frederic Warde, pictorial cloth. $20–$25.

HERITAGE PRESS. Szyk, Arthur. *Ink and Blood.* New York: Heritage Press 1946, 74 plates by the author in sepia and 6 in color, one of 1,000 copies, signed by the artist, decorative ep's, full black morocco, original slipcase. $350–$700.

HERITAGE PRESS. *See also* Bibles: Szyk, Arthur, *The Book of Ruth*; Szyk, Arthur, *The Book of Job.*

HERRICK, Robert. *See* Golden Cockerel Press.

HERSEY, John. *Hiroshima.* New York: Knopf 1946, 1st edition, quarto, wrappers. $25–$100.

HERSEY, John. *The Wall.* New York: Knopf 1950, 1st edition, DJ. $25.

HERTER, George L. *Professional Fly-Tying and Tackle-Making Manual.* Waseca: published by the author (1971), later printing, paper covers. $17.50

HERTER, George L. and Bertha. *Bull Cook and Authentic Historical Recipes and Practices.* Waseca: published by the author (1969), later printing, gold binding, 2 vols. $55.

HESSE, Herman. *Steppenwolf.* London: 1929, translated by Basil Creighton, 1st English edition, DJ. $200.

HEWLETT, Maurice. *Halfway House.* London: Chapman & Hall 1908, original red cloth. $20.

HEYERDAHL, Thor. *Sea Routes to Polynesia: American Indians and Early Asiatics in the Pacific.* Chicago: Rand McNally (1968). $20.

HEYWARD, Dubose. *Carolina Chansons: Legends of the Low Country.* New York: Macmillan 1922. $75–$125.

HEYWARD, Dubose. *Mamba's Daughters.* Garden City: Doubleday, Doran 1929, 1st edition, DJ. $50–$125.

HEYWARD, Dubose. *Porgy. Play in Four Acts.* New York: Theatre Guild Acting Version, 1928. $25–$35.

HEYWARD, Dubose and Dorothy. *Porgy. Play in Four Acts.* Garden City: Doran 1927. $75–$150.

HIGGINSON, Thomas Wentworth. *Army Life in a Black Regiment.* Boston: Fields, Osgood & Co. 1870, 1st edition. $125–$150.

HIGGINSON, Thomas Wentworth. *Army Life in a Black Regiment.* East Lansing: Michigan State University Press 1960, reprint edition. $20–$30.

HIGHSMITH, Patricia. *Strangers on a Train.* London: Cresset 1950, 1st English edition of author's first book, very scarce, DJ. $150–$400.

HIGHSMITH, Patricia. *The Talented Mr. Ripley.* New York: Coward, McCann 1955, 1st edition, precedes the English edition, DJ. $100–$200.

HILBERG, Raul. *The Destruction of the European Jews.* Chicago: Quadrangle "1961". $25–$35.

HILL, Grace Livingston. *Crimson Mountain.* New York: Grosset and Dunlap (1942), reprint edition in DJ. $10.

HILL, Grace Livingston. *Crimson Mountain.* New York: Grosset and Dunlap (1942), reprint edition. $3.50–$7.

HILL, Grace Livingston. *Spice Box.* Philadelphia: Lippincott (1943), 1st edition. $7–$9.

HILL, Grace Livingston. *Spice Box.* Philadelphia: Lippincott (1943), 1st edition, DJ. $12–$18.

HILL, Grace Livingston. *The Story of a Whim.* Boston: The Golden Rule Co. (1903), 1st edition of an early title, scarce. $25–$35.

HILL, Grace Livingston. *See also* Booth, Evangeline: *The War Romance of the Salvation Army.*

HILLYER, Robert. *The Death of Captain Nemo.* New York: 1949, 1st edition, DJ. $20.

HILTON, James. *Good-bye, Mr. Chips.* London: Hodder & Stoughton 1934, 1st edition, DJ. $50–$75.

HILTON, James. *Lost Horizon.* New York: William Morrow 1933, 1st edition, DJ. $100–$200.

HILTON, James. *Random Harvest*. Boston: 1941, 1st American edition, DJ. $40–$50.

HIMES, Chester. *Cast the First Stone*. New York: Coward, McCann (1952), 1st edition, DJ. $50–$100.

HIMES, Chester. *If He Hollers Let Him Go*. Garden City: Doubleday 1945, 1st edition of author's first book, DJ. $100–$200.

HIMES, Chester. *Pinktoes*. New York: Putnam (1965), 1st edition, DJ. $35–$50.

HISTORY. *See* "Key to Categories."

HITCHCOCK, Lucius. *See* "Key to Illustrators."

HOAGLAND, Edward. *Cat Man*. Boston: 1956, 1st edition, DJ. $50.

HOBAN, Russell. *Riddley Walker*. London: (1980), 1st edition, precedes American edition, DJ. $50–$100.

HODGSON, Ralph. *The Last Blackbird and Other Lines*. London: Allen 1907, 1st edition, original cloth. $75.

HOFFMAN, Abbie. *Steal This Book*. New York: Pirate Editions (1971), paperback original, wraps. $20–$40.

HOFFMAN, Professor. *Modern Magic, a Practical Treatise on the Art of Conjuring*. London: 1886, 5th edition. $50–$150.

HOKINSON, Helen. *See* "Key to Illustrators."

HOLE BOOK, THE. See Newell, Peter.

HOLLAND, Ray P. *My Gun Dogs*. Boston: Houghton Mifflin 1929, 1st edition, scarce. $35.

HOLLAND, Ray P. *Shotgunning in the Uplands*. New York: Barnes (1944), 2nd printing, quarto, color ills by Lynn Bogue Hunt. $65.

HOLMES, John Clellon. *Go*. New York: Scribner's 1952, 1st edition of author's first book. $200.

HOLMES, John Clellon. *The Horn*. New York: Random House 1958, 1st edition, DJ. $50–$75.

HOLMES, O.W. *The Autocrat of the Breakfast Table*. Boston: Phillips, Sampson & Co. 1858, 1st edition, 1st issue, original cloth. $200–$250.

HOPE, Anthony. *The Prisoner of Zenda*. Bristol: Arrowsmith

(1894), 1st edition, 1st issue, in original claret cloth, with list of 17, not 18, titles on page 311. $150–$200.

HOPE, Laura Lee. *See* Juvenile Series Books.

HOPKINS, Gerard Manley. *Poems of.* London: Humphrey Milford (1918), 1st edition, gray boards and beige cloth, edited by Robert Bridges, 2 portraits, 2 double-page facsimiles, 750 copies printed. $250–$500.

HOPKINS, Gerard Manley. *Poems of.* London: Humphrey Milford (1918), 1st edition, gray boards and beige cloth, edited by Robert Bridges, 2 portraits, 2 double-page facsimiles, 750 copies printed, DJ. $500–$2,000.

HOPPER, Charles Edward. *See* "Key to Illustrators."

HORBLIT, Harrison D. *See* Grolier Club.

HORGAN, Paul. *Great River: The Rio Grande in North American History.* New York: Rinehart and Co. 1954, 2 vols, 1st trade edition, slipcase. $35–$60.

HORGAN, Paul. *Great River: The Rio Grande in North American History.* New York: Rinehart and Co. 1954, 2 vols, limited edition, one of 1,000 copies, specially illustrated and signed by author, slipcase. $125–$225.

HORGAN, Paul. *The Faults of Angels.* New York: Harper 1933, 1st edition of author's first novel, DJ. $35–$100.

HOUDIN, Jean Eugene Robert. *Memoirs of Robert Houdin, Ambassador, Author and Conjuror.* Philadelphia: Porter & Coates 1859, 1st American edition. $80–$250.

HOUDIN, Jean Eugene Robert. *The Secrets of Conjuring and Magic.* London: Routledge 1878, some wear and stains. $75–$300.

HOUDINI, Harry. *Magical Rope Ties and Escapes.* London: Will Goldston (1920), dampstained, DJ. $60–$150.

HOUDINI, Harry. *The Unmasking of Robert Houdin.* New York: 1908, portrait frontis, profusely illustrated. $80–$135.

HOUDINI, Harry. *Yar, The Primeval Man.* np: 1921, 12 pages, wraps. $200–$500.

HOUGH, Emerson. *The Mississippi Bubble.* Indianapolis: Bobbs Merrill (1902), 1st edition, 1st issue, with "Houh" on spine. $35–$100.

HOUGH, Emerson. *The Singing Mouse Stories.* New York:

Forest and Stream Publishing Co. 1895, 1st edition of author's first book, scarce. $85–$150.

HOUGH, Emerson. *The Story of the Cowboy.* New York: Appleton 1897, 1st edition, 6 ills by C.M. Russell. $65–$125.

HOUGH, Emerson. *The Story of the Outlaw: A Study of the Western Desperado.* New York: Outing Co. 1907, 1st edition, ills, cloth-backed decorated boards, scarce. $65–$125.

HOUSMAN, A.E. *A Shropshire Lad.* London: Kegan Paul, Trench, Trubner & Co. 1896, parchment-backed blue-gray boards with paper spine label, 1st edition (limited to 350 copies) of author's first book. $1,000–$2,000.

HOUSMAN, A.E. *A Shropshire Lad.* New York and London: 1896, parchment spine, spine label, 1st edition of the American issue, limited to 150 copies, bound from sheets of the English edition, with a substitute New York title page. $500–$750.

HOUSMAN, A.E. *More Poems.* New York: 1936, 1st American edition, DJ. $20.

HOUSMAN, A.E. *The Collected Poems.* London: Jonathan Cape 1939, 1st collected edition, DJ. $25–$45.

HOUSMAN, A.E. *See also* Heritage Press.

HOUSMAN, Laurence. *A Farm in Fairyland.* London: Kegan Paul, Trench, Trubner and Company 1894, 1st edition of author's first book, ills and cover design by Housman. $50–$150.

HOUSMAN, Laurence. *See also* "Key to Illustrators."

HOWARD, Robert E. *Conan the Barbarian.* New York: Gnome Press (1954). $150.

HOWARD, Robert E. *Singers in the Shadows.* West Kingston: Donald Grant, 1970, 1st edition, one of 500 copies, DJ. $100.

HOWARD, Robert E. *The Coming of Conan.* New York: Gnome Press (1953), 1st edition, DJ. $125.

HUBBARD, Elbert. *A Message to Garcia.* (East Aurora: Roycrofters 1899), limp suede, decorated, covers worn and stained. $15.

HUBBARD, Elbert. *A Message to Garcia.* East Aurora: Roycrofters 1901, elaborate, handdone colors and gold—16 floral borders, 11 vignettes, 16 initials, title page; green morocco with floral-patterned gilt back, 1 of 50 on vellum signed by artist and Hubbard. $140–$160.

HUBBARD, Elbert. *Elbert Hubbard's Scrap Book*. East Aurora: Roycrofters 1923, first edition, original cloth, DJ, and box. $35.

HUBBARD, Elbert. *Hollyhocks and Golden Glow*. (East Aurora): The Roycrofters (1912), art nouveau title page, headpieces and tailpieces, wrappers, box. $20–$35.

HUBBARD, Elbert. *Lydia E. Pinkham...Her Life and Times*. East Aurora: Roycrofters 1915, frontis and one plate, suede. $25.

HUBBARD, Elbert. *So Here Cometh White Hyacinths*. (East Aurora: Roycrofters 1915), limp suede, designed by Dard Hunter, 2 photographs, moire ep's. $55.

HUBBARD, Elbert. *The City of Tagaste*. East Aurora: Roycroft Press 1900, thin, tall quarto, gilt-stamped boards with suede, one of 940 copies signed by Hubbard, decorations by Anna Paine. $200.

HUBBARD, Elbert. *The Closed or Open Shop: Which?* East Aurora: The Roycrofters 1916, title page designed by Dard Hunter, suede. $25.

HUBBARD, Elbert. *See also* Sets.

HUBBARD, L. Ron. *Dianetics.* New York: Hermitage (1950), 1st edition, DJ. $125–$250.

HUBBARD, L. Ron. *Kingslayer.* Los Angeles: Fantasy Press 1949, 1st edition, DW designed by William Benulis, DJ. $75–$150.

HUBBARD, L. Ron. *Typewriter in the Sky/Fear*. New York: Gnome Press (1951), 1st edition so stated on copyright page, DJ. $75–$175.

HUCKLEBERRY FINN. See Twain, Mark.

HUDSON, W.H. *Birds of La Plata.* London: 1920, 1st trade edition, 2 vols, 22 colored plates by H. Gronvold, DJ. $125.

HUDSON, W.H. *Far Away and Long Ago: A History of My Early Life*. London: J.M. Dent 1918, 1st edition, DJ. $85–$125.

HUDSON, W.H. *Far Away and Long Ago: A History of My Early Life*. London: J.M. Dent 1918, 1st edition. $30.

HUDSON, W.H. *Green Mansions: A Romance of the Tropical Forest*. London: Duckworth 1904, 1st edition, 1st issue, green cloth without the publisher's symbol on the rear cover. $100–$300.

HUDSON, W.H. *Idle Days in Patagonia*. London: Chapman Hall 1893, 1st edition, 1st issue, in red cloth without the publisher's symbol on rear cover, one of 1,750 copies, numerous black and white ills by Alfred Hartley and J. Smit. $50–$125.

HUDSON, W.H. *Little Boy Lost*. New York: Knopf 1920, quarto, blue pictorial cloth, teg, 8 color plates by Dorothy Lathrop, plus some full-page black and whites, 1st edition thus. $75–$150.

HUDSON, W.H. *See also* Limited Editions Club; Heritage Press; Sets.

HUGHES, Dorothy B. *Ride The Pink Horse*. New York: Duell, Sloan & Pearce 1946, 1st edition, DJ. $45.

HUGHES, Langston. *Simple Speaks His Mind*. New York: Knopf 1950, 1st edition, DJ. $50–$65.

HUGHES, Langston. *Tambourines to Glory*. New York: John Day (1958), 1st edition, pictorial DJ. $60–$75.

HUGHES, Langston. *The Big Sea*. New York: Knopf 1940, 1st edition, DJ. $150.

HUGHES, Langston. *The Weary Blues*. New York: Knopf 1926, 1st edition of author's first book, DJ. $1,000.

HUGHES, Langston. *The Weary Blues*. New York: Knopf 1926, 1st edition of author's first book. $200.

HUGHES, Langston, and DeCarava, Roy. *The Sweet Flypaper of Life*. New York: Simon & Schuster 1955, photographs by Roy DeCarava, story by Hughes, 1st printing, "first printing" on copyright page, published simultaneously in hardcover, this one in wraps. $80–$125.

HUGHES, Richard. *High Wind in Jamaica*. London: Chatto & Windus 1929, 1st British edition and 1st edition under this title, DJ, and with wraparound band still present. This was published first in America, under the title *The Innocent Voyage*. $50–$150.

HUGHES, Richard. *High Wind in Jamaica*. London: Chatto & Windfus 1929, 1st British edition and 1st edition under this title, DJ, but without the wraparound advertising band. $50–$75.

HUGHES, Richard. *The Innocent Voyage.* New York: Harper 1929, 1st edition, DJ, published in England as *A High Wind in Jamaica.* $100–$200.

HUGHES, Ted. *A Primer of Birds.* (Lurley in Devon): The Gehenna Press 1981, one of 250 copies, woodcuts by Leonard Baskin, narrow quarto, signed by artist and author. $200–$300.

HUGHES, Ted. *Selected Poems 1957-1981.* London: 1982, 1st edition, DJ. $25.

HUGHES, Ted. *The Hawk in the Rain.* London: Faber & Faber 1957, 1st edition of author's first book, DJ. $125. .

HUGHES, Ted. *The Hawk in the Rain.* New York: Harper (1957), 1st American edition, preceded by the English edition, DJ. $100.

HUGO, Ian. *See* "Key to Illustrators."

HUMOR. *See* "Key to Categories."

HUMPHREY, Maud. *Children of the Revolution.* New York: Frederick A. Stokes 1900, illustrated by Maud Humphrey, quarto, illustrated boards. $200–$300.

HUNEKER, James. *Ivory, Apes and Peacocks: Joseph Conrad, Walt Whitman, Jules LaForgue, Dostoevsky, Tolstoy.* New York: Charles Scribner's Sons 1915, 1st edition, original cloth. $35.

HUNEKER, James. *Painted Veils.* New York: Boni & Liveright (1920), 1st edition, limited to 1,200 numbered copies signed by the author, DJ. $65.

HUNT, Lynn Bogue. *See* "Key to Illustrators."

HUNTER, Dard. *See* "Key to Illustrators."

HUROK, Sol. *Impresario.* New York: Random House (1946), 1st edition, ills. $20.

HURST, Fannie. *The Hands of Veronica.* New York: Harper (1947), 1st edition, DJ. $30.

HURSTON, Zora Neale. *Jonah's Gourd Vine.* Philadelphia: Lippincott 1934, 1st edition of author's first book, DJ. $600–$800.

HURSTON, Zora Neale. *Mules and Men.* Philadelphia: Lippincott 1935, 1st edition, DJ. $350–$450.

HURSTON, Zora Neale. *Tell My Horse.* Philadelphia: Lippincott (1938), 1st edition, DJ. $200–$300.

HURSTON, Zora Neale. *Tell My Horse.* Philadelphia: Lippincott (1938), 1st edition. $55–$75.

HURSTON, Zora Neale. *Their Eyes Were Watching God.* Philadelphia: Lippincott (1937), 1st edition, DJ. $175.

HUSTED, Ida. *The Life and Work of Susan B. Anthony.* Indianapolis: The Hollenbeck Press (1898, 1908), 3 vols, voluminous, including letters, lectures, etc., 1st edition. $100–$135.

HUXLEY, Aldous. *After Many a Summer.* London: Chatto & Windus 1939, 1st edition, DJ. $100–$125.

HUXLEY, Aldous. *After Many a Summer.* New York: Harper & Brothers 1939, 1st American edition, DJ. $35.

HUXLEY, Aldous. *An Encyclopedia of Pacifism.* London: Chatto & Windus 1937, original printed yellow wrappers, uncommon. $60.

HUXLEY, Aldous. *Antic Hay.* London: Chatto & Windus 1923, 1st edition, DJ. $150.

HUXLEY, Aldous. *Ape and Essence.* London: Chatto & Windus 1949, 1st edition, DJ. $25.

HUXLEY, Aldous. *Ape and Essence.* New York: 1948, 1st American edition, DJ. $25.

HUXLEY, Aldous. *Brave New World.* London: Chatto & Windus 1932, 1st trade edition, DJ. $400–$500.

HUXLEY, Aldous. *Brave New World.* New York: Doubleday 1932, 1st American edition, DJ. $300–$350.

HUXLEY, Aldous. *Eyeless in Gaza.* London: Chatto & Windus 1936, 1st edition, DJ. $125–$225.

HUXLEY, Aldous. *Eyeless in Gaza.* London: Chatto & Windus 1936, 1st trade edition. $12–$25.

HUXLEY, Aldous. *Point Counter Point.* London: Chatto & Windus 1928, 1st edition, DJ. $125.

HUXLEY, Aldous. *Selected Poems.* Oxford: Blackwell 1926, 1st edition, without DJ as issued, scarce. $75–$125.

HUXLEY, Aldous. *The Doors of Perception.* London: Chatto & Windus 1954, 1st edition, DJ. $50–$75.

HUXLEY, Aldous. *The Perennial Philosophy.* London: Chatto & Windus 1946, 1st edition, DJ. $35.

HUXLEY, Aldous. *Time Must Have a Stop.* New York: Harper 1944, 1st American edition, DJ. $25–$35.

HYDE, Philip. *See* "Key to Illustrators."

 I

IBSEN, Henrik. *Hedda Gabler.* Copenhagen: Gyldendalske Boghandel 1890, 1st edition. $600.

IBSEN, Henrik. *Peer Gynt: A Dramatic Poem.* London: George Harrap 1935, one of 460 numbered copies signed by the artist, 12 mounted color plates by Arthur Rackham, 1st edition thus, bound in white vellum, slipcase. $500–$1,000.

IBSEN, Henrik. *Peer Gynt: A Dramatic Poem.* London: George Harrap 1935, 12 color plates and other ills by Arthur Rackham, 1st (trade) edition thus, original cloth, DJ. $100–$300.

IBSEN, Henrik. *The Doll's House.* New York: D. Appleton & Co. 1889, 1st American edition. $50.

INGOLDSBY, Thomas (R.H. Barham). *The Ingoldsby Legends; or Mirth and Marvels.* London: 1870 Richard Bentley, 2 vols, ills by George Cruikshank, John Leech, and others, annotated edition, very fine decorated morocco binding. $150–$200.

INGOLDSBY, Thomas (R.H. Barham). *The Ingoldsby Legends; or Mirth and Marvels.* London: Richard Bentley 1840, 42, 47, 3 vols, ills by George Cruikshank, John Leech, and others, original cloth, 1st edition. $500–$1,000.

INGOLDSBY, Thomas (R.H. Barham) *The Ingoldsby Legends; or Mirth and Marvels.* London: 1898, illustrated by Arthur Rackham, 1st edition thus. $250–$350.

INGOLDSBY, Thomas (R.H. Barham). *The Ingoldsby Legends; or Mirth and Marvels.* London: 1907, illustrated by Arthur Rackham, later printing cloth binding. $200–$300.

INVISIBLE SCARLET O'NEIL. See Big Little Books.

IRISH, William. *Deadline at Dawn.* Cleveland: World (1946), 1st motion picture edition, illustrated with scenes from the movie, DJ. $25–$50.

IRISH, William. *The Dancing Detective.* Philadelphia: Lippincott (1946), 1st edition, DJ, scarce in DJ. $110.

IRISH, William. *See also* Vintage Paperbacks.

IRVING, John. *Setting Free the Bears.* New York: Random House (1968), 1st edition of author's first book, DJ. $200–$300.

IRVING, John. *The 158-Pound Marriage.* New York: Random House (1974), DJ. $50–$65.

IRVING, John. *The Hotel New Hampshire.* New York: Random House (1981), 1st edition, DJ. $20–$30.

IRVING, John. *The Water-Method Man.* New York: Random House (1972), 1st edition of author's second book, DJ. $75.

IRVING, John. *The World According to Garp.* New York: Dutton (1978), 1st trade edition, DJ. $30–$40.

IRVING, Washington. *Rip Van Winkle.* New York: Russell 1897, 1st edition thus, color ills by Will Bradley. $100–$150.

ISHERWOOD, Christopher. *Goodbye to Berlin:* London 1939, 1st English edition, DJ. $400–$500.

ISHERWOOD, Christopher. *Lions and Shadows: An Education in the 'Twenties'.* London: Hogarth Press 1938, 1st edition, DJ. $350.

ISHERWOOD, Christopher. *Prater Violet.* London: Methuen (1946), 1st English edition in DJ designed by John Ross. $50–$75.

ISHERWOOD, Christopher. *Prater Violet.* New York: Random House (1945), 1st edition, DJ. $50–$75.

ISHERWOOD, Christopher. *The Berlin Stories.* (New York: New Directions 1945), 1st edition, DJ. $25–$50.

ISHERWOOD, Christopher. *The World in the Evening.* London: Methuen 1954, 1st edition, DJ. $85.

IVES, Charles. *Essays Before A Sonata.* New York: Knickerbocker 1920, 1st edition of author's first book, issued without a DJ. $200–$300.

J

JACK ARMSTRONG. See Big Little Books

JACKSON, Charles. *The Lost Weekend.* New York/Toronto: Farrar & Rinehart (1944), 1st edition of author's first book, DJ. $50–$75.

JACKSON, Holbrook. *The Anatomy of Bibliomania.* New York: Scribner's 1931, 2 vols. $135.

JACKSON, Shirley. *The Lottery.* New York: Farrar & Rinehart 1949, 1st edition of the author's second and scarcest book, DJ. $150.

JACKSON, Shirley. *See also* Vintage Paperbacks.

JAMES, P.D. *Cover Her Face.* New York: Scribner's (1962), 1st American edition of author's first book, DJ. $75–$100.

JAMES, Will. *Big-Enough.* New York/London: Scribner's 1931, 1st edition with code letter "A" on copyright page, pictorial cloth, many ills, DJ. $40–$75.

JAMES, Will. *Lone Cowboy: My Life Story.* New York: Scribner's 1930, 1st trade edition with "A" on copyright page, illustrated by the author, DJ. $50–$100.

JAMES, Will. *Look-See with Uncle Bill.* New York: Scribner's 1938, 1st edition, "A," illustrated, very scarce. $50–$75.

JAMES, Will. *Sand.* New York: Scribner's 1929, 1st edition, "A," DJ. $50–$75.

JAMES, Will. *Smoky the Cowhorse.* New York: Scribner's 1926, small quarto, 1st edition, "A," DJ. $40–$200.

JAMES, Will. *The American Cowboy.* New York: Scribner's 1942, 1st edition, "A," illustrated by the author, DJ. $75–$125.

JANEWAY, Elizabeth. *The Walsh Girls.* Garden City: Doubleday, Doran 1943, 1st American edition of author's first book, DJ. $35.

JARRELL, Randall. *Little Friend, Little Friend.* New York: Dial Press 1945, 1st edition of author's second book, 1st edition not stated, DJ. $150–$300.

Decorative Bindings, 1850-1920

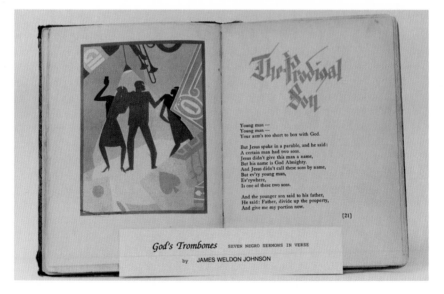

Collectibles: Circus and African American

Books from Typical Collecting Areas: Movie, Sporting, and Military . . .

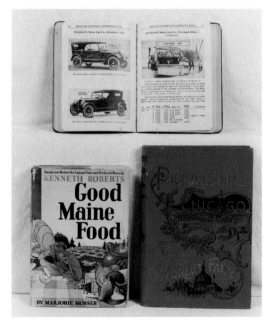

. . . As Well As Automotive, Cooking, and Expositions

Vintage Paperbacks

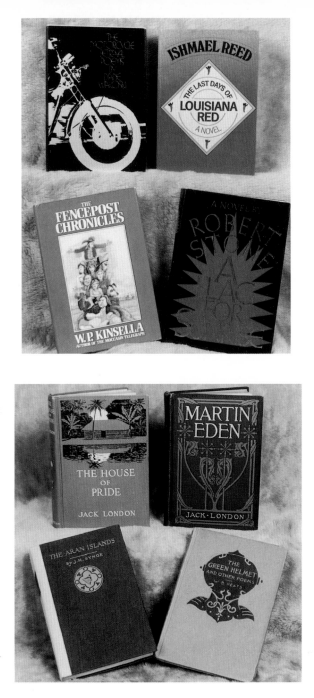

First Editions

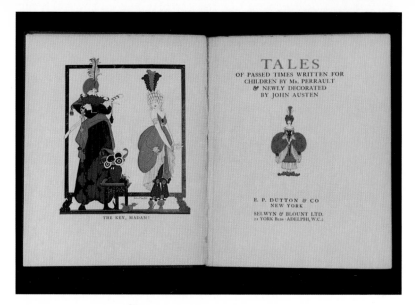

Illustrations by John Austen

Illustrated Endpapers and Book by Robert McCloskey

Collectible Children's Books

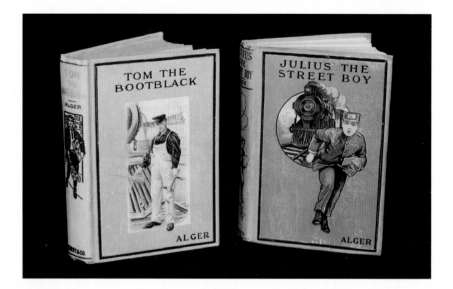

Juvenile Series Books

JARRELL, Randall. *Losses.* New York: Harcourt, Brace and Co. (1948), 1st edition so stated, DJ. $150–$250.

JARRELL, Randall. *Pictures from an Institution.* New York: Knopf 1954, 1st American edition, DJ. $100.

JARRELL, Randall. *The Complete Poems.* London: Faber & Faber (1971), 1st edition, includes poems not previously published, DJ. $100.

JARRELL, Randall. *The Complete Poems.* New York: Farrar, Straus & Giroux (1969), 1st American edition, DJ. $75.

JEFFERIES, Richard. *Bevis: The Story of a Boy.* London: 1882, 3 vols, 1st edition, later binding of half-morocco and gilt, worn. $250–$300.

JEFFERIES, Richard. *Greene Ferne Farm.* London: Smith, Elder & Co. 1880, 1st edition, original cloth. $125–$175.

JEFFERIES, Richard. *The Story of my Heart.* London: Duckworth and Co. (1923), 1st illustrated edition, 1st edition thus, 36 woodcuts by Ethelbert White, 24 of them headpieces or tailpieces, and 12 plates, limited to 225 copies, signed by the artist. $65.

JEFFERIES, Richard. *The Story of My Heart.* New York: 1924, illustrated by Ethelbert White, 1st edition thus. $50.

JEFFERS, John Robinson. *Flagons and Apples.* Los Angeles: Grafton Publishing Co. 1912, boards and cloth, 1st edition of Jeffers's first book, paper label on cover and spine. $400–$1,000.

JEFFERS, Robinson. *Cawdor and Other Poems.* New York: Liveright 1928, 1st edition, limited to 375 numbered copies signed by the author, original cerise buckram-backed boards, gilt, box. $75–$175.

JEFFERS, Robinson. *Give Your Heart to the Hawks.* New York: Random House 1933, 1st edition, DJ. $75–$100.

JEFFERS, Robinson. *Medea.* New York: Random House (1946). $75.

JEFFERS, Robinson. *Roan Stallion, Tamar and Other Poems.* London: Published by Leonard and Virginia Woolf at the Hogarth Press 1928, 1st English edition, limited to 440 copies, more than a quarter of which were destroyed, DJ. $200–$300.

JEFFERS, Robinson. *Roan Stallion, Tamar and Other Poems*. New York: The Modern Library (1933), 1st Modern Library edition, DJ. $35–$50.

JEFFERS, Robinson. *Roan Stallion, Tamar and Other Poems*. New York: Boni & Liveright 1925, 1st American edition, DJ. $125–$200.

JEFFERS, Robinson. *Such Counsels You Gave to Me and Other Poems*. New York: Random House (1937), 1st edition, decorated by Fritz Eichenberg, limited to 300 copies, half-calfskin and decorated boards, signed by Jeffers, glassine DJ, slipcase. $125–$250.

JEFFERS, Robinson. *Such Counsels You Gave to Me and Other Poems*. New York: Random House (1937), 1st trade edition, DJ. $75.

JEFFERS, Robinson. *Tamar and Other Poems*. New York City: Peter G. Boyle (1924), 1st edition, one of 500 copies, published at the author's expense, DJ. $200–$400.

JEFFERS, Robinson. *The Women at Point Sur*. New York: Boni and Liveright (1927), limited 1st edition of 265 numbered copies signed by the author, box. $75–$125.

JEFFERS, Robinson. *The Women at Point Sur*. New York: Boni and Liveright 1927, 1st trade edition, DJ. $40–$50.

JEFFERS, Robinson. *See also* Grabhorn Printing.

JEROME, Jerome K. *Three Men in a Boat*. Bristol/London: Arrowsmith/Simpkin 1889, 1st edition, 1st issue. $75–$150.

JOHNSON, James Weldon. *Autobiography of an Ex-Colored Man*. New York: Knopf 1927, 1st Knopf edition, originally published anonymously. This is the 1st reprint edition, with new introduction by Carl Van Vetchen. $40.

JOHNSON, James Weldon. *God's Trombones*. New York: Viking 1927, 1st edition, illustrated by Aaron Douglas, DJ. $150–$250.

JOHNSON, James Weldon. *Negro Americans, What Now?* New York: Viking Press 1934, 1st American edition. $30–$40.

JOHNSON, James Weldon. *Saint Peter Relates an Incident of the Resurrection Day*. New York: 1930, limited edition of 200 numbered and signed copies, in glassine dust wrapper and slipcase. Johnson's scarcest book. $200–$500.

JOHNSON, James Weldon. *Saint Peter Relates an Incident of the Resurrection Day*. New York: 1930, limited edition of 200 numbered and signed copies, Johnson's scarcest book. $100–$200.

JOHNSON, James Weldon. *The Book of American Negro Spirituals*. New York: Viking 1925, 1st edition. $30–$40.

JOHNSON, James Weldon. *See also Autobiography of an Ex-Colored Man*.

JOHNSON, Lionel. *Poems*. London and Boston: Elkin Mathews/Copeland & Day 1895, 1st edition of 750 copies for England and America. $30–$250.

JOHNSON, Lionel. *See also* Cuala Press: Yeats, William Butler, *Poetry and Ireland*.

JOHNSON, Merle. *American First Editions, Revised and Enlarged by Jacob Blanck*. New York: (1942), 4th edition. $75–$150.

JOHNSON, Owen. *The Tennessee Shad: Chronicling the Rise and Fall of the Firm of Doc MacNooder and the Tennessee Shad*. New York: 1911, 8 plates by F.R. Gruger, 1st edition. $40–$75.

JOHNSON, Robert U., and Buel, Clarence C. *Battles and Leaders of the Civil War*. New York: Century Co. 1884-88, 4 vols, 1st edition, "one of the most quoted [books] in Civil War literature." $175–$275.

JOHNSON, Robert U., and Buel, Clarence C. *Battles and Leaders of the Civil War*. New York: Yoseloff 1956, 4 vols, many ills and maps, DJs. $50–$75.

JOHNSON, Robert U., and Buel, Clarence C., editors. *Battles and Leaders of the Civil War. Being for the most part contributions by Union and Confederate Officers*. New York: Century Co. (1887-89), 1st book edition, 4 vols, 4to, 3/4 leather, ills, originally published in "Century" magazine. $200.

JOHNSTON, Annie Fellows. *The Little Colonel's Holidays*. Boston: The Page Co. (1901), 28th impression, February 1923, illustrated by L.J. Bridgman. $12–$30.

JOHNSTON, Mary. *To Have and to Hold*. Boston: Houghton Mifflin 1900, illustrated by Howard Pyle and others, 1st edition. $20–$40.

JOHNSTON, Robert. *See* "Key to Illustrators."

JOLAS, Eugene. *I Have Seen Monsters and Angels*. Paris: Transition Press (1938), wrappers, 1st edition. $40.

JONES, David. *Anathemata: Fragments of an Attempted Writing*. London: Faber & Faber (1952), 1st edition, in repaired DJ. $75–$175.

JONES, Harold. *See* "Key to Illustrators."

JONES, James. *From Here to Eternity*. New York: Charles Scribner's Sons, 1951, 1st edition of author's first book, DJ. $75–$175.

JONES, Laurian. *See* "Key to Illustrators."

JONES, LeRoi. *Blues People, Negro Music in White America*. New York: Morrow 1963, 1st edition. $30.

JONES, LeRoi. *Cuba Libre*. New York: Fair Play for Cuba Committee (1961), pamphlet, one of the author's earliest books. $150–$200.

JONES, LeRoi. *Preface to a Twenty Volume Suicide Note*. New York: Totem Press in association with Corinth Books (1961), 1st edition, stapled in white wrappers. $75.

JONES, LeRoi. *See also* Baraka, Imamu Amiri.

JONES, Shirley. *Backgrounds*. np 1979, square folio with 10 colored etchings, one of 25 numbered copies signed by the artist, printed by her in 18pt Bodoni on green paper, decorated half-morocco, marbled ep's by Mary French. $400.

JONES, Wilfred. *See* "Key to Illustrators."

JONSON, Ben. *See* Eragny Press.

JORDAN, June. *Who Look at Me*. New York: Crowell 1969, 1st edition, DJ. $100.

JOYCE, James. *A Portrait of the Artist as a Young Man*. New York: Huebsch 1916, precedes the English 1st edition because the British printers refused to set the type due to the British anti-obscenity laws, 1st edition. $500–$750.

JOYCE, James. *A Portrait of the Artist as a Young Man*. London: Egoist Ltd. (1917), 1st English edition, bound from American sheets, one of about 750 copies. $350–$700.

JOYCE, James. *A Portrait of the Artist as a Young Man*. New York: The Modern Library (1928), 1st Modern Library edition, leatherette. $25–$35.

JOYCE, James. *A Portrait of the Artist as a Young Man*. Leipzig: Tauchnitz 1930, "Copyright Edition," original white wrappers, with browning and some chipping. $25.

JOYCE, James. *Anna Livia Plurabelle*. London: Faber and Faber (1930), 1st English edition, 16mo, original brown wrappers. $50–$125.

JOYCE, James. *Anna Livia Plurabelle*. New York: Crosby Gaige 1928, one of 800 numbered copies, signed by author. $1,000–$1,500.

JOYCE, James. *Chamber Music*. Boston: Cornhill Company (1918), 1st American edition (unauthorized), 12mo, green cloth. $150.

JOYCE, James. *Chamber Music*. New York: Huebsch 1923, 2nd authorized American edition, octavo, black boards, internally repaired DJ. $300.

JOYCE, James. *Chamber Music*. Vigo St., London: Elkin Mathews (1907), 1st edition, 3rd issue. $700–$1,500.

JOYCE, James. *Chamber Music*. Vigo St., London: Elkin Mathews (1907), 1st edition, 1st issue, very small quarto, rare, author's first book. $2,000–$5,000.

JOYCE, James. *Collected Poems*. New York: Black Sun Press 1936, limited 1st edition, one of 800 numbered copies, in glassine DJ. $400–$500.

JOYCE, James. *Collected Poems*. New York: Viking 1937, 1st trade edition, DJ. $400–$500.

JOYCE, James. *Corrections of Misprints in Finnegans Wake*. As prepared by the author after publication of the 1st edition. London: Faber & Faber 1945, 1st edition, printer wrappers, quarto. $50–$100.

JOYCE, James. *Dubliners*. London: Grant Richards Limited (1914), 1st edition, scarce. $500–$1,300.

JOYCE, James. *Exiles. A Play in Six Acts*. New York: Huebsch, 1st American edition, one of 388 copies known to have been sold. $150–$250.

JOYCE, James. *Exiles*. London: Grant Richards 1918, 1st edition. $400–$650.

JOYCE, James. *Finnegans Wake*. London/New York: Faber & Faber/Viking 1939, 1st edition, one of 425 numbered copies signed by Joyce, slipcase. $3,000–$5,000.

JOYCE, James. *Finnegans Wake*. London: Faber & Faber (1939), 1st trade edition, DJ. $700–$1,200.

JOYCE, James. *Finnegans Wake*. New York: Viking Press 1939, 1st American edition, DJ. $300–$500.

JOYCE, James. *Letters of James Joyce*. New York: Viking (1966), edited by Stuart Gilbert and Richard Ellman, 3 vols, DJs. $80–$125.

JOYCE, James. *Pomes Pennyeach*. Paris: Shakespeare and Co. 1927, small octavo, with errata slip, 1st edition. $150–$275.

JOYCE, James. *Stephen Hero*. (New York): New Directions (1944), 1st American edition, DJ. $50–$125.

JOYCE, James. *Stephen Hero*. London: Jonathan Cape 1944, correct 1st edition, pictorial DJ. $100–$250.

JOYCE, James. *The Portable James Joyce*. New York: Viking 1947, 1st edition, DJ. $30–$40.

JOYCE, James. *Ulysses*. London and Paris: Published by John Rodker in Paris for Egoist Press 1922, original blue wrappers, 1st English edition of 2,000 copies, slipcase. $2,500.

JOYCE, James. *Ulysses*. London and Paris: Published by John Rodker in Paris for Egoist Press 1922, original blue wrappers, 1st English edition of 2,000 copies, slipcase lacking. $1,000–$2,000.

JOYCE, James. *Ulysses*. London: Egoist Press, 2nd English edition, original wrappers, the colophon states, "This edition of 500 copies is specially printed to replace those destroyed in transit to the USA." $7,500.

JOYCE, James. *Ulysses*. New York: Random House 1934, 1st authorized American edition, DJ. $100–$300.

JOYCE, James. *Ulysses*. Paris: Shakespeare and Co. 1922, 1st edition, 1st printing, one of 150 on Verge d'Arches paper, hardest to find issue, almost an inch taller than the other two original issues of 100 and 750. $10,000.

JOYCE, James. *See also* Limited Editions Club.

JUNG, Carl Gustav. *Psychology of the Unconscious*. New York: Moffat, Yard & Co. 1916, 1st edition in English. $150.

JUNGK, Robert. *Brighter than a Thousand Suns*. New York: Harcourt, Brace and World "1958". $25–$35.

JUVENILE SERIES BOOKS. Alger, Horatio, Jr. *Helping Himself.* Chicago: M.A. Donohue & Co., nd, 2-color pictorial cover. $5–$8.

JUVENILE SERIES BOOKS. Alger, Horatio, Jr. *Julius the Street Boy.* New York: Hurst & Co., nd, chromolithograph paste-down cover label. $10–$15.

JUVENILE SERIES BOOKS. Alger, Horatio, Jr. *Tom, The Bootblack.* New York: Hurst & Co., nd, chromolithograph paste-down cover label. $10–$15.

JUVENILE SERIES BOOKS. Appleton, Victor. *Tom Swift and his Motorcycle.* New York: Grosset & Dunlap (1910), 1st of the Tom Swift series, DJ. $25–$35.

JUVENILE SERIES BOOKS. Appleton, Victor. *Tom Swift and his Motorcycle.* New York: Grosset & Dunlap (1910), 1st of the Tom Swift series. $5–$7.

JUVENILE SERIES BOOKS. Bowen, R. Sidney. *Dave Dawson with the Air Corps.* Akron and New York: Saalfield (1942), DJ. $6–$12.

JUVENILE SERIES BOOKS. Bowen, R. Sidney. *Red Randall in the Aleutians.* New York: Grosset & Dunlap (1945), DJ. $6–$15.

JUVENILE SERIES BOOKS. Cook, Canfield. *Spitfire Pilot.* New York: Grosset & Dunlap (1942), a Lucky Terrell flying story, DJ. $6–$15.

JUVENILE SERIES BOOKS. Duncan, Gregory. *Dick Donnelly of the Paratroops.* Racine: Whitman (1944), DJ. $5–$12.

JUVENILE SERIES BOOKS. Hope, Laura Lee. *The Bobbsey Twins in the Great West.* New York: Grosset & Dunlap, 1930s, DJ. $5.

JUVENILE SERIES BOOKS. Keene, Carolyn. *Mystery of the Ivory Charm.* New York: Grosset & Dunlap (1936), orange silhouette ep's, last Nancy Drew title listed is title #19, last edition of Ivory Charm with a glossy frontis, white spine, DJ. $15–$45.

JUVENILE SERIES BOOKS. Keene, Carolyn. *Mystery of the Ivory Charm.* New York: Grosset & Dunlap (1936), orange silhouette ep's, last Nancy Drew title listed is title #19, last edition of Ivory Charm with a glossy frontis. $12–$25.

JUVENILE SERIES BOOKS. Keene, Carolyn. *Secret at Shadow Ranch.* New York: Grosset & Dunlap (1931), blue multi-figure ep's, last Nancy Drew title listed is title #37, pictorial spine, DJ. $10.

JUVENILE SERIES BOOKS. Keene, Carolyn. *Secret at Shadow Ranch*. New York: Grosset & Dunlap (1931), blue multi-figure ep's, last Nancy Drew title listed is title #37. $4–$6.

JUVENILE SERIES BOOKS. Keene, Carolyn. *Secret of the Old Clock*. New York: Grosset & Dunlap (1930), orange silhouette ep's, last Nancy Drew title listed is title #21, white spine, DJ. $12–$20.

JUVENILE SERIES BOOKS. Keene, Carolyn. *Secret of the Old Clock*. New York: Grosset & Dunlap (1930), orange silhouette ep's, last Nancy Drew title listed is title #21. $10–$15.

JUVENILE SERIES BOOKS. Keene, Carolyn. *The Haunted Showboat*. New York: Grosset & Dunlap (1958), modern pictorial hardcovers, last Nancy Drew title listed is #40. $2–$3.

JUVENILE SERIES BOOKS. Rockwood, Roy. *Bomba the Jungle Boy and the Painted Hunters*. New York: Cupples & Leon (1932), pictorial spine and DJ. $15.

JUVENILE SERIES BOOKS. Snell, Roy J. *Sparky Ames of the Ferry Command*. Racine: Whitman (1943), DJ. $5–$12.

 K ————————————————————

KAFKA, Franz. *Das Schloss*. Munich: Kurt Wolff 1926, 1st edition (of *The Castle*), light wear. $700.

KAFKA, Franz. *The Castle*. London: Martin Secker 1930, 1st edition in English, translated by Willa and Edwin Muir, DJ. $100–$300.

KAFKA, Franz. *The Castle*. New York: Knopf 1930, 1st American edition, DJ. $75–$200.

KAFKA, Franz. *The Metamorphosis*. (New York): Vanguard Press (1946). $35–$50.

KAFKA, Franz. *The Trial*. London: 1937, 1st English edition. $50.

KAISER, Henry. *See* Grabhorn Printing.

KANTOR, MacKinlay. *Andersonville*. New York: World (1955),

limited edition of 1,000 copies, signed by the author, slipcase. $75.

KANTOR, MacKinlay. *The Voice of Bugle Ann.* New York: Coward McCann (1935), 1st edition, DJ. $35.

KAUFFER, E. McKnight. *See* "Key to Illustrators."

KAVANAGH, Patrick. *See* Cuala Press.

KAYE-SMITH, Sheila. *Susan Spray.* New York: Harper and Brothers 1931, 1st American edition, DJ. $20–$35.

KAZIN, Alfred. *On Native Grounds.* New York: Reynal and Hitchcock (1941), 1st edition, DJ. $85.

KEATON, Diane. *Reservations.* New York: Knopf 1980, with photographs of America's hotel lobbies, 1st edition, DJ. $20.

KEATS, John. *Endymion: A Poetic Romance.* London: Taylor and Hessey 1818, 1st edition, contemporary half calfskin. $3,000.

KEATS, John. *See also* Golden Cockerel Press.

KEENE, Carolyn. *See* Juvenile Series Books.

KEENE, J. Harrington. *Fly-Fishing and Fly-Making for Trout, Bass, Salmon, etc.* New York: Forest and Stream 1891, 2nd edition, revised and enlarged, illustrated, and with fly-making materials attached within. $250.

KEEPING, Virginia. *See* "Key to Illustrators."

KEES, Weldon. *The Fall of the Magicians.* New York: Reynal & Hitchcock (1947), 1st edition of author's important second book, DJ. $85.

KEITH, Agnew Newton. *Land Below the Wind.* Boston: Little, Brown 1949, 1st edition of author's first book, DJ. $35.

KEITH, Elmer. *Big Game Rifles and Cartridges.* Onslow County, North Carolina: Samworth 1936. $50.

KEITH, Elmer. *Shotguns by Keith.* New York: Bonanza Books (1950), reprint edition. $30.

KELLAND, Clarence Budington. *Scattergood Baines Returns.* New York & London: 1940, 1st edition, DJ. $20.

KELLER, Arthur. *See* "Key to Illustrators."

KELMSCOTT PRESS (London). More, Sir Thomas. *Utopia.* London: Kelmscott Press 1893, one of 300. $60–$750.

KELMSCOTT PRESS (London). Morris, William. *Child Christopher and Goldilind the Fair*. London: Kelmscott Press 1895, 2 vols, hand-colored copy with some initials in gold, one of 600. $150–$350.

KELMSCOTT PRESS (London). Morris, William. *Gothic Architecture*. London: Kelmscott Press 1893, one of 1,500. $250.

KELMSCOTT PRESS (London). Morris, William. *Poems by the Way*. London: Kelmscott Press 1891, one of 300. $650.

KELMSCOTT PRESS (London). Morris, William. *The Wood Beyond the World*. London: Kelmscott Press 1894, one of 350. $750.

KELMSCOTT PRESS (London). Morris, William. *The Wood Beyond the World*. London: Kelmscott Press 1894, one of 8 on vellum. $7,000.

KELMSCOTT PRESS (London). Shelley, Percy Bysshe. *The Poetical Works*. London: Kelmscott Press 1894, one of 250, 3 vols, quarto, original vellum. $1,100.

KELMSCOTT PRESS (London). Spenser, Edmund. *The Shepheardes Calender*. London: Kelmscott Press 1896, one of 225. $1,000–$2,000.

KELMSCOTT PRESS (London). *The Tale of Beowulf*. London: Kelmscott Press 1895, one of 300. $400.

KEMBLE, E.W. *See* "Key to Illustrators."

KEMP, Harry. *Chanteys and Ballads: Sea-Chanteys, Tramp-Ballads, and Other Ballads and Poems*. New York: Brentano's 1920, 1st edition, DJ. $20–$25.

KENEALLY, Thomas. *The Place at Whitton*. London: Cassell (1964), 1st English edition of author's first book, DJ. $100.

KENNEDY, William. *Billy Phelan's Greatest Game*. New York: Viking (1978), 1st edition, DJ. $65–$100.

KENT, Rockwell. *A Northern Christmas*. New York: American Artists Group (1941), Number 1 in their American Artists Gift Book series, small format, profusely illustrated by Kent, DJ. $35.

KENT, Rockwell. *Greenland Journal*. New York: Ivan Obolensky (1962), one of 1,000 numbered copies signed by author, many text ills, 6 original lithographs in pocket in slipcase, one of them signed by Kent. $175–$275.

KENT, Rockwell. *It's Me O Lord, the Autobiography of Rockwell Kent.* New York: (1955), DJ. $200.

KENT, Rockwell. *N. By E.* New York: Brewer and Warren 1930, 1st trade edition, numerous headpieces, printed by the Lakeside Press, DJ. $65–$85.

KENT, Rockwell. *N. By E.* New York: Literary Guild 1930, DJ. $15.

KENT, Rockwell. *Rockwellkentiana: Few Words and Many Pictures.* New York: Harcourt Brace 1933, with a Bibliography and List of Prints by Karl Zigrosser, 85 pages of reproductions of Kent's engravings, DJ. $65–$85.

KENT, Rockwell. *Salamina.* New York: Harcourt Brace 1935, over 80 ills by the author, 1st edition, DJ. $65.

KENT, Rockwell. *The Bookplates and Marks of.* New York: Random House 1929, with reproductions of 85 plates, printed on special Japanese paper in an edition of 1,250 copies signed by Kent, printed by Elmer Adler at the Pynson Printers, DJ. $100–$200.

KENT, Rockwell. *See also* "Key to Illustrators."

KEROUAC, Jack. *Big Sur.* New York: Farrar, Straus & Cudahy (1962), copyright page of 1st edition reads "First printing, 1962," 1st edition, DJ. $75–$125.

KEROUAC, Jack. *Book of Dreams.* San Francisco: City Lights Books (1961), 1st printing, wraps. $75–$100.

KEROUAC, Jack. *On the Road.* New York: Viking 1957, 1st edition of author's second and most famous book, DJ. $200–$400.

KEROUAC, Jack. *The Dharma Bums.* New York: Viking 1958, 1st edition, DJ. $75–$175.

KEROUAC, Jack. *The Subterraneans.* New York: Grove (1958), copyright page of 1st edition reads (abbreviated) "*The Subterraneans* is published in 3 eds:/An Evergreen Book (E–99)/A hardbound ed/A specially bound Limited Ed/of 100 numbered copies," 1st trade edition, DJ. $275–$350.

KESEY, Ken. *One Flew Over the Cuckoo's Nest.* New York: Viking (1962), 1st edition of author's first book, DJ. $150–$350.

KESEY, Ken. *Sometimes A Great Notion.* New York: Viking (1964), 1st edition, 1st issue, with publisher's emblem on half-title page, DJ. $75–$150.

KESEY, Ken. *The Day After Superman Died*. Northridge, CA: Lord John Press 1980, one of 50, issued without DJ. $50.

KEWPIES. See O'Neill, Rose.

KILMER, Joyce. *Trees and Other Poems*. New York: George Doran (1914), 1st edition, 1st state, without "Printed in USA" on copyright page. $75–$100.

KIMBROUGH, Emily. *We Followed Our Hearts to Hollywood*. New York: Dodd, Mead 1943, drawings by Helen Hokinson, 1st edition, DJ. $20–$35.

KING ARTHUR. See Lanier, Sydney.

KING, Captain Charles. *An Apache Princess*. New York: 1903, 1st edition, illustrated in black and white by Frederic Remington and Edward Deming. $25.

KING, Stephen. *Carrie*. New York: Doubleday 1974, 1st edition of author's first book, 1st edition so stated, DJ. $200–$400.

KING, Stephen. *Christine*. New York: Viking (1983), 1st edition, DJ. $25–$35.

KING, Stephen. *Cujo*. New York: Viking 1981, 1st trade edition, DJ. $25–$35.

KING, Stephen. *Cycle of the Werewolf*. Westland, MI: The Land of Enchantment 1983, 1st trade edition, illustrated in color and black and white by Berni Wrightson, DJ. $90.

KING, Stephen. *Firestarter*. Huntington Woods: Phantasia Press 1980, 1st edition, limited to 26 signed and lettered copies, issued without DJ or slipcase. $2,000–$4,000.

KING, Stephen. *Firestarter*. New York: Viking Press (1980), 1st trade edition, DJ. $200.

KING, Stephen. *Night Shift*. New York: Doubleday 1978, 1st edition, DJ. $175–$375.

KING, Stephen. *'Salem's Lot*. Garden City: Doubleday 1975, 1st edition, 2nd issue, with front DJ flap reading both $7.95 and "Father Cody," author's second book. $225–$500.

KING, Stephen. *The Dead Zone*. New York: Viking (1979), 1st edition, DJ. $50–$85.

KING, Stephen. *The Eyes of the Dragon*. Bangor: Philtrum Press 1984, one of 1,000, illustrated by Kenneth R. Linkhauser, slipcase. $350–$550.

KING, Stephen. *The Shining*. Garden City: Doubleday & Co. 1977, 1st edition, 1st edition so stated on copyright page, DJ. $125–$150.

KING, Stephen. *The Stand*. New York: Doubleday and Co. 1977, 1st edition, DJ. $80–$175.

KING, Stephen. *See also* Bachman, Richard (Stephen King pseudonym), under Vintage Paperbacks.

KING, Stephen, and Straub, Peter. *The Talisman*. West Kingston and Boston: Donald Grant 1984, 2 vols, 1st edition, limited and signed, one of 1,200, signed by both writers, 11 color plates by 11 different fantasy artists, slipcase. $90–$400.

KINGSLEY, Charles. *The Water Babies*. New York: Dodd, Mead 1916, color plates by Jessie Wilcox Smith. $175–$250.

KINGSLEY, Charles. *The Water Babies*. New York: Dutton 1908, color plates by Margaret Tarrant. $50–$100.

KINGSTON, Maxine Hong. *China Men*. New York: Knopf 1980, 1st edition, DJ. $20.

KINGSTON, Maxine Hong. *The Woman Warrior: Memoir of a Girlhood among Ghosts*. New York: Knopf 1976, 1st edition of the author's first book, DJ. $35–$65.

KINNELL, Galway. *Flower Herding on Mount Monadnock*. Boston: Houghton Mifflin 1964, 1st American edition, DJ. $35–$50.

KINNELL, Galway. *The Last Hiding Place of Snow*. (New York): The Red Osier Press 1980, 1st edition, 2 wood engravings by Barry Moser, limited to 150 copies, signed by poet and artist. $60–$75.

KINSELLA, Thomas. *Moralities*. Dublin: Dolmen (1960), 1st edition, wraps, quarto, one of 475 copies of a total edition of 500. $150.

KINSELLA, Thomas. *Tear*. Cambridge: Pyn-Randall 1969, one of the 12 remaining copies of the 1st edition, which was suppressed on the poet's demand, because of the political significance of its orange coloring, signed. $250.

KINSELLA, W.P. *The Fencepost Chronicles*. Boston: Houghton, Mifflin (1987), 1st edition, DJ. $20–$30.

KIPLING, J. Lockwood. *See* "Key to Illustrators."

KIPLING, Rudyard. *"Captains Courageous": A Story of the Grand Banks*. London: Macmillan 1897, 1st edition with 22 ills by I.W. Taber, blue cloth pictorially gilt-stamped and with gilt edges. $150–$175.

KIPLING, Rudyard. *"Captains Courageous": A Story of the Grand Banks*. New York: Century 1897, original decorated cloth initialed by Blanche MacManus, 1st American edition with changes in text from the British, illustrated, printed at the Divinne Press. $100–$150.

KIPLING, Rudyard. *Ballads and Barrack Room Ballads*. New York: Macmillan 1892, 1st American edition. $35–$75.

KIPLING, Rudyard. *Barrack Room Ballads and Other Verses*. London: Methuen 1892, red cloth, 1st trade edition. $50–$125.

KIPLING, Rudyard. *Collected Verse*. New York: Doubleday, Page 1910, 1st illustrated edition, color plates and full-page black and white ills by W. Heath Robinson. $75–$100.

KIPLING, Rudyard. *Departmental Ditties and Other Verses*. Lahore, India 1886, 1st edition, 1st issue, octavo, original tan wraps tied with red tape. $1,000–$2,000.

KIPLING, Rudyard. *Departmental Ditties. Barrack-Room Ballads and Other Verses*. New York: United States Book Co. (1890), original cloth, 1st edition, 1st issue, with the "Lovell" imprint on spine. $125–$300.

KIPLING, Rudyard. *Just So Stories for Little Children*. London: Macmillan and Co. 1902, 1st edition, illustrated by the author, pictorial red cloth. $500.

KIPLING, Rudyard. *Kim*. Garden City: Doubleday, Page 1901, 1st American edition, original green cloth, scarce. $50–$100.

KIPLING, Rudyard. *Kim*. London: Macmillan and Co. 1901, 1st edition, illustrated with ten halftone plates by J. Lockwood Kipling, original cloth. $75–$150.

KIPLING, Rudyard. *Kim*. London: Macmillan and Co. 1901, 1st edition, illustrated with ten halftone plates by J. Lockwood Kipling, original cloth, worn DJ (DW very scarce). $300–$600.

KIPLING, Rudyard. *Land and Sea Tales for Scouts and Guides*. London: Macmillan 1923, DJ. $35–$50.

KIPLING, Rudyard. *Puck of Pook's Hill.* London: Macmillan 1906, 1st edition, original cloth. $50.

KIPLING, Rudyard. *Puck of Pook's Hill.* New York: Doubleday, Page and Co. 1906, 1st American edition and 1st illustrated edition, 4 full-page colored plates by Arthur Rackham. $75–$225.

KIPLING, Rudyard. *Songs of the Sea.* Garden City: Doubleday, Page 1927, 1st American trade edition, 34 color and black and white ills by Donald Maxwell, DJ. $65.

KIPLING, Rudyard. *The Jungle Book.* London: Macmillan 1894, 1st edition, illustrated by J. Lockwood Kipling, original blue pictorial boards. $150–$250.

KIPLING, Rudyard. *The Jungle Book.* New York: Century 1913, illustrated by Maurice and Edward Detmold with 16 color plates and pictorial borders and ep's, 1st edition thus. $75–$100.

KIPLING, Rudyard. *The Jungle Book.* New York: Century Co. 1894, 1st American edition, illustrated. $50–$75.

KIPLING, Rudyard. *The Legs of Sister Ursala.* San Francisco: Windsor Press 1927, hand set on handmade paper, one of 500 numbered copies, 1st separate edition. $25–$35.

KIRK, Maria. *See* "Key to Illustrators."

KNIGHT, Hilary. *See* "Key to Illustrators."

KNOWLES, John. *A Separate Peace.* London: Secker & Warburg 1955, 1st edition, preceded 1st American edition, DJ. $400.

KNOWLES, John. *A Separate Peace.* New York: Macmillan 1960, 1st American edition, DJ. $100.

KOESTLER, Arthur. *Darkness at Noon.* London: 1940, 1st edition, DJ, very scarce. $400.

KOESTLER, Arthur. *Scum of the Earth.* London: Victor Gollancz, Left Book Club 1941, 1st edition, an early work, DJ. $50.

KOESTLER, Arthur. *Spanish Testament.* London: Left Book Club (Gollancz) 1947, 1st edition, orange cloth. $50.

KOESTLER, Arthur. *The Yogi and the Commissar.* New York: Macmillan 1945, 1st American edition, DJ. $25.

KOESTLER, Arthur. *Thieves in the Night: Chronicles of an Experiment*. New York: Macmillan 1946, 1st American edition, DJ. $35.

KOESTLER, Arthur. *See also* Costler, Dr. A.; Vintage Paperbacks.

KOHLER, Wolfgang. *The Mentality of Apes*. New York: Harcourt, Brace 1925, translated from the 2nd revised edition, 9 plates. $20–$40.

KOONTZ, Dean R. *Oddkins*. New York: Warner 1988, 1st edition, DJ. $20.

KOONTZ, Dean R. *See also* Vintage Paperbacks.

KOTZWINKLE, William. *Doctor Rat*. New York: Knopf 1976, 1st edition, DJ. $400.

KOSINSKI, Jerzy. *The Painted Bird*. Boston: Houghton Mifflin 1965, 1st edition, 1st issue, with pages 270 and 271 beginning with the same 1st line, DJ. $150–$200.

KOSINSKI, Jerzy. *See also* Novak, Joseph.

KRAUSS, Ruth. *A Hole is to Dig*. New York: Harper Brothers (1952), illustrated by Maurice Sendak, DJ. $100–$125.

KREDEL, Fritz. *See* "Key to Illustrators."

KREYMBORG, Alfred. *Funnybone Alley*. New York: Macauley (1927), quarto, purple cloth, 1st edition, one of 500 copies, illustrated by Boris Artzybasheff with 7 tipped-in color plates, pictorial ep's and black and white ills. $100.

KUNITZ, Stanley. *Intellectual Things*. Garden City: Doubleday, Doran 1930, 1st edition of author's first book, 1st American edition, DJ. $150.

KUNITZ, Stanley. *Next-to-Last Things: New Poems and Essays*. 1985, 1st edition, DJ. $25.

KUNITZ, Stanley. *Passport to the War*. New York: Henry Holt 1944, 1st edition of author's second book of poetry, DJ. $75.

KUNITZ, Stanley. *Selected Poems 1928-1958*. Boston: Little, Brown (1958), 1st edition, DJ. $75.

KUNITZ, Stanley. *The Coat Without a Seam*. Northampton: Gehenna Press 1974, one of 150 signed copies, quarto, portrait by Leonard Baskin, printed by Harold McGrath on Italian handmade paper using Centaur types, half-vellum, paper boards. $225.

KUNITZ, Stanley. *The Poems of Stanley Kunitz 1928-1978.* Boston: Little, Brown (1979), 1st edition, DJ. $35–$40.

 L ———————————————————————

L'AMOUR, Louis. *Comstock Load.* New York: Bantam (1981), jacket art by Louis Glanzman, 1st edition, DJ. $50.

L'AMOUR, Louis. *Education of a Wandering Man, A Memoir.* New York: Bantam (1989), 1st edition, DJ. $20.

L'AMOUR, Louis. *Heller with a Gun.* New York: Bantam (1985), 1st hardcover edition, brown leatherette. $20.

L'AMOUR, Louis. *Hopalong Cassidy and the Riders of High Rock.* New York: Doubleday 1951, 1st edition, DJ. $150.

L'AMOUR, Louis. *Kilrone.* New York: Bantam (1982), 1st hardcover edition, brown leatherette. $25.

L'AMOUR, Louis. *Last Stand at Papago Wells.* New York: Bantam (1986), 1st hardcover edition, brown leatherette. $20.

L'AMOUR, Louis. *Rivers West.* New York: Dutton (1975), 1st edition, DJ. $75.

L'AMOUR, Louis. *Sackett's Land.* New York: Bantam (1982), 1st hardcover edition, brown leatherette. $30.

L'AMOUR, Louis. *The Californios.* New York: Dutton (1974), 1st edition, DJ. $75.

L'AMOUR, Louis. *The Cherokee Trail.* New York: Bantam (1982), jacket art by Louis Glanzman, 1st edition, DJ. $50.

L'AMOUR, Louis. *The Ferguson Rifle.* New York: Bantam (1982), 1st hardcover edition, brown leatherette. $25.

L'AMOUR, Louis. *The First Fast Draw.* New York: Bantam (1981), 1st hardcover edition, brown leatherette. $30.

LA FARGE, Oliver. *Laughing Boy.* Cambridge: Houghton, Mifflin 1929, 1st edition, DJ. $30.

LA ROCHEFOUCAULD. *See* Golden Cockerel Press.

LANG, Andrew. *The Green Fairy Book.* London: Longman's, Green & Co. 1892, 1st edition, black and white ills, including some full page, by H.J. Ford, original binding. $150–$275.

LANG, Andrew. *The Violet Fairy Book.* London: Longman's, Green & Co. 1901, 1st edition, 8 full-page color plates, plus black and white ills, including some full page, by J.H. Ford, original binding. $150–$275.

LANIER, Sydney. *The Boy's King Arthur.* New York: Scribner's 1917, edited by Sydney Lanier, 1st edition, 17 color plates by N.C. Wyeth. $75–$100.

LANIER, Sydney. *The Boy's King Arthur.* New York: Scribner's 1924, edited by Sydney Lanier, later edition, 17 color plates by N.C. Wyeth. $20–$35.

LARDNER, Ring. *Round Up. The Stories of Ring Lardner.* New York: Scribner's 1929, 1st edition, DJ. $50–$100.

LARDNER, Ring. *Round Up. The Stories of Ring Lardner.* New York: Scribner's 1929, 1st edition. $30.

LARDNER, Ring. *Say it with Oil.* New York: George H. Doran Co. (1923), 1st edition, with *Say it with Bricks*, by Nina Wilcox Putnam, printed back-to-back with the preceding, DJ. $65.

LARDNER, Ring. *The Portable Ring Lardner.* New York: Viking 1946, 1st edition, DJ. $20–$40.

LARDNER, Ring. *Treat 'em Rough.* Indianapolis: Bobbs-Merrill Co. (1918), 1st edition, 1st issue, without the 18-line poem that appears on page 6 in the second printing, uncommon. $75–$350.

LARDNER, Ring W. *You Know Me Al.* Cleveland and New York: The World Publishing Company (1946), reprint edition. $3.50–$8.

LARDNER, Ring W. *You Know Me Al.* Cleveland and New York: The World Publishing Company (1946), reprint edition, DJ. $8–$12.

LARKIN, Philip. *The Whitsun Weddings.* London: Faber & Faber (1964), 1st edition, DJ. $75–$175.

LARKIN, Philip. *XX Poems.* Belfast 1951, privately printed for the poet and distributed by him as gifts, in an edition of 100 copies, scarce. $1,500.

LAST OF THE MOHICANS, THE. Philadelphia: H.C. Carey & I. Lea,Chestnut Street 1826, "By the author of *The Pioneers*" (by

James Fenimore Cooper), 2 vols, 1st edition, original boards with paper labels. $3,000–$6,000.

LATHROP, Dorothy. *See* "Key to Illustrators."

LAUGHLIN, James. *Some Natural Things.* Norfolk: New Directions (1945), 1st edition, DJ. $35–$50.

LAVER, James. *See* Nonesuch Press.

LAVIGNE, Robert. *See* "Key to Illustrators."

LAWRENCE, D.H., and Miller, Henry. *Pornography and Obscenity: Handbook for Censors. Two Essays by.* Michigan City, Indiana: 1958, wraps. $85.

LAWRENCE, D.H. *Collected Poems.* London: Secker & Warburg 1928, 1st trade edition, DJ. $100–$200.

LAWRENCE, D.H. *Collected Poems.* New York: Jonathan Cape and Harrison Smith 1929, 1st American edition, cloth, tissue DW, publisher's slipcase with paper labels. $75–$150.

LAWRENCE, D.H. *Lady Chatterley's Lover.* np: Florence: 1928, privately printed, a piracy, light blue paper-covered boards with paper spine label. $35–$45.

LAWRENCE, D.H. *Lady Chatterley's Lover.* np: (Florence) 1928, privately printed, one of 1,000 numbered copies signed by author, mulberry-colored boards, plain cream-colored DJ. $2,000–$3,000.

LAWRENCE, D.H. *Pornography and Obscenity.* London: Faber & Faber (1929), 1st edition, original printed orange wrappers, #5 in Faber & Faber's "Criterion Miscellany" series. $35–$50.

LAWRENCE, D.H. *Psychoanalysis and the Unconscious.* London: Martin Secker (1923), 1st English edition, DJ. $150–$200.

LAWRENCE, D.H. *Psychoanalysis and the Unconscious.* New York: 1921, 1st edition. $75.

LAWRENCE, D.H. *Sea and Sardinia.* New York: Thomas Seltzer 1921, 8 color plates by Jan Juta, 1st edition. $75–$175.

LAWRENCE, D.H. *Sons and Lovers.* London: Duckworth 1913, 1st edition, 2nd issue, with tipped-in title page, original dark blue cloth, blind-stamped, and with gilt. $250–$500.

LAWRENCE, D.H. *The Portable D.H. Lawrence.* New York: Viking Press 1947, 1st edition, DJ. $25.

LAWRENCE, D.H. *The Rainbow.* New York: B.W. Huebsch 1916, 1st American edition. $75–$150.

LAWRENCE, D.H. *The Virgin and the Gypsy.* London: Martin Secker (1930), 1st trade edition, DJ. $75–$125.

LAWRENCE, D.H. *Women in Love.* London: Martin Secker (1921), 1st trade edition. $75–$150.

LAWRENCE, D.H. *Women in Love.* New York: Thomas Seltzer 1922, 1st American trade edition. $75.

LAWRENCE, Frieda. *"Not I, but the Wind..."* New York: Viking 1934, 1st trade edition, DJ. $25–$50.

LAWRENCE, Frieda. *"Not I, but the Wind..."* Santa Fe: privately printed by the Rydal Press (1934), one of 1,000 copies signed by the author, 1st edition, DJ. $50–$150.

LAWRENCE, T.E. *Revolt in the Desert.* Garden City: Doubleday 1927, portrait, 15 plates, folding map, 1st American edition. $25–$30.

LAWRENCE, T.E. *Revolt in the Desert.* Garden City: Doubleday 1927, later printing. $10–$20.

LAWRENCE, T.E. *Revolt in the Desert.* Garden City: Doubleday 1927, portraits and 15 plates, plus folding map, 1st American edition, DJ. $50–$85.

LAWRENCE, T.E. *Revolt in the Desert.* London: Jonathan Cape 1927, portraits, map, 1st edition. $25–$75.

LAWRENCE, T.E. *Seven Pillars of Wisdom.* Garden City: 1935, 1st American trade edition. $25.

LAWRENCE, T.E. *Seven Pillars of Wisdom.* Garden City: Doubleday 1935, 1st American trade edition, DJ. $45–$75.

LAWRENCE, T.E. *Seven Pillars of Wisdom.* Garden City: Doubleday 1935, 1st American edition, bound in half calfskin, one of 750 copies, DJ and slipcase. $125–$150.

LAWRENCE, T.E. *The Mint.* Garden City: Doubleday 1955, 1st American edition, limited to 1,000 copies. $75–$125.

LAWRENCE, T.E. *See also* Golden Cockerel Press.

LAWSON, Robert. *Rabbit Hill.* New York: Viking 1944, 1st edition, illustrated by the author, DJ. $50.

LAWSON, Robert. *See also* "Key to Illustrators."

LE BLANC, Maurice. *Arsene Lupin, Gentleman Burglar*. New York: Ogilvie 1910, 1st American edition, DJ. $20.

LE CARRÉ, John. *A Small Town in Germany*. New York: Coward-McCann (1968), 1st American edition, DJ. $50–$75.

LE CARRE, John. *The Spy Who Came in from the Cold*. London: Gollancz 1963, 1st edition, DJ. $250–$350.

LE GALLIENNE, Richard. *The Religion of a Literary Man*. London: Elkin Mathews and John Lane 1893, with 15-page publisher's catalog, 1st edition. $32.50

LE GALLIENNE, Richard. *The Romance of Perfume*. New York and Paris: Richard Hudnut 1928, 1st edition, title page and 8 full-page ills by George Barbier, laid-in Hudnut pamphlet in rear pocket, printed by William Rudge on rag paper, glassine wrapper, slipcase. $85–$150.

LE GUIN, Ursula. *The Compass Rose*. New York: Harper and Row (1982), 1st trade edition, DJ. $15.

LE GUIN, Ursula. *The Dispossessed*. New York: Harper and Row (1974), 1st edition, winner of the 1974 Nebula and 1975 Hugo awards, DJ. $100.

LE GUIN, Ursula. *The Left Hand of Darkness*. New York: Walker (1969), 1st hardcover edition, winner of the 1969 Nebula and 1970 Hugo awards, DJ. $350.

LEA, Tom. *Bullfight Manual for Spectators*. Cuidad Juarez: Nourse (1949), color pictorial wrappers, 1st edition, scarce. $35.

LEA, Tom. *The Brave Bulls*. Boston: Little, Brown 1949, 1st edition, DJ. $40.

LEA, Tom. *The King Ranch*. Boston: Little, Brown (1957), 2 vols, 1st trade edition, 1st issue, with the word "For" absent in the 1st line on page 507 of Volume 2, maps and drawings by author, design and typography by Carl Herzog, boxed. $100–$200.

LEA, Tom. *Western Beef Cattle: A Series of Eleven Paintings by Tom Lea depicting the Origin and Development of the Western Range Animal*. (El Paso: The Encino Press 1967), one of 850 copies designed by William D. Wittliff at the Encino Press, slipcase. $75–$125.

LEACOCK, Stephen. *Funny Pieces*. New York: Dodd, Mead 1936, 1st edition, DJ. $25–$50.

LEACOCK, Stephen. *Moonbeams from the Larger Lunacy*. London: John Lane 1916, 1st edition. $20.

LEAF, Munro. *The Story of Ferdinand*. New York: Viking 1936 (Sept. 1936), 1st edition, illustrated by Robert Lawson, DJ. $100–$350.

LEAF, Munro. *Wee Gillis*. New York: Viking 1938, 1st edition, illustrated by Robert Lawson, DJ. $35–$50.

LEAR, Edward, completed by Ogden Nash. *The Scroobius Pup*. New York: Harper & Row (1968), quarto, paintings and drawings by Nancy Ekholm Burkert, DJ. $30–$40.

LEARY, Timothy. *High Priest*. New York: World/New American Library (1968), 1st edition, DJ. $35–$65.

LEAVES OF GRASS. Boston: Thayer & Eldridge 1860-61, by Walt Whitman, whose name does not appear, 3rd edition, pirated version, without printer's imprint, brown cloth stamped in gilt. $250–$400.

LEAVES OF GRASS. Camden: 1876, by Walt Whitman, whose name does not appear in the book, Author's Edition, cream-colored half calfskin, marbled board sides, brown leather label, two portraits, signed. $750–$1,500.

LEAVES OF GRASS. Washington: 1872, reprint of 1871 5th edition. Whitman's name appears in copyright notice or verso of title page. $150.

LEE, William (William S. Burroughs). *See* Vintage Paperbacks.

LEECH, John. *See* "Key to Illustrators."

LEHMANN, John. *New Writing in England*. New York: Critics Group Press 1939, pictorial wrappers, 1st edition, very scarce, never published in England. $45.

LEHMANN, Rosamond. *Dusty Answer*. New York: Henry Holt 1927, 1st American edition of author's first book, DJ. $50–$75.

LEHMANN, Rosamond. *Invitation to the Waltz*. New York: Henry Holt (1932), 1st American edition, DJ. $50.

LEHMANN, Rosamond. *The Ballad and the Source*. London: Collins 1944, 1st edition, DJ. $35.

LEIBER, Fritz. *Gather, Darkness!* New York: Pellegrini and Cudahy (1950), 1st edition, DJ. $65.

LEIBER, Fritz. *Night's Black Agents.* Sauk City; Arkham House 1947, 1st edition, 3,000 copies printed, DJ. $100.

LEIBER, Fritz. *Ship of Shadows.* London: Gollancz 1979, 1st edition, DJ. $25.

LEIGHTON, Clare. *Country Matters.* New York: Macmillan 1937, 1st edition, includes over 70 wood engravings by Leighton, DJ. $50.

LEIGHTON, Clare. *Four Hedges—A Gardener's Chronicle.* New York: Macmillan Co. 1935, 1st edition, 88 wood engravings by the author, quarto, DJ. $20–$45.

LEIGHTON, Clare. *Southern Harvest.* New York: Macmillan 1942, 1st edition, full-page engravings plus headpieces by the author, DJ. $30.

LEINSTER, Murray. *City on the Moon.* New York: Avalon Books (1957), 1st edition, DJ. $75.

LEINSTER, Murray. *Four from Planet Five.* London: White Lion (1974), 1st British and 1st hardcover edition, DJ. $45.

LEINSTER, Murray. *Sidewise in Time.* Chicago: Shasta 1950, 1st edition, DJ. $75–$100.

LEINSTER, Murray. *The Murder of the USA.* New York: Crown (1946), 1st edition, DJ. $85.

LEINSTER, Murray. *Time Tunnel.* London: Sidgwick & Jackson (1971), 1st British edition and 1st hardcover edition, DJ. $50–$75.

LENSKI, Lois. *Bound Girl of Cobble Hill.* New York: Stokes 1938, 1st edition, illustrated by the author, DJ. $35–$45.

LENSKI, Lois. *See also* "Key to Illustrators."

LEONARD, William Ellery. *A Son of Earth, Collected Poems.* New York: Viking 1928, 1st edition, limited to 350 numbered copies. $25–$35.

LERMONTOV, Michael. *The Demon: A Poem.* London: Trubner & Co. 1875, gilt pictorial cloth 1875, 1st edition in English. $100.

LEROUX, Gaston. *The Mystery of the Yellow Room.* New York: Brentano's 1908, 1st US edition. $50–$80.

LEROUX, Gaston. *The Phantom of the Opera.* New York: Grosset & Dunlap (1911), movie edition, 1st thus, with two double-page ills by André Castaigne and 4 photographs from the 1925 Lon Chaney movie, DJ, scarce in jacket. $35–$65.

LESBIAN AND GAY BOOKS. *See* "Key to Categories."

LESSING, Doris. *The Golden Notebook.* London: Michael Joseph (1962), 1st edition, DJ. $100–$200.

LESSING, Doris. *The Golden Notebook.* New York: Simon & Schuster 1962, 1st American edition, DJ. $50–$100.

LESSING, Doris. *The Grass is Singing.* London: Michael Joseph (1950), 1st edition of author's first book, DJ. $300.

LEVERTOV, Denise. *The Double Image.* London: Cresset Press 1946, 1st edition of author's first book, DJ. $150–$300.

LEVERTOV, Denise. *With Eyes at the Back of Our Heads.* (Norfolk): New Directions (1959), 1st edition, DJ. $75.

LEWIS, Alfred Henry. *The Apaches of New York.* New York: 1912, 1st edition, ills. $30.

LEWIS, Alfred Henry. *Wolfville Days.* New York: Frederick A. Stokes (1902), frontis by Frederic Remington. $40–$100.

LEWIS, C.S. *Dymer.* London: 1926, 1st edition of author's second book, cover decoration and title page by R.L. Knowles. $75–$125.

LEWIS, C.S. *Out of the Silent Planet.* London: John Lane, The Bodley Head 1938, 1st edition, DJ by Harold Jones. $250–$350.

LEWIS, C.S. *Prince Caspian—The Return to Narnia.* London: Geoffrey Bles (1951), 1st edition, DJ. $150–$200.

LEWIS, C.S. *The Abolition of Man.* London: 1943, 1st edition, wrappers, scarce. $40–$65.

LEWIS, C.S. *The Abolition of Man.* New York: Macmillan 1947, 1st American edition, DJ. $20–$40.

LEWIS, C.S. *The Case for Christianity.* New York: Macmillan 1944, DJ. $20–$40.

LEWIS, C.S. *The Great Divorce.* London: Geoffrey Bles, The Centenary Press (1945), 1st edition, DJ. $30–$90.

LEWIS, C.S. *The Hideous Strength, A Modern Fairy-Tale for Grown-ups.* London: John Lane, The Bodley Head 1945. $50.

LEWIS, C.S. *The Horse and His Boy.* London: Geoffrey Bles (1954), 1st edition, DJ. $100–$150.

LEWIS, C.S. *Till We Have Faces—A Myth Retold.* London: Geoffrey Bles 1956, 1st edition. $45–$65.

LEWIS, Oscar. *Sea Routes to the Gold Fields.* New York: Knopf 1949, 1st edition, ills, DJ. $20.

LEWIS, Oscar. *See also* The Book Club of California.

LEWIS, Sinclair. *Babbitt.* New York: Harcourt, Brace and Company (1922), 1st edition, 1st state, with "Purdy" for "Lyte" in line 4, page 49, DJ. $125–$450.

LEWIS, Sinclair. *Babbitt.* New York: Harcourt, Brace and Company (1922), 1st edition, 1st state, with "Purdy" for "Lyte" in line 4, page 49. $50.

LEWIS, Sinclair. *Dodsworth.* New York: Grosset & Dunlap (1929), reprint edition. $3.50–$5.

LEWIS, Sinclair. *Dodsworth.* New York: Grosset & Dunlap (1929), reprint edition, DJ. $8–$10.

LEWIS, Sinclair. *Main Street.* New York: Harcourt, Brace 1920, 1st edition, 1st issue. $30.

LEWIS, Sinclair. *The Man Who Knew Coolidge.* New York: Harcourt, Brace (1928), 1st edition, DJ. $150–$200.

LEWIS, Sinclair. *See also* Graham, Tom.

LEWIS, Wyndham. *America and Cosmic Man.* London: Nicholas and Watson (1948), 1st trade edition, DJ. $60.

LEWIS, Wyndham. *Doom of Youth.* London: 1932, 1st English edition, withdrawn from circulation after a libel suit was threatened by Alec Waugh, and after the sale of 549 copies, the balance being destroyed. $90–$175.

LEWIS, Wyndham. *The Apes of God.* Santa Barbara: Black Sparrow Press 1981, limited edition of 26 copies, hand-bound, acetate DJ. $50–$75.

LEWIS, Wyndham. *The Childermass. Section I.* London: Chatto & Windus 1928, 1st edition, scarce in DJ. (Only Section I was ever published.) $150.

LEWIS, Wyndham. *Time and Western Man.* London: Chatto and Windus 1927, 1st edition, DJ. $60–$125.

LEWIS, Wynham. *See also* "Key to Illustrators."

LEWISOHN, Ludwig. *The Case of Mr. Crump.* Paris: Edward W. Titus 1926, 1st edition, small quarto, original printed wrappers, limited to 500 copies for America, 2nd book printed by the Black Manikin Press. $50–$150.

LEWISOHN, Ludwig. *The Case of Mr. Crump.* Paris: Edward W. Titus 1931, new edition with preface by Thomas Mann, 1st edition thus, printed wrappers. $30–$50.

LIEBLING, A.J. *The Road Back to Paris.* Garden City: Doubleday, Doran 1944, 1st edition, DJ. $40–$65.

LIEBLING, A.J. *The Sweet Science.* New York: Viking 1956, 1st edition, DJ. $75.

LIEBLING, A.J. *The Telephone Booth Indian.* Garden City: Doubleday 1947, 1st edition, DJ. $150.

LIMITED EDITIONS CLUB. Baudelaire, Charles. *Flowers of Evil.* New York: Limited Editions Club 1940, lithographs by Jacob Epstein, slipcase. $85.

LIMITED EDITIONS CLUB. Bellamy, Edward. *Looking Backward.* New York: Limited Editions Club 1941, in slipcase. $75.

LIMITED EDITIONS CLUB. Benet, Stephen Vincent. *John Brown's Body.* New York: Limited Editions Club 1948, ills by John Stuart Curry, limited edition of 1,500 copies, in slipcase. $40–$60.

LIMITED EDITIONS CLUB. Bradbury, Ray. *The Martian Chronicles.* New York: Limited Editions Club 1974, illustrated by Joseph Mugnaini, one of 2,000 numbered copies signed by the author and the artist, tissue DJ and slipcase. $150–$200.

LIMITED EDITIONS CLUB. Browning, Robert. *The Ring and the Book.* New York: Limited Editions Club 1949, 2 vols, red morocco-backed boards, slipcase. $65–$85.

LIMITED EDITIONS CLUB. Cable, George W. *Old Creole Days.* New York: Limited Editions Club 1943. Slipcase. $75.

LIMITED EDITIONS CLUB. Carson, Rachel. *The Sea Around Us.* New York: Limited Editions Club 1980, photographs by Alfred Eisenstaedt, one of 2,000 numbered copies, signed by Eisenstaedt, glassine wrappers and slipcase. $75.

LIMITED EDITIONS CLUB. Colette (Sidonie-Gabrielle). *Break of Day.* New York: Limited Editions Club 1983, translated by Enid McLeod, illustrated by Francoise Gilot, blue silk cloth, slipcase. $100–$125.

LIMITED EDITIONS CLUB. Conrad, Joseph. *Heart of Darkness.*

New York: Limited Editions Club 1969, 1st edition thus, decorated boards, slipcase. $75.

LIMITED EDITIONS CLUB. Conrad, Joseph. *The Nigger of the Narcissus.* New York: Limited Editions Club 1965, in slipcase. $50–$75.

LIMITED EDITIONS CLUB. Crane, Stephen. *The Red Badge of Courage.* New York: Limited Editions Club 1944, illustrated, morocco, slipcase. $100–$150.

LIMITED EDITIONS CLUB. Doyle, Arthur Conan. *The Adventures of Sherlock Holmes.* New York: Limited Editions Club (1950), illustrated with a selection of the original ills, 3 vols, publisher's slipcase. $175.

LIMITED EDITIONS CLUB. Fitzgerald, F. Scott. *Tender is the Night.* New York: Limited Editions Club 1982, quarto, original lithograph and 8 reproductions of colored gouaches by Fred Meyer, one of 2,000 numbered copies signed by artist and Scribner, in slipcase. $125.

LIMITED EDITIONS CLUB. France, Anatole. *The Crime of Sylvestre Bonnard.* New York: Limited Editions Club 1937, translated by Lafcadio Hearn, illustrated by Sylvan Sauvage, one of 1,500 copies signed by the illustrator. $50.

LIMITED EDITIONS CLUB. Grahame, Kenneth. *The Wind in the Willows.* New York: Limited Editions Club 1940, edited by A.A. Milne, illustrated by Arthur Rackham with 16 full-page mounted color plates, cloth-backed boards, edition of 2,000 copies signed by designer Bruce Rogers, in slipcase. $450–$750.

LIMITED EDITIONS CLUB. Hudson, W.H. *Green Mansions.* New York: Limited Editions Club, Franklin Printing Co. 1935, cloth and boards, illustrated by E.A. Wilson, limited to 1,500 copies signed by illustrator, box. $30–$60.

LIMITED EDITIONS CLUB. Joyce, James. *Ulysses.* New York: Limited Editions Club 1935, quarto, illustrated by Matisse, designed by George Macy, one of 250 signed by author and artist out of a total edition of 1,500, 1st illustrated edition, slipcase. $2,500–$3,000.

LIMITED EDITIONS CLUB. Joyce, James. *Ulysses.* New York: Limited Editions Club 1935, quarto, brown cloth stamped in gold, illustrated by Matisse, designed by George Macy; this copy is one of a total edition of 1,500, 1st illustrated edition, slipcase. $1,500.

LIMITED EDITIONS CLUB. Lewis, Sinclair. *Main Street.* Chicago: Lakeside Press for Members of the Limited Editions Club 1937, illustrated by Grant Wood, one of 1,500 copies signed by the artist, box. $100–$250.

LINCOLN, Joseph C. *Cape Cod Ballads.* Trenton: Brandt 1902, 1st edition. $75.

LINCOLN, Joseph C. *Cape Cod Ballads.* New York: Appleton 1922. $50.

LINCOLN, Joseph C. *Cy Whittaker's Place.* New York: A.L. Burt (1908), reprint edition. $5–$8.

LINCOLN, Joseph C. *Cy Whittaker's Place.* New York: A.L. Burt (1908), reprint edition, DJ. $7–$10.

LINCOLN, Joseph C. *Cy Whittaker's Place.* New York: Appleton 1908, 1st edition. $18.

LINDBERGH, Anne Morrow. *North to the Orient.* New York: Harcourt, Brace 1935, 1st edition, DJ. $20–$35.

LINDBERGH, Anne Morrow. *The Unicorn and Other Poems.* New York: Pantheon 1936, 1st edition, DJ. $20–$35.

LINDBERGH, Charles. *The Spirit of St. Louis.* New York: Scribner's 1953, 1st trade edition, DJ. $50–$100.

LINDBERGH, Charles. *We.* New York: Putnam 1927, 1st edition, limited edition of 1,000 copies in Japan vellum over tan boards, signed by author and publishers, slipcase, scarce. $500–$850.

LINDBERG, Charles. *We.* New York: Putnam 1927, 1st trade edition of author's first book, frontis portrait. $15–$30.

LINDBERG, Charles. *We.* New York: Putnam 1927, 1st trade edition of author's first book, frontis portrait, DJ. $75–$100.

LINDSAY, Vachel. *General William Booth Enters into Heaven and Other Poems.* New York: Mitchell Kennerly 1913, 1st edition of author's first regularly published book. $45–$100.

LINDSAY, Vachel. *The Chinese Nightingale and Other Poems.* New York: 1916, 1st edition. $25–$75.

LINDSAY, Vachel. *The Congo and Other Poems.* New York: Macmillan 1914, 1st edition. $25–$65.

LIPPMAN, Walter. *A Preface to Morals.* New York: 1929, 1st edition, DJ. $20–$35.

LITERATURE and ON LITERATURE. *See* "Key to Categories."

LITTLE BLACK SAMBO. Racine: Whitman (1953), square-ish 16mo, author not credited but, this is a close paraphrase of her text. Sambo is portrayed as an East Indian, pictorial paper-covered boards, color ills throughout. $8–$15.

LITTLE BLACK SAMBO. See also Bannerman, Helen.

LITTLE ENGINE THAT COULD, THE. See Piper, Watty.

LITTLE LORD FAUNTLEROY. See Burnett, Frances Hodgson.

LITTLE ORPHAN ANNIE. See Big Little Books.

LITTLE PRINCE, THE. See Saint-Exupery, Antoine de.

LLEWELLYN, Richard. *How Green was My Valley.* London: Michael Joseph (1939), 1st English edition of author's first book, DJ. $65–$100.

LLEWELLYN, Richard. *How Green was My Valley.* New York: Macmillan 1940, 1st American edition of author's first book, DJ. $35–$50.

LLEWELLYN, Richard. *None but the Lonely Heart.* New York: Macmillan 1943, 1st American edition, DJ. $25.

LOCKRIDGE, Ross. *Raintree County.* Boston: Houghton, Mifflin 1948, 1st edition, DJ. $50–$125.

LOFTING, Hugh. *Doctor Dolittle in the Moon.* New York: Stokes (1928), 1st edition, illustrated by the author in color and black and white, DJ. $75–$125.

LOFTING, Hugh. *Doctor Dolittle's Zoo.* New York: Stokes (1925), later printing, illustrated by the author in color and black and white. $20.

LOMAX, Bliss. *Pardners of the Badlands.* New York: Doubleday, Doran "1942", 1st edition, DJ. $15–$40.

LOMAX, John. *Songs of the Cattle Trail and Cow Camp.* New York: Macmillan 1919, 1st edition. $35–$50.

LONDON, Charmian. *Our Hawaii.* New York: Macmillan 1917, 1st edition. $100–$125.

LONDON, Jack. *Before Adam*. New York: Macmillan 1907, numerous ills by Charles Livingston Bull, 1st edition. $60–$80.

LONDON, Jack. *Burning Daylight*. (np): The Daily Worker (1919), 1st thus. $25–$50.

LONDON, Jack. *Burning Daylight*. New York: Macmillan 1910, 1st edition, 1st printing, with 1 blank leaf rather than 3 following text, and with "Published October, 1910" on copyright page, the latter point shared with the 2nd printing. $125–$225.

LONDON, Jack. *Jerry of the Islands*. New York: Macmillan 1917 1st edition, color frontis. $100–$150.

LONDON, Jack. *Martin Eden*. New York: Macmillan 1909, 1st published edition, 1st printing, DJ. $2,000.

LONDON, Jack. *Martin Eden:* New York: Macmillan 1909, 1st published edition, 1st printing. $150–$250.

LONDON, Jack. *Smoke Bellew*. New York: Century 1912, 1st edition, frontis and 7 plates by P.J. Monahan. $125–$200.

LONDON, Jack. *Tales of the Fish Patrol*. New York: Macmillan 1905, 1st edition. $75–$250.

LONDON, Jack. *The Abysmal Brute*. New York: Century 1913, 1st edition, 1st issue with "Published May, 1913" on copyright page and in olive green cloth stamped with black and yellow, frontis by Gordon Grant. $120–$160.

LONDON, Jack. *The Abysmal Brute*. New York: Century 1913, 1st edition, 1st issue with "Published May, 1913" on copyright page and in olive green cloth stamped with black and yellow, frontis by Gordon Grant, DJ which is lightly chipped at extremities. $650–$1,000.

LONDON, Jack. *The Call of the Wild*. London: Heinemann 1903, 1st English edition, identical with the 1st American edition except for binding and title page. $125–$250.

LONDON, Jack. *The Call of the Wild*. New York: Grosset and Dunlap (1903), DJ. $35–$75.

LONDON, Jack. *The Call of the Wild*. New York: Macmillan 1903, 1st edition, 1st binding of vertical ribbed cloth, illustrated by Charles Livingston Bull and Philip R. Goodwin, and decorations by Charles Edward Hopper, DJ. $1,000–$2,000.

LONDON, Jack. *The Call of the Wild.* New York: Macmillan 1903, 1st edition, 1st binding of vertical ribbed cloth, illustrated by Charles Livingston Bull and Philip R. Goodwin, and decorations by Hopper. $150–$300.

LONDON, Jack. *The God of his Fathers and Other Stories.* New York: McClure 1901, 1st edition of author's scarce second book. $200–$350.

LONDON, Jack. *The God of his Fathers.* London. 1902, 1st British edition of London's scarce second book. $150.

LONDON, Jack. *The God of his Fathers.* New York. McClure 1901, 1st edition of London's scarce second book, ex-library book with letter painted on spine, library marks within, bright and clean copy. $20–$35.

LONDON, Jack. *The House of Pride.* New York: Macmillan 1912, 1st issue. $175–$275.

LONDON, Jack. *The People of the Abyss.* New York: Macmillan 1903, 1st edition. $150–$450.

LONDON, Jack. *The Sea-Wolf.* New York: Grosset and Dunlap (1930), movie edition with 4 photos, DJ. $20–$75.

LONDON, Jack. *The Son of the Wolf.* New York: Grosset & Dunlap (1900), reprint edition, frontis ill. $12.

LONDON, Jack. *The Son of the Wolf.* New York: Grosset & Dunlap (1900), reprint edition, frontis ill, DJ. $20–$35.

LONDON, Jack. *White Fang.* New York: Macmillan 1906, 1st edition. $150.

LONDON, Jack. *See also* Big Little Books.

LONE RANGER. See Big Little Books.

LONGFELLOW, H.W. *The Golden Legend.* Boston: Ticknor, Reed and Fields 1851, by Henry Wadsworth Longfellow, 1st edition, 1st issue, original cloth. $200.

LONGFELLOW, H.W. *The Song of Hiawatha.* Boston: Ticknor and Fields 1855, by Henry Wadsworth Longfellow, 1st American edition, 1st issue, with "dove" on page 96, line 7, rather than "dived," and 12 pages of ads dated October 1855, original brown cloth. $300.

LONGSTREET, Stephen. *Decade 1929-1939.* New York: Random House (1940), 1st edition, author's first novel, DJ. $65.

LONGSTRETH, T. Morris. *The Silent Force.* New York and London: Century (1927), 1st edition. $35.

LOOS, Anita. *But Gentlemen Marry Brunettes.* New York: Boni & Liveright 1928, illustrated by Ralph Barton, 1st edition, DJ. $75–$100.

LOOS, Anita. *Gentlemen Prefer Blondes.* New York: Boni & Liveright 1925, illustrated by Ralph Barton, 1st edition, 1st issue with "divine" on contents leaf, DJ. $75–$100.

LOPEZ, Barry. *Crossing Open Ground.* New York: Scribner's (1988), 1st edition, DJ. $20.

LOPEZ, Barry. *Crow and Weasel.* San Francisco: North Point Press 1990, 1st edition, illustrated, 1st issue with gold stamping on front cover, DJ. $20–$45.

LORCA, Federico García. *Lament for the Death of a Bullfighter.* New York: Oxford University Press (1937), 1st edition, DJ. $45.

LORCA, Federico García. *Poems.* English translation by Stephen Spender and J.L. Gill. London: Dolphin 1939, 1st edition, DJ. $75.

LORCA, Federico García. *Three Tragedies.* (New York): New Directions (1947), 1st edition, DJ. $50.

LORD, Walter. *A Night to Remember.* New York: Holt (1955), 1st edition, illustrated with photographs, DJ. $12–$20.

LORDE, Audre. *Cool.* New York: Norton (1976), 1st edition, DJ. $25–$50.

LOUYS, Pierre. *The Collected Tales of.* New York: 1930, color and black and white ills by John Austen. $35.

LOUYS, Pierre. *The Songs of Bilitis.* New York: 1926, privately printed by Macy-Masius, 1st edition, illustrated throughout by Willy Pogany including colored pictorial ep's. $65–$100.

LOVECRAFT, Howard. *Something About Cats.* Sauk City: Arkham House 1949, 1st edition, one of 2,995 copies, DJ. $75–$200.

LOVECRAFT, Howard. *The Lurker at the Threshold.* Sauk City: Arkham House 1945, 1st edition, one of 3,041 copies, DJ. $100–$125.

LOVECRAFT, Howard. *The Shunned House.* Athol: W. Paul Cook, The Recluse Press 1928, 1st edition of author's first book of fiction, one of 300 copies, bound in crushed levant by Sangorski and Sutcliffe. $1,200–$1,500.

LOVECRAFT, Howard. *The Shuttered Room and Other Pieces.* Sauk City: Arkham House 1959, one of 2,527 copies, DJ. $75–$150.

LOWELL, Amy. *East Wind.* Boston: Houghton Mifflin 1926, 1st edition, DJ. $45.

LOWELL, Amy. *John Keats.* Boston: Riverside Press 1925, 1st edition, 2 vols, DJs, boxed. $45–$85.

LOWELL, Robert. *For the Union Dead.* New York: Farrar, Straus (1964), 1st edition, DJ. $75–$100.

LOWELL, Robert. *Life Studies.* London: Faber (1959), 1st edition, precedes American edition, DJ. $125–$200.

LOWELL, Robert. *Life Studies.* New York: Farrar, Straus (1959), 1st American edition, DJ. $75–$125.

LOWELL, Robert. *Lord Weary's Castle.* New York: Harcourt, Brace (1946), 1st edition of author's second book, DJ, scarce. $150–$300.

LOWELL, Robert. *The Mills of the Kavanaughs.* New York: Harcourt, Brace (1951), 1st edition, DJ. $150–$200.

LOWRY, Malcom. *Under the Volcano.* New York: Reynal and Hitchcock (1947), 1st edition, DJ. $500–$750.

LOWRY, Malcom. *Under the Volcano.* New York: Reynal and Hitchcock (1947), 1st edition, worn DJ. $165–$350.

LOWRY, Malcom. *Casualty.* New York: New Directions 1946, 1st edition of author's first published book, DJ. $25–$40.

LUHAN, Mabel Dodge. *Edge of the Taos Desert.* New York: (1937), includes 16 pages of halftones, 1st edition, DJ. $55.

LUHAN, Mabel Dodge. *Movers and Shakers.* New York: (1936), 16 photographs, 1st edition, DJ. $35.

LUHAN, Mabel Dodge. *Taos and its Artists.* New York: Duell, Sloan & Pearce 1947, illustrated, 1st edition, DJ. $85.

LUTES, Della T. *Millbrook.* Boston: Little, Brown 1938, illustrated by Edward Shenton, 1st edition, DJ. $35.

LYTLE, Andrew. *A Name for Evil.* Indianapolis: Bobbs-Merrill (1947), 1st edition, DJ, scarce. $125–$175.

◈ **M** ──────────────────────────────────

MABINOGION, THE. See Golden Cockerel Press.

MACAULAY, Rose. *And No Man's Wit.* London: 1940, 1st edition, DJ. $35.

MACDIARMID, Hugh. *Sangschaw.* Edinburgh: William Blackwood 1925. ("Hugh McDiarmid" is Christopher Murray Grieve.) 1st edition of author's first book, original blue cloth, scarce. $200.

MACDONALD, Betty. *The Plague and I.* Philadelphia: Lippincott 1948, 1st edition, DJ. $15–$35.

MACDONALD, George. *At the Back of the North Wind.* Philadelphia: McKay 1919, 1st edition, color plates by Jessie Wilcox Smith. $85–$100.

MACDONALD, George. *The Princess and Curdie.* New York: Macmillan 1927, 1st edition, illustrated by Dorothy Lathrop, DJ. $75–$100.

MACDONALD, John D. *Cinnamon Skin.* New York: Harper & Row (1982), 1st edition, DJ. $20.

MACDONALD, John D. *The Empty Copper Sea.* Philadelphia: Lippincott (1978), 1st edition, DJ. $25.

MACDONALD, John D. *The Ivory Grin.* New York: Knopf 1952, 1st edition, DJ. $100–$125.

MACDONALD, John Ross. *The Way Some People Die* (by Kenneth Millar). New York: Knopf 1951, 1st edition, DJ. $200–$400.

MACDONALD, Ross. *Archer in Jeopardy* (by Kenneth Millar). New York: Knopf 1979, three novels: *The Doomsters, The Zebra-Striped Hearse, The Instant Enemy,* with a foreword by the author, 1st edition of this collection. $45.

MACDONALD, Ross. *The Blue Hammer.* New York: Knopf 1976, 1st edition, DJ. $25.

MACDONALD, Ross. *The Chill.* New York: Knopf 1964, 1st edition, DJ. $75–$125.

MACDONALD, Ross. *The Underground Man.* New York: Knopf 1971, 1st edition, DJ. $35.

MACDONALD, Ross. *The Zebra-Striped Hearse*. New York: Knopf 1962, 1st edition, DJ. $75–$125.

MACFALL, Haldane. *Aubrey Beardsley: The Man and His Work*. London: John Lane, Bodley Head 1928, 1st trade edition, portrait, 12 ills. $50–$150.

MACFALL, Haldane. *The Book of Lovat*. London: J.M. Dent & Sons 1923, illustrated by Claude Lovat Fraser with 8 full-page color plates, 13 halftones, and numerous decorations in text, 1st trade edition, DJ. $50–$125.

MACHEN, Arthur. *Dreads and Drolls*. London: 1926, 1st trade edition. $25.

MACHEN, Arthur. *The Great God Pan and the Inmost Light*. London: John Lane 1894, 1st edition, title page vignette and pictorial cloth by Aubrey Beardsley. $75–$125.

MACHEN, Arthur. *The Terror: A Fantasy*. London: Duckworth (1917), 1st edition, slightly defective DJ. $50–$150.

MACKENZIE, Compton. *Kensington Rhymes*. London: 1912, 1st edition of author's first book for children, 8 color plates and many black and white drawings by J.R. Monsell, worn DJ. $50–$100.

MACKENZIE, Compton. *Poems*. Oxford and London: B.H. Blackwell 1907, 1st edition of author's first book, gray wraps. $125–$175.

MACKENZIE, Compton. *The Vital Flame*. London: 1947, 1st edition, DJ. $35–$50.

MACLEISH, Archibald. *America was Promises*. New York: Duell, Sloan & Pearce, Inc. (1939), 1st edition, DJ. $20–$25.

MACLEISH, Archibald. *Frescoes for Mr. Rockefeller's City*. New York: John Day 1933, in stiff printed wrappers, 1st edition, uncommon. $25–$60.

MACLEISH, Archibald. *Nobodaddy*. Cambridge: Dunster House 1926, 1st edition, one of 750 copies, title page design by Dwiggins, issued without DW. $45–$75.

MACMANUS, Blanche. *See* "Key to Illustrators."

MACNEICE, Louis. *Poems*. London: 1935, 1st edition, in torn DJ. $75–$100.

MACY, George. *See* "Key to Illustrators."

MADELINE. See Bemelmans, Ludwig.

MAETERLINCK, Maurice. *The Blue Bird.* New York: Dodd, Mead 1911, quarto, 25 tipped-in color plates by F. Robinson, 1st US deluxe illustrated edition. $50–$85.

MAETERLINCK, Maurice. *The Life of the Bee.* New York: Dodd, Mead 1912, 1st American edition, thick quarto, gilt pictorial cover and 13 tipped-in color plates by Edmund Detmold. $85–$125.

MAGEE, David. *Infinite Riches: Adventures of a Rare Book Dealer.* New York: Eriksson (1973), 1st edition, DJ. $50.

MAHAN, A.T. Captain. *The Influence of Sea Power Upon History.* London: Sampson Low, 1890, 1st edition, maps and plans. $70.

MAHAN, A.T. Captain. *The Life of Nelson; The Embodiment of the Sea Power of Great Britain.* London: Sampson, Low Marston & Co. 1899, 2nd edition, revised, 21 maps and battle plans, handsome cover. $35.

MAILER, Norman. *Advertisements for Myself.* New York: Putnam's (1959), 1st edition, DJ. $25–$40.

MAILER, Norman. *Barbary Shore.* New York: Rinehart (1951), 1st edition of author's second novel, DJ. $50–$125.

MAILER, Norman. *Marilyn.* (New York: Grosset and Dunlap 1973), 1st trade edition, DJ. $30–$50.

MAILER, Norman. *The Naked and the Dead.* New York: Rinehart (1948), 1st edition of author's first book, DJ. $100–$200.

MAILER, Norman. *The Naked and the Dead.* New York: Rinehart (1948), later printing, without the Rinehart monogram on the copyright page, slightly chipped DJ. $25–$35.

MAILER, Norman. *The White Negro.* San Francisco: City Lights Books 1957, issued in wraps only, later issue of the first separate edition, with a .75 rather than the earlier .35 cover price; originally appeared in "Dissent" (Little Magazine). $15–$25.

MALAMUD, Bernard. *The Assistant.* New York: Farrar, Straus and Cudahy (1957), 1st edition, DJ. $65–$150.

MALAMUD, Bernard. *The Natural.* New York: Harcourt, Brace (1952), 1st edition, 1st issue of author's first book, with 1st issue blue cloth binding, DJ. $100–$300.

MALCOLMSON, Anne. *Yankee Doodle's Cousins*. Boston: Houghton, Mifflin (1941), illustrated by Robert McCloskey, later printing. $10–$20.

MALRAUX, Andre'. *Man's Hope*. New York: Random House (1938), 1st American edition, DJ. $30–$50.

MALRAUX, Andre'. *The Psychology of Art*. London: A. Zwemmer 1949 and Pantheon 1950, 3 vols, quarto, 400 ills including many color plates, DJs. $125–$250.

MANDRAKE THE MAGICIAN. See Big Little Books.

MANN, Erika. *A Gang of Ten*. New York: L.B. Fischer (1942), 1st American edition. $35.

MANN, Thomas. *Buddenbrooks*. Berlin: Verfall einer Familie 1901, 1st edition of author's first book, 2 vols, rare. $5,000.

MANN, Thomas. *Buddenbrooks*. New York: Knopf 1924, 2 vols, 1st American edition. $30–$50.

MANN, Thomas. *Buddenbrooks*. New York: Knopf 1924, 2 vols, 1st American edition, DJs. $100–$150.

MANN, Thomas. *Joseph in Egypt*. New York: Knopf 1938, 2 vols, 1st American edition, in moderately worn slipcase. $25–$50.

MANNING, David. *Bandit's Honor*. New York: Chelsea House "1927", 1st edition, DJ. $20–$50.

MANSFIELD, Katherine. *In a German Pension*. New York: Knopf 1926, 1st American edition of author's first book, which had been suppressed during her lifetime, DJ. $75–$100.

MANSFIELD, Katherine. *Journal of Katherine Mansfield*. New York: Knopf 1927, 1st American edition. $100.

MANSFIELD, Katherine. *The Garden Party and Other Stories*. London: Constable (1922), 1st trade edition. $25–$65.

MARANDE, H. *See* "Key to Illustrators."

MARKHAM, Edwin. *The Man with the Hoe and Other Poems*. New York: McClure, Phillips and Co. 1902, later printing. $15.

MARKHAM, Edwin. *The Man with the Hoe and Other Poems*. New York: Doubleday, Doran and McClure 1899, 1st edition, 1st issue, with "fruitless" for "milkless" on page 35. $75–$150.

MARKHAM, Edwin. *The Man with the Hoe*. San Francisco: Robertson 1899, 1st book edition, wraps. $300–$400.

MARQUAND, John P. *Lord Timothy Dexter of Newburyport, Mass.* New York: Minton, Balch 1925, 1st edition, DJ. $75–$150.

MARQUAND, John P. *Mr. Moto is So Sorry.* Boston: Little, Brown 1938, 1st edition, DJ. $200.

MARQUAND, John P. *The Late George Apley.* Boston: Little, Brown 1937, 1st edition, 1st printing, with "Pretty Pearl" on page 19, line 1, DJ. $100–$150.

MARQUEZ, Gabriel Garcia. *See* Garcia Marquez, Gabriel.

MARQUIS, Don. *Archy's Life of Mehitable.* Garden City: Doubleday, Doran 1933, 1st edition, DJ. $35–$90.

MARSHALL, S.L.A. *Bastogne.* Washington: Infantry Journal Press "1946". $35–$45.

MARSHALL, S.L.A. *Night Drop.* Boston: Atlantic-Little, Brown "1962". $25–$40.

MARX, Groucho. *Beds.* New York: Farrar & Rinehart (1930), 1st edition, 4 black and white photos, in paper boards with colored photograph on cover. $100–$150.

MARY FRANCIS. See Fryer, Jane Eayre.

MARY POPPINS. See Travers, P.L.

MASEFIELD, John. *Salt Water Ballads.* London: Grant Richards 1902, 1st edition and rare 1st issue of author's first book, with Richards imprint on title page and error in "Sea Fever." $200–$400.

MASEFIELD, John. *Selected Poems.* New York: Macmillan 1923, 1st American edition, DJ. $25.

MASEREEL, Frans. *My Book of Hours. 167 Designs Engraved on Wood.* Foreword by Romain Rolland, privately printed 1922, limited edition of 600 signed and numbered copies, tissue DJ. $250–$350.

MASEREEL, Frans. *Passionate Journey. A Novel in 165 woodcuts.* New York: (1948), introduction by Thomas Mann, 1st American editions, both book and DJ with a few rather minor flaws. $30.

MASTERS, Edgar Lee. *Spoon River Anthology.* New York: Macmillan 1915, 1st edition, 1st issue, measuring 7/8" across top of covers. $225–$325.

MATHESON, Richard. *Born of Man and Woman*. Philadelphia: The Chamberlain Press, Inc. 1954, 1st edition of author's first book published in hardcover, scarce, DJ. $125–$200.

MATHESON, Richard. *The Beardless Warriors*. Boston: Little, Brown (1960), 1st edition, DJ. $50–$100.

MATHESON, Richard. *See also* Vintage Paperbacks.

MATISSE, Henri. *See* "Key to Illustrators."

MATTHEWS, William F. *See* Grolier Club.

MATTHIESSEN, Peter. *At Play in the Fields of the Lord*. New York: Random House (1965), 1st edition, DJ. $100.

MATTHIESSEN, Peter. *In the Spirit of Crazy Horse*. New York: Viking (1983), 1st edition, DJ; scarce because of political and legal implications and complications; publisher recalled book. $75–$150.

MAUGHAM, Somerset. *Cakes and Ale, or the Skeleton in the Cupboard*. Garden City: Doubleday, Doran 1930, 1st American edition, DJ. $50–$100.

MAUGHAM, Somerset. *The Moon and Sixpence, A Novel*. London: Heinemann 1919, 1st edition, later state of ads, with 7 (not 6) Phillpott titles. $150–$250.

MAUGHAM, Somerset. *The Razor's Edge*. London: Heinemann (1944), 1st English edition, DJ. $25–$100.

MAUGHAM, Somerset. *The Razor's Edge*. New York: Doubleday, Doran 1944, 1st edition, limited to 750 copies numbered and signed by Maugham, in slipcase, issued without DJ. $100–$300.

MAUGHAM, Somerset. *The Razor's Edge*. New York: Doubleday, Doran 1944, 1st trade edition, DJ. $25–$50.

MAULDIN, Bill. *Back Home*. New York: William Sloane (1947), jacket designed by Oscar Ogg, text and cartoons by the author, 1st edition, DJ. $35–$50.

MAULDIN, Bill. *Mud, Mules and Mountains*. Italy: The Stars & Stripes "1944", 2-color, stapled wrappers, scarce. $50–$60.

MAULDIN, Bill. *This Damn Tree Leaks. A Collection of War Cartoons*. Italy: The Stars and Stripes Mediterranean 1945, 1st edition, wrappers. $25.

MAURIAC, Francois. *Therese.* New York: Henry Holt (1947), 1st American edition, DJ. $30.

MAUROIS, Andre'. *The Silence of Colonel Bramble.* New York: 1920, 1st American edition of author's first book to be published in English. $50–$100.

MAXWELL, Donald. *See* "Key to Illustrators."

MAYO, Wm. (MD) and Charles (MD). *Collection of Papers Published Previous to 1909.* Philadelphia and London: Saunders 1912, 1st edition, 2 vols, plates. $65.

MCALMON, Robert. *Being Geniuses Together.* London: Secker & Warburg (1938), 1st edition, very scarce. $350–$550.

MCALMON, Robert. *Being Geniuses Together.* London: Secker & Warburg (1938), 1st edition, very scarce, DJ. $750–$1,000.

MCCAFFREY, Anne. *Moreta: Dragonlady of Pern.* (London): Severn House (1983), 1st edition, 1984 Hugo nominee, DJ. $15–$25.

MCCAFFREY, Anne. *Moreta: Dragonlady of Pern.* New York: Ballantine Books (1983), 1st edition, 1984 Hugo nominee, DJ. $10–$20.

MCCAFFREY, Anne. *The Ship who Sang.* (London): Rapp & Whiting/Andre' Deutsch (1971), 1st British edition (published first in the US), DJ. $45–$55.

MCCAFFREY, Anne. *The Ship who Sang.* New York: Walker (1969), 1st edition, precedes the British, includes "Dramatic Mission," nominee for both Nebula and Hugo awards, DJ. $200–$275.

MCCAFFREY, Anne. *To Ride Pegasus.* London: Dent (1974), 1st British edition and 1st hardcover edition, DJ. $75–$100.

MCCAFFREY, Anne. *To Ride Pegasus.* New York: Ballantine Books (1990), 1st US hardcover edition, DJ. $10–$15.

MCCARTHY, Mary. *Cast a Cold Eye.* New York: Harcourt, Brace (1950), 1st edition, DJ. $35–$85.

MCCARTHY, Mary. *Memories of a Catholic Girlhood.* New York: Harcourt, Brace (1957), 1st edition, DJ. $35–$50.

MCCARTHY, Mary. *The Company She Keeps.* New York: Simon & Schuster 1942, 1st edition of author's first book written under her own name, DJ. $100–$200.

MCCARTHY, Mary. *The Groves of Academe.* New York: Harcourt, Brace 1951, 1st edition, DJ. $35–$85.

MCCAUSLAND, Elizabeth. *See* Abbott, Berenice.

MCCLURE, Michael. *The Cherub.* Santa Rosa, CA: Black Sparrow Press 1970, quarto, one of 250 numbered and signed copies, acetate DJ. $40.

MCCOY, Horace. *Kiss Tomorrow Good-Bye.* New York: Random House 1948, 1st edition, DJ. $35–$50.

MCCOY, Horace. *They Shoot Horses, Don't They?* New York: Simon & Schuster 1935, 1st edition of author's first book, DJ. $150–$250.

MCCOY, Horace. *They Shoot Horses, Don't They?* New York: Simon & Schuster 1935, 1st edition of author's first book. $40.

MCCRAE, John. *In Flanders Fields and Other Poems.* New York: 1919, 1st edition, in scarce DJ. $50–$75.

MCCRAE, John. *In Flanders Fields and Other Poems.* New York: 1919, 1st edition. $20–$35.

MCCULLERS, Carson. *Reflections in a Golden Eye.* (New York: New Directions 1950), 1st New Directions edition, worn DJ. $20.

MCCULLERS, Carson. *Reflections in a Golden Eye.* Cambridge: Houghton, Mifflin 1941, 1st edition of author's second book, DJ. $125–$225.

MCCULLERS, Carson. *The Ballad of the Sad Café.* Boston: Houghton, Mifflin 1951, 1st edition, DJ. $75–$125.

MCCULLERS, Carson. *The Heart is a Lonely Hunter.* Boston: Houghton, Mifflin 1940, 1st edition of author's first book, DJ. $150–$300.

MCCULLERS, Carson. *The Heart is a Lonely Hunter.* Boston: Houghton, Mifflin 1940, 1st edition of author's first book, ragged DJ. $50–$200.

MCCULLERS, Carson. *The Member of the Wedding.* Boston: Houghton, Mifflin 1946, 1st edition of author's third book, DJ. $100–$150.

MCCULLEY, Johnston. *Mark of Zorro.* New York: 1924, 1st edition, DJ. $50–$100.

MCCUTCHEON, George Barr. *Brewster's Millions*. New York: Grosset & Dunlap (1902), reprint edition, black and white ills. $3.50–$8.

MCCUTCHEON, George Barr. *Brewster's Millions*. New York: Grosset & Dunlap (1902), reprint edition, black and white ills, DJ. $8–$12.

MCCUTCHEON, George Barr. *Graustark, the Story of a Love behind a Throne*. Chicago: Herbert S. Stone 1901, 1st edition of author's first book. $45–$60.

MCELROY, Joseph. *A Smuggler's Bible*. New York: Harcourt, Brace and World, Inc. (1966), 1st edition of author's first book, DJ. $75–$125.

MCFEE, William. *Casuals of the Sea*. London: Secker & Warburg 1916, 1st edition. $50.

MCGRATH, Harold. *The Carpet from Bagdad*. Indianapolis: Bobbs-Merrill 1911, 1st edition, full-color, full-page ills by André Castaigne, DJ. $20–$40.

MCGRATH, Thomas. *Movie at the End of the World*. Chicago: Allen Swallow 1980, 1st edition, wraps. $10.

MCKAY, Claude. *Banana Bottom*. New York: Harper 1933, 1st edition, very scarce, somewhat worn and soiled DJ. $300–$400.

MCKAY, Claude. *Banjo*. New York: Harper & Brothers 1929, 1st edition, DJ. $100–$225.

MCKAY, Claude. *Banjo*. New York: Harper & Brothers 1929, 1st edition. $25–$60.

MCKAY, Claude. *Harlem Shadows: The Poems of Claude McKay*. New York: Harcourt, Brace (1922), 1st edition, DJ. $275–$450.

MCKAY, Claude. *Harlem Shadows: The Poems of Claude McKay*. New York: Harcourt, Brace (1922), 1st edition. $40–$75.

MCKAY, Claude. *Selected Poems of Claude McKay*. New York: Bookmen Associates 1953, 1st edition, introduction by John Dewey, autobiographical note by Max Eastman, posthumous but mainly collected by Claude McKay before his death in 1948, DJ. $25–$45.

MCKAY, Claude. *Spring in New Hampshire and Other Poems*. London: Grant Richards 1920, true 1st edition, published before the American, tan paper wraps, frontis is photograph of author. $200–$300.

MCKENNEY, Ruth. *My Sister Eileen.* New York: Harcourt, Brace (1938), 1st edition, DJ. $35–$50.

MCMURTRY, Larry. *All My Friends are Going to be Strangers.* New York: Simon & Schuster (1972), 1st edition, DJ. $50–$75.

MCMURTRY, Larry. *Horseman, Pass By.* New York: Harper (1961), 1st edition of author's first book, DJ. $200–$600.

MCMURTRY, Larry. *Horseman, Pass By.* New York: Harper (1961), 1st edition of author's first book. $25–$50.

MCMURTRY, Larry. *Leaving Cheyenne.* New York: Harper & Row (1963), 1st edition of author's second book, DJ. $125–$300.

MCMURTRY, Larry. *Lonesome Dove.* New York: Simon & Schuster (1985), 1st edition, DJ. $50–$150.

MCMURTRY, Larry. *The Last Picture Show.* New York: Dial 1966, 1st edition, DJ. $65–$150.

MCMURTRY, Larry. *Moving On.* New York: Simon & Schuster (1970), 1st edition, DJ. $50–$135.

MCMURTRY, Larry. *Terms of Endearment.* New York: Simon & Schuster (1975), 1st edition, DJ. $50–$100.

MCMURTRY, Larry. *The Desert Rose.* New York: Simon & Schuster 1983, 1st edition, DJ. $30.

MCPHEE, John. *A Room Full of Hovings.* New York: Farrar, Straus & Giroux (1968), 1st edition, DJ. $45–$65.

MCPHEE, John. *A Sense of Where You Are.* New York: Farrar, Straus & Giroux (1965), 1st edition of author's first book, DJ. $100–$200.

MCPHEE, John. *Basin and Range.* New York: Farrar, Straus & Giroux (1981), 1st edition, DJ. $25.

MCPHEE, John. *Encounters with the Archidruid.* New York: Farrar, Straus & Giroux (1971), 1st edition, DJ. $35–$55.

MCPHEE, John. *Oranges.* New York: Farrar, Straus 1967, 1st edition, DJ. $45–$65.

MCPHEE, John. *The Curve of Binding Energy.* New York: Farrar, Straus & Giroux (1974), 1st edition, DJ. $35–$45.

MCPHEE, John. *The Deltoid Pumpkin Seed.* New York: Farrar, Straus & Giroux (1973), 1st edition, DJ. $35–$45.

MCPHEE, John. *The Headmaster.* New York: Farrar, Straus & Giroux (1966), 1st edition, DJ. $50–$75.

MELVILLE, Herman. *Moby Dick.* New York: Random House (1930), illustrated by Rockwell Kent, DJ. $60–$80.

MELVILLE, Herman. *Moby Dick.* New York: Random House (1930), illustrated by Rockwell Kent. $20–$35.

MELVILLE, Herman. *Moby Dick; or, The Whale.* New York: Harper & Brothers 1851, 1st American edition, original cloth. *Moby Dick* was published first in England, in a 3-vol edition, as *The Whale* (see entry). $7,000–$20,000.

MELVILLE, Herman. *Omoo: A Narrative of Adventures in the South Seas.* New York: Harper and Brothers 1847, 1st American edition, original cloth with gilt-stamped ship on front cover. (First printed in England.) $1,500–$2,000.

MELVILLE, Herman. *The Whale.* London: Richard Bentley 1851, 1st edition, 3 vols. The first publication of *Moby Dick*, in the original half-cloth. $75,000–$90,000.

MELVILLE, Herman. *See also* Grabhorn Printing.

MENCKEN, H.L. *Prejudices. Sixth Series.* New York: Knopf (1927), 1st trade edition, DJ. $50–$125.

MENCKEN, H.L. *Prejudices. Third Series.* New York: Knopf (1922), 1st trade edition. $15–$50.

MENCKEN, H.L. *The American Language.* New York: Knopf 1937, 4th edition, corrected, enlarged, and rewritten; his final version, followed by 2 supplements in 1945 and 1948; an abridged version encompassing the supplements was published in 1963 after his death. $20–$40.

MENCKEN, H.L. *The American Language.* New York: Knopf (1919), 1st edition, DJ. $175–$300.

MENCKEN, H.L. *Treatise on the Gods.* New York: Knopf 1930, 1st edition, chipped DJ. $50–$75.

MENDELEEF, Dmitry Ivanovich. *The Principles of Chemistry.* London: Longman's, Green & Co. 1891, 1st English edition, 2 vols, original cloth, fairly worn. $125–$200.

MENEN, Aubrey. *The Prevalence of Witches.* London: Chatto and Windus 1947, 1st edition of author's first book, DJ. $25–$35.

MERRILL, James. *The Country of a Thousand Years of Peace.* New York: Knopf 1959, 1st edition, DJ. $100–$150.

MERRITT, A. *The Moon Pool.* New York: Putnam's 1919, 1st edition of author's first novel. $100–$150.

MERRITT, A. *The Ship of Ishtar.* New York: Putnam 1926, 1st edition. $65–$75.

MERTON, Thomas. *Seeds of Contemplation.* (Norfolk): New Directions (1949), 1st trade edition, DJ. $50–$100.

MERTON, Thomas. *The Tears of Blind Lions.* (New York): New Directions (1949), 1st edition, DJ. $40–$100.

MERTON, Thomas. *The Waters of Siloe.* New York: Harcourt, Brace 1949, 1st edition, DJ. $35–$45.

MEYER, Fred. *See* "Key to Illustrators."

MEYNELL, Alice. *The Children.* New York and London: John Lane, the Bodley Head, 1897, 1st edition. $25–$35.

MEYNELL, Francis. *English Printed Books.* London: Collins 1948, 1st edition, full-page color plates of various illustrators including Kate Greenaway, DJ. $25.

MICHENER, James. *Sayonara.* New York: Random House (1954), 1st edition, DJ. $50–$100.

MICHENER, James. *Tales of the South Pacific.* New York: Macmillan 1947, 1st edition, author's first work of fiction, DJ. $125–$250.

MICHENER, James. *The Floating World. The Story of Japanese Prints.* New York: Random House 1954, 1st edition, profusely illustrated in color and black and white, DJ. $65–$100.

MICKEY MOUSE. See Big Little Books.

MILITARY. *See* "Key to Categories."

MILL, James. *Elements of Political Economy.* London: Baldwin, Cradock and Joy 1821, 1st edition, with pages 237-40 containing ads, later half-morocco, minor to moderate defects. $650–$1,275.

MILL, John Stuart. *A System of Logic, Ratiocinative and Inductive.* London: Longmans 1843, 1st edition, 2 vols, in original cloth-backed boards, ex-library but nice set, rare. $750–$1,500.

MILL, John Stuart. *Autobiography.* London: Longmans 1873, 1st edition, original green cloth. $50–$150.

MILL, John Stuart. *The Subjection of Women.* London: Longmans, Green, Reader, & Dyer 1869, 1st edition, original cloth. $500–$900.

MILLAR, Kenneth. *See* MacDonald, Ross; MacDonald, John Ross.

MILLAR, H.R. *See* "Key to Illustrators."

MILLAY, Edna St. Vincent. *Collected Sonnets.* New York: Harper 1941, 1st edition, DJ. $25–$35.

MILLAY, Edna St. Vincent. *Renascence and Other Poems.* New York: Mitchell Kennerly 1917, 1st edition, 1st issue, on Glaslan (watermarked) paper, DJ. $300–$600.

MILLAY, Edna St. Vincent. *Renascence and Other Poems.* New York: Mitchell Kennerly 1917, 1st edition, 1st issue, on Glaslan (watermarked) paper. $75–$200.

MILLAY, Edna St. Vincent. *Renascence and Other Poems.* New York: Mitchell Kennerly 1917, 1st edition, 2nd issue, on Ingres D'Arches paper. $50.

MILLAY, Edna St. Vincent. *The Buck in the Snow.* New York: Harper 1928, 1st edition, DJ. $50.

MILLER, Alice Duer. *The White Cliffs.* New York: Coward-McCann 1940, 1st edition, DJ. $12–$35.

MILLER, Arthur. *Death of a Salesman.* New York: Viking 1949, 1st edition, DJ. $40–$150.

MILLER, Arthur. *Focus.* New York: Reynal and Hitchcock (1945), 1st edition of author's first novel, DJ. $35.

MILLER, Francis T., edited by. *The Photographic History of the Civil War.* New York: The Review of Reviews Co. 1911-12, 10 vols, 1st edition. $400–$900.

MILLER, Francis T., edited by. *The Photographic History of the Civil War.* New York: T. Yoseloff 1957, 10 vols in 5, boxed. $150–$225.

MILLER, Francis T., edited by. *The World in the Air: The Story of Flying in Pictures.* New York: Putnam's 1930, 2 vols, over 1,200 photos and other ills from government and private sources, issued without DJs. $75–$350.

MILLER, Henry. *The Air-Conditioned Nightmare.* New York: New Directions (1945), correct 1st edition in tan cloth with tipped-in photographs on coated stock, DJ. $50–$85.

MILLER, Henry. *The Cosmological Eye*. Norfolk: New Directions (1939), 1st edition of the first of the author's books to be published in the US, DJ. $75–$150.

MILLER, Henry. *Tropic of Cancer*. New York: Medusa 1940, 1st American edition of author's first book, printed in Mexico and sold under the counter in the US, came out in both cloth and wraps; this edition cloth, which is more scarce. $125–$200.

MILLER, Henry. *Tropic of Cancer*. Paris: Obelisk Press 1934, 1st edition of author's first book with "First published September 1934" on copyright page, in original pictorial wrappers. $5,000.

MILLER, Henry. *See also* Lawrence, D.H. and Miller, Henry; Grabhorn Printing.

MILNE, A.A. *The House at Pooh Corner*. London: Methuen (1928), 1st edition, illustrated by Ernest Shepard, pink cloth, DJ. $300–$500.

MILNE, A.A. *The House at Pooh Corner*. London: Methuen (1928), 1st edition, illustrated by Ernest Shepard, pink cloth. $100–$200.

MILNE, A.A. *The House at Pooh Corner*. New York: Dutton (1928), 1st American edition, illustrated by Ernest Shepard, DJ. $200.

MILNE, A.A. *The House at Pooh Corner*. New York: Dutton (1928), 1st American edition, illustrated by Ernest Shepard. $50–$75.

MILNE, A.A. *The House at Pooh Corner*. Toronto: McClelland & Stewart (1925), later printing (1970s), illustrated by Ernest Shepard, pictorial paper-covered boards. $3.50–$8.

MILNE, A.A. *The House at Pooh Corner*. Toronto: McClelland & Stewart (1925), later printing (1970s), illustrated by Ernest Shepard, pictorial paper-covered boards, DJ. $8–$12.

MILNE, A.A. *Winnie the Pooh*. London: Methuen (1926), decorated by E.H. Shepard, 1st trade edition, green cloth with gold Pooh and Christopher Robin, cream ep's, DJ. $500–$750.

MILNE, A.A. *Winnie the Pooh*. London: Methuen (1926), decorated by E.H. Shepard, 1st trade edition, green cloth with gold Pooh and Christopher Robin, cream ep's. $200–$400.

MILNE, A.A. *Winnie the Pooh*. New York: Dutton (1926), decorated by E.H. Shepard, 1st trade edition, green cloth with gold Pooh and Christopher Robin, DJ. $250–$500.

MILNE, A.A. *Winnie the Pooh.* New York: Dutton (1926), decorated by E.H. Shepard, 1st trade edition, green cloth with gold Pooh and Christopher Robin. $100.

MILTON, John. *See* Doves Press; Ashendene Press (in *Three Elegies*); Golden Cockerel Press.

MINER, L.R. *See* "Key to Illustrators."

MITCHELL, Margaret. *Gone with the Wind.* New York: Macmillan 1936, 1st edition, 1st issue with "Published May 1936" on copyright page and with no further printing dates, DJ. $1,200–$3,000.

MITCHELL, Margaret. *Gone with the Wind.* New York: Macmillan 1939, 1st movie edition, colored pictorial wraps, illustrated with color photographs from the movie. $65.

MITCHELL, Margaret. *Gone with the Wind.* New York: Macmillan 1940, green cloth, color scenes from the movie, DJ. $25–$50.

MITCHELL, Margaret. *Gone with the Wind.* New York: Macmillan 1936, 1st edition, 1st issue with "Published May 1936" on copyright page and with no further printing dates, beat-up DJ. $125–$350.

MITCHELL, Margaret. *Gone with the Wind.* New York: Macmillan 1936, 1st edition, 1st issue with "Published May 1936" on copyright page and with no further printing dates. $100–$300.

MITFORD, Nancy. *Love in a Cold Climate.* New York: Random House 1949, 1st American edition, DJ. $25.

MITSCHERLICH, Alexandern, and Mielke, Fred. *Doctors of Infamy: The Story of the Nazi Medical Crimes.* New York: McGraw-Hill "1956". $40.

MODERN FIRSTS. *See* "Key to Categories."

MOMADAY, N. Scott. *House Made of Dawn.* New York: Harper & Row (1968) 1st edition, DJ. $50–$100.

MOMADAY, N. Scott. *The Names. A Memoir.* New York: Harper & Row 1976, 1st edition, DJ. $25.

MONAHAN, P.J. *See* "Key to Illustrators."

MONSELL, J.R. *See* "Key to Illustrators."

MONTGOMERY, L.M. *Anne of Avonlea*. Boston: L.C. Page 1909, 3rd impression, September 1909. $20–$30.

MONTGOMERY, L.M. *Anne of Green Gables*. Boston: L.C. Page 1908, 1st edition. $100–$225.

MOORE, Brian. *Judith Hearne*. (London): Deutsch (1955), 1st edition of author's first book, DJ. $150–$200.

MOORE, Brian. *The Lonely Passion of Judith Hearne*. Boston: (1955), 1st American edition, DJ. $75–$125.

MOORE, Brian. *The Luck of Ginger Coffey*. (London): Andre Deutsch (1960), 1st edition, DJ. $75.

MOORE, Clement C. *Denslow's Night Before Christmas*. New York: G.W. Dillingham 1902, 1st edition thus, 2nd binding state, of brown-stamped gray cloth with color pictorial paste-on label (first was pictorial boards), illustrated in color throughout by W.W. Denslow. $250–$300.

MOORE, Clement C. *The Night Before Christmas*. New York: Grosset and Dunlap (1961), illustrated in color by Gyo Fujikawa, quarto, illustrated boards. $15.

MOORE, Clement C. *The Night Before Christmas*. Akron: Saalfield nd (about 1940s), illustrated by Frances Brundage, quarto, colored pictorial wraps. $40.

MOORE, George. *Esther Waters, A Novel*. London: 1894, 1st edition. $25–$75.

MOORE, Marianne. *Poems*. London: Egoist Press 1921, 1st edition of author's first book, wrappers. $200–$450.

MOORE, Marianne. *Selected Poems*. New York: Macmillan 1935, 1st edition. $50–$175.

MOORE, Marianne. *What are Years*. New York: Macmillan 1941, 1st edition, DJ. $100–$175.

MOORE, Merrill. *Clinical Sonnets*. New York: Trayne (1949), 1st edition, DJ. $25.

MOORE, T. Sturge. *See* "Key to Illustrators."

MORE, Sir Thomas. *See* Golden Cockerel Press; Kelmscott Press.

MORISON, Samuel Eliot. *History of United States Naval Operations in World War II*. Boston: Little, Brown 1947-1962, 1st edition, 15 vols, DJs. $275.

MORISON, Samuel Eliot. *New Guinea and the Marianas, March 1944-August 1944*. Boston: Little Brown 1962, 1st edition, illustrated, DJ. $25.

MORISON, Samuel Eliot. *New Guinea and the Marianas, March 1944-August 1944*. Boston: Little Brown 1962, 7th printing, illustrated, Volume VIII of History of U.S. Naval Operations in World War II. $15.

MORISON, Samuel Eliot. *The Two-Ocean War*. Boston: Little, Brown "1963". $25–$40.

MORLEY, Christopher. *Plum Pudding*. New York: Doubleday, Page 1921, 1st edition, DJ. $50–$65.

MORLEY, Christopher. *The Haunted Bookshop*. Garden City: Doubleday, Page & Co. 1919, 1st edition, 1st issue, DJ. $300–$400.

MORLEY, Christopher. *Where the Blue Begins*. Philadelphia: Lippincott (1922), 1st American Rackham edition, 4 color plates and 16 line drawings by Arthur Rackham, DJ. $75.

MORRIS, William. *See* Kelmscott Press.

MORRIS, Wright. *My Uncle Dudley*. New York: Harcourt, Brace 1942, 1st edition of author's first book, DJ. $200–$600.

MORRIS, Wright. *The Inhabitants*. New York: Scribner's 1946, 1st edition, DJ. $100–$150.

MORRISON, Toni. *Sula*. New York: Knopf 1974, 1st edition of author's second book, uncommon, DJ. $75–$150.

MORRISON, Toni. *Tar Baby*. New York: Knopf 1981, 1st edition, DJ. $35–$75.

MORRISON, Toni. *The Bluest Eye*. New York: Holt, Rinehart (1970), 1st edition of author's first book, uncommon, DJ. $125–$325.

MORROW, Honoré. *We Must March*. New York: Stokes "1925", 1st edition, DJ. $25–$50.

MOSER, Barry. *See* "Key to Illustrators."

MOSKOWITZ, Ira. *See* "Key to Illustrators."

MOSSER, Marjorie. *Good Maine Food*. New York: Doubleday, Doran 1940, 3rd issue, introduction and notes by Kenneth Roberts, DJ. $35.

MOTHER GOOSE. Boston: Little, Brown 1940, 1st edition, illustrated in full color by Gustaf Tenggren. $50–$75.

MOTHER GOOSE PICTURE BOOK. Racine: (1928), full-color ills by Charlotte Stone, wrappers. $25–$40.

MOTLEY, Willard. *Knock on any Door.* New York: Appleton (1947), 1st edition of author's first book, DJ. $75–$100.

MOVIES, THE. *See* "Key to Categories."

MRS. WIGGS OF THE CABBAGE PATCH. See Rice, Alice Hegan.

MUGNAINI, Joseph. *See* "Key to Illustrators."

MUIR, Edwin. *Journeys and Places.* London: Dent 1937, 1st edition, DJ. $50–$100.

MUIR, Edwin. *The Structure of the Novel.* (Hogarth Lectures, First Series, #6.) London: Hogarth Press 1925, DJ. $50–$75.

MUIR, John. *A Thousand-Mile Walk to the Gulf,* edited by W.F. Bade. Boston: Houghton, Mifflin 1916, 1st edition. $75.

MUIR, John. *My First Summer in the Sierra.* Boston and New York: Houghton, Mifflin, 1st edition. $75–$150.

MUIR, John. *Steep Trails.* Boston: Houghton, Mifflin 1918, 1st edition. $110–$150.

MUIR, John. *The Mountains of California.* New York: Century 1894, 1st edition. $175–$250.

MUIR, Percy H. *English Children's Books 1600-1900.* New York: 1954, 1st American edition, illustrated, DJ. $75.

MULFORD, Clarence. *The Coming of Cassidy and the Others.* Chicago: A.C. McClurg Co. "1913", 1st edition, ills in color by Maynard Dixon, DJ. $50–$150.

MUNDY, Talbot. *Jimgrim and Allah's Peace.* New York: Appleton-Century 1936, 1st edition, with "(1)" at base of text on page 279, DJ. $100–$135.

MUNDY, Talbot. *Purple Perate.* New York: Appleton-Century 1935, 1st edition, 1st printing, with "(1)" on page 367; the third Tros novel. $100–$135.

MUNDY, Talbot. *The Ivory Trail.* New York: A.L. Burt (1919), reprint edition, black and white frontis. $5–$10.

MUNDY, Talbot. *The Ivory Trail*. New York: A.L. Burt (1919), reprint edition, black and white frontis, DJ. $8–$18.

MUNGO, Raymond. *Tropical Detective Story*. New York: E.P. Dutton 1972, 1st edition, DJ. $20–$40.

MURDOCH, Iris. *The Sandcastle*. London: 1957, 1st edition, DJ. $100–$150.

MURDOCH, Iris. *The Sovereignty of Good over Other Concepts*. Cambridge: 1967, 1st English edition, wraps. $60–$75.

MURRY, John Middleton. *Shakespeare*. New York: Harcourt, Brace (1936), 1st American edition, DJ. $35–$65.

MY FARM BOOK. England: Raphael Tuck & Sons (1930s?), full-color ills, wrappers. $25–$35.

MYSTERIES. *See* "Key to Categories."

 N ————————————————————————

NABOKOV, Vladimir. *Laughter in the Dark*. Indianapolis: Bobbs-Merrill (1938), 1st edition of author's first book published in the US, DJ. $100–$300.

NABOKOV, Vladimir. *Lolita*. New York: Putnam's (1958), 1st American edition, DJ. $100–$125.

NAEF, Weston (with Lucien Goldschmidt). *See* Grolier Club

NAIPAUL, V.S. *The Mystic Masseur*. New York: Vanguard 1959, 1st American edition of author's first book, DJ. $35–$75.

NANSEN, Fridtjof. *Farthest North*. New York: Harper's 1897, 2 vols, color plates, 4 maps in pocket, 1st American edition. $95.

NANSEN, Fridtjof. *Farthest North*. London: Harper 1898, 2nd London edition, 2 vols. $50–$75.

NANSEN, Fridtjof. *Farthest North*. New York: Harper 1898, popular edition, 1 vol. $30.

NANSEN, Fridtjof. *First Crossing of Greenland*. London: Longman's Green 1890, 2 vols, 4 folding maps, 12 plates, 1st edition in English. $200.

NAPOLEON I. *See* Golden Cockerel Press.

NASH, Ogden. *The Bad Parent's Garden of Verse.* New York: Simon & Schuster 1936, 1st edition, frontis and ills by Reginald Birch, DJ. $25–$40.

NASH, Ogden. *The Face is Familiar: the Selected Verse of.* Boston: Little, Brown and Co. 1940, 1st edition, DJ. $20–$35.

NASH, Ogden. *See also* Lear, Edward: *The Scroobius Pup.*

NAST, Thomas. *See* "Key to Illustrators."

NATIVE AMERICAN. *See* "Key to Categories."

NATHAN, Geroge Jean. *Bottoms Up. An Application of the Slapstick to Satire.* New York: Philip Goodman Co. 1917, 1st edition, DJ. $50–$85.

NATHAN, George Jean. *Passing Judgements.* New York: 1935, 1st edition, DJ. $35.

NATHAN, Robert. *A Journal for Josephine.* New York: Knopf 1943, 1st edition, DJ. $35.

NATURAL HISTORY. *See* "Key to Categories."

NAUTICAL. *See* "Key to Categories."

NEARING, Scott. *Black America.* New York: Vanguard Press 1929, 1st edition, photographs. $35–$50.

NEARING, Scott. *United World.* New Jersey: Open Road Press 1944, 1st edition, DJ. $25–$50.

NEIHARDT, John G. *Black Elk Speaks.* New York: 1932, 1st edition, illustrated by Standing Bear, color plates. $35–$75.

NEIHARDT, John G. *Indian Tales & Others.* New York: Macmillan "1926", 1st edition, DJ. $35–$75.

NEILL, John R. *See* "Key to Illustrators."

NEMEROV, Howard. *The Image and the Law.* (New York: 1947), 1st edition of author's first book, DJ. $50–$100.

NERUDA, Pablo. *Residence on Earth and Other Poems.* Norfolk: New Directions (1946), 1st American edition. $20–$30.

NESBIT, Edith. *Leaves of Life.* London: Longmans, Green & Co. 1888, 1st edition. $75–$150.

NESBIT, Edith. *The Phoenix and the Carpet.* London: Newnes (1904), 1st edition, colored frontis and black and white drawings by H.R. Millar. $200–$500.

NESBIT, Edith. *The Phoenix and the Carpet.* New York: Macmillan 1904, 1st American edition, frontis and 1 black and white plate by H.R. Millar. $65–$125.

NESBIT, Edith. *The Railway Children.* London: 1906, 1st edition, 20 black and white drawings by C.E. Brock. $200–$500.

NEWELL, Peter. *The Hole Book.* New York: Harper (1908), 1st edition, illustrated by the author. $100–$200.

NEWELL, Peter. *See also* "Key to Illustrators."

NEWTON, A. Edward. *A Magnificent Farce and Other Diversions of a Book Collector.* Boston: The Atlantic Monthly Press (1921), 1st edition, DJ. $40–$50.

NEWTON, A. Edward. *A Magnificent Farce and Other Diversions of a Book Collector.* Boston: The Atlantic Monthly Press (1921), 2nd impression. $12–$15.

NEWTON, A. Edward. *Amenities of Book Collecting.* Boston: Atlantic Monthly Press 1922, later impression. $10–$20.

NEWTON, A. Edward. T*he Amenities of Book Collecting and Kindred Affections.* Boston: The Atlantic Monthly Press 1918, 1st edition, 1st issue. $20–$60.

NEWTON, Isaac. *Optiks.* London: 1704, 1st edition, folding plates. $13,000.

NEWTON, Isaac. *Optiks.* London: printed for Willian Innys 1730, 4th edition, 12 engraved folding plates, contemporary calfskin, nicely decorated binding. $800.

NEWTON, Isaac. *Philosophiae Naturalis Principia Mathematica.* London: 1687, 1st edition, 1st issue, quarto, various flaws. $65,000.

NICHOLS, Beverly. *A Thatched Roof.* London: 1933, 1st edition, 5 full-page and four half-page black and white ills by Rex Whistler, DJ. $25–$40.

NICHOLS, John. *The Sterile Cuckoo.* New York: David McKay (1965), 1st edition of author's first book, DJ. $50–$75.

NICHOLSON, Meredith. *A Hoosier Chronicle.* Boston: Houghton, Mifflin 1912, 1st edition. $15.

NICOLSON, Harold. *Public Faces.* Boston: Houghton, Mifflin 1933, 1st American edition, DJ. $35.

NIELSEN, Kay. *See* "Key to Illustrators."

NIGHT BEFORE CHRISTMAS, THE. See Moore, Clement C., three entries.

NIN, Anais. *Children of the Albatross.* New York: Dutton 1947, 1st American edition, DJ. $75–$125.

NIN, Anais. *Ladders to Fire.* New York: E.P. Dutton and Co. 1946, 1st American edition, engravings by Ian Hugo, DJ. $75–$125.

NONESUCH PRESS. Laver, James. *Ladies' Mistake.* Bloomsbury: Nonesuch Press 1933, octavo, ills by Thomas Lowinsky, 9 plates, marbled boards, one of 300 copies printed at the Fanfare Press, marbled slipcase. $75–$125.

NONESUCH PRESS. Laver, James. *Love's Progress: or, The Education of Araminta.* Bloomsbury: Nonesuch Press 1929, octavo, marbled boards, one of 1,500 copies printed by Walter Lewis at the University Press, Cambridge. $30–$50.

NONESUCH PRESS. Lawrence, D.H. *Love Among the Haystacks and Other Pieces.* London: Nonesuch Press 1930, 1st edition, one of 1,600 numbered copies printed at the Curwen Press on handmade paper, DJ and glassine wrapper. $75–$125.

NORDHOFF, Charles. *The Bounty Trilogy.* Boston: Little, Brown 1940, 1st edition thus, ep maps, 12 color plates by N.C. Wyeth, DJ. $75–$150.

NORDHOFF, Charles. *Whaling and Fishing.* Cincinnati: Moore, Wilstach, Keys & Co. 1856, 1st edition, original cloth. $250.

NORDHOFF, Charles B., and Hall, James Norman. *Mutiny on the Bounty.* Boston: Little, Brown 1932, 1st edition, DJ. $75–$150.

NORRIS, Frank. *McTeague, A Story of San Francisco.* New York: Doubleday and McClure 1899, 1st edition, 1st printing, with "moment" as the last word on page 106. $150–$400.

NORTON, André. *Fur Magic.* Cleveland: World (1968), 1st edition, DJ. $75–$125.

NORTON, André. *Jargoon Pard.* New York: Atheneum 1974, 1st edition, DJ. $25–$35.

NOTESTEIN, Wallace. *A History of Witchcraft in England from 1558 to 1718.* Washington: American Historical Association 1911, 1st edition, rebound. $25.

NOVAK, Joseph. *No Third Path*. Garden City: Doubleday 1962, by Jerzy Kosinski, 1st edition of author's second book, DJ. $75–$125.

NOVAK, Joseph. *The Future is Ours, Comrade*. New York: Doubleday 1950, by Jerzy Kosinski, 1st edition of author's first book, DJ. $150–$250.

NOYES, Alfred. *Ballads and Poems*. Edinburgh and London: William Blackwood and Sons 1928, 1st edition, DJ. $25.

NUREMBERG CHRONICLE. Schedel, Hartmann. *Liber Chronicarum*. Nuremberg: Anton Koberger 12 July, 1493, 1st edition, Latin text, over 1,800 woodcuts (some being repeats), 325 of 328 leaves present, some worming, some repaired tears, bound in old vellum. $20,000–$30,000.

 O

O'CASEY, Sean. *Two Plays: Juno and the Paycock, The Shadow of a Gunman*. London: Macmillan 1925, 1st edition, DJ. $50–$100.

O'BRIEN, Tim. *Going After Cacciato*. New York: Delacorte/ Lawrence (1978), 1st edition of author's third book, winner of National Book Award, DJ. $35–$75.

O'BRIEN, Tim. *If I Die in a Combat Zone, Box Me Up and Send Me Home*. New York: Delacorte/Lawrence (1973), 1st edition of author's first book, scarce, DJ. $200–$600.

O'BRIEN, Tim. *Northern Lights*. New York: Delacorte/Lawrence (1975), 1st edition of author's second book, DJ. $35–$75.

O'CONNOR, Flannery. *Everything that Rises must Converge*. New York: Farrar, Straus & Giroux (1956), 1st edition, DJ. $75–$125.

O'CONNOR, Flannery. *Wise Blood*. New York: Harcourt, Brace 1952, 1st edition of author's first book, DJ. $250–$500.

O'CONNOR, Frank. *Death in Dublin. Michael Collins and the Irish Revolution*. Garden City: Doubleday, Doran 1937, 1st American edition, DJ. $25–$40.

O'CONNOR, Frank. *See also* Cuala Press.

O'DAY, Dean, editor. *Shirley Temple Story Book, Authorized Ed.* Akron and New York: Saalfield (1935), illustrated. $20–$30.

O'DELL, Scott. *Island of the Blue Dolphins.* Boston: Houghton, Mifflin 1960, 1st edition, DJ, winner of Newbery Award 1960. $35–$60.

O'DELL, Scott. *The King's Fifth.* Boston: Houghton, Mifflin "1966", 1st edition, DJ. $20.

O'DONNELL, E.P. *Green Margins.* Boston: Houghton, Mifflin 1936, 1st edition; this was a Fellowship Prize novel, DJ. $35.

O'FAOLAIN, Sean. *A Purse of Coppers. Short Stories.* London: Jonathan Cape (1937), 1st edition, DJ. $50–$100.

O'FLAHERTY, Liam. *The Informer.* London: 1925, 1st edition, DJ. $150–$250.

O'HARA, John. *Pal Joey.* New York: Duell, Sloan (1940), 1st edition, DJ. $100–$200.

O'NEILL, Eugene. *The Emperor Jones, Diff'rent, The Straw.* New York: Boni and Liveright (1921), 1st edition, one of 2,200 copies printed, DJ. $150–$200.

O'NEILL, Eugene. *The Iceman Cometh.* New York: Random House (1946), 1st edition, DJ. $50–$75.

O'NEILL, Rose. *The Kewpies Their Book.* New York: Stokes (1913), 1st edition, kewpies by the author. $100–$200.

OATES, Joyce Carol. *By the North Gate.* New York: Vanguard Press 1963, 1st edition, DJ. $65–$125.

OATES, Joyce Carol. *Crossing the Border.* New York: Vanguard 1976, 1st edition, DJ. $35–$60.

OATES, Joyce Carol. *Luxury of Sin.* Northridge: Lord John Press 1984, 1st edition, one of 26 specially bound copies, lettered and signed by author, original half-morocco. $100.

ODETS, Clifford. *Three Plays: Awake and Sing, Waiting for Lefty, Till the Day I Die.* New York: Covici, Friede (1935), 1st edition, 1st printing (the Random House edition of 1935 was published later, printed from the Covici, Friede plates), DJ. $50–$100.

OLSEN, Tillie. *Silences.* New York: Delacorte 1978, 1st edition, DJ. $20–$35.

OLSEN, Tillie. *Tell Me a Riddle.* Philadelphia: Lippincott (1961), 1st edition of author's first book, DJ. $100–$200.

OLSON, Charles. *The Maximus Poems.* New York: Jargon/Corinth 1960, 1st trade edition, wraps. $25–$40.

OMAR KHAYYAM, THE RUBAIYAT OF. See Golden Cockerel Press; Grolier Club.

OPPENHEIM, E. Phillips. *Havoc.* New York: A.L. Burt (1911), reprint edition, color ills by Howard Chandler Christy. $3.50–$8.

OPPENHEIM, E. Phillips. *Havoc.* New York: A.L. Burt (1911), reprint edition, color ills by Howard Chandler Christy, DJ. $8–$12.

OPPENHEIM, E. Phillips. *The Battle of Basinghall Street.* Boston: Little, Brown 1935, 1st American edition, DJ. $20.

ORWELL, George. *Animal Farm.* London: Secker and Warburg 1945, 1st edition, DJ. $200–$1,100.

ORWELL, George. *Animal Farm.* New York: Harcourt, Brace (1946), 1st American edition, DJ. $50–$150.

ORWELL, George. *Animal Farm.* New York: Harcourt, Brace (1946), 1st American edition. $15–$35.

ORWELL, George. *Nineteen Eighty-Four.* New York: Harcourt (1949), 1st American edition, 1st issue, in red DJ. $125–$300.

ORWELL, George. *The English People.* London: Collins 1947, 1st edition, DJ. $25–$40.

OSGOOD, Henry O. *So this is Jazz.* Boston: Little, Brown 1926, 1st edition, illustrated, DJ. $50–$75.

OSLER, William. *Principles and Practice of Medicine.* New York: Appleton 1896, 2nd edition. $225.

OSLER, William. *Principles and Practice of Medicine.* New York: Appleton 1899, 3rd edition. $200.

OSLER, William. *Principles and Practice of Medicine.* New York: Appleton 1935, 12th edition. $50.

OSLER, William. *Principles and Practice of Medicine.* New York: Appleton 1892, 1st edition, 2nd issue, includes ads dated later than March. $350–$650.

OSLER, William. *Principles and Practice of Medicine.* New York: Appleton 1893, 1st edition, later printing. $300–$400.

OSLER, William. *Principles and Practice of Medicine.* New York: Appleton 1892, 1st edition, 1st issue, with last ads in back of book dated March, 1892. $500–$1,200.

OSLER, William. *Principles and Practice of Medicine.* New York: Appleton 1912, 8th edition, revised. $100.

OUTCAULT, F. *Buster Brown, His Dog Tige, and Their Troubles.* London: (1900), oblong folio, colored ills throughout by the author, stiff pictorial wrappers, rebacked, new rear cover and repaired front cover (author's name usually given as R.F. Outcault). $75.

OVERALL BOYS, THE. See Grover, Eulalie Osgood.

OVID. *See* Golden Cockerel Press.

OWEN, Wilfred. *Poems. New Complete Edition.* London: 1931, edited and introduced by Edmund Blunden with a 40-page memoir; many new poems included, DJ. $50–$100.

OZ BOOKS. *See* Baum, L. Frank; Thompson, Ruth Plumly.

OZICK, Cynthia. *Trust.* New York: 1966, 1st edition of author's first book, DJ. $75–$125.

P

PAGE, Thomas Nelson. *Red Rock.* New York: Scribner's 1898, 1st edition. $15–$25.

PAGE, Thomas Nelson. *Santa Claus's Partner.* New York: Scribner's 1899, 1st edition. $20.

PAGET, Sidney. *See* "Key to Illustrators."

PAINE, Anna. *See* "Key to Illustrators."

PAINE, Thomas. *Common Sense.* Philadelphia: R. Bell 1776, 1st issue, lacking last leaf, browned and damp-stained throughout, soiled and frayed; price at auction. $8,500.

PALEY, Grace. *The Little Disturbances of Man.* New York: Doubleday 1959, 1st edition of author's first book, DJ. $75–$150.

PALGRAVE, F.T. *A Golden Treasury of Songs and Lyrics.* New

York: Duffield & Co. 1911, 1st Parrish edition, 8 color plates after paintings by Maxfield Parrish, quarto. $85.

PANKHURST, E. Sylvia. *The Suffragette*. New York: Sturgis & Walton 1911, 1st US edition. $65–$75.

PARKER, Dorothy. *Death and Taxes*. New York: Viking 1931, 1st edition, DJ. $75–$125.

PARKER, Dorothy. *Not so Deep as a Well*. New York: Viking 1936, 1st edition, DJ. $50–$75.

PARKER, Gilbert. *The Seats of the Mighty*. New York: 1902, 1st edition. $20.

PARKER, Robert B. *Mortal Stakes*. Boston: Houghton, Mifflin 1975, 1st edition, DJ. $50–$100.

PARKER, Robert B. *The Godwulf Manuscript*. Boston: Houghton, Mifflin 1974, 1st edition of Parker's first Spenser book, DJ. $150.

PARKS, Gordon. *Camera Portraits: The Techniques and Principles of Documentary Portraiture*. New York: Franklin Watts 1948, 1st edition, DJ. $75–$125.

PARNELL, Thomas. *See* Cuala Press.

PARRISH, Maxfield. *See* "Key to Illustrators."

PATCHEN, Kenneth. *Memoirs of a Shy Pornographer*. (New York): New Directions (1945), 1st edition, DJ. $50–$100.

PATCHEN, Kenneth. *See You in the Morning*. New York: Padell (1947). $15.

PATER, Walter. *Imaginary Portraits*. London: 1887, 1st edition. $50–$100.

PATTON, George S. *War as I Knew It*. Boston: Houghton, Mifflin "1947". $35–$50.

PAUL, Elliot. *Hugger-Mugger in the Louvre*. New York: (1940), 1st edition, DJ. $35–$65.

PEAKE, Mervyn. *Gormenghast*. London: Eyre and Spottiswoode 1950, 1st edition of the second book in the Gormenghast trilogy, DJ. $100–$300.

PEAKE, Mervyn. *Titus Groan*. New York: Reynal and Hitchcock (1946), 1st American edition of author's first novel and the first book of the Gormenghast trilogy, DJ. $50–$100.

PEAT, Fern Bisel. *See* "Key to Illustrators."

PERCY, Walker. *Love in the Ruins.* New York: Farrar, Straus & Giroux (1971), 1st edition of author's third book, DJ. $35–$75.

PERCY, Walker. *The Moviegoer.* New York: Knopf 1961, 1st edition of author's first novel, DJ. $500–$750.

PERELMAN, S.J. *Dawn Ginsberg's Revenge.* New York: Horace Liveright (1929), 1st edition, 2nd printing, with silver cloth binding, DJ. $325–$500.

PERELMAN, S.J. *The Swiss Family Perelman.* New York: Simon & Schuster 1950, 1st edition, DJ. $25.

PERFORMING ARTS: DRAMA, MUSIC, MAGIC. *See* "Key to Categories."

PERKINS, Lucy Fitch. *The Spanish Twins.* Boston: Houghton, Mifflin (1934), small format, illustrated by the author. $15–$30.

PERRAULT, Charles. *Tales of Passed Times Written for Children by Mr. Perrault, Newly Decorated by John Austen.* New York: E.P. Dutton & Co. nd. $50–$75.

PERRAULT, M. (Charles). *Histories, or Tales of Past Times; Told by Mother Goose.* London: J. Harris (1803), early nineteenth-century edition of Perrault's fairy tales, includes "Red Riding Hood," "Sleeping Beauty"; original dutch-flowered boards, engraved frontis and headpieces. $1,500–$2,500.

PERRY, Commodore Matthew. *Narrative of the Expedition of an American Squadron...* Washington: Nicholson 1856, 1st edition, 3 vols, 4to, plates, lithos, maps, some color, and with the suppressed nude bathing scene. $500–$1,000.

PETER PAN. See Barrie, James.

PETER RABBIT. See Potter, Beatrix.

PETERKIN, Julia. *Black April.* Indianapolis: Bobbs-Merrill 1927, 1st edition, DJ. $35–$75.

PETERKIN, Julia. *Scarlet Sister Mary.* Indianapolis. Bobbs-Merrill (1928), 1st edition, DJ. $50–$75.

PETERKIN, Julia, and Ulmann, Doris. *Roll, Jordan, Roll.* New York: Robert O. Ballou 1933, 1st edition, DJ. $100–$225.

PETERSHAM, Maud and Miska. *See* "Key to Illustrators."

PETRY, Ann. *The Street.* Boston: Houghton, Mifflin 1946, 1st edition of author's first book, DJ. $50–$125.

PHILLIPS, Jayne Anne. *How Mickey Made It*. St. Paul: Bookslinger Editions 1981, 1st trade edition, issued without DJ. $25–$50.

PHILLPOTTS, Eden. *A Clue from the Stars*. New York: Macmillan 1932, 1st American edition, DJ. $15–$30.

PHIZ (H.K. Browne). *See* "Key to Illustrators."

PHOTOGRAPHY. *See* "Key to Categories."

PICTURESQUE CHICAGO AND GUIDE TO THE WORLD'S FAIR. Baltimore: R.H. Woodward & Co. 1892, illustrated. $25–$35.

PIED PIPER OF HAMELIN, THE. See Browning, Robert.

PIGS IS PIGS. (By Ellis Parker Butler.) Chicago/New York: 1905, "Compliments of Railway Appliances Co.," 1st American edition of author's first and very popular book, thin paper wrappers. $75–$175.

PINOCCHIO. See Collodi, Carlo.

PINTER, Harold. *Five Screenplays*. London: 1971, 1st edition, DJ. $35.

PIPER, Watty. *The Little Engine That Could*. New York: Platt & Munk (1930), retold by Watty Piper from *The Pony Engine*, illustrated by Lois Lenski. $50–$75.

PIPER, Watty. *See also* Bannerman, Helen; *Little Black Sambo*, edited by Watty Piper.

PIRSIG, Robert M. *Zen and the Art of Motorcycle Maintenance*. New York: 1974, 1st edition, DJ. $50.

PITTER, Ruth. *A Mad Lady's Garland*. London: 1934, 1st edition, DJ. $25–$35.

PITTER, Ruth. *A Trophy of Arms: Poems 1926-1936*. London: (nd), 1st edition, DJ. $25–$35.

PLANCK, Max. *Einfehrung in die Theorie der Elektrizitatund des Magnetismus*. Leipzig: S. Hirzel 1922, 1st edition. $165.

PLATH, Sylvia. *Ariel*. London: Faber & Faber 1965, 1st edition, author's second book, preceded American publication by a year, DJ. $50–$150.

PLATH, Sylvia. *The Bell Jar*. New York: Harper & Row 1971, 1st American edition, DJ. $75–$125.

PLATH, Sylvia. *The Colossus: Poems*. London: 1960, 1st edition, DJ, rare. $400–$750.

PLATH, Sylvia. *The Colossus: Poems*. New York: Knopf 1962, 1st American edition, DJ. $75–$125.

PLATO. *See* Golden Cockerel Press.

PLOMER, William. *The Family Tree*. London: Hogarth Press 1929, Hogarth Living Poets #10, one of 400 copies printed. $30–$40.

POE, E.A. *The Conchologist's First Book*. Philadelphia: Published for the author by Haswell, Barrington, and Haswell 1839, 1st edition, 1st state, by Edgar Allan Poe, original boards. $750–$1,000.

POE, Edgar Allan. *Tales*. New York: Wiley & Putnam 1845, 1st American edition, 2nd printing, with the imprints of "Smith, Stereotyper" and "H. Ludwig, Printer" on the copyright page; bookseller catalog price. $5,500.

POE, Edgar Allan. *See also* Grabhorn Printing.

POETRY. *See* "Key to Categories."

POGANY, Willy. *See* "Key to Illustrators."

POHL, Frederik. *Slave Ship*. New York: Ballantine Books (1957), 1st edition, DJ. $200–$300.

POHL, Frederik. *Starburst*. New York: Ballantine Books (1982), 1st edition, DJ. $20–$25.

POPEYE. See Big Little Books.

PORTER, David D. *The Naval History of the Civil War*. Glendale: Castle 1970, DJ. $25–$40.

PORTER, David D. *The Naval History of the Civil War*. New York: the Sherman Publishing Co. 1886, 1st edition, quarto, scarce. $175–$250.

PORTER, Katherine Anne. *A Christmas Story*. New York: Delacorte Press (1967), 1st edition, drawings by Ben Shahn, one of 500 copies signed by author and artist, issued without a DJ. $50–$100.

PORTER, Katherine Anne. *Flowering Judas*. New York: Harcourt, Brace (1929), 1st edition, one of 600 copies, DJ. $75–$200.

PORTER, Katherine Anne. *Ship of Fools*. Boston: Little, Brown (1962), 1st edition, DJ. $35–$65.

PORTER, Katherine Anne. *The Leaning Tower and Other Stories*. New York: Harcourt, Brace (1944), 1st edition, DJ. $40–$75.

PORTER, Luther H. *Cycling for Health and Pleasure: An Indispensable Guide to the Successful Use of the Wheel.* New York: Dodd, Mead 1895, 1st edition, decorated yellow cloth, illustrated. $60–$75.

POST, Melville Davidson. *Uncle Abner.* New York: Appleton 1918, 1st edition. $50–$125.

POTTER, Beatrix. *The Tailor of Gloucester.* London: Warne nd (about 1970), color ills by Potter, DJ. $12–$20.

POTTER, Beatrix. *The Tale of Mr. Toad.* London: Warne (1939), color ills by Potter, DJ. $20–$35.

POTTER, Beatrix. *The Tale of Mrs. Tiggy-Winkle.* London and New York: Warne 1905, 1st edition, color plates plus black and white; green boards. $100–$350.

POTTER, Beatrix. *The Tale of Mrs. Tittlemouse.* London and New York: Warne 1910, 1st edition, color plates, blue cloth. $100–$350.

POTTER, Beatrix. *The Tale of Peter Rabbit.* London and New York: Warne nd (1902), 1st edition. $150–$750.

POTTER, Beatrix. *The Tale of the Flopsy Bunnies.* London and New York: Warne 1909, 1st edition, color plates, green boards. $150–$400.

(POTTER, Beatrix). *The Tale of Peter Rabbit.* Philadelphia: Altemus (1904) "Wee Books for Wee Folks" series. Due to a misunderstanding between the US and London branches of Warne, *The Tale of Peter Rabbit* wasn't copyrighted in the US. Once copied by Altemus, it was too late for Warne to copyright it. Potter's name does not appear on this edition. $15–$50.

POTTER, Beatrix, imitation. Almond, Linda. *Peter Rabbit's Easter.* Philadelphia: Altemus (1921), color plates, and pictorial paste-on on cover. $20–$50.

POUND, Ezra. *Canzoni.* London: Mathews 1911, 1st edition, one of about 500 copies. $150–$250.

POUND, Ezra. *Eleven New Cantos XXXI-XLI.* New York: Farrar & Rinehart (1934), 1st edition, DJ. $75–$125.

POUND, Ezra. *The Pisan Cantos.* (New York): New Directions (1948), 1st edition, DJ. $100–$175.

POWELL, Anthony. *A Dance to the Music of Time*. London: Heinemann 1951-75, complete in 12 vols, from *A Question of Upbringing* to the last book, *Hearing Secret Harmonies*, 1st editions, DJs. $750–$1,500.

POWELL, Anthony. *A Question of Upbringing*. New York: Scribner's 1951, 1st American edition, DJ. $75–$150.

POWELL, Lawrence Clark. *Recollections of an Ex-Bookseller*. Los Angeles: 1850, one of 500 copies, engravings by Ilya Shor, wrappers. $35–$50.

POWERS, James F. *Prince of Darkness and Other Stories*. London: John Lehman 1948, 1st English edition of author's first book, DJ. $50–$75.

POWYS, John Cowper. *A Glastonbury Romance*. New York: Simon and Schuster 1932, 1st trade edition, DJ. $75–$200.

POWYS, John Cowper. *Wolf Solent*. New York: 1929, 2 vols, DJs, slipcase. $75–$150.

POWYS, Llewelyn. *Black Laughter*. London: 1925, 1st English edition. $35.

POWYS, Llewelyn. *See also* Golden Cockerel Press.

POWYS, Theodore Francis. *Mockery Gap*. London: 1925. $50–$75.

POWYS, Theodore Francis. *Mr. Weston's Good Wine*. London: Chatto & Windus 1927, 1st edition, one of 660 signed copies, 6 woodcuts from drawings by George Charlton. $50–$100.

POWYS, Theodore Francis. *See also* Golden Cockerel Press.

PRESTON, May Wilson. *See* "Key to Illustrators."

PRICE, George. *It's Smart to be People*. New York: (1942), 1st edition, DJ. $25–$50.

PRICE, Reynolds. *A Long and Happy Life*. New York: Atheneum 1966, 1st edition of author's first book, DJ. $50–$100.

PRIESTLY, J.B. *Angel Pavement*. London: Heinemann 1930, 1st edition, DJ. $35.

PRIESTLY, Joseph. *The History and Present State of Electricity, with Original Experiments*. London: Bathurst & Lowndes 1775, 3rd edition, corrected and enlarged, 8 folding plates. $450.

PRIVATE PRESS BOOKS. *See* "Key to Categories."

PROKOSCH, Frederic. *The Assassins*. New York: Harper 1936, 1st edition, DJ. $20–$35.

PROUST, Marcel. *A La Recherche du Temps Perdu.* Paris: (1913–17), 1st edition throughout, 13 vols, original printed wrappers. $8,000–$10,000.

PROUST, Marcel. *Remembrance of Things Past.* New York: Random House (1932), 2 vols, later American edition, boxed. $25–$40.

PROUST, Marcel. *Remembrance of Things Past.* New York: Random House (1932), 2 vols, later American edition. $20–$30.

PROUST, Marcel. *The Past Recaptured.* New York: Boni 1932, 1st American edition of the final vol of *Remembrance of Things Past*, DJ. $50.

PSYCHOLOGY, MEDICINE, SCIENCE. *See* "Key to Categories."

PURDY, James. *Malcolm.* New York: Farrar, Straus & Giroux 1959, 1st edition, DJ. $35–$50.

PYLE, Ernie. *Brave Men.* New York: Holt (1944), 1st edition, DJ. $25–$35.

PYM, Barbara. *Excellent Women.* London: Jonathan Cape (1952), 1st English edition, DJ. $150–$200.

PYNCHON, Thomas. *Gravity's Rainbow.* New York: Viking (1973), 1st edition, DJ. $75–$125.

PYNCHON, Thomas. *The Crying of Lot 49.* Philadelphia: Lippincott (1965), 1st edition, DJ. $100–$150.

 Q ——————————————————————

QUEEN, Ellery. *See* Vintage Paperbacks.

QUENNELL, Peter. *Poems.* New York: Jonathan Cape and Harrison Smith (nd), printed in Holland, wide quarto, patterned cloth, one of 500 copies. $25.

QUILLER-COUCH, Sir Arthur. *In Powder and Crinoline.* (London): Hodder and Stoughton (1913), quarto, illustrated by Kay Nielsen with 24 tipped-in color plates, pictorial ep's, and tissue guards. $250–$350.

QUILLER-COUCH, Sir Arthur. *The Twelve Dancing Princesses and Other Fairy Tales Retold by.* New York: Doran (nd), 1st American edition, 16 tipped-in color plates by Kay Nielsen, plus decorated binding by the artist as well as black and white drawings in text, DJ. $75–$250.

 R ————————————————————————

RACHE, Elmer. *See* "Key to Illustrators."

RACKHAM, Arthur. *The Arthur Rackham Fairy Book.* Philadelphia: Lippincott (1933), 1st American edition, 8 color plates plus numerous black and white silhouettes in text, introduction by Rackham, DJ. $150–$200.

RACKHAM, Arthur. *See* "Key to Illustrators."

RADIN, Edward. *Lizzie Borden: The Untold Story.* New York: Simon & Schuster 1961, 1st edition, DJ. $25.

RAGGEDY ANN. See Gruelle, Johnny.

RAINE, Kathleen. *The Lion's Mouth.* London: Hamish Hamilton 1977, 1st edition, DJ. $25.

RAINE, William MacLeod. *Arkansas Guns.* Boston: Houghton, Mifflin "1954", 1st edition, DJ. $10–$40.

RAINE, William MacLeod. *Bucky O'Conner.* New York: Grosset & Dunlap (1910), reprint edition, black and white ills by Clarence Rowe. $3–$7.

RAINE, William MacLeod. *Bucky O'Conner.* New York: Grosset & Dunlap (1910), reprint edition, black and white ills by Clarence Rowe, DJ. $7–$12.

RAINE, William MacLeod, *Famous Sheriffs and Western Outlaws.* New York: Doubleday 1929, 1st edition, DJ. $75–$125.

RAND, Ayn. *Atlas Shrugged.* New York: Random House (1957), 1st edition, DJ. $100–$200.

RAND, Ayn. *See also* Vintage Paperbacks.

RANSOM, John Crowe. *Chills and Fever*. New York: Knopf 1924, 1st edition, 1st issue, DJ, scarce thus. $100–$175.

RANSOM, John Crowe. *The New Criticism—An Examination of the Critical Theories of I.A. Richards, T.S. Eliot, Yvor Winters, and William Empson*. Norfolk: New Directions (1941), 1st edition, DJ. $50–$100.

RANSOME, Arthur. *Swallows and Amazons*. London: Jonathan Cape 1937, 11th impression of the 1st illustrated edition, published in 1931 (1st edition was 1930, unillustrated), illustrated by Clifford Webb, ep's by Stephen Spurrier. $25–$50.

RAWLINGS, Marjorie Kinnan. *Cross Creek Cookery*. New York: Scribner's 1942, 1st edition with drawings by Robert Camp, pictorial cover and endpapers, DJ. $50–$100.

RAWLINGS, Marjorie Kinnan. *Cross Creek Cookery*. New York: Scribner's 1942, 1st edition, 2nd printing, with white ep's, DJ. $25–$35.

RAWLINGS, Marjorie Kinnan. *The Yearling*. New York: Scribner's 1938, 1st edition, decorations by Edward Shenton, DJ. $35–$75.

RAWLINGS, Marjorie Kinnan. *The Yearling*. New York: Scribner's 1939, 1st edition thus (1st trade edition of this 1939 Pulitzer Prize edition), beige pictorial linen binding, top page edges stained pale green, 14 color plates and colored ep's by N.C. Wyeth, DJ. $65–$100

RAWLINGS, Marjorie Kinnan. *The Yearling*. New York: Scribner's 1939, 1st edition thus (1st trade edition of this 1939 Pulitzer Prize edition), beige pictorial linen binding, top page edges stained pale green, 14 color plates and colored ep's by N.C. Wyeth. $25–$40.

RAWLINGS, Marjorie Kinnan. *See also* Scribner's Illustrated Classics.

READ, Herbert. *Art Now*. London: Faber & Faber 1936, new and Revised edition, small quarto, 128 plates, DJ designed by E. McKnight Kauffer, as in the 1st edition, with DJ. $25–$40.

REBECCA OF SUNNYBROOK FARM. See Wiggin, Kate Douglas.

RED RYDER. See Big Little Books.

REED, John. *Ten Days That Shook the World*. New York: Boni & Liveright 1919, ills, 1st edition. $100–$250.

REED, Myrtle. *Old Rose and Silver*. New York and London: G.P.Putnam's 1909, Margaret Armstrong decorative binding. $25–$35.

REED, Ishmael. *The Last Days of Louisiana Red*. New York: Random House (1974), 1st edition, DJ. $20–$35.

REFERENCE BOOKS. *See* "Key to Categories."

REMARQUE, Erich Maria. *All Quiet on the Western Front*. London: Putnam's 1929, 1st edition in English, DJ. $50–$150.

REMINGTON, Frederick. *See* "Key to Illustrators."

REPPLIER, Agnes. *Pere Marquette*. New York: Doubleday, Doran 1929, 1st edition, DJ. $20–$50.

REXROTH, Kenneth. *Morning Star*. New York: New Directions 1979, 1st edition, DJ. $20–$25.

REZNIKOFF, Charles. *The Lionhearted*. Philadelphia: Jewish Publication Society 1944, 1st edition, DJ, scarce. $50–$75.

RHEAD, Louis. *See* "Key to Illustrators."

RHYS, Jean. *The Left Bank—Sketches and Studies of Present-Day Bohemian Paris*. London: 1927, 1st edition of author's first book, DJ. $250–$500.

RHYS, Jean. *The Left Bank—Sketches and Studies of Present-Day Bohemian Paris*. New York: 1927, 1st American edition of author's first book, DJ. $65–$100.

RICE, Alice Hegan. *Mrs. Wiggs of the Cabbage Patch*. New York: 1901, 1st edition, 1st issue, illustrated. $75–$100.

RICE, Anne. *Interview with a Vampire*. New York: 1976, 1st edition, DJ. $400–$500.

RICE, Craig. *See* Vintage Paperbacks.

RICE, Elmer. *Street Scene*. New York: French 1929, wrappers, 1st edition. $30.

RICH, Adrienne. *Diving into the Wreck*. New York: Norton 1973, 1st edition, DJ. $20–$35.

RICH, Adrienne. *The Diamond Cutters*. New York: Harper & Brothers (1955), 1st edition of author's second book as an adult, DJ. $75–$200.

RICHARDSON, Dorothy. *Deadlock*. London: Duckworth and Co. (1921), 1st edition, DJ. $150–$225.

RICHARDSON, Dorothy. *John Austen and the Inseparables*. London: William Jackson 1930, self-portrait and 5 other engravings by Austen, 1st trade edition. $25–$50.

RICHTER, Conrad. *The Sea of Grass*. New York: Knopf 1937, 1st trade edition, DJ. $35–$75.

RIDGE, Lola. *Firehead*. New York: Payson and Clarke 1929, 1st trade edition, DJ. $25–$95.

RIDING, Laura. *Collected Poems*. London: 1938, 1st English edition, DJ. $100–$200.

RIDING, Laura. *The Left Heresy in Literature and Life*. London: 1939, 1st English edition, DJ. $75–$200.

RIDLER, Anne. *Cain*. London: 1943, 1st edition, DJ. $25–$50.

RILEY, James Whitcomb. *An Old Sweetheart of Mine*. Indianapolis: Bobbs-Merrill (1902), 1st edition, ills by Howard Chandler Christy, decorated cloth binding, floral decorations within by Virginia Keep, front cover has pictorial paste-on. $20–$50.

RILEY, James Whitcomb. *Out to Old Aunt Mary's*. Indianapolis: Bobbs-Merrill (1904), 1st edition, decorative binding, illustrated throughout by Howard Chandler Christy, decorative borders by Margaret Armstrong. $20–$50.

RILEY, James Whitcomb. *Riley Child Verse*. Indianapolis: Bowen-Merrill (1906), 8 color plates and many other colored ills by Ethel Franklin Betts, the whole on heavy coated stock. $50–$100

RILEY, James Whitcomb. *Riley Child-Rymes*. Indianapolis: Bowen-Merrill 1899, 1st edition, later printing, 80 ills by Will Vawter, pictorial cloth. $30.

RILEY, James Whitcomb. *The Flying Islands of the Night*. Indianapolis: Bowen-Merrill 1892, 1st edition, 1st printing, Binding A (white boards). $150.

RILEY, James Whitcomb. *See also* Sets.

RILKE, Rainer Maria. *Duineser Elegien.* Leipzig: Insel Verlag 1923, 1st edition, DJ. $150–$300.

RILKE, Rainer Maria. *Duino Elegies*, translated with commentary by J.B.Leishman and Stephen Spender. New York: Norton (1939), 1st American edition, DJ. $50–$150.

RILKE, Rainer Maria. *Poems from the Book of Hours 'Das Studenbuch'*, translated by Babette Deutsch. Norfolk: New Directions (1941), 1st edition, DJ. $20–$35.

RILKE, Rainer Maria. *The Notebooks of Malte Laurids Brigge.* London: Hogarth Press 1930, 1st edition, DJ. $100–$200.

RIMBAUD, Arthur. *A Season in Hell*, translated by Delmore Schwartz. Norfolk: New Directions (1939), 1st edition of this translation, one of 750 copies printed by Edmund Thompson at Hawthorn House, DJ. $40–$75.

RIMBAUD, Arthur. *Une Saison En Enfer.* Brussels: 1873, 1st edition, one of 250, original wraps. $5,500.

RINEHART, Mary Roberts. *Nomad's Land.* New York: Doran 1926, 1st edition, DJ. $25–$50.

RIP VAN WINKLE. See Irving, Washington.

ROBBINS, Tom. *Even Cowgirls Get the Blues.* Boston: Houghton Mifflin 1976, 1st edition, DJ. $75–$150.

ROBERTS, Elizabeth Madox. *The Great Meadow.* New York: Viking Press 1930, 1st edition, DJ. $20–$50.

ROBERTS, Kenneth. *Europe's Morning After.* New York: Harper & Brothers 1921, 1st edition, DJ. $125–$250.

ROBERTS, Kenneth. *Lydia Bailey.* Garden City: New York: Doubleday 1947, 1st trade edition, DJ. $25–$50.

ROBERTS, Kenneth. *Northwest Passage.* Garden City: Doubleday, Doran 1937, special 2-vol edition limited to 1,051 numbered sets signed by the author, with tipped-in page from Robert's working manuscript, DJs, boxed. $125–$200.

ROBERTSON, Frank C. *The Outlaw of Antler.* New York: Dutton "1937", 1st edition, DJ. $25–$50.

ROBIN HOOD. Philadelphia: McKay 1917, 1st edition, plates by N.C. Wyeth. $35–$65.

ROBINSON CRUSOE. See Defoe, Daniel.

ROBINSON, Charles. *See* "Key to Illustrators."

ROBINSON, Edwin Arlington. *Sonnets, 1889-1927*. New York: Macmillan 1928, 1st trade edition, DJ. $20–$50.

ROBINSON, F. *See* "Key to Illustrators."

ROBINSON, Jackie. *I Never Had it Made*. New York: Putnam (1972), 1st edition, DJ. $20–$35

ROBINSON, W. Heath. *Bill the Minder*. New York: Holt 1912, 1st American edition, includes 16 color plates by Robinson. $200.

ROBINSON, W. Heath. *See* "Key to Illustrators."

ROCKMORE, Noel. *See* "Key to Illustrators."

ROCKWOOD, Roy. *See* Juvenile Series Books.

ROETHKE, Theodore. *Collected Poems*. Garden City: Doubleday 1966, 1st edition, DJ. $30–$50.

ROETHKE, Theodore. *The Lost Son and Other Poems*. Garden City: Doubleday 1948, 1st edition, DJ. $150–$200.

ROETHKE, Theodore. *Words for the Wind*. London: Secker & Warburg 1957, 1st edition, DJ. $75–$125.

ROGERS, Bruce. *See* "Key to Illustrators."

ROGERS, Will. *There's Not a Bathing Suit in Russia and Other Bare Facts*. New York: Boni 1927, 1st edition, illustrated by Herb Roth. $15–$35.

ROHMER, Sax. *Daughter of Fu Manchu*. Garden City: Doubleday 1931, 1st edition, DJ. $75–$150.

ROHMER, Sax. *Tales of Secret Egypt*. New York: McKinlay, Stone & Mackenzie (1919), reprint edition, black and white frontis. $3.50–$8.

ROHMER, Sax. *The Return of Dr. Fu-Manchu*. New York: McKinlay, Stone & Mackenzie (1916), reprint edition, black and white frontis. $3.50–$8.

ROHMER, Sax. *The Romance of Sorcery*. London: (1914), thick octavo, somewhat worn. $100–$150.

ROLVAAG, O.E. *Giants in the Earth. A Saga of the Prairie*. New York and London: Harper's 1927, 1st trade edition, DJ. $50–$100.

ROSENBERG, Isaac. *Poems.* London: Heinemann 1922, 1st edition, introduction by Laurence Binyon, DJ, scarce. $150–$350.

ROSETTI, Christina. *Goblin Market.* London: 1893, illustrated by Laurence Housman, 1st thus, 12 plates, aeg. $225–$540.

ROSETTI, Christina. *See also* Eragny Press.

ROSS, M.T. *See* "Key to Illustrators."

ROTH, Herb. *See* "Key to Illustrators."

ROTH, Philip. *Portnoy's Complaint.* New York: Random House (1969), 1st trade edition, DJ. $35–$50.

ROWE, Clarence. *See* "Key to Illustrators."

RUARK, Robert. *Honey Badger.* New York: McGraw-Hill 1965, 1st edition, DJ. $30.

RUARK, Robert. *Old Man and the Boy.* New York: Houghton Mifflin 1960, 1st printing, DJ. $45–$75.

RUBIN, Jerry. *We are Everywhere.* New York: Harper & Row (1971), 1st edition, DJ. $25–$50.

RUKEYSER, Muriel. *Beast in View.* New York: Doubleday, Doran 1944, 1st edition, DJ. $35–$50.

RUKEYSER, Muriel. *The Life of Poetry.* New York: Current Books, Inc., A.A. Wynn, Publisher 1949, 1st edition, DJ. $35–$50.

RUKEYSER, Muriel. *Theory of Flight.* New Haven: 1935, 1st edition of author's first book, DJ. $150–$250.

RUNYON, Damon. *In Our Town.* New York: Creative Age Press (1946), 1st edition, illustrated by Garth Williams, DJ. $40–$65.

RUSH, Benjamin. *Medical Inquiries and Observations.* Philadelphia: Printed by Griggs and Dickenson for M. Carey 1815, 4th edition, 4 vols in 2, newly rebound. $150–$200.

RUSHDIE, Salman. *The Satanic Verses.* New York: Viking (1988), 1st edition of author's 4th novel, 3rd in a series given important awards by France and Britain, and to which the fundamentalist government of Iran responded with a death sentence on its author for blasphemy, DJ. $50–$125.

RUSKIN, John. *See* Doves Press.

RUSSELL, Bertrand. *Mysticism and Logic*. New York: Norton (1929), 1st American edition, DJ. $35–$65.

RUSSELL, Bertrand. *See also* Whitehead, Alfred North.

RUSSELL, George W. ("AE"). *See* Cuala Press.

 S ─────────────────────────────────

SABATINI, Rafael. *See* Sets.

SACKVILLE-WEST, Vita. *All Passion Spent*. London: Hogarth Press 1931, 1st edition, DJ. $75–$125.

SACKVILLE-WEST, Vita. *All Passion Spent*. New York: 1931, 1st American edition, DJ. $25–$50.

SAINT-EXUPERY, Antoine de. *The Little Prince*. New York: Reynal & Hitchcock (1943), 1st trade edition in English, ills in color by the author, DJ. $50–$150.

SAKI. *The Novels and Plays of Saki*. New York: Viking Press 1933, 1-vol edition, DJ. $50.

SAKI. *The Unbearable Bassington*. London: Eyre and Spottiswoode (Century Library #5) 1947, 1st edition, DJ. $30–$75.

SAKI. *The Westminster Alice*. London: Westminster Gazette 1902, 1st edition, original wrappers, with black and white drawings by F.Carruthers Gould, parodying Tenniel. $150–$200.

SALINGER, J.D. *Nine Stories*. Boston: Little, Brown (1953), 1st edition of author's second book, DJ. $400–$750.

SALINGER, J.D. *The Catcher in the Rye*. New York: Little, Brown 1951, 1st edition of author's first book with "first edition" so stated. DJ of book club edition has Book of the Month Clud statement on rear flap. DJ. $400–$1,500.

SALINGER, J.D. *The Catcher in the Rye*. New York: Little, Brown 1951, Book of the Month Club edition, DJ. $35–$125.

SALINGER, J.D. *The Complete Uncollected Short Stories of J.D.*

Salinger. Piracy, np, nd, 2 vols; the 1st edition, with printed, not pictorial, wraps. $550.

SALINGER, J.D. *See also* Barrows, R.M., for Salinger's first appearance in book form.

SAMSON AND DELILAH. See Golden Cockerel Press.

SANDBURG, Carl. *Abraham Lincoln: The Prairie Years.* New York: Harcourt, Brace (1926), 1st trade edition, 2 vols, 118 ills, 5 maps. $35–$40.

SANDBURG, Carl. *Abraham Lincoln: The War Years.* New York: Harcourt, Brace (1939–40), 1st trade edition, 4 vols, illustrated with 414 halftones from photographs and 249 reproductions of cartoons, letters, documents, etc., boxed. $60–$125.

SANDBURG, Carl. *Cornhuskers.* New York: Harcourt, Brace 1918, 1st edition, 1st state. $30–$50.

SANDBURG, Carl. *The People, Yes.* New York: Harcourt, Brace (1936), 1st trade edition, DJ. $25–$30.

SANDOZ, Mari. *Slogum House.* Boston: Little, Brown "1937", 1st edition of her second book and first novel, DJ. $50.

SANTEE, Ross. *The Rummy Kid Goes Home and Other Stories of the Southwest.* New York: Hastings "1965", 1st edition, illustrated by the author, DJ. $20.

SARG, Tony. *See* "Key to Illustrators."

SAROYAN, William. *The Human Comedy.* New York: Harcourt, Brace (1943), 1st edition, ills by Don Freeman, DJ. $75–$100.

SAROYAN, William. *See also* Grabhorn Printing.

SARTON, May. *Encounter in April.* Boston: Little, Brown 1938, 1st edition of author's first book, DJ. $150–$250.

SARTON, May. *Mrs. Stevens Hears the Mermaids Singing.* New York: Norton (1965), 1st edition, DJ. $50.

SARTON, May. *The Education of Harriet Hatfield.* New York: Norton (1989), 1st edition, DJ. $20.

SARTON, May. *The House by the Sea.* New York: Norton (1977), 1st edition, DJ. $35.

SARTON, May. *The Magnificent Spinster.* New York: Norton (1985), 1st edition, DJ. $25.

SARTRE, Jean Paul. *The Emotions.* New York: Philosophical Library (1948), 1st American edition, DJ. $30–$50.

SAUNDERS, Louise. *The Knave of Hearts.* New York: Scribner 1925, 1st edition, large quarto, 23 full-page and other smaller color ills, pictorial ep's and colored pictorial cover label, all by Maxfield Parrish. $500–$900.

SAUNDERS, Louise. *The Knave of Hearts.* Racine: Whitman nd, later edition, quarto, 10 full-page and other smaller color ills, pictorial title page and half title and frontis, all by Maxfield Parrish. $300–$400.

SAUVAGE, Sylvan. *See* "Key to Illustrators."

SAY, Allen. *See* "Key to Illustrators."

SAYERS, Dorothy. *Strong Poison.* New York: Brewer & Warren (1930), 1st American edition, DJ. $150–$200.

SAYERS, Dorothy. *The Nine Taylors.* London: Gollancz 1934, 1st edition, DJ. $75–$100.

SAYERS, Dorothy. *Unpopular Opinions.* London: Gollancz 1946, 1st edition, DJ. $45–$60.

SCHINDELMAN, Joseph. *See* "Key to Illustrators."

SCHOONOVER, Frank. *See* "Key to Illustrators."

SCHREINER, Olive. *Story of an African Farm.* Chicago: Donahue, Henneberry & Co. nd (about 1895), presumed 1st American edition. $75–$100.

SCHULBERG, Budd. *What Makes Sammy Run?* New York: Random House 1941, 1st edition of author's first book, DJ. $150–$350.

SCHWARTZ, Delmore. *The World is a Wedding.* Norfolk: New Directions 1948, 1st edition, DJ. $75–$125.

SCIENCE FICTION, FANTASY, HORROR. *See* "Key to Categories."

SCORESBY, William, Jr. *An Account of the Arctic Regions, with a History and Description of the Northern Whale-Fishery.* Edinburgh: 1820, 1st edition, 2 vols. $900–$1,200.

SCOTT, Peter. *See* "Key to Illustrators."

SCOUTING. Seton, Ernest Thompson, and Baden-Powell, Lieutenant-General Sir Robert. *Boy Scouts of America.* 1910, soft cover, cover soiled and worn. $150–$400.

SCOUTING. *Brownie Scout Handbook*. New York: Girl Scouts of the United States of America 1954. $5.

SCOUTING. Camp Fire Girls, *see also* Trade Catalogs.

SCOUTING. *Den Mother's Den Book*. New York: Boy Scouts of America 1947. $10.

SCOUTING. *Explorer Manual*. New York: Boy Scouts of America 1950. $7.

SCOUTING. *Girl Scout Handbook*. 3rd impression. New York: Girl Scouts of the United States of America (1933). $12.

SCOUTING. *Handbook for Boys*. New York: Boy Scouts of America 1916, 1st edition, 14th printing. $85.

SCOUTING. *Handbook for Boys*. New York: Boy Scouts of America 1919, 1st edition, 20th printing. $85.

SCOUTING. *Handbook for Boys*. New York: Boy Scouts of America 1922, 1st edition, 26th printing. $70.

SCOUTING. *Handbook for Boys*. New York: Boy Scouts of America 1926, 1st edition, 35th printing. $40.

SCOUTING. *Handbook for Boys*. New York: Boy Scouts of America 1912, 1st edition, 4th printing. $135.

SCOUTING. *Handbook for Boys*. New York: Boy Scouts of America 1911, 1st edition, 400 pages. $165.

SCOUTING. *Handbook for Boys*. New York: Boy Scouts of America 1943, 4th edition, 36th printing. $15.

SCOUTING. *Handbook for Boys*. New York: Boy Scouts of America 1976, 8th edition, 4th printing. $6.

SCOUTING. *Handbook for Boys*. New York: Boy Scouts of America 1911. $160.

SCOUTING. *Handbook for Patrol Leaders*. New York: Boy Scouts of America 1929, 1st edition, 2nd printing. $25.

SCOUTING. *Handbook for Scoutmasters*. New York: Boy Scouts of America 1918, 1st edition. $120.

SCOUTING. *Handbook for Scoutmasters*. New York: Boy Scouts of America 1920, 2nd edition, 2nd printing. $50.

SCOUTING. *Handbook for Scoutmasters*. New York: Boy Scouts of America 1923, 2nd edition, 4th printing. $40.

SCOUTING. *Handbook for Scoutmasters.* New York: Boy Scouts of America 1930, 2nd edition, 15th printing. $30.

SCOUTING. *Handbook for Scoutmasters.* New York: Boy Scouts of America 1953, 4th edition, 7th printing. $10.

SCOUTING. *How Girls Can Help Their Country.* New York: The Camp Fire Girls, Inc. 1917; this was the first Camp Fire Girls handbook. $75.

SCOUTING. *Leader's Guide to the Brownie Scout Program.* New York: The Girl Scouts of the United States of America (1945), 2nd printing. $10.

SCOUTING. *Patrols and their Court of Honor/Girl Scouts.* New York: The Girl Scouts of the United States of America 1929, has brown silhouette. $18.

SCOUTING. *Revised Handbook for Boys.* New York: Boy Scouts of America 1932, 17th printing. $25.

SCOUTING. *Revised Handbook for Boys.* New York: Boy Scouts of America 1940, 32nd printing. $25.

SCOUTING. *Scouting for Girls, Official Handbook.* New York: Girl Scouts, Inc. 1926, 8th reprint. $15.

SCOUTING. *Scouting for Girls.* New York: Girl Scouts, Inc. 1920, 1st edition. $25.

SCOUTING. *Scouting for Girls.* New York: Girl Scouts, Inc. 1920, 2nd edition. $20.

SCOUTING. *Sea Scout Manual.* New York: Boy Scouts of America 1929. $30.

SCOUTING. *Senior Girl Scouting.* New York: The Girl Scouts of the United States of America 1945. $12.

SCOUTING. *The Book of the Campfire Girls.* New York: Campfire Girls, Inc. 1922, 10th printing. $30.

SCOUTING. *The Book of the Campfire Girls.* New York: Campfire Girls, Inc. 1942. $10.

SCOUTING. *The Wolf Cubbook, Cubs B.S.A.* New York: Boy Scouts of America 1939. $12.

SCOUTING. *Wo-He-Lo, The Story of the Camp Fire Girls, 1910-1960.* New York: Campfire Girls, Inc. 1961, 1st edition. $10.

SCRIBNER'S ILLUSTRATED CLASSICS. Rawlings, Marjorie

Kinnan. *The Yearling*. New York: Scribner's 1940, Scribner Illustrated Classics edition, black cloth binding with paste-on pictorial label, 12 color plates by N.C. Wyeth, as well as pictorial title page and ep's, DJ. $125–$250.

SCRIBNER'S ILLUSTRATED CLASSICS. Rawlings, Marjorie Kinnan. *The Yearling*. New York: Scribner's 1940, Scribner's Illustrated Classics edition, black cloth binding with paste-on pictorial label, 12 color plates by N.C. Wyeth, as well as pictorial title page and ep's. $50–$125.

SCRIBNER'S ILLUSTRATED CLASSICS. James, Will. *Smoky the Cowhorse*. (New York: Scribner's 1929), square 8vo, 1st printing of "Illustrated Classics Edition," 6 full-page color plates and title page in color by author. This series has black cloth, pictorial paste-on labels. $35.

SCRIBNER'S ILLUSTRATED CLASSICS. *See also* Stevenson, Robert Louis, 2 entries.

SENDAK, Maurice. *Seven Little Monsters*. New York: Harper & Row (1975), 1st American edition, illustrated by Sendak, DJ. $35–$45.

SENDAK, Maurice. *See also* "Key to Illustrators."

SERVICE, Robert. *Rhymes of a Red Cross Man*. Toronto: Briggs 1916, 1st edition. $20–$40.

SERVICE, Robert. *Rhymes of a Rolling Stone*. Toronto: Briggs (1912), later printing. $7.50–$15.

SETON, Ernest Thompson. *Lives of the Hunted*. New York: Scribner's 1901, 1st edition, over 200 drawings by the author, decorated cloth. $40–$60.

SETON, Ernest Thompson. *See also* Scouting.

SETS. Barrie, James. *The Works of*. London: New York: Scribner's 1929-31; the Peter Pan Edition; 14 vols, limited to 1,030 sets, signed by the publisher. $75–$400.

SETS. Bierce, Ambrose. *The Collected Works of*. New York: The Neale Publishing Co. 1901-12, 1st edition, limited to 250 copies, 12 vols. $500–$750.

SETS. Casanova, Jacques. *The Memoirs of Jacques Casanova, an Autobiography*. London: 1929, translated by Arthur Machen, 12 vols, limited edition of 550 sets. $150–$175.

SETS. Crane, Stephen. *The Work of.* New York: Knopf (1925-26), 12 vols, limited edition of 750 sets, boxes showing wear, DJs. $300.

SETS. Firbank, Ronald. *The Works.* London: 1928, 5 vols, in yellow buckram, one of 235 sets. $500.

SETS. Glasgow, Ellen. *The Virginia Edition of the Works of Ellen Glasgow.* New York: 1938, signed and limited edition of 810 sets, 12 vols, in glassine and slipcases. $300–$600.

SETS. Hudson, W.H. *The Collected Works.* London: Dent 1922, 24 vols, green cloth, gilt lettering, raised profile, teg, portrait frontis, limited to 750 numbered sets, DJs. $1,000.

SETS. Hubbard, Elbert. *Little Journeys to the Homes of the Great.* East Aurora: The Roycrofters 1928, 14 vols, DJs, pictorial ep's, beige cloth with paper labels. $65–$100.

SETS. Machen, Arthur. *The Works of Arthur Machen.* London: Martin Secker (1923), 9 vols, the Caerleon edition, limited to 1,000 numbered sets signed by Machen. $400–$800.

SETS. Riley, James Whitcomb. *The Works of.* New York: Scribner's 1910-16, 16 vols, Homestead Edition. $75–$125.

SETS. Sabatini, Rafael. *The Writings of.* Boston: Houghton, Mifflin 1924-31, 29 vols, cloth, definitive edition. $150.

SETS. *The Yellow Book.* London: Elkin Mathews and John Lane; later issues John Lane, the Bodley Head, London and New York, April 1894-April 1897, 13 vols, complete set, decorated cloth. $450–$600.

SETS. Thoreau, Henry David. *Works of.* Boston: Riverside Edition, (1893-94), 11 vols, some rubbing. $650.

SEUSS, Dr. *The Cat in the Hat Comes Back.* New York: Beginner Books, Inc. (1958), 1st printing, illustrated by Dr. Seuss. $50–$75.

SEUSS, Dr. *The Cat in the Hat Comes Back.* New York: Beginner Books, Inc. (1958), later printing, illustrated by Dr. Seuss. $1.25–$5.

SEWELL, Helen. *See* "Key to Illustrators," then Wheelright, Rowland.

SEXTON, Anne. *To Bedlam and Part Way Back.* Boston: Houghton, Mifflin 1960, 1st edition of author's first book, DJ. $75–$125.

SHAHN, Ben. *See* "Key to Illustrators."

SHAKESPEARE, William. *Collected Works of.* London: 1723–25, edited by Alexander Pope, 6 vols, quarto, cloth, library markings, single price at auction. $475.

SHAKESPEARE, William. Facsimile edition. New York: New York Folio 1968, The Norton Facsimile. $50–$150.

SHAKESPEARE, William. (Set of all four folios.) London: 1623–1685, 1st issue of 2nd folio, 2nd issue of 3rd folio, 1st state of 1st issue of 4th folio, the Garden copy. $2,090,000.

SHAKESPEARE, William. *See also* Grabhorn Printing; Doves Press.

SHAPIRO, Karl. *Person, Place and Thing.* (New York): Reynal & Hitchcock (1942), 1st edition, DJ. $25–$50.

SHAW, Charles. *See* "Key to Illustrators."

SHAW, George Bernard. *Ellen Terry and Bernard Shaw.* New York: The Fountain Press 1931, one of 3,000 numbered copies, publisher's slipcase. $50–$60.

SHAW, George Bernard. *Pygmalion.* New York: 1914, 1st complete edition of the play, bound for promotional purposes, and the 1st in hard covers; illustrated by May Wilson Preston. $100.

SHAW, George Bernard. *Saint Joan.* New York: Brentano's 1924, 1st American edition, DJ. $20–$35.

SHELLEY, Percy Bysshe. *Hellas.* London: 1822, 1st edition. $1,000–$1,500.

SHELLEY, Percy Bysshe. *See* Ashendene Press: *Three Elegies;* Kelmscott Press.

SHENTON, Edward. *See* "Key to Illustrators."

SHEPARD, Ernest H. *See* "Key to Illustrators."

SHEPARD, Mary. *See* "Key to Illustrators."

SHIRER, William. *The Rise and Fall of the Third Reich.* New York: Simon and Schuster "1960." $20–$30.

SHUTE, Nevil. *A Town Like Alice.* London: Heinemann (1960), 1st edition, DJ. $50–$65.

SHUTE, Nevil. *On the Beach.* New York: Morrow 1957, 1st American edition, DJ. $35–$75.

SIDNEY, Margaret. *Five Little Peppers and How They Grew.* Boston: Lothrop 1880, 1st edition, 1st issue, with ". . . said Polly" in line beneath picture on page 231, and 1880 copyright date. $200–$300.

SILVERBERG, Robert. *Hawksbill Station.* Garden City: Doubleday 1968, 1st edition; nominated for Hugo Award in 1968 and for Nebula Award in 1967, DJ. $50–$100.

SILVERBERG, Robert. *Lord of Darkness.* New York: Arbor House (1983), 1st edition, DJ. $20–$25.

SIMON, Neil. *Last of the Red Hot Lovers.* New York: Random House (1970), DJ. $35.

SIMONT, Marc. *See* "Key to Illustrators."

SIMPSON, Sir George. *Narrative of a Journey Round the World, During the Years 1841 and 1842.* London: Harry Colburn 1847, 2 vols, 1st edition, original cloth. $300–$600.

SINCLAIR, Upton. *The Jungle.* New York: Doubleday, Page & Co. 1906, the 1st Doubleday edition, later printing with the "1" in the "1906" on the copyright page in imperfect type (the same plates were used as in the Jungle Publishing Co. edition). $35–$75.

SINCLAIR, Upton. *The Jungle.* New York: The Jungle Publishing Co. (1906), "Sustainer's Edition," with the "Jungle" imprint and "Sustainer's" slip; earliest state with "1906" in unbroken type in the copyright notice. $50–$200.

SINGER, Isaac Bashevis. *The Family Moskat.* New York: Knopf 1950, 1st edition of the first of Singer's books in English, DJ. $65–$100.

SINGER, Isaac Bashevis. *Zlateth the Goat and Other Stories.* New York: Harper & Row 1966, 1st trade edition, pictures by Maurice Sendak, DJ. $25.

SIR GAWAIN AND THE GREEN KNIGHT. See Golden Cockerel Press.

SITWELL, Edith. *The Canticle of the Rose: Selected Poems 1920-1947.* London: Macmillan 1949, 1st edition, DJ. $25–$35.

SITWELL, Osbert. *Left Hand, Right Hand: An Autobiography.* London: 1945–50, 1st edition, 5 vols, ills, DJs. $45–$85.

SKIPPY. See Big Little Books.

SLOCUM, Joshua. *Sailing Alone Around the World.* New York: Century 1900, 1st edition. Probably the most famous of the solo voyages, on a small sailing sloop. $100.

SMILIN' JACK. See Big Little Books.

SMITH, Betty. *A Tree Grows in Brooklyn.* New York: Harper's 1943, 1st issue, DJ. $25–$35.

SMITH, E. Boyd. *See* "Key to Illustrators."

SMITH, Jessie Wilcox. *See* "Key to Illustrators."

SMITH, Stevie. *Mother, What is Man?* London: 1942, 1st edition, many black and white drawings by the author, DJ. $35–$125.

SMITH, Thorne. *Topper Takes a Trip.* Garden City: Doubleday 1932, 1st edition, DJ. $75–$150.

SMITH, Wilhelm. *See* "Key to Illustrators."

SNELL, Roy J. *See* Juvenile Series Books.

SNOW, Edgar Rowe. *Famous Lighthouses of New England.* Boston: Yankee Publishing Co. (October 1945), "first edition" so stated. $20–$40.

SNOW, Edgar Rowe. *New England Sea Tragedies.* New York: Dodd, Mead & Co. 1960, 1st edition, DJ. $12–$25.

SNOW, Edgar Rowe. *Prirates and Buccaneers of the Atlantic Coast.* Boston: Yankee Publishing Co. (December 1944), 1st edition, illustrated, DJ. $25–$45.

SNYDER, Gary. *Axe Handles. Poems.* San Francisco: Northpoint Press 1983, 1st edition, wraps. $20.

SONG OF SONGS, THE. See Golden Cockerel Press.

SONTAG, Susan. *Against Interpretation and Other Essays.* New York: 1966, 1st edition of author's second book, DJ. $25–$40.

SOUTHERN, Terry. *Red-Dirt Marijuana and Other Tastes.* (New York): New American Library (1967), 1st edition, DJ. $50.

SPARK, Muriel. *The Prime of Miss Jean Brodie.* London: Macmillan 1961, 1st edition, DJ. $50–$100.

SPENDER, Stephen. *Poems.* London: Faber & Faber 1933, 1st edition, DJ. $125–$150.

SPENDER, Stephen. *Poems.* New York: Random House 1934, 1st American edition, DJ. $35–$75.

SPENSER, Edmund. *See* Ashendene Press; Kelmscott Press.

SPILLANE, Mickey. *I, The Jury.* New York: E.P. Dutton 1947, 1st edition of author's first book, DJ. $150–$250.

SPRINGER, John S. *Forest Life and Forest Trees comprising Winter Camp-Life Among the Loggers, and Wild-Wood Adventure.* New York: 1851, woodcut ills. $125.

SPYRI, Johanna. *Heidi.* Boston: 1885, translated by Louise Brooks, 1st American edition. $200–$350.

SPYRI, Johanna. *Heidi.* New York: Grosset and Dunlap (1925), reprint edition, pictorial ep's, otherwise no ills. $2.50–$4.

SPYRI, Johanna. *Heidi.* Philadelphia: Lippincott 1919, illustrated by Maria Kirk, quarto, 14 tipped-in color plates. $75–$125.

STACKPOLE, Edouard A. *The Sea Hunters.* Philadelphia: Lippincott 1953, 16 plates. $18–$35.

STAFFORD, Jean. *Boston Adventure.* New York: Harcourt, Brace (1944), 1st edition of author's first book, DJ. $60.

STARBUCK, Alexander. *History of the American Whale Fishery from its Earliest Inception to the Year 1876.* Waltham: published by the author 1876 (actually published 1878), 1st edition, 6 plates, attractively rebound. $350–$550.

STARBUCK, Alexander. *History of the American Whale Fishery.* New York: 1964, 2 vols, later edition, one of 750 sets. $200.

STEEN, Marguerite. *The Sun is My Undoing.* New York: The Viking Press 1941, 1st edition, DJ. $25.

STEGNER, Wallace. *The Big Rock Candy Mountain.* New York: Duell, Sloane and Pearce (1943), 1st edition, DJ. $75–$250.

STEIG, William. *The Lonely Ones.* New York: Duell, Sloan & Pearce (1942), 1st edition, DJ. $35–$60.

STEIN, Gertrude. *Four Saints in Three Acts, An Opera to be Sung.* New York: Random House 1934, 1st edition, "First printing, February, 1934," DJ. $75–$225.

STEIN, Gertrude. *Matisse, Picasso and Gertrude Stein.* Paris: Plain Edition (1933), 1st edition, stiff printed wrappers, publisher's printed slipcase dated 1932, one of 500 copies. $200–$400.

STEIN, Gertrude. *Tender Buttons Objects Food Rooms.* New York: Claire Marie 1914, 1st edition, limited to 1,000 copies, paper-covered boards. $400.

STEIN, Gertrude. *Three Lives. Stories of the Good Anna, Melanctha, and the Gentle Lena.* New York: Grafton Press 1909, 1st edition of author's first book, one of 1,000 copies printed, 300 of which were used for the 1st English publication. $500–$1,000.

STEINBECK, John. *Cannery Row.* New York: Viking 1945, 1st edition, with "First published by the Viking Press in January, 1945" on copyright page, DJ. $50–$100.

STEINBECK, John. *East of Eden.* New York: Viking Press 1952, 1st trade edition, with "First published by the Viking Press in September 1952" on copyright page, DJ. $75–$225.

STEINBECK, John. *Of Mice and Men.* New York: Covici Friede (1937), 1st edition, 1st issue, with "heavy hands were pendula" on page 9, changed in later printings. $200–$400.

STEINBECK, John. *The Grapes of Wrath.* New York: Viking (1939), 1st edition, 1st issue, with "first published in April, 1939" on copyright page and "first edition" at bottom of front DW flap, DJ. $250–$1,000.

STEINBECK, John. *The Red Pony.* New York: Viking Press 1945, 1st illustrated edition, ills by Wesley Dennis, publisher's box. $25–$50.

STEINER-PRAG. *See* "Key to Illustrators."

STEPHENS, Alice B., and Wyeth, N.C. *See* "Key to Illustrators."

STERNE, Laurence. *See* Golden Cockerel Press.

STEVENS, Wallace. *Harmonium.* New York: Knopf 1923, 1st edition, 1st issue of author's first book, with "Published September, 1923" on copyright page, with binding of checkered paper-covered boards in blue, red, yellow, and white, DJ. $1,000–$1,200.

STEVENS, Wallace. *Harmonium.* New York: Knopf 1923, 1st edition, 1st issue of author's first book, with "Published September, 1923" on copyright page, with binding of checkered paper-covered boards in blue, red, yellow, and white. $200–$300.

STEVENS, Wallace. *Ideas of Order.* New York: Knopf 1936, 1st trade edition, 1st binding (striped cloth); includes 3 poems that were not in the earlier Alcestis Press edition of only 165 copies, DJ. $150–$300.

STEVENS, Wallace. *The Auroras of Autumn*. New York: Knopf 1950, 1st edition, DJ. $100–$150.

STEVENSON, Robert Louis. *A Child's Garden of Verses*. New York: Oxford University Press 1947, illustrated by Tasha Tudor, 1st thus, color and black and white, DJ. $75–$125.

STEVENSON, Robert Louis. *Kidnapped*. New York: Scribner's (1913), 1st edition, Scribner's Illustrated Classics, 17 color plates by N.C. Wyeth. $100–$200.

STEVENSON, Robert Louis. *Treasure Island*. New York: Scribner's 1911, 1st edition of the first of Scribner's Illustrated Classics, 17 color plates by N.C. Wyeth. $125–$250.

STOKER, Bram. *Dracula*. New York: 1899, 1st American edition, original pictorial cloth. $250–$650.

STOKER, Bram. *Dracula*. New York: Doubleday, Page & Co. 1904, early American edition, original decorated brown cloth. $100–$150.

STOKER, Bram. *Dracula*. Westminster: Archibald Constable & Co. 1897, 1st edition, 1st issue, with page 392 blank, and no ads bound in, original yellow cloth binding, tight but not fine. $1,200–$2,500.

STONE, I.F. *The Haunted Fifties*. New York: Random House 1963, 1st edition, DJ. $35–$50.

STONE, Robert. *A Flag for Sunrise*. New York: Knopf (1981), 1st edition, DJ. $20–$30.

STONE, Robert. *A Hall of Mirrors*. Boston: Houghton, Mifflin 1967, 1st edition of author's first book, DJ. $150–$350.

STONE, Robert. *Dog Soldiers*. Boston: Houghton, Mifflin 1974, 1st edition of author's second book, National Book Award winner, DJ. $30–$60.

STOPPARD, Tom. *Rosencrantz and Guidenstern are Dead*. London: 1967, 1st edition, DJ. $175–$225.

STOVER, Mary E. and Wallace. *See* "Key to Illustrators."

STRATTON-PORTER, Gene. *Birds of the Bible*. Cincinnati: Jennings and Graham 1909, 1st edition, illustrated with photos. $125–$300.

STRATTON-PORTER, Gene. *Firebird*. New York: Doubleday 1922, 1st edition, pictorial boards. $240–$400.

STRATTON-PORTER, Gene. *Freckles.* New York: Grosset & Dunlap (1904), early reprint edition. $12–$15.

STRATTON-PORTER, Gene. *Girl of the Limberlost.* New York: Doubleday 1909, 1st edition, illustrated by W.T. Benda, DJ. $50–$150.

STRATTON-PORTER, Gene. *Girl of the Limberlost.* New York: Doubleday 1909, 1st edition, illustrated by W.T. Benda. $12–$40.

STRATTON-PORTER, Gene. *Jesus of the Emerald.* New York: Doubleday, Page 1923, 1st edition. $400–$600.

STRATTON-PORTER, Gene. *Michael O'Halloran.* New York: Doubleday 1915, 1st edition, illustrated by F. Rogers. $10–$15.

STRATTON-PORTER, Gene. *Michael O'Halloran.* New York: Doubleday 1915, 1st edition, illustrated by F. Rogers, DJ. $15–$35.

STRATTON-PORTER, Gene. *Michael O'Halloran.* New York: Grosset & Dunlap (1915), reprint edition, DJ. $10–$15.

STRATTON-PORTER, Gene. *Michael O'Halloran.* New York: Grosset & Dunlap (1915), reprint edition. $5–$8.

STRATTON-PORTER, Gene. *Morning Face.* New York: Doubleday 1916, 1st edition, photographs. $50–$175.

STRATTON-PORTER, Gene. *The Magic Garden.* New York: Doubleday, Page 1927, 1st edition, ills and decorations by Thayer, DJ, fairly scarce in DJ. $60–$125.

STRATTON-PORTER, Gene. *What I Have Done with Birds.* Indianapolis: Bobbs-Merrill (1907), 1st edition, quarto. $100–$200.

STRAUB, Peter. *Koko.* New York: Dutton 1988, 1st edition, DJ. $20–$25.

STRAUB, Peter. *See also* King, Stephen: *The Talisman.*

STREATFIELD, Noel. *Circus Shoes.* New York: Random House (1939), 1st American edition, 2nd printing of her third book, issued in England as *The Circus is Coming,* issued as *Circus Shoes* in the US for the sake of the association with the earlier *Ballet Shoes* and *Tennis Shoes,* illustrated by R. Floethe. $10–$15.

STUART, Jesse. *Man with a Bull-Tongue Plow.* New York: Dutton 1934, 1st edition, DJ. $200–$300.

STUART, Jesse. *Taps For Private Tussie*. New York: Dutton 1943, 1st edition, DJ. $50–$100.

STUART, John. *See* "Key to Illustrators."

STYRON, William. *Lie Down in Darkness*. Indianapolis/New York: Bobbs-Merrill (1951), 1st edition, DJ. $100–$150.

SUTHERLAND, Graham. *See* "Key to Illustrators."

SWARTHOUT, Glendon. *They Came to Cordura*. New York: Random House "1958", 1st edition, made into a western (movie) with Gary Cooper, DJ. $35.

SWIFT, Jonathan. *See* Golden Cockerel Press.

SWINBURNE, Algernon Charles. *See* Golden Cockerel Press.

SWISS FAMILY ROBINSON. *See* Wyss, David.

SYLVESTER, Herbert Milton. *Indian Wars of New England*. Boston: W.B. Clarke 1910, 3 vols, 1st edition. $325.

SYNGE, John Millington. *The Playboy of the Western World*. Boston: Luce 1911, 1st American edition, vellum and boards. $35–$125.

SYNGE, John Millington. *Riders to the Sea*. Boston: Luce 1911, 1st American edition, vellum on spine. $35–$125.

SYNGE, John Millington. *See also* Cuala Press.

SZYK, Arthur. *The Hagaddah*, edited by Cecil Roth. Jerusalem: Massadah 1957, large quarto, text in English and Hebrew, blue velvet, stamped in gold, original lined folding box. $100–$350.

SZYK, Arthur. *The New Order*. New York: Putnam (1941), 1st edition, quarto, pictorial title page, 9 full color plates, 30 black and white ills by Szyk, DJ. $75–$200.

SZYK, Arthur. *See also* "Key to Illustrators."

 T ────────────────────────

TABER, Gladys. *Conversations with Amber*. Philadelphia: Lippincott (1978), 1st printing, DJ. $15–$25.

TABER, Gladys. *Especially Spaniels*. Philadelphia: Macrae-Smith Co. (1945), 1st edition, DJ. $15–$25.

TABER, Gladys. *Stillmeadow Calendar.* Philadelphia: Lippincott 1967, book club edition, DJ. $9–$15.

TABER, I.W. *See* "Key to Illustrators."

TAGORE, Rabindranath. *Fireflies.* New York: Macmillan 1928, 1st edition, decorated and pictorial DJ by Boris Artzybasheff. $35–$75.

TAGORE, Rabindranath. *Fruit-Gathering.* New York: Macmillan 1916, 1st trade edition. $15–$25.

TAILSPIN TOMMY. See Big Little Books.

TALE OF BEOWULF, THE. See Kelmscott Press.

TAN, Amy. *The Joy Luck Club.* New York: Putnam 1989, 1st edition of author's first book, DJ. $75–$150.

TARKINGTON, Booth. *Penrod.* Garden City: Doubleday, Page 1914, 1st edition, 1st issue, with "sence" for "sense" on page 19. $75–$125.

TARRANT, Margaret. *See* "Key to Illustrators."

TATE, Allen. *Poems: 1922-1947.* New York: Scribner's 1948, 1st edition, DJ. $35–$75.

TATE, James. *Absences, New Poems.* Boston: Little, Brown 1972, 1st edition, DJ. $15–$20.

TCHELITCHEW, Pavel. *See* "Key to Illustrators" under Whistler, Rex.

TENGGREN, Gustaf. *See* "Key to Illustrators."

TENNIEL, John. *See* "Key to Illustrators."

TENNYSON, Alfred. *See* Doves Press.

TENNYSON, Alfred, Lord. *Poems.* London: 1842, 2 vols. $300–$500.

THE ANGORA TWINNIES. Rochester, N.Y.: Stecher Litho. Co. (1917), illustrated by Margaret E. Price. $30–$50.

THE BOOK CLUB OF CALIFORNIA. Lewis, Oscar. *The Wonderful City of Carrie Van Wie: Paintings of San Francisco at the Turn of the Century.* Printed for the Book Club of California at the Grabhorn Press (1963), folio, 21 color plates, limited to 525 copies, DJ. $80–$100.

THE BOOK CLUB OF CALIFORNIA. Lewis, Oscar. *The Origin of the Celebrated Jumping Frog of Calaveras County.* San Francisco:

The Book Club of California 1931, one of 250 copies, frog decorations and decorative initials by Valenti Angelo, facsimile of 1853 newspaper insert. $125–$175.

THE DARK SIDE OF THE MOON. New York: Scribner's 1947, 1st edition. The author "for obvious reasons prefers to remain anonymous," DJ. $20.

THE LITTLE COLONEL. See Johnston, Annie Fellows.

THE NAVIGATOR. . . . Directions for Navigating the Monongahela, Allegheny, Ohio & Mississippi Rivers. Pittsburgh: Cramer, Spear & Eichbaum 1817 by Zadok Cramer, 9th edition, 12mo, "most used guide to western waters," many river charts, full-page woodcuts, maps. $700.

THE QUEEN OF HEARTS. London: Warne (1881), illustrated by Randolph Caldecott, every page is illustrated as are the ep's, plus 5 color plates tipped-in. $25–$40.

THE SEVEN LITTLE SISTERS WHO LIVE on the Round Ball that Floats in the Air. Boston 1861, 1st edition of Jane Andrew's first book, published anonymously. $75–$150.

THEROUX, Paul. *Waldo.* Boston: Houghton, Mifflin 1967, 1st edition of author's first book, DJ. $25–$150.

THOMAS, Dylan. *Collected Poems, 1934-1952.* London: Dent (1952), 1st edition, DJ. $75–$175.

THOMAS, Dylan. *Deaths and Entrances.* London: J.M. Dent and Sons, Ltd. (1946), 1st edition, DJ. $100–$200.

THOMAS, Edward. *Collected Poems.* London: Selwyn and Blount 1920, 1st edition, portraits, DJ. $75.

THOMPSON, Hunter S. *Fear and Loathing in Las Vegas: A Savage Journey to the Heart of the American Dream.* New York: Random House (1971), 1st edition, DJ. $125–$175.

THOMPSON, Hunter S. *Fear and Loathing in Las Vegas: A Savage Journey to the Heart of the American Dream.* New York: Random House 1971, 1st edition. $10–$20.

THOMPSON, Jim. *See* Vintage Paperbacks.

THOMPSON, Kay. *Eloise.* New York: Simon & Schuster 1955, 1st edition, 1st printing, illustrated by Hilary Knight, large quarto, DJ. $150–$200.

THOMPSON, Ruth Plumly. *Jack Pumpkinhead of Oz.* Chicago:

Reilly & Lee (1929), illustrated by John R. Neill, 1st edition, having 12 color plates, DJ (scarce in DJ). $200–$300.

THOMPSON, Ruth Plumly. *Jack Pumpkinhead of Oz*. Chicago: Reilly & Lee (about 1945), illustrated by John R. Neill, black and white ills, spine sun-faded, covers have some moderate wear and staining. $20–$40.

THOMPSON, Ruth Plumly. *Speedy in Oz*. Chicago: Reilly & Lee (1941), illustrated by John R. Neill, a reprint from 1941, the 28th Oz book and Thompson's 14th, numerous black and white ills, lightly worn but bright, DJ slightly soiled and chipped. $45–$60.

THOREAU, Henry David. *A Week on the Concord and Merrimack Rivers*. Boston and Cambridge: James Monroe 1849, Thoreau's first book, one of about 1,000 copies, 1st edition with 3 lines dropped from the foot of page 396, original cloth. $1,500–$3,000.

THOREAU, Henry David. *Cape Cod*. Boston: Ticknor & Fields 1865, original cloth. $400–$500.

THOREAU, Henry David. *Cape Cod*. Boston: Houghton Mifflin 1896, 2 vols, 1st printing of what is commonly called the 2nd edition, illustrated with lovely small watercolors by Amelia M. Watson. $150–$250.

THOREAU, Henry David. *Walden, or A Life in the Woods*. Boston: Ticknor & Fields 1854, 1st edition, spine ends frayed. $950–$1,600.

THOREAU, Henry David. *Walden, or Life in the Woods*. Chicago: Lakeside Press 1930, first of this edition, limited to 1,000 copies, slipcase. $135.

THOREAU, Henry David. *See also* Golden Cockerel Press; Sets.

THUCYDIDES. *See* Ashendene Press.

THURBER, James. *The Thirteen Clocks*. New York: Simon & Schuster (1950), illustrated by Marc Simont, 1st state. $125.

TIMLIN, William. *The Ship that Sailed to Mars*. New York: Stokes (1923), 1st American edition; 48 mounted color plates and 48 mounted, decorated, colored pages of calligraphic text. $1,000.

TOLKIEN, J.R.R. *The Hobbit or There and Back Again*. Boston: Houghton-Mifflin Co. 1938, 1st American edition, 1st printing, without a half-title page, with a bowing hobbit on title page, and with front and back ep maps reversed in list of ills; ills by author, DJ. $500–$1,000.

TOLKIEN, J.R.R. *The Hobbit or There and Back Again*. London: Allen & Unwin (1937), 1st edition, 1st state of DJ, with misprinting "Dodgeson" on rear inner flap; ills, ep maps, DJ. $2,000–$4,000.

TOLSTOY, Leo. *See* Ashendene Press.

TOM MIX. *See* Big Little Books.

TOM SAWYER. *See* Twain, Mark.

TOM SWIFT. *See* Juvenile Series Books; Appleton, Victor.

TOOMER, Jean. *Cane*. New York: Boni & Liveright (1923), 2nd printing. $150.

TRADE CATALOGS. *1924 Camp Fire Girls Equipment Catalog*. $27.50.

TRADE CATALOGS. *The Biggest Variety of Boat Supplies for Immediate Delivery Found Anywhere in America*. New York: E.J. Willis Co. 1937, 264 pages. $15–$20.

TRADE CATALOGS. Lawrence, Bradley and Pardee. Illustrated catalog of carriages, sleighs, harnesses, saddles, etc. New Haven 1862, 147 pages, numerous fine ills, "one of the best and earliest pictorial records." $250–$500.

TRAVEN, B. *The Death Ship: The Story of an American Sailor*. London: 1934, 1st edition in English of author's first book, translated by Eric Sutton, DJ. $300–$700.

TRAVEN, B. *The Death Ship: The Story of an American Sailor*. New York: Knopf 1934, 1st American edition, DJ. $200–$350.

TRAVEN, B. *The Treasure of the Sierra Madre*. New York: 1934, 1st American edition, DJ. $150–$350.

TRAVERS, P.L. *Mary Poppins Comes Back*. New York: Reynal & Hitchcock (1935), 4th printing, illustrated by Mary Shepard. $12–$35.

TRAVERS, P.L. *Mary Poppins*. New York: Reynal & Hitchcock (1934), 1st American edition, illustrated by Mary Shepard, DJ. $150–$200.

TREASURE ISLAND. See Stevenson, Robert Louis.

TRUMBO, Dalton. *Johnny Got His Gun*. Philadelphia: Lippincott 1939, 1st edition, DJ. $75–$150.

TUDOR, Tasha. *See* "Key to Illustrators."

TUTTLE, W.C. *Shotgun Gold*. Boston: Houghton, Mifflin "1940", 1st edition, DJ. $20–$50.

TWAIN, Mark. *A Connecticut Yankee in King Arthur's Court*. New York: Charles L. Webster 1889, 1st edition. $150–$300.

TWAIN, Mark. *Following the Equator: A Journey Around the World*. Hartford: American Publishing Co. 1897, 1st trade edition. $75–$150.

TWAIN, Mark. *The Adventures of Huckleberry Finn*. New York: Charles L. Webster & Co. 1885, 1st American edition, 1st state, with blue cloth, title page tipped in, with copyright date on verso (1884), numerous other points. $1,000–$3,000.

TWAIN, Mark. *The Adventures of Tom Sawyer*. Hartford, Chicago, Cincinnati: American Publishing Co.; San Francisco: A. Roman & Co. 1876, 1st American edition (published after the British), 1st printing, on woven paper plus more complex points, blue cloth. $2,000–$4,000.

TWAIN, Mark. *The Adventures of Tom Sawyer*. Hartford: American Publishing Co. 1894, later printing by the original publisher, pictorially stamped brown cloth, frontis ill and drawings throughout. $35–$50.

TWAIN, Mark. *The Adventures of Tom Sawyer*. New York: Grosset and Dunlap (1936), illustrated ep's, no ills, DJ. $3.50–$6.

TWAIN, Mark. *The Adventures of Tom Sawyer*. New York: Harper and Brothers (1875, 1903, 1910, 1917) (about 1928), illustrated by Worth Brehm with color frontis, the same ill as paste-on pictorial label on front cover, plus 15 black and white glossy plates. $25–$45.

TYLER, Anne. *A Slipping-Down Life*. New York: Knopf 1976, 1st edition, DJ. $100–$150.

TYLER, Anne. *Dinner at the Homesick Restaurant*. New York: Knopf 1982, 1st edition, DJ. $45–$65.

TYLER, Anne. *The Accidental Tourist*. New York: Knopf 1985, 1st edition, DJ. $25–$35.

TYNAN, Katherine. *See* Cuala Press.

 U ——————————————————————

U.S. LIGHT-HOUSE BOARD. *Annual Report of the Light-House Board to the Secretary of the Treasury for the Fiscal Year Ended June 30, 1885*. Washington: GPO 1885, 40 maps and plates, original cloth. $45–$65.

U.S. COAST SURVEY. *Report of the Superintendent of the Coast Survey, Showing the Progress of the Survey during the Year 1852*. Washington: Robert Armstrong 1853, original cloth. $125.

U.S. INFANTRY TACTICS. Philadelphia: published by the US government 1861. $75.

ULMANN, Doris. *See* Peterkin, Julia: *Roll, Jordan, Roll*.

UNCLE REMUS. *See* Harris, Joel Chandler.

UNCLE WIGGILY. *See* Garis, Howard.

UNDERWOOD, J.L. *The Women of the Confederacy*. New York and Washington: Neale 1906, 1st edition. $225.

UPDIKE, John. *Rabbit is Rich*. New York: Knopf 1981, 1st trade edition, DJ. $15–$35.

UPDIKE, John. *Rabbit, Run*. New York: Knopf 1960, 1st edition of the first Rabbit book, DJ. $75–$150.

UPDIKE, John. *The Carpentered Hen and Other Tame Creatures*. New York: Harper's (1958), 1st edition of author's first book, DJ. $200–$350.

UPFIELD, Arthur. *Death of a Swagman*. London: Aldor 1946, 1st edition, DJ. $50–$75.

UPTON, Bertha. *The Golliwog's Circus*. London: Longman's Green & Co. 1903, 1st edition, with pictures by Florence K. Upton, oblong quarto, cloth-backed pictorial boards, color plates and more ills in text. $125–$300.

UPTON, Florence K. *See* Upton, Bertha.

US GEOLOGICAL SURVEY. *2nd Annual Report, 1880-81.* Washington: US GPO 1882. $65.

 V ——————————————————————

VAN DINE, S.S. *The Benson Murder Case. A Philo Vance Story.* New York: Grosset and Dunlap (1926), reprint edition, scarce title, DJ. $35.

VAN DINE, S.S. *The Bishop Murder Case. A Philo Vance Story.* New York: Scribner's 1929, 1st edition, DJ. $75–$125.

VAN DINE, S.S. *The Canary Murder Case. A Philo Vance Story.* New York: Scribner's 1928, 2nd printing, DJ. $35.

VAN DINE, S.S. *The Kennel Murder Case. A Philo Vance Story.* New York: Scribner's 1933, 1st edition, DJ. $85–$100.

VAN DINE, S.S. *The Kennel Murder Case. A Philo Vance Story.* New York: Scribner's 1933, 1st edition. $30–$50.

VAN DINE, S.S. *The Kidnap Murder Case. A Philo Vance Story.* New York: Scribner's 1936, 1st edition, DJ. $70.

VAN DINE, S.S. *The Kidnap Murder Case. A Philo Vance Story.* New York: Scribner's 1936, 1st edition. $20–$35.

VAN DYKE, Henry. *The Broken Soldier and the Maid of France.* New York: Harper 1919, ills by Frank Schoonover, 1st edition. $17.50.

VAN DYNE, Edith. *Aunt Jane's Nieces Out West.* Chicago: Reilly & Britton (1914), 1st edition, 1st state, with ad on the verso of the half-title page listing all the titles in the series, including this title. $45–$65.

VAN GULIK, Robert. *The Chinese Bell Murders.* London: Michael Joseph (1958), 1st edition, DJ. $75–$175.

VAN LOON, Hendrick Willem. *Van Loon's Geography.* New York: Simon & Schuster 1932, 1st edition, illustrated by the author, DJ. $15–$40.

VAN VETCHEN, Carl. *Nigger Heaven.* New York: Knopf 1926, 1st trade edition, DJ. $100.

VAN VETCHEN, Carl. *Tiger in the House.* New York: Knopf 1920, 1st edition, DJ. $75–$125.

VAN VOGT, A.E. *The Mind Cage.* New York: Simon & Schuster 1957, 1st edition. $25–$35.

VAN VOGT, A.E. *The World of A.* New York: Simon & Schuster 1948, 1st edition, DJ. $100–$175.

VAN WIE, Carrie. *See* "Key to Illustrators."

VANCE, Jack. *Big Planet.* New York: Avalon Books (1957), 1st edition, DJ. $150–$225.

VANCE, Jack. *Cugel's Saga.* New York: Timescape Books (1983), 1st edition, DJ. $20–$25.

VANCOUVER, George. *Voyage of Discovery to the North Pacific to Ascertain the Existence of any Navigable Communication between the North Pacific and the Atlantic 1790-95.* London: Robinson & Edwards 1798, 1st edition, 3 vols, quarto plus folio atlas. $9,000–$13,000.

VANCOUVER, George. *Voyage of Discovery to the North Pacific to Ascertain the Existence of any Navigable Communication between the North Pacific and the Atlantic 1790-95.* London: Robinson & Edwards 1798, 1st edition, 3 vols, 4to, without the atlas. $2,000–$3,000.

VANCOUVER, George. *Voyage of Discovery to the North Pacific Ocean to Ascertain the Existence of any Navigable Communication between the North Pacific and the Atlantic Oceans 1790-95.* London: Robinson & Edwards 1798, 1st edition, atlas vol only. $2,800.

VASSOS, John. *See* "Key to Illustrators."

VAVRA, Robert. *Romany Free.* New York: Reynal (1977), illustrated by Fleur Cowles, 1st edition. $20–$40.

VAWTER, Will. *See* "Key to Illustrators."

VERNE, Jules. *Adventures in the Land of the Behemoth.* Boston: 1874, 1st American edition. $75–$125.

VERNE, Jules. *Journey to the Center of the Earth.* London: Griffeth & Farran 1872, 1st edition. $150–$225.

VERNE, Jules. *Journey to the Center of the Earth.* New York: Scribner, Armstrong 1874, 1st American edition. $100–$150.

VIDAL, Gore. *The City and the Pillar.* New York: Dutton 1946, 1st edition of the author's third book, DJ. $50–$100.

VILLIERS, Alan. *The Coral Sea.* New York: Whittlesey House (1949). $15.

VILLIERS, Alan. *Whalers of the Midnight Sun: A Story of Modern Whaling in the Antarctic.* New York: 1934, 1st edition. $20.

VILLON, Francois. *See* Eragny Press.

VINTAGE PAPERBACKS. Algren, Nelson. *Nelson Algren's Own Book of Lonesome Monsters.* New York: Lancer (1962), wraps, 1st edition, a paperback original. $35.

VINTAGE PAPERBACKS. Bachman, Richard (Stephen King). *Rage.* New York: Signet Books (1981), paperback original, thus true 1st. $40–$70.

VINTAGE PAPERBACKS. Bachman, Richard (Stephen King). *Roadwork.* New York: Signet Books (1981), paperback original, thus true 1st. $40–$70.

VINTAGE PAPERBACKS. Bachman, Richard (Stephen King). *Silver Bullet.* New York: New American Library (1985), collects *Cycle of the Werewolf* and "Silver Bullet," King's screenplay based on his novella, 1st edition thus, includes movie stills, foreward by King. $15.

VINTAGE PAPERBACKS. Bachman, Richard (Stephen King). *The Long Walk.* New York: Signet Books (1981), paperback original, thus true 1st. $40–$70.

VINTAGE PAPERBACKS. Bachman, Richard (Stephen King). *The Running Man.* New York: Signet Books (1981), paperback original, thus true 1st. $40–$70.

VINTAGE PAPERBACKS. Benet, Stephen Vincent. *A Book of Americans.* New York: Armed Forces Edition (1944), illustrated by Charles Guild. $20.

VINTAGE PAPERBACKS. Brock, Stuart. *Just Around the Corner.* New York: Dell 337 (1942). $9.

VINTAGE PAPERBACKS. Brooke, Rupert. *The Collected Poems of.* New York: Armed Services Edition (1924). $35.

VINTAGE PAPERBACKS. Chandler, Raymond. *Five Murderers.* New York: Avon (1944), Avon Mystery Monthly #19, paperback original, true 1st, scarce. $100–$150.

VINTAGE PAPERBACKS. Eberhart, Mignon. *With This Ring.* New York: Dell Mystery (1941), #83. $10.

VINTAGE PAPERBACKS. Goodis, David. *Dark Passage.* New York: Dell 221 (1948), 1st edition. $25.

VINTAGE PAPERBACKS. Hammett, Dashiell. *Dead Yellow Women.* New York: Lawrence Spivak, Jonathan Press Mystery #J29 (1947), 1st edition, wrappers. $50.

VINTAGE PAPERBACKS. Hammett, Dashiell. *The Continental Op.* New York: Lawrence E. Spivak (1945), Jonathan Press Mystery #B62, 1st edition, digest size, wrappers; this is the true 1st edition. $75–$100.

VINTAGE PAPERBACKS. Hammett, Dashiell. *The Maltese Falcon.* New York: Pocket Books (1944), 1st Pocket Books edition, pictorial wrappers, in scarce DJ. $75.

VINTAGE PAPERBACKS. Irish, William. *If I Should Die Before I Wake.* New York: Avon 104, 1946, wrappers, a paperback original, not previously published in hardcover, 1st printing. $45.

VINTAGE PAPERBACKS. Jackson, Shirley. *The Lottery.* np: Lion Books #14 (Jan. 1950), a story collection. $25.

VINTAGE PAPERBACKS. Koestler, Arthur. *Darkness at Noon.* New York: Penguin (1948), Signet 671, 1st printing. $25.

VINTAGE PAPERBACKS. Koontz, Dean. *The Flesh in the Furnace.* New York: Bantam S-6977 (1972), paperback original, 1st edition. $17.50.

VINTAGE PAPERBACKS. Lee, William. *Junkie.* New York: Ace Books (1953) (bound as 1 paperback vol with Helbrant, Maurice, *Narcotic Agent*). This is William Burroughs's first book, scarce, 1st edition. $125–$200.

VINTAGE PAPERBACKS. Matheson, Richard. *Ride the Nightmare.* New York: Ballantine 301-K (1959), paperback original, 1st edition. $45.

VINTAGE PAPERBACKS. Queen, Ellery. *The Dragon's Teeth.* New York: Pocket Books 459 (1947), 1st printing. $7.50.

VINTAGE PAPERBACKS. Rand, Ayn. *The Virtue of Selfishness.*

(New York): New American Library (1964), a Signet book, 1st edition, preceding the hardcover; pictorial wraps. $30.

VINTAGE PAPERBACKS. Rice, Craig. *The Corpse Steps Out.* New York: Pocket Book 476 (1947), 1st printing. $7.50.

VINTAGE PAPERBACKS. Thompson, Jim. *The Criminal.* New York: Lion 184 (1953), paperback original, 1st edition. $85.

VINTAGE PAPERBACKS. Willeford, Charles. *Honey Gal.* New York: Beacon Books B-160 (1958), paperback original, 1st edition. $75.

VINTAGE PAPERBACKS. Wodehouse, P.G. *Leave it to Psmith.* New York: Dell (1924), reprint, pictorial wrappers, showing moderate wear. $25.

VONNEGUT, Kurt. *Cat's Cradle.* New York: Holt, Rinehart & Winston (1963), 1st edition, DJ. $50–$75.

VONNEGUT, Kurt. *Slaughterhouse-Five.* (New York): Delacorte (1969), 1st edition, DJ. $100–$125.

VOYAGES. *See* "Key to Categories."

 W

WAKOSKI, Diane. *The Magellanic Clouds.* Los Angeles: Black Sparrow Press 1970, 1st trade edition, wraps. $20–$35.

WAKOSKI, Diane. *The Motorcycle Betrayal Poems.* New York: Simon & Schuster (1971), 1st printing. $65.

WALCOTT, Derek. *In a Green Night—Poems 1948-1960.* London: Cape 1962, 1st British edition of Walcott's 1st book, after a small island printing—"a landmark in Caribbean literature," DJ, wraparound band with printed comment from Robert Graves. $100–$300.

WALCOTT, Derek. *Selected Poems.* New York: Farrar, Straus 1964, 1st edition, DJ. $75.

WALEY, Arthur. *A Hundred and Seventy Chinese Poems.* London: Constable 1918, 1st edition, linen-backed boards, printed at the Chiswick Press. $50–$75.

WALKER, Alice. *Horses Make a Landscape Look More Beautiful: Poems.* San Diego: Harcourt, Brace (1979), 1st edition. $35.

WALKER, Alice. *Once.* New York: Harcourt, Brace & World (1968), 1st edition of author's first book, a selection of poems, DJ. $200–$350.

WALKER, Alice. *The Color Purple.* New York: Harcourt (1982), 1st edition, DJ. $100–$200.

WALKER, Alice. *The Third Life of Grange Copeland.* New York: Harcourt Brace Jovanovich (1970), 1st edition of author's second book, DJ. $100–$200.

WALLACE, Edgar. *The Man at the Carlton.* New York: A.L. Burt (1932), reprint edition. $3.50–$8.

WALLACE, Edgar. *The Man at the Carlton.* New York: A.L. Burt (1932), reprint edition, DJ. $8–$12.

WALLACE, Willard M. *Soul of the Lion, a Biography of General Joshua L. Chamberlain.* New York: Thomas Nelson 1960, 1st edition, DJ. $40–$65.

WALPOLE, Hugh. *Vanessa.* London: Macmillan 1933, 1st edition, DJ. $15–$20.

WARD, Lynd. *God's Man.* New York: Jonathan Cape (1929), 1st edition of the author's first book, a story in pictures. $75–$125.

WARNER, Rex. *The Cult of Power.* London: 1946, 1st edition, DJ. $25–$65.

WARNER, Sylvia Townsend. *The Museum of Cheats.* New York: Viking Press 1947, 1st edition, DJ. $20–$30.

WARREN, Robert Penn. *Band of Angels.* New York: Random House 1955, 1st edition, DJ. $50–$75.

WARREN, Robert Penn. *Selected Poems: New and Old 1923-1966.* New York: Random House (1966), 1st trade edition, DJ. $35–$60.

WASHINGTON, Booker T. *Up from Slavery.* New York: Doubleday, Page 1901, 1st edition. $50–$100.

WATSON, Amelia M. *See* "Key to Illustrators."

WAUGH, Evelyn. *Love Among the Ruins.* London: Chapman & Hall 1953, 1st trade edition, DJ. $150.

WAUGH, Evelyn. *The Loved One.* Boston: Little, Brown 1948, 1st American edition, DJ. $30–$50.

WAUGH, Evelyn. *The Loved One*. London: Chapman & Hall 1948, 1st edition, DJ. $150.

WEBB, Clifford. *See* "Key to Illustrators."

WEBB, Mary. *Precious Bane*. London: Jonathan Cape "1924", 1st edition. $65–$175.

WEEGEE. *Naked Hollywood*, text by Mel Harris. New York: Pellagrini and Cudahy 1953, quarto, photographs, DJ. $55–$75.

WEEGEE. *Weegee's People*. New York: Duell, Sloan & Pearce 1946, 1st edtion, photographs, DJ. $55–$75.

WEISGARD, Leonard. *See* "Key to Illustrators."

WELLS, H.G. *The History of Mr. Polly*. London: Nelson 1910, 1st edition. $40.

WELLS, H.G. *The History of Mr. Polly*. New York: The Press of the Reader's Club 1941, 1st edition thus, introduction by Sinclair Lewis; this is in effect a book club edition; DJ. $25.

WELLS, H.G. *The Invisible Man. A Grotesque Romance*. London: C. Arthur Pearson 1897, 1st edition, with 2 pages of publisher's ads. $150–$200.

WELLS, H.G. *The Outline of History*. New York: Macmillan Co. 1926, "New Illustrated Edition, Revised and Rewritten," 2 vols, DJs. $15–$35.

WELLS, H.G. *The War of the Worlds*. London: William Heinemann 1898, 1st edition, with 6-page publisher's catalog dated Autumn 1897, scarce. $150–$350.

WELLS, H.G. *The War of the Worlds*. New York: Harper's 1898, 1st American edition, differing textually from the English edition, and containing 15 ills from the original Pearson's Magazine appearance that are not present in the British 1st; uncommon. $150–$350.

WELLS, H.G. *See also* Golden Cockerel Press.

WELTY, Eudora. *Delta Wedding*. New York: Harcourt, Brace (1946), 1st edition of author's fourth book, DJ. $100–$200.

WELTY, Eudora. *Delta Wedding*. New York: Harcourt, Brace (1946), 1st edition of author's fourth book. $20–$40.

WELTY, Eudora. *The Optimist's Daughter*. New York: Random House (1972), 1st trade edition, DJ. $35–$75.

WELTY, Eudora. *The Robber Bridegroom*. Garden City: Doubleday 1942, 1st edition of author's second book, DJ. $350–$500.

WEST, Mae. *She Done Him Wrong (Diamond Lil)*. New York: 1932, 1st edition, DJ. $50–$150.

WEST, Nathanael. *A Cool Million*. New York: Covici-Friede (1934), 1st edition, 1st binding of light tan cloth. $100–$150.

WEST, Nathanael. *A Cool Million*. New York: Covici-Friede (1934), 1st edition, 1st binding of light tan cloth, DJ. $800–$1,000.

WEST, Nathanael. *Miss Lonelyhearts*. New York: Liveright (1933), 1st edition, DJ. $1,200–$2,000.

WEST, Nathanael. *Miss Lonelyhearts*. (New York): New Directions (1933), 1st "New Classics" edition, DJ. $40.

WEST, Nathanael. *The Day of the Locust*. New York: Random House (1939), 1st edition, DJ. $500–$1,000.

WEST, Rebecca. *Black Lamb and Grey Falcon*. New York: Viking 1941, 1st American edition, DJ, slipcase. $35–$100.

WEST, Rebecca. *Return of the Soldier*. London: Nisbet (1918), 1st edition of author's second book and first novel, DJ. $75–$100.

WESTERNERS BRAND BOOK, THE. Book Eight. Los Angeles: Los Angeles Corral of the Westerners (1959). Limited to 525 copies. $35–$95.

WESTERNS AND NORTHERNS. *See* "Key to Categories."

WESTON, Edward. *Nudes*. Milerton: Aperture 1977, 1st edition, quarto, with a remembrance by Charis Wilson and accompanied by excerpts from the Daybooks and Letters, DJ. $35–$45.

WHARTON, Edith. *Ethan Frome*. New York: Scribner 1911, 1st edition, 1st printing, with perfect type at the foot of page 135. $100–$200.

WHARTON, Edith. *French Ways and Their Meaning*. New York: Appleton 1919, 1st edition. $20–$50.

WHARTON, Edith. *Italian Villas and Their Gardens*. New York: Century 1904, 1st edition, quarto, 15 color and 11 black and white ills by Maxfield Parrish, also photos, pictorial and decorative binding by the Decorative Designers, signed "DD." $100–$300.

WHARTON, Edith. *The Children.* (New York): Grosset & Dunlap (1928), reprint edition. $3.50–$8.

WHARTON, Edith. *The Children.* (New York): Grosset & Dunlap (1928), reprint edition, DJ. $8–$12.

WHEELOCK, John Hall. *The Bright Doom.* New York: Scribner's 1927, 1st edition, DJ. $35.

WHEELRIGHT, Rowland. *See* "Key to Illustrators."

WHIPPLE, A.B.C. *Yankee Whalers in the South Seas.* Garden City: Doubleday 1954, 1st edition, DJ. $22.50.

WHISTLER, Rex. *Four Fantastic Tales.* London: 1932. $50.

WHISTLER, Rex. *See also* "Key to Illustrators."

WHITE, E.B. *Charlotte's Web.* New York: Harper's (1952), 1st edition, illustrated by Garth Williams, DJ. $150–$250.

WHITE, E.B. *One Man's Meat.* New York: Harper's 1942, 1st edition, DJ. $35–$100.

WHITE, E.B. *Stuart Little.* New York: Harper's (1945), illustrated by Garth Williams, 1st edition, pictorial cloth, DJ. $75–$125.

WHITE, E.B. *Stuart Little.* New York: Harper's (1945), illustrated by Garth Williams, 1st edition. $25–$40.

WHITE, E.B. *The Second Tree from the Corner.* New York: Harper's (1954), 1st trade edition, DJ. $15–$75.

WHITE, T.H. *The Once and Future King.* London: Collins 1958, 1st edition, DJ. $75–$200.

WHITE, T.H. *The Sword in the Stone.* London: 1938, 1st edition, DJ. $300–$400.

WHITE, T.H. *The Sword in the Stone.* New York: Putnam's 1939, 1st American edition, DJ. $75.

WHITEHEAD, Alfred North, and Russell, Bertrand. *Principia Mathematica.* Cambridge: University Press 1910-12-13, 1st editions, 3 vols, of 750 copies of Volume I, and 500 copies each of Volumes II and III, original blue cloth. $7,500.

WHITMAN, Walt. *See Leaves of Grass.*

WIESE, Kurt. *See* "Key to Illustrators."

WIGGIN, Kate Douglas. *Arabian Nights.* New York: Scribner's 1925, edited by Kate Douglas Wiggin, illustrated by Maxfield Parrish, later printing. $40–$60.

WIGGIN, Kate Douglas. *Rebecca of Sunnybrook Farm.* Boston: Houghton, Mifflin 1903, 1st edition. $75–$150.

WIGGIN, Kate Douglas. *Susanna and Sue.* Boston and New York: Houghton, Mifflin; the Riverside Press, Cambridge 1909, 1st edition ("Published October 1909"), illustrated by N.C. Wyeth and Alice Barber Stephens. $50–$75.

WIGGIN, Kate Douglas. *The Birds' Christmas Carol.* Boston: Houghton, Mifflin 1912, illustrated by K. Wireman, later printing of author's second book, first privately printed to raise money for the first free kindergarten west of the Rockies. $20–$40.

WILDE, Oscar. *The Ballad of Reading Gaol.* London: Leonard Smithers 1898, 1st edition, one of 800 copies. $400–$800.

WILDE, Oscar. *The Ballad of Reading Gaol.* New York: E.P. Dutton 1928, 16 full-page ills by John Vassos. $40–$75.

WILDE, Oscar. *The Happy Prince.* New York: Putnam's (1913), quarto, 1st US edition (printed in England); 12 tipped-in color plates with lettered tissue guards by Charles Robinson, many drawings within text, ep's, and title page. $150–$175.

WILDE, Oscar. *The Harlot's House.* New York: Dutton 1929, illustrated by John Vassos; small quarto, edition limited to 200 copies. $200.

WILDE, Oscar. *The Picture of Dorian Gray.* New York: M.J. Ivers & Co. (1890), 1st edition, with ads at end, published the year before the British edition, in original blue printed wrappers. $750.

WILDER, Laura Ingalls. *On the Banks of Plum Creek.* New York: Harper and Brothers 1937, illustrated by Helen Sewell and Mildred Boyle, 1st edition, DJ. $50–$100.

WILDER, Thornton. *The Bridge of San Luis Rey.* New York: Boni 1927, 1st American trade edition, illustrated by Amy Drevenstedt, DJ. $100–$200.

WILEY, Bell I. *The Common Soldier of the Civil War, The Life of Billy Yank, The Life of Johnny Reb.* Indianapolis: Bobbs-Merrill 1943 and 1952, 1st edition, photographs, slipcase; based on soldiers' diaries and letters, many previously unpublished. $60–$85.

WILLEFORD, Charles. *See* Vintage Paperbacks.

WILLIAMS, Charles. *All Hallow's Eve.* New York: Pellegrini and Cudahy (1948), 1st US edition, DJ. $20–$35.

WILLIAMS, Charles. *Descent into Hell*. London: Faber & Faber (1937), 1st edition, DJ, scarce. $225–$275.

WILLIAMS, Charles. *Descent into Hell*. London: Faber & Faber (1937), 1st edition, scarce. $50–$65.

WILLIAMS, Charles. *The Place of the Lion*. London: Mundanus/Gollancz 1931, 1st edition, wrappers. $50.

WILLIAMS, Garth. *See* "Key to Illustrators."

WILLIAMS, Gluyas. *See* "Key to Illustrators."

WILLIAMS, Tennessee. *A Streetcar Named Desire*. (Norfolk): New Directions (1947), 1st edition, DJ. $300–$500.

WILLIAMS, Tennessee. *Cat on a Hot Tin Roof*. (New York): New Directions (1955), 1st edition, DJ. $75.

WILLIAMS, Tennessee. *The Glass Menagerie*. New York: Random House (1945), 1st edition, DJ. $150–$250.

WILLIAMS, Tennessee. *The Rose Tattoo*. (New York): New Directions (1950), 1st edition, DJ. $75.

WILLIAMS, William Carlos. *In the American Grain*. New York: Boni 1925, 1st edition, DJ. $125–$225.

WILLIAMS, William Carlos. *Paterson*. (Norfolk: New Directions 1946), Book One, 1st edition, one of 1,000 copies printed at the Van Vetchen Press, DJ. $150–$300.

WILLIAMS, William Carlos. *Paterson*. (Norfolk: New Directions 1946), Book One, 1st edition, one of 1,000 copies printed at the Van Vetchen Press. $65–$95.

WILLIAMS, William Carlos. *Paterson*. (Norfolk: New Directions 1946), Book Five, 1st edition, DJ. $75–$150.

WILLIAMS, William Carlos. *Paterson. Books One through Five*. (New York): New Directions (1946-1958), 5 vols, DJs. $900–$1,200.

WILLIAMS, William Carlos. *The Autobiography*. New York: Random House (1951), 1st edition, DJ. $50–$75.

WILLIAMS, William Carlos. *The Complete Collected Poems of William Carlos Williams 1906-1938*, 1st edition. $35–$50.

WILLINGHAM, Calder. *End as a Man*. New York: Vanguard (1947), 1st edition of author's first book, DJ. $50–$100.

WILSON, E.A. *See* "Key to Illustrators."

WILSON, Edmund. *Axel's Castle*. New York: Scribner's 1931, 1st edition, DJ. $125–$250.

WILSON, Edmund. *Memoirs of Hecate County*. New York: Doubleday 1946, 1st edition, DJ. $50–$125.

WILSON, Edmund. *Patriotic Gore—Studies in the Literature of the American Civil War*. New York: Farrar, Straus & Giroux 1962, 1st edition, DJ. $50–$65.

WILSON, Edmund. *The Wound and the Bow*. Boston: Houghton Mifflin 1941, 1st edition, DJ. $75–$100.

WILSON, Edmund. *To The Finland Station*. New York: Harcourt, Brace (1940), 1st edition, DJ. $175–$250.

WINNIE THE POOH. *See* Milne, A.A.

WINSOR, Kathleen. *Forever Amber*. New York: 1944, 1st edition of author's first book, DJ. $50.

WINTERS, Yvor. *The Journey and Other Poems*. Ithaca: Dragon Press 1931, 1st edition, wraps. $35–$55.

WIREMAN, K. *See* "Key to Illustrators."

WISTER, Owen. *The Virginian, A Horseman of the Plains*. New York: Macmillan 1902, 1st edition. $100–$200.

WODEHOUSE, P.G. *Carry On, Jeeves*. London: Jenkins 1925, 1st edition. The author's name is pronounced "Woodhouse." $50.

WODEHOUSE, P.G. *Carry On, Jeeves*. New York: A.L. Burt (1927), reprint edition, DJ. $25.

WODEHOUSE, P.G. *Leave it to Psmith*. New York: A.L. Burt (1924), reprint edition, DJ. $20–$25.

WODEHOUSE, P.G. *Leave it to Psmith*. New York: George H. Doran Co. (1924), 1st American edition, defective DJ. $125–$175.

WODEHOUSE, P.G. *Leave it to Psmith*. New York: George H. Doran Co. (1924), 1st American edition, reading copy. $25–$35.

WODEHOUSE, P.G. *Meet Mr. Mulliner*. Garden City: Doubleday, Doran 1928, 1st American edition, DJ. $300.

WODEHOUSE, P.G. *My Man Jeeves*. London: George Newnes (1919), 1st edition, DJ. $3,000.

WODEHOUSE, P.G. *My Man Jeeves*. London: George Newnes (1919), 1st edition. $350.

WODEHOUSE, P.G. *The Code of the Woosters.* London: Jenkins (1938), 1st British edition. $60–$75.

WODEHOUSE, P.G. *The Crime Wave at Blandings.* Garden City: Doubleday, Doran 1937, 1st American edition, DJ. $90–$125.

WOLFE, Thomas. *A Stone, A Leaf, A Door: Poems.* New York: Scribner's 1945, 1st edition, DJ. $25–$45.

WOLFE, Thomas. *Look Homeward, Angel.* New York: Scribner's 1929, 1st edition, 1st issue, with lowercase "g" on page 308, line 26, and missing "t" in "stationed" on page 506, line 23, Scribner's seal present on copyright page, portrait on rear panel cover of jacket, DJ. $1,000–$1,500.

WOLFE, Thomas. *Of Time and the River.* New York: Scribner's 1935, 1st edition, DJ. $100–$250.

WOLFE, Thomas. *The Portable Thomas Wolfe.* New York: Viking Press 1946, 1st edition, DJ. $35.

WOLFE, Thomas. *The Web and the Rock.* New York: Harper's 1939, 1st edition, DJ. $75–$150.

WOLFE, Thomas. *You Can't Go Home Again.* New York: Harper's 1940, 1st edition, DJ. $50–$100.

WOLFE, Tom. *The Bonfire of the Vanities.* New York: Farrar, Straus & Giroux (1987), 1st edition, DJ. $20–$50.

WOLFE, Tom. *The Electric Kool-Aid Acid Test.* New York: Farrar, Straus & Giroux (1968), 1st edition, DJ. $75–$100.

WOLFE, Tom. *The Kandy Kolored Tangerine Flake Streamline Baby.* New York: Farrar, Straus & Giroux (1965), 1st edition of author's first book, DJ. $75–$125.

WOMEN'S BOOKS. *See* "Key to Categories" under Women's Studies."

WOMEN'S STUDIES. *See* "Key to Categories."

WONDERFUL WIZARD OF OZ, THE. See Baum, L. Frank.

WOOD, Grant. *See* "Key to Illustrators."

WOODY WOODPECKER. See Big Little Books.

WOOLF, Leonard. *Fear and Politics—A Debate at the Zoo.* London: Hogarth Press 1925, 1st edition, stiff wrappers. $35–$75.

WOOLF, Virginia. *A Room of One's Own.* London: The Hogarth Press 1929, 1st trade edition, DW designed by Vanessa Bell, DJ. $150–$225.

WOOLF, Virginia. *A Room of One's Own*. New York and London: Fountain Press/Hogarth Press, 1929, 1st edition, limited to 492 numbered copies signed by the author. $300–$800.

WOOLF, Virginia. *Flush—A Biography*. New York: Harcourt, Brace 1933, 1st American edition, DJ. $35.

WOOLF, Virginia. *Mrs. Dalloway*. London: Hogarth Press 1925, 1st edition, with moderate defects. $100.

WOOLF, Virginia. *Orlando*. London: Hogarth Press 1928, 1st English edition, DJ. $250–$400.

WOOLF, Virginia. *Orlando*. New York: Crosby Gaige 1928, 1st edition, limited to 861 copies on rag paper, signed by the author, issued without DJ. $250–$525.

WOOLF, Virginia. *Orlando*. New York: Harcourt, Brace (1928), 1st American trade edition, DJ. $75–$100.

WOOLF, Virginia. *The Second Common Reader*. New York: Harcourt, Brace (1932), 1st American edition, DJ. $65–$75.

WOOLF, Virginia. *The Waves*. London: Hogarth 1931, 1st edition, jacket designed by Vanessa Bell, DJ. $150–$500.

WOOLF, Virginia. *The Waves*. New York: Harcourt, Brace (1931), 1st American edition, DJ. $75–$150.

WOOLF, Virginia. *To the Lighthouse*. London: Hogarth Press 1927, 1st edition, DJ designed by Vanessa Bell. $300–$1,000.

WOOLRICH, Cornell. *Rendezvous in Black*. New York: Rinehart 1948, 1st edition, DJ. $75–$175.

WOOLRICH, Cornell. *The Black Path of Fear*. Garden City: The Crime Club 1944, DJ. $75–$175.

WORDSWORTH, William. *Poems*. London: printed for Longman, etc. 1807, 2 vols, 1st issue, original binding. $1,200–$1,500.

WORLD'S FAIR. *Picturesque Chicago and Guide to the World's Fair*. Baltimore: R.H. Woodward & Co. 1892, illustrated. $25–$35.

WOUK, Herman. *The Caine Mutiny. A Novel of World War II*. New York: Doubleday 1951, 1st edition, DJ. $50–$100.

WRIGHT, Austin Tappan. *Islandia*. New York: Farrar &

Rinehart (1942), 1st edition, DJ (has a tissue overwrapper, which is scarce). $75–$150.

WRIGHT, Frank Lloyd. *Genius and Mobocracy*. New York: 1949, 1st edition, folio, DJ. $100–$150.

WRIGHT, Harold Bell. *The Winning of Barbara Worth*. Chicago: The Book Supply Company (1911), 1st edition, ills by F. Graham Cootes, DJ. $75.

WRIGHT, Harold Bell. *The Winning of Barbara Worth*. Chicago: The Book Supply Company (1911), reprint edition, black and white ills by F. Graham Cootes. $3.50–$8.

WRIGHT, Harold Bell. *The Winning of Barbara Worth*. Chicago: The Book Supply Company (1911), reprint edition, black and white ills by F. Graham Cootes, DJ. $8–$12.

WRIGHT, John Buckland. *See* "Key to Illustrators."

WRIGHT, Richard. *Black Boy*. New York: Harper's (1945), 1st edition, DJ. $35–$75.

WRIGHT, Richard. *Native Son*. New York: Harper's (1940), 1st edition, 1st state, with blue binding and yellow and green DJ. $75–$150.

WRIGHTSON, Bernie. *See* "Key to Illustrators."

WROTH, Lawrence C. *See* Grolier Club.

WURTH, Anne. *Rag Doll Susie*. Akron and New York: Saalfield (1939), illustrated by Fern Bisel Peat, illustrated stiff board covers with illustrated DJ. $30–$50.

WYETH, Andrew. *See* "Key to Illustrators."

WYETH, N.C. *See* "Key to Illustrators."

WYLIE, Elinor. *Collected Poems*. New York: Knopf 1932, 1st edition, DJ. $35.

WYLIE, Elinor. *Nets to Catch the Wind*. New York: Harcourt, Brace 1921, 1st edition, 1st issue, on paper not watermarked, preceded only by a book of immature poetry 9 years previously which had been published anonymously, DJ. $150–$200.

WYLIE, Philip. *Generation of Vipers*. New York and Toronto: Farrar & Rinehart (1942), 1st edition, DJ. $100.

WYNDHAM, John. *The Day of the Triffids*. London: Michael

Joseph (1951), 1st English edition (preceded by the American edition), DJ. $175.

WYSS, David. *The Swiss Family Robinson*. New York and London: Harper's (1909), illustrated by Louis Rhead with color frontis and numerous black and white ills, black cloth with color pictorial label (same as frontis). $35–$60.

 Y —————————————————————————

YEATS, William Butler. *Collected Poems of*. New York: Macmillan 1933, 1st American edition of this collection, DJ. $50.

YEATS, William Butler. *Responsibilities and Other Poems*. London: Macmillan 1916, 1st edition, cover design in gilt by T. Sturge Moore, one of 1,000 copies. $100–$125.

YEATS, William Butler. *The Celtic Twilight. Men and Women, Ghouls and Fairies*. London: Lawrence and Bullen 1893, frontis by Jack B. Yeats, 1st edition, 1st binding. $150–$250.

YEATS, William Butler. *The Tower*. London: Macmillan 1928, 1st edition, DJ. $100–$225.

YEATS, William Butler. *The Tower*. New York: Macmillan 1928, green cloth, 1st American edition. $30–$40.

YEATS, William Butler. *The Wild Swans at Coole. Poems*. London: 1919, 1st trade edition. $50–$85.

YEATS, William Butler. *The Wind among the Reeds*. London: Elkin Mathews 1899, 1st edition. $125–$175.

YEATS, William Butler. *The Winding Stair*. London: Macmillan 1933, 1st British edition, DJ. $100–$150.

YEATS, William Butler. *See also* Cuala Press.

YELLOW BOOK, THE. See Sets.

YOUNG, Marguerite. *Prismatic Ground*. New York: 1937, 1st edition, DJ. $50–$75.

Z

ZANGWILL, Israel. *Children of the Ghetto*. London: 1892, 1st edition, 3 vols. $150.

ZANGWILL, Israel. *Dreamers of the Ghetto*. Philadelphia: Jewish Publication Society of America 1898, 1st edition. $40.

ZELAZNY, Roger. *Blood of Amber*. New York: Arbor House (1986), 1st edition, DJ. $25–$35.

ZELAZNY, Roger. *The Doors of His Face, The Lamps of His Mouth and Other Stories*. Garden City: Doubleday 1971, 1st edition. *The Doors of His Face* won the Nebula Award for 1965, DJ. $150–$250.

ZUKOVSKY, Louis. *A Test of Poetry*. (New York): The Objectivist Press 1948, 1st American edition, DJ. $75–$100.

ZWEIG, Arnold. *The Case of Sergeant Grischa*. London: Secker 1928, 1st English edition, DJ. $25–$50.

Appendix A

Key to Categories

AFRICAN-AMERICANA

Angelou, Maya
Anthologies
Autobiography of an Ex-Colored Man
Bailey, Pearl
Baldwin, James
Baldwin, James, and Avedon, Richard
Bambara, Toni Cade
Baraka, Imamu Amiri
Black Photographers Annual, The
Bontemps, Arna
Bradford, Roark
Brooks, Gwendolyn
Cable, George W.
Campanella, Roy
Chase-Riboud, Barbara
Chestnutt, Charles W.
Cleaver, Eldridge
Cullen, Countee
Du Bois, W.E.B.
Dunbar, Paul Laurence
Ellison, Ralph
Giovanni, Nikki
Haley, Alex
Himes, Chester
Hughes, Langston
Hurston, Zora Neale

Johnson, James Weldon
Jones, LeRoi
Jordan, June
Lorde, Audre
McKay, Claude
Morrison, Toni
Motley, Willard
Nearing, Scott
Osgood, Henry O.
Parks, Gordon
Peterkin, Julia
Peterkin, Julia, and Ulmann, Doris
Petry, Ann
Robinson, Jackie
Toomer, Jean
Van Vetchen, Carl
Walker, Alice
Washington, Booker T.
Wright, Richard

AMERICANA

Abbott, E.C.
Adams, Ramon
Almanacs
Austin, Mary
Benet, Stephen Vincent
Blevins, Winfred
Boas, Franz, editor

Book Club of California
Cable, George W.
Carmer, Carl
Catlin, George
Chittenden, Hiram
Clark, Walter Van Tilburg
Coates, Robert M.
Collier, John (born 1884, American)
Crevecoeur, Michel-Guillaume St. Jean de
Custer, Elizabeth
Dana, E[dmund]
Garland, Hamlin
Grabhorn Printing (San Francisco)
Horgan, Paul
Hough, Emerson
James, Will
King, Captain Charles
Lea, Tom
Lewis, Alfred Henry
Lewis, Oscar
Lomax, John
Luhan, Mabel Dodge
Lutes, Della T.
Muir, John
Nearing, Scott
Neihardt, John G.
Paine, Thomas
Raine, William MacLeod
Sandberg, Carl
Scribner's Illustrated Classics
Sylvester, Herbert Milton
The Navigator
Westerners Brand Book

BOOKS ABOUT BOOKS
Bader, Barbara

Carter, John
Garis, Roger
Grolier Club (New York)
Jackson, Holbrook
Johnson, Merle
Kent, Rockwell
Magee, David
Meynell, Francis
Muir, Percy H.
Newton, A. Edward
Powell, Lawrence Clark
Van Vetchen, Carl

BOOKS WITH PLATES, MAPS, ENGRAVINGS
Abbey, Edward
Adams, Henry
Aesop
Alcott, Louisa May
Allen, Hervey
Arbus, Diane
Audubon, John James
Austin, Mary
Bacon, Peggy
BAE (Bureau of American Ethnology)
Baedeker, Karl
Barrie, James
Baum, L. Frank
Beardsley, Aubrey
Beaton, Cecil
Beebe, Lucius
Beerbohm, Max
Bilbo, Jack
Binyon, Laurence
Black Photographers Annual, The
Blackmore, Richard D.
Book Club of California
Bourke-White, Margaret

Bourke-White, Margaret,
    and Caldwell, Erskine
Bradley, Will
Bronte, Emily
Browning, Robert
Burgess, Thornton
Burnett, Frances Hodgson
Butts, Mary
Cabell, James Branch
Caldwell, Erskine, and
    Bourke-White, Margaret
Capa, Robert
Capote, Truman
Cartier-Bresson, Henri
Castle, Agnes
Catlin, George
Chagall, Marc
Collier, John (born 1884,
    American)
Collodi, Carlo
Colum, Padraic
Covarrubias, Miguel
Crane, Hart
Cruikshank, George
Da Vinci, Leonardo
Dahl, Roald
Dahlberg, Edward
Dana, Richard Henry
Darling, Esther Birdsall
Defoe, Daniel
Denison, Muriel
Denslow's Mother Goose
Derrydale Press
Detmold, E.J.
Dickens, Charles
Dodge, M.E.
Dowson, Ernest
Dunbar, Paul Laurence
Eaton, Seymour
Evans, Walker

Fabre, Jean Henri
Farrington, S. Kip, Jr.
Fleming, Ian
Fox, John
France, Anatole
Gallico, Paul
Gauguin, Paul
Gibbings, Robert
Gibson, Charles Dana
Gill, Eric
Golden Cockerel Press
Gordon, Elizabeth
Gould, John (1804–1881)
Grabhorn Printing
Grahame, Kenneth
Greenaway, Kate
Grimm, Jakob Ludwig Carl,
    and Grimm, Wilhelm Carl
Grolier Club
Grosz, George
Grover, Eulalie Osgood
Harris, Joel Chandler
Hawkins, Anthony Hope
Heritage Press
Holland, Ray P.
Hudson, W.H.
Ibsen, Henrik
Ingoldsby, Thomas (R.H.
    Barham)
Irving, Washington
Johnson, Robert U., and
    Buel, Clarence C.
Johnston, Annie Fellows
Jones, Shirley
Keaton, Diane
Kent, Rockwell
King, Stephen
King, Stephen, and Straub,
    Peter
Kingsley, Charles

Kinnell, Galway
Kipling, Rudyard
Kohler, Wolfgang
Lang, Andrew
Lanier, Sydney
Lawrence, T.E.
Lea, Tom
Limited Editions Club
Lofting, Hugh
Luhan, Mabel Dodge
MacDonald, George
MacFall, Haldane
Maeterlinck, Maurice
Mailer, Norman
Melville, Herman
Meynell, Francis
Michener, James
Miller, Francis T., edited by
Morley, Christopher
Mother Goose
Mulford, Clarence
Nansen, Fridtjof
Newell, Peter
Newton, Isaac
O'Neill, Rose
Palgrave, F.T.
Parks, Gordon
Perrault, M. (Charles)
Perry, Commodore
    Matthew
Potter, Beatrix
Rawlings, Marjorie Kinnan
Read, Herbert
Riley, James Whitcomb
Robin Hood
Robinson, W. Heath
Saunders, Louise
Scribner's Illustrated
    Classics
Spyri, Johanna

Stevenson, Robert Louis
The Queen of Hearts
Thompson, Ruth Plumly
Timlin, William
Weegee
Weston, Edward
Wiggin, Kate Douglas
Wilde, Oscar
Wiley, Bell I.

CHILDREN'S BOOKS

A Visit to the Circus
Adams, Richard
Akers, Floyd
Alcott, Louisa May
Andersen, Hans Christian
Ardizzone, Edward
Bailey, Pearl
Baldwin, James
Bannerman, Helen
Barrie, James
Baum, L. Frank
Belloc, Hilaire
Bemelmans, Ludwig
Big Little Books
Blaine, John
Bond, Michael
Bontemps, Arna
Brooks, Gwendolyn
Brown, Margaret Wise
Browning, Robert
Buck, Pearl
Burgess, Gelett
Burgess, Thornton
Burnett, Frances Hodgson
Burton, Virginia Lee
Canfield, Dorothy
Carroll, Lewis
Collodi, Carlo

Colum, Padraic
Cox, Palmer
Cruikshank, George
Dahl, Roald
Daugherty, James
De Angeli, Marguerite
De Brunhoff, Jean
De la Mare, Walter
Defoe, Daniel
Denison, Muriel
Denslow's Mother Goose
Detmold, E.J.
Dickens, Charles
Disney
Dodge, M.E.
Eaton, Seymour
Enright, Elizabeth
Field, Eugene
Finley, Martha
Flack, Marjorie
Fleming, Ian
Forester, C.S.
France, Anatole
Fryer, Jane Eayre
Gag, Wanda
Gallico, Paul
Garis, Howard
Gates, Josephine Scribner
Gordon, Elizabeth
Graham, Tom (Sinclair
    Lewis)
Grahame, Kenneth
Greenaway, Kate
Grimm, Jakob Ludwig Carl,
    and Grimm, Wilhelm Carl
Grover, Eulalie Osgood
Gruelle, Johnny
Gury, Jeremy
Harris, Joel Chandler
Hawthorne, Nathaniel

Hearn, Lafcadio
Hecht, Ben
Henry, Robert S.
Hudson, W.H.
Hughes, Langston, and
    DeCarava, Roy
Humphrey, Maud
Irving, Washington
Johnston, Annie Fellows
Jordan, June
Kingsley, Charles
Kipling, Rudyard
Krauss, Ruth
Kreymborg, Alfred
La Farge, Oliver
Lang, Andrew
Lanier, Sydney
Lawson, Robert
Leaf, Munro
Lear, Edward, completed by
    Ogden Nash
Lenski, Lois
Lewis, C.S.
Lofting, Hugh
Lopez, Barry
MacDonald, George
MacKenzie, Compton
Maeterlinck, Maurice
Malcolmson, Anne
Milne, A.A.
Montgomery, L.M.
Moore, Clement C.
Mother Goose
Mother Goose Picture Book
My Farm Book
Nesbit, Edith
Newell, Peter
O'Dell, Scott
O'Neill, Rose
Outcault, F.

Perkins, Lucy Fitch
Perrault, Charles
Perrault, M. (Charles)
Piper, Watty
Potter, Beatrix
Quiller-Couch, Sir Arthur
Rackham, Arthur
Ransome, Arthur
Rawlings, Marjorie Kinnan
Rice, Alice Hegan
Riley, James Whitcomb
Robin Hood
Saint-Exupery, Antoine de
Scribner's Illustrated
    Classics
Sendak, Maurice
Sidney, Margaret
Spyri, Johanna
Stevenson, Robert Louis
Stratton-Porter, Gene
Streatfield, Noel
Tarkington, Booth
The Angora Twinnies
The Queen of Hearts
The Seven Little Sisters who
    Live...
Thompson, Kay
Thompson, Ruth Plumly
Thurber, James
Timlin, William
Tolkien, J.R.R.
Travers, P.L.
Twain, Mark
Upton, Bertha
Van Dyke, Edith
Vavra, Robert
White, E.B.
White, T.H.
Wiggin, Kate Douglas
Wilde, Oscar

Wilder, Laura Ingalls
Wurth, Anne
Wyss, David

COOKBOOKS

Beebe, Lucius
Cassell's
Early, Eleanor
Farmer, Fannie Merritt
Fisher, M.F.K.
Herter, George L., and
    Bertha
Mosser, Marjorie

HISTORY

Ashendene Press
Churchill, Winston S.
Gibbon, Edward
Grabhorn Printing
Heritage Press
Koestler, Arthur
Perry, Commodore
    Matthew
Roberts, Kenneth
Sandberg, Carl
Stone, I.F.
Trumbo, Dalton
West, Rebecca

HUMOR

Anthologies
Benchley, Robert
Cuppy, Will
Dunne, Peter Finley
Gross, Milt
Kimbrough, Emily
Leacock, Stephen

Marquis, Don
Parker, Dorothy
Perelman, S.J.
Pigs is Pigs
Price, George
Rogers, Will
Runyon, Damon
Smith, Thorne
Steig, William
Wodehouse, P.G.

LESBIAN AND GAY BOOKS

Carpenter, Edward
Douglas, Lord Alfred
Farnan, Dorothy J.
Grumbach, Doris
Hall, Radclyffe
Hansen, Joseph
Isherwood, Christopher
Lehmann, Rosamond
Lorde, Audre
Sarton, May
Wilde, Oscar

LITERATURE AND ON LITERATURE

Achebe, Chinua
Alcott, Louisa May
Anderson, Sherwood
Ashendene Press
Austen, Jane
Blackmore, Richard D.
Blake, William
Bronte, Charlotte
Brooks, Cleanth, and
    Warren, Robert Penn
Brooks, Van Wyck

Browning, Elizabeth Barrett
Browning, Robert
Byron, George Gordon,
    Lord
*Cambridge Bibliography of
    English Literature*
*Cambridge History of English
    Literature*
Coleridge, Samuel Taylor
Cooper, James Fenimore
Crane, Stephen
Cuala Press
Dickens, Charles
Donne, John
Doves Press
Emerson, Ralph Waldo
Eragny Press
Faulkner, William
Golden Cockerel Press
Grabhorn Printing
Grolier Club
Hawthorne, Nathaniel
Holmes, O.W.
Housman, Laurence
Huneker, James
Jolas, Eugene
Jones, David
Joyce, James
Keats, John
Kelmscott Press
Last of the Mohicans, The
Lawrence, Frieda
Le Gallienne, Richard
Leaves of Grass
Lehmann, John
Leonard, William Ellery
Lermontov, Michael
Lindsay, Vachel
Longfellow, H.W.
Masters, Edgar Lee

Mauriac, Francois
Melville, Herman
Mencken, H.L.
Meynell, Alice
Muir, Edwin
Murry, John Middleton
Nathan, George Jean
Newton, A. Edward
Nonesuch Press
Poe, Edgar Allan
Ransom, John Crowe
Rhys, Jean
Richardson, Dorothy
Riding, Laura
Rilke, Rainer Maria
Rosetti, Christina
Rukeyser, Muriel
Shakespeare, William
Shelley, Percy Bysshe
Sitwell, Osbert
Sontag, Susan
Stein, Gertrude
Tennyson, Alfred, Lord
Thoreau, Henry David
Twain, Mark
Wilson, Edmund
Wordsworth, William
Yeats, William Butler

Military

Allen, William
Austin, A.B.
Ayling, K.
Barnard, J.G.
Billings, John D.
Bourke-White, Margaret
Capa, Robert
Chamberlain, Joshua L.
Chestnut, Mary Boykin

Freeman, Donald Southall
Grant, Ulysses S.
Guderian, Heinz
Higginson, Thomas
    Wentworth
Hilberg, Raul
Johnson, Robert U., and
    Buel, Clarence C.
Johnson, Robert U., and
    Buel, Clarence C., editors
Marshall, S.L.A.
Mauldin, Bill
McCrae, John
Miller, Francis T., edited by
Mitscherlich, Alexandern,
    and Mielke, Fred
Morison, Samuel Eliot
O'Brien, Tim
Patton, George S.
Porter, David D.
Remarque, Erich Maria
Shirer, William
U.S. Infantry Tactics
Underwood, J.L.
Wallace, Willard M.
Wiley, Bell I.

Modern Firsts

Abbey, Edward
Achebe, Chinua
Ackerly, J.R.
Adams, Leonie
Adams, Richard
Agee, James
Aiken, Conrad
Albee, Edward
Aldington, Richard
Aleichem, Sholem
Algren, Nelson

Allen, Hervey
Allen, Woody
Amado, Jorge
Ambler, Eric
Amis, Kingsley
Anderson, Maxwell
Anderson, Poul
Anderson, Sherwood
Angelou, Maya
Anthologies
Antoninus, Brother
Asch, Sholem
Ashbery, John
Asimov, Isaac
Atwood, Margaret
Auchincloss, Louis
Auden, W.H.
Auel, Jean
Auslander, Joseph
Bagnold, Enid
Bailey, H.C.
Baldwin, James, and
    Avedon, Richard
Ballard, J.G.
Bambara, Toni Cade
Banks, Russell
Baraka, Imamu Amiri
Barker, George
Barnes, Djuna
Barrie, James
Barrows, R.M., editor
Barth, John
Barthelme, Donald
Bates, H.E.
Baum, Vicki
Beagle, Peter S.
Beardsley, Aubrey
Beaton, Cecil
Beattie, Ann
Beckett, Samuel

Beebe, Lucius
Beerbohm, Max
Bell, Clive
Belloc, Hilaire
Bellow, Saul
Bemelmans, Ludwig
Benchley, Robert
Benet, Stephen Vincent
Bennett, Arnold
Benson, E.F.
Benson, Sally
Bentley, E.C.
Berger, Thomas
Berry, Wendell
Berryman, John
Bester, Alfred
Betjeman, John
Bierce, Ambrose
Biggers, Earl Derr
Bishop, Elizabeth
Bishop, John Peale
Blanding, Don
Blish, James
Bloch, Robert
Bogan, Louise
Bond, Nelson
Bontemps, Arna
Borges, Jorge Luis
Boulle, Pierre
Bowen, Elizabeth
Bowles, Jane
Bowles, Paul
Boyd, James
Boyd, William
Bradbury, Ray
Bradford, Roark
Braine, John
Brautigan, Richard
Bridges, Robert
Bromfield, Louis

Brooke, Rupert
Brooks, Gwendolyn
Brown, Frederic
Buchan, John
Buck, Pearl
Bukowski, Charles
Bunin, Ivan
Burgess, Anthony
Burke, James Lee
Burke, Thomas
Burnett, W.R.
Burroughs, Edgar Rice
Burroughs, William
Bush, Christopher
Bynner, Witter
Byrne, Donn
Cabell, James Branch
Cain, James M.
Caldwell, Erskine
Calisher, Hortense
Callaghan, Morley
Campbell, Roy
Camus, Albert
Canetti, Elias
Canfield, Dorothy
Capek, Karel
Capote, Truman
Capote, Truman, and
    Avedon, Richard
Carmer, Carl
Carson, Rachel
Carter, Forrest
Cary, Joyce
Cather, Willa
Celine, Louis-Ferdinand
Cendrars, Blaise
Chambers, Robert W.
Chandler, Raymond
Chase-Riboud, Barbara
Cheever, John

Chesterton, G.K.
Christie, Agatha
Chute, Carolyn
Clancy, Tom
Clark, Walter Van Tilburg
Clarke, Arthur C.
Clavell, James
Cleaver, Eldridge
Coffin, Robert Tristram
Cohen, Leonard
Colette (Sidonie-Gabrielle)
Collier, John (born 1901,
    English)
Compton-Burnett, Ivy
Connell, Evan S.
Connolly, Cyril
Conrad, Joseph
Coppard, A.E.
Cornell, Catherine
Corso, Gregory
Corvo, Baron
Crane, Hart
Creeley, Robert
Crews, Harry
Cronin, A.J.
Crosby, Caresse
Crosby, Harry
Crowley, Aleister
Croy, Homer
Cullen, Countee
Cummings, e.e.
Cunard, Nancy
Cuppy, Will
Dahl, Roald
Dahlberg, Edward
Dane, Clemence
Davies, Rhys
Davies, W.H.
Davis, H.L.
Day, Clarence

Deighton, Len
DeLillo, Don
Derleth, August
Deutsch, Babette
Devries, Peter
Di Prima, Diane
Dick, Philip K.
Dick, R.A.
Dickey, James
Didion, Joan
Dinesen, Isak
Doctorow, E.L.
Donleavy, J.P.
Dos Passos, John
Douglas, Lloyd C.
Douglas, Lord Alfred
Douglas, Norman
Doyle, Arthur Conan
Dreiser, Theodore
Drinkwater, John
Du Maurier, Daphne
Dunbar, Paul Laurence
Durrell, Lawrence
Eastlake, William
Eberhart, Richard
Eddison, E.R.
Edmonds, Walter D.
Eliot, T.S.
Ellison, Ralph
Ellson, Hal
Erdrich, Louise
Evans, Abbie Huston
Farmer, Philip José
Farrell, James T.
Fast, Howard
Faulkner, William
Fearing, Kenneth
Ferber, Edna
Feutchwanger, Leon
Firbank, Ronald

Fitzgerald, F. Scott
Fleming, Ian
Ford, Ford Madox
Forester, C.S.
Forster, E.M.
Fournier, Alain
Fowles, John
Francis, Dick
Fraser, George MacDonald
Friedman, Bruce Jay
Frost, Robert
Fuller, R. Buckminster
Fuller, Roy
Gaddis, William
Gallico, Paul
Garcia Marquez, Gabriel
Gardner, John
Garland, Hamlin
Garnett, David
Gascoyne, David
Gass, William
Genet, Jean
Gibbings, Robert
Gibran, Kahlil
Gide, André
Gilbert, Michael
Gill, Brendan
Gill, Eric
Ginsberg, Allen
Giovanni, Nikki
Giradoux, Jean
Glasgow, Ellen
Godden, Rumer
Gogarty, Oliver St. John
Gold, Michael
Golding, Louis
Golding, William
Goodman, Paul
Gorey, Edward
Gordimer, Nadine

Gorki, Maxim
Goyen, William
Grafton, Sue
Grass, Gunther
Graves, Robert
Green, Anna Katherine
Green, Henry
Green, Julian
Greene, Graham
Gregory, Lady (Isabella
    Augusta)
Gresham, William
Gross, Milt
Grumbach, Doris
Guiney, Louise Imogen
Gunn, Thom
Guthrie, A.B.
Haggard, H. Rider
Haley, Alex
Hall, Donald
Hall, James Norman
Hall, Radclyffe
Hammett, Dashiell
Hanley, James
Hannah, Barry
Hansen, Joseph
Hardwick, Elizabeth
Harris, Frank
Harris, Mark
Harrison, Jim
Hartley, Marsden
Hawkes, John
Heany, Seamus
Heard, H.F.
Hearn, Lafcadio
Hecht, Ben
Heinlein, Robert
Heller, Joseph
Hemingway, Ernest
Herbert, Frank

Hersey, John
Hesse, Herman
Heyward, Dubose
Highsmith, Patricia
Hillyer, Robert
Hilton, James
Himes, Chester
Hoagland, Edward
Hoban, Russell
Hoffman, Abbie
Holmes, John Clellon
Hopkins, Gerard Manley
Horgan, Paul
Housman, A.E.
Housman, Laurence
Howard, Robert E.
Hughes, Dorothy B.
Hughes, Langston
Hughes, Richard
Hughes, Ted
Huxley, Aldous
Ibsen, Henrik
Irish, William
Irving, John
Isherwood, Christopher
Jackson, Shirley
James, P.D.
James, Will
Janeway, Elizabeth
Jarrell, Randall
Jeffers, Robinson
Johnson, James Weldon
Johnson, Lionel
Jones, James
Jones, LeRoi
Joyce, James
Kafka, Franz
Kantor, MacKinlay
Kaye-Smith, Sheila
Keneally, Thomas

Kennedy, William
Kerouac, Jack
Kesey, Ken
King, Stephen
Kingston, Maxine Hong
Kinnell, Galway
Kinsella, Thomas
Kinsella, W.P.
Kipling, Rudyard
Knowles, John
Koestler, Arthur
Koontz, Dean R.
Kotzwinkle, William
Kreymborg, Alfred
Kunitz, Stanley
Lardner, Ring
Larkin, Philip
Laughlin, James
Lawrence, D.H.
Lawrence, Frieda
La Blanc, Maurice
Le Carré, John
Le Gallienne, Richard
Le Guin, Ursula
Lea, Tom
Leacock, Stephen
Leary, Timothy
Lehmann, John
Lehmann, Rosamond
Leiber, Fritz
Leighton, Clare
Leinster, Murray
Leonard, William Ellery
Lessing, Doris
Levertov, Denise
Lewis, C.S.
Lewis, Sinclair
Lewis, Wyndham
Lewisohn, Ludwig
Liebling, A.J.

Lindbergh, Anne Morrow
Lindsay, Vachel
Llewellyn, Richard
Lockridge, Ross
London, Charmian
London, Jack
Longstreet, Stephen
Loos, Anita
Lopez, Barry
Lorca, Federico García
Lorde, Audre
Louys, Pierre
Lovecraft, Howard
Lowell, Amy
Lowell, Robert
Lowry, Malcom
Lowry, Robert
Luhan, Mabel Dodge
Lytle, Andrew
Macaulay, Rose
MacDiarmid, Hugh
MacDonald, Betty
MacDonald, John D.
MacDonald, Ross
Machen, Arthur
MacKenzie, Compton
MacLeish, Archibald
MacNeice, Louis
Mailer, Norman
Malamud, Bernard
Malraux, André
Mann, Erika
Mann, Thomas
Mansfield, Katherine
Markham, Edwin
Marquand, John P.
Marquis, Don
Masefield, John
Masereel, Frans
Masters, Edgar Lee

Matheson, Richard
Matthiessen, Peter
Maugham, Somerset
Mauriac, Francois
Maurois, André
McAlmon, Robert
McCaffrey, Anne
McCarthy, Mary
McClure, Michael
McCoy, Horace
McCullers, Carson
McCulley, Johnston
McFee, William
McGrath, Thomas
McKay, Claude
McKenney, Ruth
McMurtry, Larry
McPhee, John
Mencken, H.L.
Menen, Aubrey
Merrill, James
Merritt, A.
Merton, Thomas
Michener, James
Miller, Alice Duer
Miller, Arthur
Miller, Henry
Mitchell, Margaret
Mitford, Nancy
Momaday, N. Scott
Moore, Brian
Moore, Marianne
Moore, Merrill
Morley, Christopher
Morris, Wright
Morrison, Toni
Motley, Willard
Muir, Edwin
Mundy, Talbot
Mungo, Raymond

Murdoch, Iris
Murry, John Middleton
Nabokov, Vladimir
Naipaul, V.S.
Nash, Ogden
Nathan, Robert
Nemerov, Howard
Neruda, Pablo
Nesbit, Edith
Nichols, Beverly
Nichols, John
Nicolson, Harold
Nin, Anais
Nordhoff, Charles
Nordhoff, Charles B., and
    Hall, James Norman
Norris, Frank
Norton, André
Novak, Joseph
Noyes, Alfred
O'Brien, Tim
O'Connor, Flannery
O'Donnell, E.P.
O'Faolain, Sean
O'Flaherty, Liam
O'Hara, John
O'Neill, Eugene
Oates, Joyce Carol
Odets, Clifford
Olsen, Tillie
Olson, Charles
Oppenheim, E. Phillips
Orwell, George
Ozick, Cynthia
Paley, Grace
Parker, Dorothy
Parker, Robert B.
Patchen, Kenneth
Paul, Elliot
Peake, Mervyn

Percy, Walker
Perelman, S.J.
Peterkin, Julia
Peterkin, Julia, and Ulmann,
    Doris
Petry, Ann
Phillips, Jayne Anne
Pinter, Harold
Pirsig, Robert M.
Pitter, Ruth
Plath, Sylvia
Plomer, William
Pohl, Frederik
Porter, Katherine Anne
Post, Melville Davidson
Pound, Ezra
Powell, Anthony
Powers, James F.
Powys, John Cowper
Powys, Llewelyn
Powys, Theodore Francis
Price, Reynolds
Priestly, J.B.
Prokosch, Frederic
Proust, Marcel
Purdy, James
Pym, Barbara
Pynchon, Thomas
Quiller-Couch, Sir Arthur
Raine, Kathleen
Rand, Ayn
Ransom, John Crowe
Rawlings, Marjorie Kinnan
Remarque, Erich Maria
Repplier, Agnes
Rexroth, Kenneth
Reznikoff, Charles
Rhys, Jean
Rice, Anne
Rich, Adrienne

Richardson, Dorothy
Richter, Conrad
Ridge, Lola
Riding, Laura
Ridler, Anne
Rilke, Rainer Maria
Rimbaud, Arthur
Rinehart, Mary Roberts
Robbins, Tom
Roberts, Elizabeth Madox
Roberts, Kenneth
Robinson, Edwin Arlington
Roethke, Theodore
Rogers, Will
Rohmer, Sax
Rolvaag, O.E.
Rosenberg, Isaac
Roth, Philip
Ruark, Robert
Rubin, Jerry
Rukeyser, Muriel
Runyon, Damon
Rushdie, Salman
Sackville-West, Vita
Saint-Exupery, Antoine de
Saki
Salinger, J.D.
Sandberg, Carl
Sandoz, Mari
Santee, Ross
Saroyan, William
Sarton, May
Sartre, Jean Paul
Sayers, Dorothy
Schreiner, Olive
Schulberg, Budd
Schwartz, Delmore
Service, Robert
Sexton, Anne
Shapiro, Karl

Shaw, George Bernard
Shute, Nevil
Silverberg, Robert
Simon, Neil
Sinclair, Upton
Singer, Isaac Bashevis
Sitwell, Edith
Sitwell, Osbert
Smith, Betty
Smith, Stevie
Smith, Thorne
Snyder, Gary
Sontag, Susan
Southern, Terry
Spark, Muriel
Spender, Stephen
Spillane, Mickey
Stafford, Jean
Stegner, Wallace
Steig, William
Stein, Gertrude
Steinbeck, John
Stevens, Wallace
Stone, Robert
Stoppard, Tom
Straub, Peter
Stuart, Jesse
Styron, William
Synge, John Millington
Tagore, Rabindranath
Tan, Amy
Tarkington, Booth
Tate, Allen
Tate, James
The Dark Side of the Moon
Theroux, Paul
Thomas, Dylan
Thomas, Edward
Thompson, Hunter S.
Thurber, James

Tolkien, J.R.R.
Traven, B.
Trumbo, Dalton
Tyler, Anne
Updike, John
Upfield, Arthur
Van Dine, S.S.
Van Gulik, Robert
Van Vetchen, Carl
Van Vogt, A.E.
Vance, Jack
Vidal, Gore
Vintage Paperbacks
Vonnegut, Kurt
Wakoski, Diane
Walcott, Derek
Waley, Arthur
Walker, Alice
Walpole, Hugh
Ward, Lynd
Warner, Rex
Warner, Sylvia Townsend
Warren, Robert Penn
Washington, Booker T.
Waugh, Evelyn
Webb, Mary
Wells, H.G.
Welty, Eudora
West, Mae
West, Nathanael
West, Rebecca
Wharton, Edith
Wheelock, John Hall
Whistler, Rex
White, E.B.
White, T.H.
Wiggin, Kate Douglas
Wilde, Oscar
Wilder, Thornton
Williams, Charles

Williams, Tennessee
Williams, William Carlos
Willingham, Calder
Wilson, Edmund
Winters, Yvor
Wodehouse, P.G.
Wolfe, Thomas
Wolfe, Tom
Woolf, Leonard
Woolf, Virginia
Woolrich, Cornell
Wouk, Herman
Wright, Austin Tappan
Wright, Richard
Wylie, Elinor
Wylie, Philip
Wyndham, John
Yeats, William Butler
Young, Marguerite
Zelazny, Roger
Zukovsky, Louis
Zweig, Arnold

MOVIES, THE

Biggers, Earl Derr
Cather, Willa
Chandler, Raymond
Denison, Muriel
Hart, William S.
Irish, William
Leroux, Gaston
London, Jack
Marx, Groucho
Mitchell, Margaret
O'Day, Dean, editor
Shute, Nevil
Swarthout, Glendon
Weegee
West, Mae

Williams, Tennessee

MYSTERIES

Ambler, Eric
Bailey, H.C.
Bentley, E.C.
Big Little Books
Biggers, Earl Derr
Bloch, Robert
Bramah, Ernest
Brown, Frederic
Burke, James Lee
Burnett, W.R.
Bush, Christopher
Carr, John Dickson
Chandler, Raymond
Chesterton, G.K.
Christie, Agatha
Clancy, Tom
Deighton, Len
Doyle, Arthur Conan
Eastlake, William
Fleming, Ian
Francis, Dick
Grafton, Sue
Green, Anna Katherine
Hammett, Dashiell
Harrison, Jim
Heard, H.F.
Heritage Press
Highsmith, Patricia
Himes, Chester
Hughes, Dorothy B.
Irish, William
James, P.D.
Le Blanc, Maurice
Le Carré, John
Leroux, Gaston
Limited Editions Club

MacDonald, John D.
MacDonald, Ross
Marquand, John P.
Oppenheim, E. Phillips
Parker, Robert B.
Paul, Elliot
Post, Melville Davidson
Rohmer, Sax
Sayers, Dorothy
Spillane, Mickey
Upfield, Arthur
Van Dine, S.S.
Van Gulik, Robert
Vintage Paperbacks
Woolrich, Cornell

NATIVE AMERICAN

Austin, Mary
BAE (Bureau of American
    Ethnology)
Catlin, George
Collier, John (born 1884,
    American)
Covarrubias, Miquel
Garland, Hamlin
La Farge, Oliver
Sylvester, Herbert Milton
Boas, Franz, editor
Carter, Forrest
Erdrich, Louise
Kinsella, W.P.
Matthiessen, Peter
Neihardt, John G.

NATURAL HISTORY

Audubon, John James
Burroughs, John
Caras, Roger

Carrighar, Sally
Carson, Rachel
Culpepper, Nicholas
Gould, John (1804–1881)
Grieve, Maud
Hudson, W.H.
Muir, John
Seton, Ernest Thompson
Stratton-Porter, Gene
US Geological Survey

NAUTICAL

Ashley, Clifford
Blunt, Edmund M.
Bowditch, Nathaniel
Brassey, Anne
Bullen, Frank T.
Carse, Robert
Chapelle, Howard I.
Chapman, Charles
Chatterton, E.K.
Chichester, F.
Clowes, G.S. Laird
Cutler, Carl C.
Dana, Richard Henry
Fanning, Edmund
Gardner, John
Gatty, Harold
Golden Cockerel Press
Hawkesworth, John
Heyerdahl, Thor
Lord, Walter
Mahan, A.T. Captain
Masefield, John
McFee, William
Morison, Samuel Eliot
Nordhoff, Charles
Nordhoff, Charles B., and
    Hall, James Norman
Porter, David D.

Scoresby, William, Jr.
Simpson, Sir George
Slocum, Joshua
Snow, Edgar Rowe
Stackpole, Edouard A.
Starbuck, Alexander
Trade Catalogs
U.S. Light-House Board
U.S. Coast Survey
Vancouver, George
Villiers, Alan
Whipple, A.B.C.

PERFORMING ARTS: DRAMA, MUSIC, MAGIC

Albee, Edward
Anderson, Maxwell
Anthologies
Baraka, Imamu Amiri
Beckett, Samuel
Connelly, Marc
Cornell, Catherine
Coward, Noel
Day, Clarence
Doves Press
Dunsany, Lord
Epstein, Brian
Goldberg, Isaac
Grabhorn Printing
Hall, Trevor
Hart, Moss
Hellman, Lillian
Heyward, Dubose
Hoffman, Professor
Houdin, Jean Eugene Robert
Houdini, Harry
Hurok, Sol
Ibsen, Henrik
Ives, Charles
Jones, LeRoi

McKenney, Ruth
Miller, Arthur
Nathan, George Jean
O'Casey, Sean
O'Neill, Eugene
Odets, Clifford
Osgood, Henry O.
Pinter, Harold
Rice, Elmer
Rohmer, Sax
Shakespeare, William
Shaw, George Bernard
Synge, John Millington
Williams, Tennessee

PHOTOGRAPHY

Abbey, Edward
Abbott, Berenice
Adams, Ansel
Agee, James
Antoninus, Brother
Arbus, Diane
Austin, Mary
Baldwin, James, and
    Avedon, Richard
Black Photographers Annual,
    The
Bourke-White, Margaret,
    and Caldwell, Erskine
Caldwell, Erskine, and
    Bourke-White, Margaret
Capa, Robert
Capote, Truman
Capote, Truman, and
    Avedon, Richard
Cartier-Bresson, Henri
Dunbar, Paul Laurence
Evans, Walker
Grabhorn Printing
Grolier Club

Keaton, Diane
Mailer, Norman
Miller, Francis T., edited by
Parks, Gordon
Peterkin, Julia, and Ulmann, Doris
Weegee
Weston, Edward

POETRY

Adams, Leonie
Aiken, Conrad
Anthologies
Antoninus, Brother
Ashbery, John
Ashendene Press
Auden, W.H.
Barker, George
Barrett, Elizabeth
Benet, Stephen Vincent
Berryman, John
Betjeman, John
Bishop, Elizabeth
Bishop, John Peale
Blake, William
Blanding, Don
Bogan, Louise
Bridges, Robert
Brooke, Rupert
Brooks, Gwendolyn
Browning, Elizabeth Barrett
Browning, Robert
Bukowski, Charles
Bynner, Witter
Byron, George Gordon, Lord
Campbell, Roy
Carleton, Will
Cohen, Leonard
Coleridge, Samuel Taylor
Corso, Gregory
Crane, Hart
Crane, Nathalia
Crane, Stephen
Creeley, Robert
Cuala Press
Cullen, Countee
Cummings, e.e.
Davies, W.H.
Day-Lewis, Cecil
De la Mare, Walter
Deutsch, Babette
Di Prima, Diane
Dickey, James
Donne, John
Doves Press
Drinkwater, John
Dunbar, Paul Laurence
Eberhart, Richard
Eliot, T.S.
Eragny Press
Erdrich, Louise
Evans, Abbie Huston
Ferlinghetti, Lawrence
Frost, Robert
Gascoyne, David
Ginsberg, Allen
Giovanni, Nikki
Golden Cockerel Press
Grabhorn Printing
Graves, Robert
Grolier Club
Guest, Edgar
Guiney, Louise Imogen
Gunn, Thom
Hall, Donald
Hall, Radclyffe
Hartley, Marsden
Heany, Seamus

Hillyer, Robert
Hodgson, Ralph
Hopkins, Gerard Manley
Housman, A.E.
Hughes, Langston
Hughes, Ted
Jarrell, Randall
Jeffers, Robinson
Johnson, James Weldon
Johnson, Lionel
Joyce, James
Keats, John
Kees, Weldon
Kelmscott Press
Kemp, Harry
Kilmer, Joyce
Kinnell, Galway
Kinsella, Thomas
Kipling, Rudyard
Kunitz, Stanley
Larkin, Philip
Laughlin, James
Lawrence, D.H.
Leaves of Grass
Leonard, William Ellery
Levertov, Denise
Lincoln, Joseph C.
Lindbergh, Anne Morrow
Lindsay, Vachel
Longfellow, H.W.
Lorca, Federico García
Lorde, Audre
Lowell, Amy
Lowell, Robert
MacDiarmid, Hugh
MacKenzie, Compton
MacLeish, Archibald
MacNeice, Louis
Markham, Edwin
Masefield, John

Masters, Edgar Lee
McClure, Michael
McCrae, John
McGrath, Thomas
McKay, Claude
Merrill, James
Millay, Edna St. Vincent
Miller, Alice Duer
Moore, Marianne
Moore, Merrill
Muir, Edwin
Nemerov, Howard
Neruda, Pablo
Noyes, Alfred
Olson, Charles
Owen, Wilfres
Palgrave, F.T.
Pitter, Ruth
Plath, Sylvia
Plomer, William
Pound, Ezra
Raine, Kathleen
Ransom, John Crowe
Rexroth, Kenneth
Reznikoff, Charles
Rich, Adrienne
Ridge, Lola
Riding, Laura
Ridler, Anne
Riley, James Whitcomb
Rilke, Rainer Maria
Rimbaud, Arthur
Robinson, Edwin Arlington
Roethke, Theodore
Rosenberg, Isaac
Rukeyser, Muriel
Sandberg, Carl
Service, Robert
Sexton, Anne
Shakespeare, William

Shapiro, Karl
Shelley, Percy Bysshe
Sitwell, Edith
Smith, Stevie
Snyder, Gary
Spender, Stephen
Stevens, Wallace
Tagore, Rabindranath
Tate, Allen
Tate, James
Tennyson, Alfred, Lord
Thomas, Dylan
Thomas, Edward
Wakoski, Diane
Walcott, Derek
Waley, Arthur
Walker, Alice
Warren, Robert Penn
Wheelock, John Hall
Wilde, Oscar
Williams, William Carlos
Winters, Yvor
Wolfe, Thomas
Wordsworth, William
Wylie, Elinor
Yeats, William Butler
Young, Marguerite
Zukovsky, Louis

PRIVATE PRESS BOOKS

Ashendene Press
Cuala Press
Doves Press
Eragny Press
Golden Cockerel Press
Grabhorn Printing
Grolier Club
Kelmscott Press
Nonesuch Press

PSYCHOLOGY, MEDICINE, SCIENCE

Abraham, Karl
Culpepper, Nicholas
Darwin, Charles
Eddington, Sir Arthur S.
Einstein, Albert
Faraday, Michael
Freud, Sigmund
Grolier Club
Hubbard, L. Ron
Jung, Carl Gustav
Jungk, Robert
Kohler, Wolfgang
Lawrence, D.H.
Mayo, Wm. (MD) and
    Charles (MD)
Mendeleef, Dmitry
    Ivanovich
Newton, Isaac
Osler, William
Planck, Max
Priestly, Joseph
Rush, Benjamin
Sartre, Jean Paul

REFERENCE BOOKS

Bader, Barbara
Baedeker, Karl
Bailey, L.H.
*Cambridge Bibliography of
    English Literature*
*Cambridge History of English
    Literature*
Carter, John
Cassell's
Johnson, Merle
Mencken, H.L.

Meynell, Francis
Miller, Francis T., edited by
Muir, Percy H.
Porter, David D.
Wells, H.G.
Westerners Brand Book

SCIENCE FICTION, FANTASY, HORROR

Aldiss, Brian W.
Anderson, Poul
Asimov, Isaac
Auel, Jean
Ballard, J.G.
Bear, Greg
Bester, Alfred
Big Little Books
Blish, James
Bradbury, Ray
Capek, Karel
Chambers, Robert W.
Clarke, Arthur C.
Derleth, August
Dick, Philip K.
Farmer, Philip José
Heinlein, Robert
Herbert, Frank
Howard, Robert E.
Hubbard, L. Ron
King, Stephen
Koontz, Dean R.
Le Guin, Ursula
Leiber, Fritz
Leinster, Murray
Lewis, C.S.
Lovecraft, Howard
Machen, Arthur
Matheson, Richard

McCaffrey, Anne
Merritt, A.
Mundy, Talbot
Norton, André
Peake, Mervyn
Pohl, Frederik
Rice, Anne
Sets
Shute, Nevil
Silverberg, Robert
Stoker, Bram
Straub, Peter
Tolkien, J.R.R.
Van Vogt, A.E.
Vance, Jack
Verne, Jules
Vintage Paperbacks
Wells, H.G.
White, T.H.
Williams, Charles
Wright, Austin Tappan
Wyndham, John
Zelazny, Roger

VOYAGES

Brassey, Anne
Cook, Captain James
Cook, Frederick
Dana, Richard Henry
Doughty, Charles Montague
Fanning, Edmund
Franklin, John
Freuchen, Peter
Grabhorn Printing
Hawkesworth, John
Heyerdahl, Thor
Melville, Herman
Nansen, Fridtjof

Nordhoff, Charles B., and
  Hall, James Norman
Perry, Commodore
  Matthew
Simpson, Sir George
Slocum, Joshua
Vancouver, George
Villiers, Alan

WESTERNS AND
NORTHERNS

Bennett, Robert A.
Big Little Books
Bonham, Frank
Bower, B.M.
Brand, Max
Burt, Katherine Newlin
Cullum, Ridgewell
Cunningham, Eugene
Curwood, James Oliver
Field, Peter
Gill, Tom
Gregory, Jackson
Grey, Zane
Gruber, Frank
Haycox, Ernest
Hendryx, James B.
L'Amour, Louis
Lea, Tom
Lomax, Bliss
Manning, David
McCulley, Johnston
McMurtry, Larry
Morrow, Honore´
Mulford, Clarence
O'Dell, Scott
Raine, William MacLeod
Robertson, Frank C.
Tuttle, W.C.

WOMEN'S STUDIES,
WOMEN'S BOOKS

Abbott, Berenice
Adams, Leonie
Alcott, Louisa May
Angelou, Maya
Antin, Mary
Arbus, Diane
Atherton, Gertrude
Atwood, Margaret
Auel, Jean
Austen, Jane
Austin, Mary
Bader, Barbara
Bagnold, Enid
Bailey, Carolyn
Bailey, Pearl
Bambara, Toni Cade
Bannerman, Helen
Barnes, Djuna
Barrett, Elizabeth
Baum, Vicki
Beattie, Ann
Birney, Catherine
Bishop, Elizabeth
Black Photographers Annual,
  The
Bogan, Louise
Book Club of California
Bourke-White, Margaret
Bourke-White, Margaret,
  and Caldwell, Erskine
Bowen, Elizabeth
Bower, B.M.
Bowles, Jane
Bronte, Charlotte
Bronte, Emily
Brooks, Gwendolyn
Brown, Alice
Brown, Margaret Wise

Browning, Elizabeth Barrett
Buck, Pearl
Burnett, Frances Hodgson
Burt, Katherine Newlin
Burton, Virginia Lee
Caldwell, Erskine, and
    Bourke-White, Margaret
Calisher, Hortense
Canfield, Dorothy
Carrighar, Sally
Carson, Rachel
Cather, Willa
Chase, Mary Ellen
Chase-Riboud, Barbara
Chestnut, Mary Boykin
Christie, Agatha
Chute, Carolyn
Colette (Sidonie-Gabrielle)
Compton-Burnett, Ivy
Corelli, Marie
Cornell, Catherine
Crane, Nathalia
Cuala Press
Cunard, Nancy
Custer, Elizabeth
De Angeli, Marguerite
Denison, Muriel
Deutsch, Babette
Di Prima, Diane
Dick, R.A.
Didion, Joan
Dinesen, Isak
Dodge, M.E.
Du Maurier, Daphne
Early, Eleanor
Enright, Elizabeth
Erdrich, Louise
Evans, Abbie Huston
Fairbrother, Nan
Farmer, Fannie Merritt

Farnan, Dorothy J.
Freeman, Mary E. Wilkins
Fryer, Jane Eayre
Gag, Wanda
Gates, Josephine Scribner
Giovanni, Nikki
Glasgow, Ellen
Golden Cockerel Press
Gordon, Elizabeth
Gordimer, Nadine
Grafton, Sue
Green, Anna Katherine
Greenaway, Kate
Gregory, Lady (Isabella
    Augusta)
Grieve, Maud
Grover, Eulalie Osgood
Grumbach, Doris
Guiney, Louise Imogen
Hall, Radclyffe
Hardwick, Elizabeth
Hill, Grace Livingston
Hurston, Zora Neale
Husted, Ida
James, P.D.
Janeway, Elizabeth
Johnston, Annie Fellows
Jones, Shirley
Jordan, June
Juvenile Series Books
Kaye-Smith, Sheila
Keaton, Diane
Keith, Agnew Newton
Kimbrough, Emily
Kingston, Maxine Hong
Kipling, Rudyard
Krauss, Ruth
Lawrence, Frieda
Le Guin, Ursula
Lehmann, Rosamond

Leighton, Clare
Lenski, Lois
Lessing, Doris
Levertov, Denise
Limited Editions Club
Lindbergh, Anne Morrow
London, Charmian
Lorde, Audre
Lowell, Amy
Luhan, Mabel Dodge
Lutes, Della T.
Macaulay, Rose
MacDonald, Betty
MacKenzie, Compton
Malcolmson, Anne
Mansfield, Katherine
McCaffrey, Anne
McCarthy, Mary
McCullers, Carson
McKenney, Ruth
Meynell, Alice
Mill, John Stuart
Millay, Edna St. Vincent
Miller, Alice Duer
Mitchell, Margaret
Mitford, Nancy
Montgomery, L.M.
Moore, Marianne
Morrison, Toni
Morrow, Honore'
Murdoch, Iris
Nesbit, Edith
Nin, Anais
Norton, Andre'
Notestein, Wallace
O'Connor, Flannery
O'Neill, Rose
Oates, Joyce Carol
Olsen, Tillie
Ozick, Cynthia

Paley, Grace
Pankhurst, E. Sylvia
Parker, Dorothy
Perkins, Lucy Fitch
Peterkin, Julia
Peterkin, Julia, and Ulmann,
    Doris
Petry, Ann
Phillips, Jayne Anne
Pitter, Ruth
Plath, Sylvia
Porter, Katherine Anne
Potter, Beatrix
Pym, Barbara
Raine, Kathleen
Rand, Ayn
Rawlings, Marjorie Kinnan
Reed, Myrtle
Repplier, Agnes
Rhys, Jean
Rice, Alice Hegan
Rice, Anne
Rich, Adrienne
Richardson, Dorothy
Ridge, Lola
Riding, Laura
Ridler, Anne
Rinehart, Mary Roberts
Roberts, Elizabeth Madox
Rosetti, Christina
Rukeyser, Muriel
Sackville-West, Vita
Sandoz, Mari
Sarton, May
Sayers, Dorothy
Schreiner, Olive
Sexton, Anne
Sidney, Margaret
Sitwell, Edith
Smith, Betty

Smith, Stevie
Sontag, Susan
Spark, Muriel
Spyri, Johanna
Stafford, Jean
Steen, Marguerite
Stein, Gertrude
Stratton-Porter, Gene
Taber, Gladys
Tan, Amy
*The Seven Little Sisters Who
    Live...*
Thompson, Kay
Thompson, Ruth Plumly
Travers, P.L.
Tyler, Anne

Underwood, J.L.
Upton, Bertha
Vintage Paperbacks
Wakoski, Diane
Walker, Alice
Warner, Sylvia Townsend
Webb, Mary
Welty, Eudora
West, Mae
West, Rebecca
Wharton, Edith
Wilder, Laura Ingalls
Winsor, Kathleen
Woolf, Virginia
Wylie, Elinor
Young, Marguerite

APPENDIX B

Key to Illustrators

ILLUSTRATORS	⇒	AUTHORS

Adams, Ansel — Austin, Mary
Adams, Ansel — Grabhorn, Printing
African-American photographers — *Black Photographers Annual, The*
Angelo, Valenti — Angelo, Valenti
Angelo, Valenti — Ashendene Press
Angelo, Valenti — Douglas, Norman
Angelo, Valenti — The Book Club of California
Arbus, Diane — Arbus, Diane
Ardizzone, Edward — Ardizzone, Edward
Armstrong, Margaret — Dunbar, Paul Laurence
Armstrong, Margaret — Reed, Myrtle
Armstrong, Margaret — Riley, James Whitcomb
Artzybasheff, Boris — Colum, Padraic
Artzybasheff, Boris — Kreymborg, Alfred
Artzybasheff, Boris — Tagore, Rabindranath
Atwell, Mabel Lucie — Barrie James
Audubon, John James — Audubon, John James
Austen, John — Louys, Pierre
Austen, John — Perrault, Charles
Avedon, Richard — Baldwin, James, and Avedon, Richard

Avedon, Richard — Capote, Truman, and Avedon, Richard

Bacon, Peggy — Bacon, Peggy
Bacon, Peggy — Hecht, Ben
Barbier, George — Le Gallienne, Richard
Barton, Ralph — Loos, Anita

ILLUSTRATORS	⇒	AUTHORS

ILLUSTRATORS	AUTHORS
Beardsley, Aubrey	Dowson, Ernest
Beardsley, Aubrey	MacFall, Haldane
Beardsley, Aubrey	Beardsley, Aubrey
Beaton, Cecil	Beaton, Cecil
Beerbohm, Max	Beerbohm, Max
Bemelmans, Ludwig	Bemelmans, Ludwig
Benda, W.T.	Stratton-Porter, Gene
Betts, Ethel Franklin	Burnett, Frances Hodgson
Betts, Ethel Franklin	Riley, James Whitcomb
Birch, Reginald	Burnett, Frances Hodgson
Birch, Reginald	Nash, Ogden
Bischoff, Ilse	Bontemps, Arna
Blackwood, Basil	Belloc, Hilaire
Blaine, Mahlon	Burke, Thomas
Blake, William	Binyon, Laurence
Bourke-White, Margaret	Bourke-White, Margaret
Bourke-White, Margaret	Caldwell, Erskine, and Bourke-White, Margaret
Boyer, Jane Allen	Fryer, Jane Eayre
Bradley, Will	Bradley, Will
Bradley, Will	Irving, Washington
Bradley, Will H.	Blackmore, Richard D.
Bridgman, L.J.	Johnston, Annie Fellows
Brock, C.E.	Nesbit, Edith
Brundage, Frances	Moore, Clement C.
Bull, Charles Livingston	London, Jack
Burgess, Gelett	Burgess, Gelett
Burkert, Nancy Ekholm	Andersen, Hans Christian
Burkert, Nancy Ekholm	Lear, Edward, completed by Ogden Nash
Burton, Virginia Lee	Burton, Virginia Lee
Cady, Harrison	Burgess, Thornton
Caldecott, Randolph	*The Queen of Hearts*
Campbell, Lang	Garis, Howard
Campbell, V. Floyd	Eaton, Seymour
Caniff, Milton	Caniff, Milton
Capa, Robert	Capa, Robert
Cartier-Bresson, Henri	Capote, Truman

ILLUSTRATORS   ⇒   AUTHORS

Cartier-Bresson, Henri	Cartier-Bresson, Henri
Catlin, George	Catlin, George
Cazac, Yoran	Baldwin, James
Chagall, Marc	Chagall, Marc
Christy, Howard Chandler	Ford, Paul Leicester
Christy, Howard Chandler	Hawkins, Anthony Hope
Christy, Howard Chandler	Oppenheim, E. Phillips
Christy, Howard Chandler	Riley, James Whitcomb
Cimino, Harry	Cendrars, Blaise
Cocteau, Jean	Butts, Mary
Cootes, F. Graham	Wright, Harold Bell
Covarrubias, Miguel	Covarrubias, Miguel
Covarrubias, Miguel	Heritage Press
Cowles, Fleur	Vavra, Robert
Cruikshank, George	Grimm, Jakob Ludwig Carl, and Grimm, Wilhelm Carl
Cruikshank, George	Ingoldsby, Thomas (R.H. Barham)
Cruikshank, John	Dickens, Charles
Crum, R.	Abbey, Edward
Crum, R.	Bukowski, Charles
Cullen, Charles	Cullen, Countee
Cullen, Charles	Anthologies
Curry, John Stuart	Limited Editions Club
Daugherty, James	Daugherty, James
De Angeli, Marguerite	De Angeli, Marguerite
De Brunhoff, Jean	De Brunhoff, Jean
de Monvel, Boutet	France, Anatole
DeCarava, Roy	Hughes, Langston, and DeCarava, Roy
Dennis, Wesley	Steinbeck, John
Denslow, W.W.	Baum, L. Frank
Denslow, W.W.	*Denslow's Mother Goose*
Denslow, W.W.	Moore, Clement C.
Detmold, E.J.	Aesop
Detmold, E.J.	Detmold, E.J.
Detmold, E.J.	Fabre, Jean Henri
Detmold, Edmund	Maeterlinck, Maurice

ILLUSTRATORS   ⇒   AUTHORS

Detmold, Maurice and Edward	Kipling, Rudyard
Disney Studios	Dahl, Roald
Dixon, Maynard	Mulford, Clarence
Douglas, Aaron	Johnson, James Weldon
Drevenstedt, Amy	Wilder, Thornton
Eichenberg, Fritz	Bronte, Emily
Eichenberg, Kent, Gropper	Hellman, Lillian
Eisenstaedt, Alfred	Limited Editions Club
eleven fantasy artists	King, Stephen, and Straub, Peter
Epstein, Jacob	Limited Editions Club
Eulalie	Bannerman, Helen
Evans, Walker	Agee, James
Evans, Walker	Crane, Hart
Evans, Walker	Evans, Walker
Flack, Marjorie	Flack, Marjorie
Floethe, Richard	Streatfield, Noel
Ford, H.J.	Lang, Andrew
Fortnum, Peggy	Bond, Michael
Fraser, Claude Lovat	De la Mare, Walter
Fraser, Claude Lovat	MacFall, Haldane
Fujikawa, Gyo	Moore, Clement C.
Gannett, Ruth	Bailey, Carolyn
Gauguin, Paul	Gauguin, Paul
Genthe, Arnold	Genthe, Arnold
Gibbings, Robert	Gibbings, Robert
Gibson, Charles Dana	Davis, Richard Harding
Gibson, Charles Dana	Gibson, Charles Dana
Gill, Eric	Gill, Eric
Gilot, Francoise	Limited Editions Club
Glanzman, Louis	L'Amour, Louis
Goodman, Percival	Goodman, Paul
Goodwin, Philip R.	Jack London
Gorey, Edward	Gorey, Edward
Gould, John	Gould, John (1804–1881)
Grant, Gordon	London, Jack
Greenaway, Kate	Browning, Robert
Greenaway, Kate	Greenaway, Kate

ILLUSTRATORS	⇒	AUTHORS

ILLUSTRATORS	AUTHORS
Greenaway, Kate, and others	Meynell, Francis
Gronvold, H.	Hudson, W.H.
Grosz, George	Grosz, George
Grover, Eulalie Osgood	Grover, Eulalie Osgood
Gruelle, Johnny	Gruelle, Johnny
Gruger, F.R.	Johnson, Owen
Hammack, E.S.	Beebe, Lucius
Hearn, Lafcadio	Hearn, Lafcadio
Hitchcock, Lucius	Deland, Margaret
Hokinson, Helen	Kimbrough, Emily
Hopper, Charles Edward	London, Jack
Housman, Laurence	Housman, Laurence
Housman, Laurence	Rosetti, Christina
Hugo, Ian	Nin, Anais
Humphrey, Maud	Humphrey, Maud
Hunt, Lynn Bogue	Farrington, S. Kip, Jr.
Hunt, Lynn Bogue	Holland, Ray P.
Hunter, Dard	Hubbard, Elbert
Hyde, Philip	Abbey, Edward
James, Will	James, Will
James, Will·	Scribner's Illustrated Classics
Johnston, Robert	Doves Press
Jones, Harold	Lewis, C.S.
Jones, Laurian	Bagnold, Enid
Jones, Shirley	Jones, Shirley
Jones, Wilfred	Hemon, Louis
Kauffer, E. McKnight	Read, Herbert
Keeping, Virginia	Gates, Josephine Scribner
Keller, Arthur	Farnol, Jeffrey
Kemble, E.W.	Harris, Joel Chandler
Kent, Rockwell	Kent, Rockwell
Kent, Rockwell	Melville, Herman
Kipling, J. Lockwood	Kipling, Rudyard
Kipling, Rudyard	Kipling, Rudyard
Kirk, Maria	Burnett, Frances Hodgson
Kirk, Maria	Spyri, Johanna
Knight, Hilary	Thompson, Kay

ILLUSTRATORS ⇒	AUTHORS
Kredel, Fritz	Grimm, The Brothers
Lathrop, Dorothy	De la Mare, Walter
Lathrop, Dorothy	Hudson, W.H.
Lathrop, Dorothy	MacDonald, George
Lavigne, Robert	Ginsberg, Allen
Lawson, Robert	Forester, C.S.
Lawson, Robert	Lawson, Robert
Lawson, Robert	Leaf, Munro
Lea, Tom	Lea, Tom
Leech, John	Ingoldsby, Thomas (R.H. Barham)
Leighton, Clare	Leighton, Clare
Lenski, Lois	Lenski, Lois
Lenski, Lois	Piper, Watty
Lewis, Wyndham	Cunard, Nancy
Lofting, Hugh	Lofting, Hugh
MacManus, Blanche	Kipling, Rudyard
Macy, George	Limited Editions Club
Marande, H.	Colette (Sidonie-Gabrielle)
Masereel, Frans	Masereel, Frans
Matisse, Henri	Limited Editions Club
Maxwell, Donald	Kipling, Rudyard
McCloskey, Robert	Malcolmson, Anne
Meyer, Fred	Limited Editions Club
Millar, H.R.	Nesbit, Edith
Miner, L.R.	Dunbar, Paul Laurence
Monahan, P.J.	London, Jack
Monsell, J.R.	MacKenzie, Compton
Moore, T. Sturge	Yeats, William Butler
Moser, Barry	Kinnell, Galway
Moskowitz, Ira	Collier, John (born 1884, American)
Mugnaini, Joseph	Limited Editions Club
Nast, Thomas	Dodge, M.E.
Neill, John R.	Baum, L. Frank
Neill, John. R.	Thompson, Ruth Plumly
Newell, Peter	Carroll, Lewis
Newell, Peter	Newell, Peter

ILLUSTRATORS	⇒	AUTHORS

ILLUSTRATORS	AUTHORS
Nielsen, Kay	Quiller-Couch, Sir Arthur
Outcault, R.F.	Outcault, F.
Paget, Sydney	Doyle, Arthur Conan
Paine, Anna	Hubbard, Elbert
Parks, Gordon	Parks, Gordon
Parrish, Maxfield	Field, Eugene
Parrish, Maxfield	Palgrave, F.T.
Parrish, Maxfield	Saunders, Louise
Parrish, Maxfield	Wiggin, Kate Douglas
Peat, Fern Bisel	Field, Eugene
Perkins, Lucy Fitch	Perkins, Lucy Fitch
Petersham, Maud and Miska	Collodi, Carlo
Phiz	Dickens, Charles
Pogany, Willy	Louys, Pierre
Potter, Beatrix	Potter, Beatrix
Preston, May Wilson	Shaw, George Bernard
Rache, Elmer	Garis, Howard
Rackham, Arthur	Browning, Robert
Rackham, Arthur	Dickens, Charles
Rackham, Arthur	Grahame, Kenneth
Rackham, Arthur	Ibsen, Henrik
Rackham, Arthur	Ingoldsby, Thomas (R.H. Barham)
Rackham, Arthur	Kipling, Rudyard
Rackham, Arthur	Limited Editions Club
Rackham, Arthur	Morley, Christopher
Rackham, Arthur	Rackham, Arthur
Remington, F., and Deming, E.	King, Captain Charles
Rhead, Louis	Wyss, David
Robinson, Charles	Castle, Agnes
Robinson, Charles	Wilde, Oscar
Robinson, F.	Maeterlinck, Maurice
Robinson, W. Heath	Kipling, Rudyard
Robinson, W. Heath	De la Mare, Walter
Robinson, W. Heath	Robinson, W. Heath
Rockmore, Noel	Bukowski, Charles
Rogers, Bruce	Limited Editions Club
Ross, M.T.	Gordon, Elizabeth

ILLUSTRATORS ⇒	AUTHORS
Roth, Herb	Rogers, Will
Rowe, Clarence	Raine, William MacLeod
Saint-Exupery, Antoine de	Saint-Exupery, Antoine de
Santee, Ross	Santee, Ross
Sarg, Tony	Cobb, Irvin
Sauvage, Sylvan	Limited Editions Club
Say, Allen	Antoninus, Brother
Schindelman, Joseph	Dahl, Roald
Schoonover, Frank	Van Dyke, Henry
Scott, Peter	Gallico, Paul
Sendak, Maurice	Krauss, Ruth
Sendak, Maurice	Sendak, Maurice
Seton, Ernest Thompson	Seton, Ernest Thompson
Seuss, Dr.	Seuss, Dr.
Sewell, Helen and Mildred B.	Wilder, Laura Ingalls
Shahn, Ben	Berry, Wendell
Shahn, Ben	Berryman, John
Shahn, Ben	Dahlberg, Edward
Shahn, Ben	Porter, Katherine Anne
Shaw, Charles	Brown, Margaret Wise
Shenton, Edward	Lutes, Della T.
Shenton, Edward	Rawlings, Marjorie Kinnan
Shepard, Ernest H.	Milne, A.A.
Shepard, Mary	Travers, P.L.
Simont, Marc	Thurber, James
Smith, E. Boyd	Austin, Mary
Smith, Jessie Wilcox	Alcott, Louisa May
Smith, Jessie Wilcox	Kingsley, Charles
Smith, Jessie Wilcox	MacDonald, George
Smith, Wilhelm	Grey, Zane
Steiner-Prag	Hart, Moss
Stephens, Alice B., and Wyeth, N.C.	Wiggin, Kate Douglas
Stover, Mary E. and Wallace	Garis, Howard
Sutherland, Graham	Gascoyne, David
Szyk, Arthur	Bibles
Szyk, Arthur	Szyk, Arthur

ILLUSTRATORS	⇒	AUTHORS

Taber, I.W.	Kipling, Rudyard
Tarrant, Margaret	Kingsley, Charles
Tenggren, Gustaf	*Mother Goose*
Tenniel, John	Carroll, Lewis
Timlin, William	Timlin, William
Tudor, Tasha	Burnett, Frances Hodgson
Tudor, Tasha	Stevenson, Robert Louis
Ullman, Doris	Peterkin, Julia, and
	Ulmann, Doris
Upton, Florence K.	Upton, Bertha
Van Loon, Hendrick Willem	Van Loon, Hendrick Willem
Van Wie, Carrie	Book Club of California
Vassos, John	Wilde, Oscar
Vawter, Will	Riley, James Whitcomb
Ward, Lynd	Ward, Lynd
Warde, Frederic	Heritage Press
Watson, Amelia M.	Thoreau, Henry David
Webb, Clifford	Ransome, Arthur
Weegee	Weegee
Weisgard, Leonard	Brown, Margaret Wise
Weston, Edward	Weston, Edward
Wheelright, Roland, and	Blackmore, Richard D.
Sewell, Helen	
Whistler, Rex	Beaton, Cecil
Whistler, Rex	Dane, Clemence
Whistler, Rex	Nichols, Beverly
Wiese, Kurt	Flack, Marjorie
Williams, Garth	White, E.B.
Williams, Gluyas	Benchley, Robert
Wilson, E.A.	Heritage Press
Wilson, Edward A.	Limited Editions Club
Wireman, K.	Wiggin, Kate Douglas
Wood, Grant	Limited Editions Club
Wright, John Buckland	Cabell, James Branch
Wrightson, Bernie	King, Stephen
Wyeth, Andrew	Allen, Hervey
Wyeth, N.C.	Boyd, James
Wyeth, N.C.	Defoe, Daniel

ILLUSTRATORS	⇒	AUTHORS
Wyeth, N.C.		Fox, John
Wyeth, N.C.		Lanier, Sydney
Wyeth, N.C.		Nordhoff, Charles
Wyeth, N.C.		Rawlings, Marjorie Kinnan
Wyeth, N.C.		*Robin Hood*
Wyeth, N.C.		Scribner's Illustrated Classics
Wyeth, N.C.		Stevenson, Robert Louis
Yeats, Jack Butler		Yeats, William Butler

APPENDIX C

Glossary

12MO—(Read "twelve-mo," the "mo" rhyming with "go.") Short for duodecimo, a rather small book size, about seven or more inches tall; see *book size*.

16MO—(Read "sixteen-mo.") A small book size, about six to seven inches; see *book size*.

4TO—(Read "quarto.") A large book size, about twelve inches tall; see *book size*.

8VO—(Read "eight-vo" or "octavo," which rhymes with "bravo.") A medium-sized book, eight to nine inches tall, the most common book size; see *book size*.

ADVANCE COPY, ADVANCE REVIEW COPY, ADVANCE READING COPY—A copy of a book, ordinarily in wraps, run off the press and distributed before publication. Advance copies are prior to first editions, and are distributed to reviewers or others in the book industry. There also exist copies of the regular trade edition, with a slip laid in identifying each as a book sent out for review. These may also be called advance copies; the former are of greater value.

ASSOCIATION COPY—A book valued for its association with an individual; for instance, one owned by the author's mother, lover, or famous friend that has some evidence of the association (as a signature).

BACKSTRIP—The covering of the spine of a book.

BLIND-STAMPED—Embossed, but without color or gilt.

BOARDS—Stiff material used for the covers of a book.

BOARDS, PAPER-COVERED—See *paper-covered boards*.

BOOK SIZE—Quarto, octavo, folio, and duodecimo are old terms from the history of book-making. Pages were originally made from large sheets which when folded in four produced a book about twelve inches high (a "quarto" volume), or when folded in eight, an eight-inches-high book or "octavo," and so on. In addition to the four sizes mentioned above, with their variant forms—("4to," etc.), there are also "32mo's" and "24mo's" and others. The larger the number, the smaller the book. "Large quarto," "small quarto," "large octavo," and "elephant folio" (twenty-three or more inches tall), are all terms in frequent use. The British system for indicating book size is different.

COATED STOCK—Glossy paper used for the pages of a book.

COPYRIGHT PAGE—The reverse side of the title page, containing the copyright date and usually other information.

CORRECT FIRST EDITION—A shorthand way of saying that a book has those identifying characteristics which make it a first edition. Usually used where there have been complications or confusions or misunderstandings about the marks of a true first.

DUODECIMO—See *12mo*.

DUST JACKET—The removable paper cover of a hardcover book.

DUST WRAPPER — Same as dust jacket.

EDITION—The word *edition* has two clear and distinct meanings as used among booksellers, in whose everyday discourse the meaning is made clear by the context. A *first edition*, in the original and basic sense of the word, consists of all the printings of a book that come out before a specific set of significant changes is made. A *printing* is all those copies of a book that are run off during one brief time period, and *first printing* means the first printing of the first edition. The collecting and selling of first printings (called *first editions*) is of such central interest that the term "first edition" is used now most frequently in the out-of-print book business in its second meaning, "first printing." *First impression* is the same as "first printing." A *first issue* is an intermediate state of the first printing. Since priority of appearance is of concern to collectors of first editions, attention has been paid to any discernable differences in priority within the first printing. These differences occur when a change is made, most often to correct an error, in typography, spelling, fact, etc., or to make a change in the binding, and the changes are ferreted out by the writer of a bibliography or reference book or other student of first editions. *First state* is nowadays used virtually interchangeably with "first issue."

EDGES—The part of the pages visible when the book is closed

ELEPHANT FOLIO—*Very* oversize volume; "atlas folio" and "double elephant folio" are bigger still.

ENDPAPERS—The first and last leaves of a book, including the "paste-down" endpapers which cover the inner surfaces of the book covers. They may be plain or decorated. Physically, they are not a part of the bound pages of the book proper.

FICTION—A story; invented; a novel or short story.

FIRST EDITION—See *edition*.

FIRST EDITION SO STATED—An edition that has "first edition" printed on the copyright page.

FIRST EDITION THUS—The first printing of an edition printed later than the original edition and having different illustrations and design, or other features which make it distinctly different from the original edition, so that it's now really a first printing of a new and different edition. "First edition" in the phrase "first edition thus" is to be understood as meaning "first printing." See *edition*. Despite its name, it is nevertheless not "a true first," and as such, collectible, since it is not the original edition of that title.

FIRST IMPRESSION—Same as a first printing.

FIRST ISSUE—See *edition*.

FIRST PRINTING—See *edition*.

FIRST STATE—See *edition*.

FIRST TRADE EDITION—The "ordinary" first edition, the phrase usually being used to distinguish it from a limited edition, an advance edition, or other.

FOLIO—Oversize volume, thirteen or more inches tall; see *book size*. "Folio" has other meanings, but this is the most frequent.

FORE-EDGE—The page edges opposite the spine.

FRONTIS, FRONTISPIECE—The illustration opposite the title page.

HALF-LEATHER—Having the spine covered with leather which extends onto the front and back covers of the book.

HALF-TITLE—The page preceding the title page, which has on it the title and nothing else.

INCUNABULA—Books printed in the sixteenth century.

INSCRIBED—autographed.

INSCRIPTION—autograph.

LATER PRINTING—Any printing of a given edition except the first one.

LIMITED EDITION—An edition published only in limited numbers, usually before the first edition.

MINIATURE—A very small book, some years ago defined as no larger than two inches by one and one-half inches; now, apparently up to three inches.

MOROCCO—A kind of leather originally from Morocco, made of goatskin tanned with sumac, and much used by bookbinders because of its combined suppleness and durability.

NONFICTION—A true account.

OCTAVO—See *8vo* and *book size*.

ORIGINAL CLOTH—The cloth binding in which the book was originally introduced by the publisher.

OUT-OF-PRINT—Books the publisher no longer has in stock; available only on the out-of-print book market.

PAPER-COVERED BOARDS—Very stiff and strong paper-covered cardboard or composition book covers.

PAPERBACK ORIGINAL—A paperback that has not been published previously, in hardcover or otherwise.

PASTE-ON—Usually seen in "pictorial paste-on" or "paste-on label," and referring to a large paper square or rectangle pasted to and often almost covering the front cover of a book. It is most often illustrated.

PASTE-DOWN—See *endpapers*.

POINTS—Characteristics of an issue or printing of a particular book that are used to identify that issue or printing and discriminate it from other issues or printings.

PRESENTATION COPY—A book that has been given by the author, with a signed, personal note.

PROOF COPY—A pre-publication copy in wraps—usually short for *uncorrected proof*.

PROVENANCE—The book's ownership history.

PSEUDONYM—An adopted name, not the author's own, under which he writes.

PUBLISHER'S BOX—Permanent formal slipcase in which the book was issued by the publisher.

QUARTO—See *4to* and *book size*.

READING COPY—Sometimes it means just that, as in "My first edition is on the shelf, and this one is my reading copy"; the rest of the time it means a book in terrible condition with all text present.

REBACKED—Having a replaced spine.

RUBBED—Surface of book binding worn.

SLIPCASE—A cardboard box with an open side, made to house a book.

TIPPED IN—Said of an illustration, page, or map lightly inserted and secured with paste.

TITLE PAGE—The page ordinarily bearing the full title, author, publisher, and sometimes publication date.

TRADE EDITION—The ordinary commercial edition of a book.

UNCORRECTED PROOF—A pre-publication state of a book, bound in wraps; on the rare book market, demands a higher asking price than an advance copy.

VELLUM—A fine-grained animal skin prepared with lime for writing on or covering books; sometimes refers to its imitation.

WRAPS, WRAPPERS—Paper covers or very thin cardboard covers.

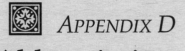 *Appendix D*

Abbreviations

The following abbreviated forms used by booksellers are listed here as they are most often used—i.e., without the period. Since the purpose of abbreviating is to save space, and since the periods have not been found necessary for clarity, they are now usually omitted in classified book ads and in sales lists.

1st ed—first edition.

1st pr—first printing.

aeg—all edges gilt (i.e., page edges).

Am—American.

av—average.

bg—binding.

b&w—black and white.

c—copyright or approximately.

cl—cloth.

col—color or colored.

cov—cover.

DJ—dust jacket.

DW—dust wrapper.

ed—edition or edited.

ep's—endpapers.

ex-lib—ex-library, formerly used in a public or institutional library.

f—usually "fine," but sometimes "fair."

F—fine.

fp—full page.

frontis—frontispiece (illustration opposite title page).

g—good.

ills—illustrations.

illus—illustrated.

L—London.

lea—leather.

lt—light.

nd—no date (meaning "no date given").

np—no place (meaning "no place of publication given").

op—out-of-print.

orig—original.

p; pp—page, pages.

plt—plate.

ow—otherwise.

pub—published or publisher.

rev—revised.

sev—several.

sgd—signed.

sm—small.

sp—spine.

teg—top edge gilt (i.e., top edge of pages).

tp—title page.

tr—translated.

unk—unknown.

vg—very good.

vg/f—very good/fine, meaning "very good to fine" or very good (condition) book in fine dust jacket.

vg/F—very good book in fine dust jacket.

vol—volume.

w—with.

waf—with all faults.

wr; wraps—wrappers.

Appendix E

References

Resources on bibliographies

Blanck, Jacob. *Bibliography of American Literature.* New Haven and London: Yale University Press, 1955.

Bruccoli, Matthew J., and Clark, C.E. Frazer, Jr. *First Printings of American Authors.* Detroit: Gale Research Inc. 1977–79. Five volumes with over 100 bibliographies per volume—includes reproductions of many title pages and some author photos.

Currey, L.W. *Science Fiction and Fantasy Authors: A Bibliography of First Printings of Their Fiction.* Boston: G.K. Hall & Co., 1979.

Howes, Wright. *U.S. INANA.* New York: Bowker, 1962.

Johnson, Mark. *American First Editions.* Waltham: Mark Press, 1969.

Lepper, Gary M. *A Bibliographical Introduction to Seventy-Five Modern Authors.* Berkeley: Serendipity Books, 1976.

St. John, Judith. *The Osborne Catalog of Early Children's Books: 1476–1910.* Toronto: Toronto Public Library, 1975.

Resources on book collecting

Ahearn, Allen. *Book Collecting: A Comprehensive Guide.* New York: Putnam, 1989.

Carter, John. *ABC For Book Collectors.* New York: Knopf, 1981.

Haller, Margaret. *Book Collector's Fact Book.* New York: Arco, 1976.

Stewart, Seumas. *Book Collecting.* New York: Dutton, 1973.

Resources on first printings and first issues

McBride, Bill, comp. *Identification of First Editions—A Pocket Guide.* McBride, publisher, Hartford, CT 06105. (Phone: 203-532-1622.) A very inexpensive guide to the habits of more than 2,500 publishers in their identification of first editions.

————. *Points of Issue: A Compendium of Points of Issue of Books by 19th and 20th Century Authors.* McBride, publisher, Hartford, CT 06105. (Phone: 203-523-1622.) Another inexpensive pocket guide, a companion to McBride's other title.

Zempel, Edward N., and Verkler, Linda A., eds. *First Editions: A Guide to Identification.* Spoon River Press, Peoria, IL 61604-5072. (Phone: 309-672-2665.) Consists of the statements of over 1,000 publishers, including many from the British Commonwealth, and for various dates, on their means of identifying their first editions.

Resources on pricing a collection

Ahearn, Allen. *Book Collecting: A Comprehensive Guide.* New York: Putnam, 1989. A price guide to the first books of 3,500 collected authors—with glossary and other material.

Ahearn, Allen and Patricia. *Collected Books: The Guide to Values.* New York: Putnam, 1991. A price guide to 15,000 first editions, with identifying data, plus a breakdown of publisher first edition identification systems and other material.

American Book Prices Current. (np): Bancroft-Parkman. (Phone: 212-737-2715 or 203-868-7408.) A record, published annually, of auction prices of books, autographs, maps, and manuscripts, with identifying data on all books sold, covering the important book auction houses in this country, England, and Europe.

Author Price Guides. Rockville, MD 20848. (Phone: 301-460-3700. Fax: 301-871-5425.) Very inexpensive separate price guides to individual authors, mainly modern first edition authors, with much useful information.

Bookman's Price Index. Gale Research Inc., Detroit, MI 48226-4094. Published twice per year, with the vital statistics and catalog prices of 30–35,000 antiquarian books per volume, from catalogs of 200 booksellers of the United States, Canada, and the British Isles.

International Rare Book Price Guide Series. Spoon River Press, Peoria, IL 61604-5072. (Phone: 309-672-2665.) Six annual price guides: *The Arts and Architecture, Early Printed Books, Literature, Modern First Editions, Science and Medicine,* and *Voyages, Travel and Exploration.* Each volume is about 250 pages with 5,000 entries. The information is taken from dealer catalogs—more than half of the material is British.

Used Book Price Guide. Mandeville Price Guide Publishers, Kenmore, WA 98028. Several volumes, the latest covering the five-year period ending in December 1888—fills a very useful niche in its reporting of dealer catalog prices of the generally lower priced books, but because it is not up to date, extrapolation is required in order to use it for pricing books.

PERIODICALS

AB Bookman's Weekly, Clifton, NJ 07015. (Phone: 201-772-0020.) The almost 45-year-old publication "for the Specialist Book World"; extensive listings of books wanted and books for sale; articles; book fair calendar; review; "Catalogs Received"; and more.

Book Quote, Peoria, IL 61604-5072. (Phone: 309-672-2665.) A biweekly, also a smaller and less expensive periodical; consists mostly of lists of books wanted and books for sale, but also has "Catalogs Received," and shows some notices and letters. What textual material it prints is of very good quality.

Book Source Monthly, Casenovia, NY 13035-0567. A very inexpensive and very packed monthly for book people; books for sale and wanted; auction calendar; auction reports; book fair calendar; "Catalogs Received"; bibliographies; specialists' directories; and more.

Firsts–Collecting Modern First Editions, P.O. Box 16945, North Hollywood, CA 91615. A fairly new, slick monthly with interesting and useful material.

Other **CONFIDENT COLLECTOR** *Titles*
of Interest
from Avon Books

ADVERTISING
IDENTIFICATION AND PRICE GUIDE
by Dawn E. Reno

ART DECO
IDENTIFICATION AND PRICE GUIDE
by Tony Fusco

COLLECTIBLE MAGAZINES
IDENTIFICATION AND PRICE GUIDE
by David K. Henkel

FINE ART
IDENTIFICATION AND PRICE GUIDE
by Susan Theran

ORIGINAL COMIC ART
IDENTIFICATION AND PRICE GUIDE
by Jerry Weist

PRINTS, POSTERS & PHOTOGRAPHS
IDENTIFICATION AND PRICE GUIDE
by Susan Theran

QUILTS
IDENTIFICATION AND PRICE GUIDE
by Liz Greenbacker & Kathleen Barach